To the Brownsville Library

In Memory Of

Philip & Helen Parkinson

by son Phil

Beat 'em, Bucs!

Jim O'Brien

12-5-98

WE HAD 'EM ALL THE WAY

Bob Prince
And His Pittsburgh Pirates

By Jim O'Brien

Betty and Bob Prince in a rare moment, relaxing on the patio outside their home in Upper St. Clair in 1965.

This book is dedicated to the memory of Bob Prince, one of the nice people who helped me along the way, and to his wife, Betty, who helped me with this book.

James P. O'Brien — Publishing
P.O. Box 12580
Pittsburgh PA 15241
Phone: (412) 221-3580

First printing, September, 1998

Manufactured in the United States of America

Printed by Geyer Printing Company, Inc.
3700 Bigelow Boulevard
Pittsburgh PA 15213

Typography by Cold-Comp
810 Penn Avenue
Pittsburgh PA 15222

ISBN 1-886348-03-0

Books By Jim O'Brien

COMPLETE HANDBOOK OF PRO BASKETBALL 1970-1971

COMPLETE HANDBOOK OF PRO BASKETBALL 1971-1972

ABA ALL-STARS

PITTSBURGH: THE STORY OF THE CITY OF CHAMPIONS

HAIL TO PITT: A SPORTS HISTORY OF
THE UNIVERSITY OF PITTSBURGH

DOING IT RIGHT

WHATEVER IT TAKES

MAZ AND THE '60 BUCS

REMEMBER ROBERTO

PENGUIN PROFILES

DARE TO DREAM

KEEP THE FAITH

WE HAD 'EM ALL THE WAY

To order copies of these titles directly from the publisher, send $26.95 for hardcover edition. Please send $3.50 to cover shipping and handling costs per book. Pennsylvania residents add 6% sales tax to price of book only. Allegheny County residents add an additional 1% sales tax for a total of 7% sales tax. Copies will be signed by author at your request. Discounts available for large orders. Contact publisher regarding availability and prices of all books in *Pittsburgh Proud* series, or to request an order form. Several of them are sold out or are available only in hardcover editions.

Contents

Other Writers on Bob Prince:

Acknowledgments

The most rewarding aspect of this book project was the delightful time I spent with Betty Prince, the wife of the late Bob Prince. She is a special person. She was excited that I was writing this book, and gave her fullest cooperation and support. She is 81, razor-sharp in her wit and recall, and tells stories in dialogue — a writer's dream. Her daughter, Nancy Thomas, and son, Bob Jr., were also good fun, and shared some personal thoughts about their dad. Their love for, and bemusement with, Bob Prince was evident throughout our meetings. Theirs are among my favorite stories.

I'll always be grateful to have known Bob Prince and to have been blessed by his good humor and great support. He ranks right up there with Art Rooney, Doc Carlson and Frank Gustine as great boosters who have impacted my life and career.

One of Bob Prince's dearest friends and proteges, Sally O'Leary, who retired two years ago after 32 years in the publicity office of the Pittsburgh Pirates, helped me in so many ways with this publishing project, as did his broadcast partner, Nellie King, and other Pirates.

My "Pittsburgh Proud" sports book series would not have been possible without the encouragement and financial support of some wonderful people in the Pittsburgh business and corporate community. Special thanks is offered for loyal and strong support from Alex Pociask of Stevens Painton Corporation and Tom Snyder of Continental Design & Management Group. They have been my biggest boosters through the years.

Other loyal patrons include Dennis Astorino of LD Astorino Associates, Ltd.; Ronald B. Livingston Sr. of Babb, Inc.; Bill Baierl of The Baierl Auto Group; Baseball Hall of Fame and Museum; Paul Lang of Bayer Corp.; Andrew F. Komer of Bowne of Pittsburgh; Miles R. Bryan of Bryan Mechanical Inc.; John T. Scalo and Jack Scalo of Burns & Scalo Roofing, Inc.

Don Carlucci of Carlucci Construction Co.; Rich Corson of C&R Limousine Service; Walter Sapp of Daniel-Sapp-Boorn Associates; Armand Dellovade of A.C. Dellovade, Inc.; Jim Broadhurst of Eat'n Park Restaurants; Everett Burns of E-Z Overhead Door & Window Co.; Ron Parkinson of J. Messner, Inc. and the Greater Pittsburgh Chevrolet Dealers Association.

John R. McGinley Jr. of Grogan, Graffan, McGinley & Lucchino, P.C.; Frank B. Fuhrer Wholesale Co.; Frank Gustine Jr. of The Gustine Company; Ed Harmon of F.E. Harmon Construction, Inc.; Steve Fedell of Ikon Office Solutions; Mike Hagan of Iron & Glass Bank; Jack Mascaro of Mascaro Construction Company; Joseph A. Massaro, Jr. of The Massaro Company; Jack B. Piatt of Millcraft Industries, Inc.

F. James McCarl and Robert B. Santillo of McCarl's, Inc.; Clem Gigliotti of Merit Contracting, Inc.; David S. Jancisin of Merrill Lynch; John C. Williams Jr. of National City Bank of Pennsylvania;

6

Jack Perkins of Mr. P's in Greensburg; A. Robert Scott of *Point*; Joe Browne Sr. of the National Football League; and the National Football League Hall of Fame.

Lloyd Gibson and John Schultz of North Side Bank; Pat Rooney of Palm Beach Kennel Club; Patrick J. Santelli of Pfizer Labs; Thomas H. O'Brien, James E. Rohr and Sy Holzer of PNC Bank Corp.; Dennis S. Meteny of Respironics, Inc.; Fred B. Sargent of Sargent Electric Co.

Jim Roddey and Michael J. Fetchko of SportsWave, Inc. (International Sports Marketing); Daniel A. Goetz of Stylette, Inc.; Dick Swanson of Swanson Group Ltd.; Barbara and Ted Frantz of Tedco Construction Corp.; W. Harrison Vail of Three Rivers Bank.

John Paul of University of Pittsburgh Medical Center; Thomas J. Usher of USX Corporation; Clark Nicklas of Vista Resources, Inc.; Charles and Stephen Previs of Waddell & Reed Financial Services; W.R. Utley of Westinghouse Electric Co. (Commercial Nuclear Fuel Division); and Ray Conaway of Zimmer Kunz. Don Schwall and Ken Wenger of Bob Prince Charities were helpful, as was Joe Tucker's daughter, Mrs. Lynne Levenbach.

Friends who have been boosters include John Bruno, Beano Cook, Art Cipriani, Tommy Kehoe, George Morris, Andy Ondrey, Arthur J. Rooney Jr., Ted Taylor. Friends who have offered special encouragement and prayer and those who have opened up doors for our endeavors include Bill Priatko, Ron Temple, Bob Shearer, Foge Fazio, Pete Mervosh, Mike Ference of Ference Marketing & Communications; Bob Lovett and Art Stroyd of Reed Smith Shaw & McClay; Bob Harper and Art Rooney II of Klett Lieber Rooney & Schorling; Rev. Laird Stuart and Rev. Bob Norris of Westminster Presbyterian Church, Darrell Hess, Jim Meston, and Robert F. Wolf.

There is a strong belief on our part that these books should be produced entirely in Pittsburgh. Bruce McGough and Tom Samuels and their staff at Geyer Printing have printed all of the books in this series. Keith and Denise Maiden and Cathy Pawlowski of Cold-Comp Typographers did their usual first-rate effort. The cover design was done by Giuseppe Francioni of Prisma, Inc. This team has worked on all of my All-Pittsburgh books. I can't forget Ed Lutz and Stan Goldmann, who believed in me from the beginning, and envy them their retirement status and wide smiles. *The Almanac* newspaper in the South Hills, for which I have been writing a man-about-town column for the past decade, has promoted my book signing appearances through the years. Now the *Valley Mirror* does the same.

Thanks to Kevin S. McClatchy and Nellie Briles of the Pittsburgh Pirates, their media relations staff, especially Jim Trdinich, Ben Bouma and Mike Kennedy, and the team's official photographer, David Arrigo, for their outstanding cooperation.

None of this would be as satisfying without the love and support of my wife, Kathie, our daughters, Sarah and Rebecca, and my mother, Mary M. O'Brien. Thank you all.

— Jim O'Brien,
June 15, 1998

Did you know?
Learning about a Prince

"The shot heard round the world."

Bob Prince never saw Bill Mazeroski's home run that won the 1960 World Series at Forbes Field and Steelers owner Art Rooney missed the "Immaculate Reception" by Franco Harris in the 1972 playoffs with the Oakland Raiders at Three Rivers Stadium.

I knew that before I researched and wrote this book, the first one ever written about the legendary Bob Prince, and you may have as well. They are interesting sidelights to two of the most magic moments in Pittsburgh sports history.

What I didn't know was that Prince was present to see Bobby Thomson's home run that won the National League pennant for the New York Giants in a 1952 playoff contest with the Brooklyn Dodgers. The Giants and Dodgers had finished in a tie for first place in the regular schedule.

Thomson's home run was heralded as "the shot heard round the world." When he hit it, Giants' broadcaster Russ Hodges hollered, "The Giants win the pennant . . . the Giants win the pennant . . . the Giants win the pennant." It's a famous sports call.

Then, because he was eager to run to the Giants' clubhouse to join in the celebration, Hodges turned to Bob Prince, who happened to be visiting in the booth, and pleaded, "Hey, Bob, do me a favor . . . take over and wrap this up for me!"

So Prince closed the show.

Thomson's memorable home run came in the last of the ninth in the Polo Grounds on October 3, 1951. It came on a 1-0 pitch by Ralph Branca. It went into the left field stands.

Maz's home run also came on a 1-0 pitch in the last of the ninth on October 13, 1960. The pitcher was Ralph Terry. It went over the left field wall, just to the right of the scoreboard. The Pirates beat the Yankees on that blow, 10-9.

Prince had been dispatched to the Pirates' clubhouse with the Pirates leading 9-7 after eight innings. When the Yankees tied the game, 9-9, in the top of the ninth, Prince was ordered to return to the broadcast booth.

He was making his way back to the booth when he heard the roar of the crowd. He was told to go to the Pirates' clubhouse. He had no idea how the game ended. He dismissed Maz with a single question — "How's it feel to be on the world championship team?" — when Maz was the first player pushed his way in the post-game interview.

Prince said the most thrilling game was watching Don Larsen of the Yankees pitching the perfect game in the 1956 World Series.

Prior to undertaking this project, I also didn't know that Prince was a broadcaster for Steelers games, along with Joe Tucker, for 11 seasons, and did Penn State football for nine seasons. He did Duquesne University basketball for six years with Tucker. He later did Ohio State basketball briefly. He also did the Pittsburgh Hornets with Tucker, and the Pittsburgh Penguins during his long and storied career. Prince said hockey was the toughest assignment.

"The action is so quick that it requires a broadcaster to always be on his toes," said Prince.

His father played football at West Point, and Prince, an Army brat, attended 18 different schools in his lifetime, including four colleges — Pittsburgh, Stanford, Oklahoma (where he got his degree) and Harvard Law for a year before dropping out to pursue other interests. Schools couldn't accommodate his outsized personality.

He was a pencil-thin 6-1½, 170 pounds, but quite the competitor. He was an all-around college athlete. He earned letters in baseball (first baseman), track (low hurdles and the 440), polo and swimming. He was quite the swimmer, but he was better known for a swan dive he once took from a hotel room into a swimming pool at a hotel in St. Louis.

Bob Prince had a passion for life and for baseball that made him the fan's announcer.

From Murray Tucker

Classic shot from late '40s shows Bob Prince lighting up cigarette in field level seats on third base line. Seated ahead of him in hat is sportscaster Joe Tucker, next to Baz Bastien of the Pittsburgh Hornets. Note the big pocket handkerchief brandished by Prince and bottled drinks held by Tucker and woman fan. Prince was often pictured with cigarette in hand and a fancy hanky in his breastpocket.

Bob Prince
The perpetual Army brat

"I had more fun than any of them."

Bob Prince, the lean and lively sports broadcaster for the Pittsburgh Pirates, must have been caught up in a midtown mob of fans asking erudite questions like "Who's going to win tonight, Bob?" or "Are we going to have a game tonight, Bob?"

Prince was nearly an hour late for our mid-afternoon meeting in the summer of 1963 at the Pittsburgh Athletic Association (P.A.A.) in Oakland, just two blocks from Forbes Field, where he said we could have a few drinks and chat. Somehow Prince can't quite catch up to his appointments.

He was 45 minutes late, but he walked in with a let's-get-going stride, and a smile and a wink. I was soon to start my senior year at the University of Pittsburgh, and I was interviewing Prince for the introductory edition of *Pittsburgh Weekly Sports*, a tabloid that Prince was eager to see come off the presses. I was grateful that Prince was giving me his time, even if he was late.

Prince was a popular figure in the P.A.A. and always created a commotion when he moved through the lobby. Prince loosened up the otherwise often staid atmosphere of the private club, just across Fifth Avenue from Pitt's Cathedral of Learning. I was a little nervous because I had always regarded the P.A.A. as off-bounds for someone lacking pedigree papers, but he made me feel instantly at home and at ease.

Prince had the run of the P.A.A. After all, he had been the Pirates broadcaster since 1948, starting out as a sidekick to Rosey Rowswell, so everybody in Pittsburgh knew him, or thought they did, anyhow. Rosey died six years later, and Prince took control of the buttons on the baseball broadcasts for the 1955 season. Prince was friendly to everybody, and his name suited him well.

While baseball was his best sport, by far, he also did football, basketball, swimming, golf and, early and late in his career, hockey. He never took any of those sports or himself seriously. He always sounded like he was having a good time, and his listeners loved going along for the ride. "How sweet it is!" Prince would say, and his listeners would nod in agreement.

He was involved in many charity activities, notably the Ham-Am golf tournament for the benefit of the West Penn Caddie Scholarship Fund, the annual HYPO game which benefited amateur baseball, and he was a major magnet in raising money for the Allegheny Valley School, which became his pet project. It is a private, non-profit multi-campus residential care and educational agency serving mentally retarded children and adults, many of whom are also physically

Overhead shot shows how Forbes Field fit into Oakland and University of Pittsburgh campus setting. In upper right corner, the Cathedral of Learning is located just across Fifth Avenue from the P.A.A., a private club frequented by Bob Prince before and after Pirates' games.

KDKA Teen Night promotion featured, left to right, Rege Cordic and Sterling Yates, two of the most popular radio personalities in Pittsburgh history, addressing early arrivals at Forbes Field.

handicapped. The school's main campus in Robinson Township contains many mementos and plaques memorializing Prince's special contributions to its successful operation. His good friend Myron Cope replaced Prince as the prime fund-raising figure for Allegheny Valley School.

On his dizzy whirl on the hand-shaking merry-go-round at the P.A.A. that day we got together, Prince peeked into every nook and cranny of the club, making sure he did not miss anyone.

He apologized for being late, autographed a baseball at the desk, and asked the manager there if anyone had called for his tickets. "Now let's go downstairs and get away from all these crazy people," he said, and moved out three paces ahead in his dark dressed-for-action slacks, his bright hazel eyes, a mischievous twinkle in them, searching for familiar faces.

He cracked two quick jokes and then descended a semi-circular stairway as if he were trying to get a running start for a parachute jump.

Prince seated himself at a table near the bar in a new wing of the P.A.A. There was a meticulous setting for four for dinner. "You don't want this stuff in front of you," he said, piling the plates and silverware on a corner of the table.

Seated there, he stirred up an image of King Arthur greeting his knights at the Round Table, as a few score of his friends digressed from their original path to walk by his table.

"Can you bring Murtaugh and Casey Stengel over Friday?" one asked.

"I don't know," Prince sighed. "I'll have to ask them."

"How about stopping back later on in the Walnut Room, Bob?" another inquired. "We need a quorum for our meeting, and we're a few short. Just make an appearance, huh? You know a man like you counts five."

"Flattery will get you nowhere, brother," Prince said in that familiar velvet-like tone, grinning. Prince made the meeting, although he was a bit late.

An old schoolmate of Prince approached him and asked him to take a $25 chance on $2,000. "The Bishop will probably win it, but I'll take one," said Prince. This was typical Prince. He had a hard time saying no to anyone, and he was always tossing money and gag lines around.

Prince drew a cigarette from his pack, and the waiter was there to strike a match. Now Prince was ready to talk. In between standing up and down like a school kid practicing for a fire drill, while I shook the hands of another dozen friends, we talked. I learned that Prince was the best-known man in town.

Prince affected worldliness in his manner and speech. Some said he was a show-off and too gabby. His craggy face grew warm and his lips moved like a flying carpet as he talked about his life.

"I had a helluva youth!" Prince exclaimed, twisting in his seat, and fetching another pretzel.

Prince was the son of a regular Army officer, and he moved from one Army post to another as a youth and then from school to school (Pitt, Stanford, Oklahoma, and Harvard Law).

"One day I counted them up," he said, "and I found that I've been to 18 schools in my life. We moved every two years, and we lived in ten different states. I was a real Army brat.

"Man, I lived like a king — even during the Depression. People in the Army had no trouble. I even took care of my father's polo ponies (he had 12 to 14). I had to get up every morning and exercise those damn things at four o'clock before I'd go to school.

"I even went out and broke wild stallions at Fort Lewis, Washington. There aren't too many places you can do that today. I had all the fine horses I ever wanted. I rode in steeplechases and fox hunts.

"I lived like a millionaire. I could play all the golf I wanted to. Swim all I wanted. I fired thousands of rounds of ammo on the machine guns. And even learned to fence with a champion. I'm pretty good at the epee and foil.

"If my father had been a civilian I couldn't have done it," Prince added, and paused for his second wind. "I got to play golf on the finest courses. Heck, I shoot in the '70s now. And, man, I can really whip 'em in table tennis."

(I had since heard from others that he was damn good playing table tennis, or ping pong. I checked this out with Pat Livingston, the former sports editor of *The Pittsburgh Press*. "He was good at everything," allowed Livingston. "He was a very competitive individual. He dared you to challenge him in a lot of ways.")

After running the gamut of American high schools, Prince finished up at Schenley High School in Pittsburgh, but never actually graduated. "I was a half-credit short," he explained. "But my father was a man of influence here in Pittsburgh in those days. And he exerted his influence, and promised I would make up the missing credit in night school. But I never did.

"You know," Prince pointed out with an extended finger, "my father had this town under martial law during the flood of 1936. He gave all the orders in that crisis. He was running the show. I remember going in a rowboat with my father down Liberty Avenue."

Well, Prince entered Pitt where he was "sensational in writing," by his own admission, and distinguished himself as the "craps shooting" champ in the hallways during his free periods.

He belonged to the Phi Delta fraternity chapter and was on the men's council as a sophomore.

He was on the swimming team at Pitt in 1936 where he tested the patience of Coach Pat Corr on a regular basis. Prince was a sprinter on the swim team and known as "Rapid Robert."

On a bitter winter day, Prince arrived late — as usual — for practice, wearing a full-length fur coat that was a mark of distinction on campus in those days of jazz, flappers, goldfish swallowers and stuffing guys in phone booths.

13

In the swim

Bob Prince as Pitt swimmer in 1936

Prince cuts an athletic figure as 23-year-old in summer of 1939 in Delafield, Wisconsin.

Bob Prince poses next to coach Bruce Drake and the 1938 Oklahoma University swim team. In photo on opposite page, Prince gets playful on 3-meter diving board with Coach Drake. His diving training would later serve him in good stead during his early years as a Pirate broadcaster.

Photos from Nancy Prince Thomas

Coach Corr sternly chewed out Prince. "You're always late! Where the hell have you been?"

Prince flipped off his fur coat, revealing only swim trunks and the skinniest of long bodies underneath, and informed the startled coach, "Hey, Pat, I'm ready!"

At a meet with CCNY, "Rapid Robert" arrived with a cigarette dangling from his lips. Before Corr could admonish him for smoking, Prince disarmed him by saying, "Here, Coach, hold this fag for me. What's Weismuller's record? Good, I'll be back in 51 seconds." Which was close to Johnny Weismuller's world record at the time in the 100 yard freestyle event.

Prince may have been Pitt's most famous swimmer because he publicized his involvement through the years at so many sports banquets, mostly poking fun at himself and his stick-like body.

"I never set any records until I reached Oklahoma," he said.

He would save his most celebrated performance at a swimming pool for a high dive act from the balcony overlooking the Chase Hotel pool in St. Louis when he was broadcasting Pirates games. He cleared a good 50 feet of concrete with his "Swannie" on a dare wager, noting "I'll do anything for twenty bucks."

He balked when his father was uprooted again, and he was to enroll in Stanford. He went there, however, and deliberately flunked out. Then his father was transferred to Fort Sill, Oklahoma, and young Bob enrolled at the University of Oklahoma. "Greatest school I ever went to," Prince volunteered. "They were a real friendly bunch of people. Stanford was snobbish."

Prince ended his educational swing at Harvard Law School. He was there the same time that John F. Kennedy was an undergraduate student. Prince won an audition for a radio broadcaster's job by "accident" and quit Harvard just shy of a degree.

"About eight of my relatives went through Harvard with flying colors," Prince remarked. "I failed in the family tradition. But I've had more fun than any of them."

Prince was fun to be around.

He was a booster. He was always trying to help other people. His wife, Betty, a Grove City College grad who was always active in alumni affairs, is a lovely woman. They had two children, Nancy and Bob Jr. Betty still chuckles when I relate stories to her about her husband. His name and his stories still pop up at sports banquets, and still draw laughs. Betty has always been a good sport about Bob.

Her husband's ashes are in a columbarium in the courtyard at Westminster Presbyterian Church in Upper St. Clair, where the Prince family lived for many years. "It's nice that he's here," Betty once disclosed. "The grandkids drive by on Route 19, and honk the horn to Bob."

Prince and I teamed up as the co-emcees when the Curbstone Coaches were reactivated at the Allegheny Club in the early '70s under the sponsorship of The Pittsburgh Brewing Company and *The Pittsburgh Press*.

Forbes Field and downtown streets were fun-filled sites back in early '60s.

Every time I was with him, whether it was in the P.A.A., the St. Clair Country Club, the Allegheny Club or Toots Shor's in New York, Prince always picked up the check and usually bought the bar a round or two. He spent money like it was burning a hole in the pocket of his latest wild slacks.

In the off-season between 1975 and 1976, the Pirates announced that Bob Prince and Nellie King would no longer serve as their broadcast team. Prince had rumpled the feathers of some of his bosses. The fans were shocked and upset. Prince was more than a radio broadcaster in Pittsburgh. He was an institution. He was unique, an original, and he was as closely linked to the Pirates as the team's nickname. Prince had rooted for the Pirates on the air, and never apologized for it. He was remembered for several phrases he repeatedly used on broadcasts such as: "You can kiss it goodbye." "Closer than fuzz on a tick's ear." "By a gnat's eyelash." "We had 'em all the way." "Sufferin' catfish." "Can of corn." "He picked that up like a Hoover sweeper." "Alabaster blasters." "A bloop and a blast." "Bug on a rug."

He also created the "green weenie" and popularized "babushka power." He delighted banquet audiences with his quick wit, such as when he introduced Stan Musial by saying, "I think it is ridiculous that we are gathered here tonight to honor a man who made more than 7,000 outs."

There has never been a better banquet emcee than Prince in Pittsburgh. He had a remarkable voice, a wonderful way of saying things, sometimes outrageous things, sometimes irreverent things. He knew how to tell a story, how to set the scene during a baseball game. He was a delightful entertainer. His voice was unmistakable, and there was a reassurance about it, especially late at night listening to him in the dark as he was doing a game out on the west coast.

The Pirates were never the same without Prince, and Prince was never quite the same without the Pirates. He continued to make appearances on local radio and TV, and got involved with other sports and commentaries, but it was never what it used to be. Pittsburgh and the Pirates were the poorer for Prince not being at the mike. And Prince was poorer for not making as much money, and lacking the vehicle to carry on his public career. He was finally brought back to the Pirates broadcast booth on May 3, 1985. Incredibly, the Pirates scored nine runs against the Los Angeles Dodgers in the first inning he worked, and went on to win the game, 16-2.

Prince was dying of cancer at the time, though it had not yet been made public. He died before the season was over. He was inducted into the broadcasters wing of the Baseball Hall of Fame in Cooperstown, New York, on August 3, 1986.

"Bob Prince's huckstering was so slickly colorful and cozening as to be entertaining, not resented. If there isn't some kind of drink served in Pittsburgh called a Bloop and a Blast, there ought to be one."
—Dick Shippy,
Akron Beacon-Journal

Some Prince Nicknames

Bill "Quail" Virdon

Bob "Dog" Skinner

Bob "Bart" Friend

Harvey "The Kitten" Haddix

"Hurryin' Joe" Christopher

Donn "Clink" Clendenon

Billy "Digger" O'Dell

Manny "Road Runner" Sanguillen

Way Up Yonder With Jesse Gonder

"Chicken on the Hill" Will Stargell

Ronnie "The Callery Pa. Hummer" Kline

Dick "Ducky" Schofield

Vernon "Deacon" Law

Bob "Beetle" Bailey

"Arriba" Roberto Clemente

Al "Scoop" Oliver

Gene "Augie" Freese

Gene "Little Angry" Clines

Ed "Spanky" Kirkpatrick

Don "Tiger" Hoak

Jim "Possum" Woods

Some Pet Prince Phrases

"Bloop and a blast" — hits needed to start a rally

"a radio ball" — a pitch that could be heard and not seen

"a Hoover" — a ball that can be scooped up easily

"by a gnat's eyelash" — close call, or near-miss

"close as fuzz on a tick's ear" — same as above

"tweener" — a hit that falls between two fielders

"We had 'em all the way" — after a comeback victory

"How sweet it is!" — saluting any special thrill

"can of corn" — easy-to-catch fly ball

Bob Prince went to work at WJAS Radio in 1941 without the benefit of any formal training as an announcer: "Whatever you call it — glib or B.S., or whatever — I was born with it, I guess."

Prince file

Family History
- Born in Los Angeles, California July 1, 1916
  Son of Col. and Mrs. F. A. Prince
- Married to Elizabeth Casey of Pittsburgh in 1941
  Daughter: Nancy   Son: Robert F. Prince Jr.
  Granddaughters: Kimberly and Casey.
  Grandson: Bob Jr.

Education
- Attended University of Pittsburgh, Stanford University and Oklahoma University.
- Graduated from Oklahoma University, 1938.
- Varsity letter winner in swimming at University of Pittsburgh and Oklahoma University.
- Attended Harvard Law School, 1939-40.

Career
- Commenced sports broadcasting — 1941.
- Announcer for Mr. Anthony Program — Mutual — Mid '40s.
- Joined Pittsburgh Pirates in 1948, with the late Rosey Rowswell. Became chief announcer in 1955 and served in that capacity through 1975.
- Announced Houston Astros baseball, 1976.
- First play-by-play announcer, ABC-TV Monday Night Baseball, 1976.
- Broadcast first baseball Championship Series between New York Mets and Atlanta Braves — Bob Wolff Enterprises.
- Broadcast three World Series, two All-Star Games — NBC-TV and Radio.
- Broadcast College World Series — Omaha, Nebraska for Home Box Office.
- Football broadcasting activities included nine years with Penn State, eleven years with the Pittsburgh Steelers, two years with CBS. College Football Game of the Week.
- Gator Bowl, CBS; Tangerine Bowl, Mutual; East-West Shrine Game, NBC.
- Broadcast Duquesne University and Ohio State basketball.
- Three NIT championship tournaments.
- Pittsburgh Hornets

- Pittsburgh Penguins
- Three American Hockey League playoffs.
- Five years of blow-by-blow in boxing, including eight World Championship fights.
- NCAA Swimming and Diving Championships. Ames, Iowa — Hughes Sports Network — Television.
- Bob Hope Desert Classic — NBC-TV.
- U.S. Open at Oakmont — Mutual Radio.

Bob Prince Enterprises
- Iron City Brewery — Member of executive staff.
- WIXZ — Daily sports talk show and commentaries
- WTAE-TV — Commentaries and special events
- Gunner Network — Saturday sports talk show on network of radio stations covering western Pennsylvania and eastern Ohio.
- CMU Football — WIXZ Radio.
- Total Communications — Special sports events on commercial and pay TV.
- Commercial radio and TV for selected sponsors.

Affiliations
- Westminster Presbyterian Church, Washington Lodge, Bellefield Lodge, Ascalon, Syria Temple, Pittsburgh Forest, South Hills Caravan, Scottish Rite, Royal Order of Jesters Court #2, Phi Delta Theta Fraternity

Awards
- Sportcaster of the Year — fourteen consecutive years. Selected by fellow sportscasters and writers.
- Jewish War Veterans
- Jaycee Man of the Year in Communications.
- Jaycee Man of the Year in Human Relations.
- Jaycee Citizens — for outstanding work on behalf of the City of Pittsburgh.
- Pittsburgh Jaycees Man of the Year.
- Pittsburgh Chamber of Commerce Man of the Year.
- Distinguished Pittsburgher — Dapper Dan Club.
- Dapper Dan Man of the Year — Cumberland, Md.
- National Disabled American Veterans — from national commander.
- American Legion Distinguished Service

- Variety Club Showman of the Year
- Connie Mack Youth Award — American Legion in Philadelphia.
- Salvation Army Centennial Medallion
- Service to Mankind — Sertoma International. Presented with authentic moon rock from first lunar landing.
- Pride of Pennsylvania
- Bob Prince Night — July 28, 1972 — commemorating 25 years of broadcasting Pirates baseball. Only major league announcer who had been with the same club for 25 consecutive years.
- Tommy Davies Award — Pittsburgh Collegiate Football Hall of Fame. First recipient.
- Art Rooney Award — Catholic Youth Association. First recipient.
- YMCA Distinguished Service
- Pittsburgh Pirates Media Hall of Fame
- National Sportswriters and Sportscasters Hall of Fame, Salisbury, N.C.
- Western Chapter of Pennsylvania Sports Hall of Fame and state enshrinee.

Activities

- *Allegheny Valley School* — Co-founder, director and executive vice-president — school for handicapped individuals.
- *George Trautman Award* — Founder of award, chairman of committee which recognizes outstanding college baseball players.
- *Fred Hutchinson Memorial* — Founder, national chairman of committee which recognizes annually a major league player by vote of major league writers and broadcasters. Financial benefit of Fred Hutchinson Cancer Research Center in Seattle.
- *Roberto Clemente Boys Club* — Chairman and director.
- *Lou Gehrig Memorial* — National director, helps in annual selection of major league baseball player awardee.
- *Ham-Am Golf Tournament* — Founder and chairman of the board for pro-celebrity amateur golf tournament. Proceeds go to caddies for college expenses. Graduate student of program was sent to England for work on master's degree.
- *Ira "Rat" Rogers Trophy* — presented by Bob Prince to outstanding scholar-athlete at West Virginia University. This is an annual award at the Touchdown Club banquet.

- *Boys' Baseball* — National director. Organization supervises league play for 120,000 boys in the U.S., Canada and Mexico.
- *HYPO* — Executive vice-president and director, organization designed to keep youth of Western Pennsylvania busily engaged in playing baseball.
- *Youth Guidance* — Member, organization works with Juvenile Court.
- *National Sportscasters and Sportswriters of America* — Director and co-founder of organization headquartered in Salisbury, N.C.
- *Dapper Dan Club* — Director and emcee for 18 years.
- *Variety Club* — Chief Barker, 1968-69. One of three men to hold office at Tent #1, the founding tent for a two-year period.
- *Thompson Club* — Master of ceremonies for annual sports night dinner, 1960-1984.

Club Memberships
- Harvard-Yale-Princeton Club, Pittsburgh Athletic Association*, Variety Club*, Dapper Dan Club*, Pittsburgh Press Club, The Allegheny Club*, Missouri Athletic Club, St. Clair Country Club, Stadium clubs in St. Louis, Los Angeles, San Francisco, Bradenton, Fla. Country Club, St. Petersburg Yacht Club

* Member Board of Directors

Allegheny Valley School

Bob Prince was prime fund-raiser for Allegheny Valley School, now a statewide service for mentally retarded individuals, based in Robinson Township.

23

On Sunnyside Street
A love affair begins with
Bob Prince and the Bucs

"How sweet it is!"

My mother would be doing her ironing in the kitchen of our home at 5410 Sunnyside Street. She had the ironing board set up in front of the Frigidaire refrigerator, with the Westinghouse stove at her back, and Westinghouse clothes washer and dryer side by side between the stove and the sink. A gray formica-topped table, where we ate all our meals, was along the opposite wall. My mother never had to iron a tablecloth because I don't remember ever seeing one on that table.

There was a black Zenith radio sitting on a ledge just big enough to hold it, high on the wall by the stairway. The radio was just above the Westinghouse roaster and cabinet. My mother would be listening to the Pirates' games on the radio as she ironed our clothes. There was a certain clean smell in the air as the iron glided over and smoothed out a white shirt or a blouse.

I'd sit on the steps in our kitchen to keep my mother company, and listen to the game with her. We talked about all kinds of things and we listened to the game. Sometimes she'd test me on my spelling, or help me with my homework while the game provided background music. Artist Norman Rockwell would have liked the scene.

Once I was in grade school, my mother always had a job, as a sales clerk or secretary. She worked a swing shift, and some days I'd join her for lunch at a restaurant on Second Avenue, which was our main street, or somewhere nearby. I thought that was the greatest, whether we were eating at Isaly's, Duffy's, the Virginia Lounge or the Lawrence Drug Store.

We lived in a row house, one of four with the same set of Koolvent awnings, green and white except for the house at the other end that, for some strange reason, broke the pattern and had burgundy and white slats instead. That seemed so stupid. Those same awnings are still there, 45 years later, with one or two slats missing or twisted, but so much else is gone. There are houses missing, like the Metro house which seemed indestructible in its heyday. There is trash blocking walkways, weeds grown high, rust, ruin, decay everywhere, pride in appearances no longer evident. I can still see the way it used to be. Sometimes we'd sit on a glider out on the porch back then, admire our yardwork, and listen to the Pirates' games on the radio.

I remember that this was especially great if the Pirates were playing somewhere on the road, such as St. Louis or Chicago and Milwaukee, and it was raining in Pittsburgh. There was something about the sound of the rain pelting those aluminum awnings, listening to Bob Prince, waiting for my dad to come home, feeling safe and secure sitting with my mother. There was always something reassuring about Bob Prince's velvet-like voice.

Our row house was 15 feet wide and two stories high if you looked at it from the front, on Sunnyside Street, and three stories high if you looked at it from the back alley, which had the rich-sounding name of Gatelodge Way. Our plot of ground was called Blair Estates — sounds good, too — on the map that accompanied the deed. The steps in the kitchen led up to our basement, which was partitioned off for a bathroom after we'd been there a few years and had a major renovation on the lower levels. I remember how excited we were when we got a separate bathroom, with a built-in bathtub/shower.

Not many people in Hazelwood, or anywhere for that matter, had a basement that was a half-level above their kitchen. I spent most of the first 24 years of my life on Sunnyside Street, the first five years at 5413 Sunnyside Street. My father, Dan O'Brien, was born on a couch in that first home, also an end house of a row of three brick houses. My mother lost a baby to a miscarriage in my parents' bedroom in that house. I remember vaguely the frenetic scene in our house that day.

It was sitting on the kitchen steps of our home on Sunnyside Street where I was first introduced to Bob Prince. He was "the voice of the Pirates." You just had to listen to Bob Prince. There was something about his rich, raspy voice. His vocal chords should have been insured by Lloyds of London. It didn't seem right somehow that the cancer that killed him was in his mouth.

Two famous sports broadcasters died at the outset of 1998. They were Harry Caray and Ray Scott. Harry Caray was an outrageous baseball broadcaster who gained fame for his phrasing and madcap behavior with the St. Louis Cardinals, the Chicago White Sox, the Oakland A's and the Chicago Cubs. Caray was a character who, like Prince, had a loyal legion of fans and just as many detractors. Scott was a straight man out of Johnstown, Pennsylvania who went from doing play-by-play for Pitt football to the Green Bay Packers during the glory days of Vince Lombardi. He was respected for his spare commentary and his professionalism. He was the opposite of Prince and Caray. Restraint was his byword. Their deaths moved sports fans throughout the country; they had left that kind of mark. Scott was mentioned as a possible successor for Prince when he was fired as the Pirates' announcer. "Bob Prince was a friend of mine," said Scott in his own succinct style when reporters called to see if he was a candidate. "So I'm not interested."

> *"I suppose I would have to credit my mother for my feelings. In our family, no one ever told me a white person was better than a black person. I always try to treat everyone fairly. I wanted black athletes to have the opportunity to play."*
> — Bob Prince

Roamin' Around in the P-G

My brother Danny delivered the morning newspaper, the *Pittsburgh Post-Gazette,* and I helped him. He was 15 and I was ten when I first started going with him on his route. We had 88 customers at our peak, and it took us about an hour to deliver all of the papers. We had to get up an hour or so earlier than most of our friends in order to deliver the papers before we went off to school.

I loved reading the sports section and comic section of the newspaper each morning at the breakfast table. Starting the day with Al Abrams and Jack Sell and Jack Hernon, Jimmy Jordan and Jimmy Miller, Phil "Alley Addenda" Gundelfinger on bowling, plus Archie, Dick Tracy, Terry and the Pirates, and Li'l Abner. I especially remember how exciting it was to read the annual tabloid supplement before the Pirates opened spring training. It was full of photographs and stories and all sorts of splendid information, thumbnail shots and bios of all the ballplayers. Jack Hernon had the Bucs' beat back then. Myron Cope was misused at the time, working the desk, taking Little League line scores over the telephone, except when he got out each year to cover the Pittsburgh Golden Gloves amateur boxing tournament. He was easily the most talented writer on the staff, I loved reading the newspaper. I just ate it up along with the Cheerios or Wheaties. It was special.

It was the start of a love affair with sports and newspapers and all kinds of printed materials about my main interest in life: the world of fun and games. When I grew up, I wanted to be like Al Abrams, the sports editor and columnist of the *Post-Gazette.* Seemed to me like he got to go to a lot of neat places, meet a lot of interesting people — Count Phil and the Japanese Ambassador, Billy Conn and Fritzi Zivic — and he got paid to watch games. He wrote simply, telling us where he went, who he met, what they said, and what he thought about all that. LaMarba, as he referred to himself, was the greatest. He held court at the Carlton House. Danny and I shared a bedroom and, at night, we'd listen to radio serials like "The Shadow" and "Mr. and Mrs. North," "Amos 'n Andy" or a Pirates' game on the radio. We'd turn out the lights and listen in the dark. You could see the game better that way, with Prince painting a picture of what was going on.

"Bob Prince was the voice under the pillow for a little kid in New Castle," wrote a fan, Dr. Louis Zona, when he heard I was writing a book about "The Gunner."

A woman in Johnstown was speaking to her husband as I was signing a book for them before the Christmas holidays in November of 1997. "How many times when you were a kid," she asked him, "and you went to bed at night listening to the ballgame, was Bob Prince the last voice you heard before you fell asleep?"

Another woman told me that her parents had gone to about 25 Pirate games during the 1960 season, but were away in Europe when the Pirates won the World Series. She was 12 at the time. She remembers her brothers and sisters sending their parents a telegram somewhere in Europe that read simply: WE HAD 'EM ALL THE WAY.

Such Prince phrases remain with those of us who followed the Pirates during his long tenure. "By a gnat's eyelash," with proper attribution, popped up in a Sunday sermon when I was working on this book.

"We felt wanted."
— Chuck Adams

When I was nine, one Christmas season I talked my mother   into buying me a toy printing press, an Ace model, at the Hazelwood Variety Store. I organized most of the games on Sunnyside Street, putting up a first-rate basketball hoop with a backboard that extended out over the street from a telephone pole. You could drive under it for a lay-up without coming away with creosote stains on your shirt from bumping into the telephone pole. I cleared a nearby vacant lot and laid out an infield, and set the ground rules, so we could play ball there. I remember how unreasonable and nasty we thought the people were who lived alongside the lot when they complained about a foul ball striking the side of their houses.

I built a broad-jumping pit and fashioned a discus with wood scraps and wood putty and used a black duckpin bowling ball for a shot put and started my own track & field team on our street. When I was 11 or 12, I started the Sunnyside A.C. and had black and white T-shirts made up with the name of our club on the front and our names on the back. Our mothers ironed on each letter, one by one. We had our own basketball league under the lights just below my parents' bedroom window.

I imported speedy black kids from other neighborhoods for my track & field team, and bought little plastic trophies at Murphy's 5 & 10 that said "World's Greatest Athlete" and presented them to the winners of different events when we'd hold a meet on Sunnyside Street. "We felt wanted, which was not our experience everywhere in those days," said Chuck Adams, one of those young blacks who ran for my Sunnyside A.C. team and later as a back for Joe Paterno's Penn State football team.

I remember getting my dad to run the 440-yard oval I'd laid out and worrying that, at age 45 or something, he might keel over and die from the exertion. After all, he seemed so old to me then, and he was winded when he finished his run.

I kept statistics for all our games, and started writing stories and put out a one-sheet newspaper now and then, which I tacked to my front door so all the kids in the neighborhood could read about themselves. It didn't cause as much commotion as Martin Luther putting his letter of protest on the doors of the Cathedral at Wittenberg, but it was an attention-getter. I cut photographs out of the newspapers and sports magazines I treasured and changed the identities of those pictured to the names of the neighborhood kids. Players at Pitt, Penn State and Notre Dame became Larry and Butchie Buffo, Butchie Boyle, Johnny Metro, Toby Lewis, Marty Wendell, Gary Ferko, Billy Fonzi, Snooky Pison, Patty and Tommy Murtha.

Johnny's dad, Homer Metro, was a big sports fan. I didn't know it then, but he liked to put bets on the games. He worked at the post office and was always wearing a dress shirt and a tie when he came home from work, so he looked a lot better than most of our dads who labored in the nearby mills and railroad yards — Jones & Laughlin Steel, U.S. Steel, Mesta Machine Company and the Baltimore & Ohio Railroad, the Monongahela Connecting Railroad — and were always dirty when they came home. Homer always had the radio on when he was sitting on his front porch, and it was always for a ballgame. We liked to sit on the porch with Homer and talk about baseball and listen to Bob Prince. They both knew what they were talking about. They were voices of authority.

Back in those days, a lot of people sat on porches and listened to the Pirate baseball games in the summer. No one had air-conditioning then, few had television sets, and there was little, if any, sports on the tube. It was that way for years. There was no cable TV or ESPN, let alone ESPN2. You could walk in certain blocks, especially in Oakland out near Forbes Field where the Pirates played their games, and listen to the ballgame on the radio as you walked by one home and then another, because somebody was on the front porch listening to Bob Prince doing the Pirates games. I didn't get to go to many at Forbes Field, so the local sandlot stars at nearby Burgwin Field were my heroes.

My dad wasn't much of a sports fan. He just wasn't into it, and that was OK. He'd won some medals in swimming as a kid, just like Prince, but that was about it. He got interested in sports because his three sons, Richard, Danny and I all liked sports, and so did my sister Carole. We were all five years apart, and I was the youngest.

Richard was 18 and a cook in the U.S. Navy in the Pacific when I was three, and he got married when he came home and lived in Ohio, so he always seemed like a second cousin, at best. He was a big sports fan, and often brought his buddies from Bridgeport, Ohio to Pittsburgh, as well as to Cleveland, to catch the baseball games. It was always a big deal when Dick and his buddies came to our house. I remember them being a noisy bunch. They'd buy five seats for four fellows and use the fifth seat to stack their cases of beer. You could bring your own beer into the ballpark in those days, and they'd come up for Sunday doubleheaders and drink their way through 18 or more innings. Imagine being able to bring your own beer to the ballpark.

My dad never took me to a Pirates game. Frank Casne, whom I still run into once in a while in the South Hills, took me to my first

Pirates game and a few more after that. Casne was the director at the Burgwin Field Recreation Center near my home. He passed out the balls so we could play basketball or softball, and brought some semblance of order and harmony whenever we were playing games under his supervision. He had a quick whistle that hung from his neck. We went to the Pirates' games as members of the "Knot-Hole Gang," and got in for a mere 50 cents a game.

We entered Forbes Field through a gate in right centerfield and we sat in the stands out in right field, in the so-called cheap seats. We were sitting just above Roberto Clemente, or folks like Carl Furillo or Stan Musial. They looked up through the screen and our bubble gum card collection came alive before our wide eyes. Cheap seats, huh? It was like having a box at the opera. God, it would be great to be able to go out to the ballpark tomorrow night and find them out in right field. Sort of like in the movie "Field of Dreams."

"We'll talk about your plans."
— Bob Prince,
Madison Square Garden,
New York, New York

I started slipping some short stories about the ballgames we played at Burgwin Field or in our neighborhood under the door of the local newspaper, *The Hazelwood Envoy*, and they started printing them and, before you knew it, I was hired as the sports editor. I was 14 and I was a professional sports writer, paid the princely sum of $5 to produce enough stories to fill two pages of a tabloid newspaper every two weeks. I played all sorts of sandlot sports, never really distinguishing myself in any of them, and wrote about all the activity.

When I went to the University of Pittsburgh, I signed up for duty on *The Pitt News*, the campus newspaper, before I signed up for classes. I was also writing for the student yearbook and doing color for basketball games on the student radio station, WPGH. It was the beginning of a love affair and a way to make a living without having to work too hard. I had two half scholarships as a reward for my campus activity, so I was going to school for free.

I arrived at Pitt in September of 1960 and one month later the Pirates were playing the New York Yankees in the World Series right on our campus. I thought it had to be the greatest place possible to go to school. Oakland was then the center for all sports and cultural activity. The Pittsburgh Steelers and the Pittsburgh Symphony were all playing there.

Beano Cook and I started a newspaper called *Pittsburgh Weekly Sports* in my senior year, 1963, at Pitt, and he introduced me personally to the best sportswriters and sportswriting in the nation, much of which we reprinted in our irreverent sheet at a fee of $2.50 or a 13-week free subscription to *PWS* per article. I interviewed Bob Prince for a feature story in the introductory issue we used to line up patrons and advertisers in advance of printing our paper on a regular basis. After two years in the U.S. Army, in Louisville, Kansas City and, finally, Delta Junction, Alaska, I returned home to Hazelwood, got married within the year to Kathleen Churchman of White Oak. I was still turning out *Pittsburgh Weekly Sports,* having a good time and learning a lot, but not making much money.

Kathie thought it would be a good idea if I got a real job. She still thinks that way, even today. So a year-and-a-half later I went off to cover the Dolphins in their last year in the American Football League for *The Miami News*, then moved to *The New York Post* for nine years.

I felt like I had arrived when I was sent to cover a baseball game at Yankee Stadium. I was more impressed with the company I was keeping in the press box than the ballplayers on the hallowed field. Sitting on both sides of me were the likes of Pulitzer Prize winning writers like Arthur Daley and Dave Anderson and Red Smith, and famous writers like Jimmy Cannon, Milton Gross, Larry Merchant, Stan Isaacs, Vic Zeigel, Maury Allen, George Vecsey, Frank Deford, Dan Jenkins, Murray Chass, Jack Lang and Joe Durso.

Sometimes famous authors would show up at sports events or press conferences in New York such as Jimmy Breslin, Norman Mailer, Budd Schulburg and William Saroyan or movie people like Horace McMahon, Joe E. Lewis, Dustin Hoffman, Robert Redford and Woody Allen. I met Phil Foster, Alan King, Milton Berle, Billy Crystal and Red Skeleton at such get-togethers.

I remember meeting Toots Shor, the famous saloon keeper, at his just-off-Broadway joint, and he mentioned that Bob Prince was one of his favorite visitors among the sports media. Toots Shor hosted the biggest showbiz, TV, radio and newspaper headliners, yet he talked about Prince endlessly because I was from Pittsburgh. He said Prince liked to line up shot glasses and keep a little glass of Coke at the end of the line. Prince was every saloon keeper's best customer. Shor figured I had to be OK, too, if Prince was a friend.

When Jackie Gleason came to town to promote "The Great One" on TV, he, too, could talk about Bob Prince. Some insist that Gleason got his "how sweet it is" line from Prince. Gleason and Prince would have been a great pair at any bar.

It was during my last year at *The Post* that I bumped into Bob Prince. He was at New York's Madison Square Garden to do a broadcast of a Penguins-Rangers game there. I spoke to him in the press room before the game, as I had when I was covering a game involving the Pirates through the years, and told him I had taken a job at *The Pittsburgh Press* and would be moving back home to Pittsburgh in the coming summer. I had been a copy boy in the classified ad section of *The Press* during my junior and senior years at Taylor Allderdice High

Pittsburgh author Jim O'Brien compares notes with Ken Burns, who produced the award-winning PBS series *Baseball* and *The Civil War* at a pre-All-Star Game party by the wall at Forbes Field in the summer of 1994. Below, O'Brien is flanked by two of the most famous one-shot home run hitters in history, Bobby Thomson of the Giants and Bill Mazeroski of the Pirates.

School, and was on a *Wall Street Journal* scholarship as a city-side intern in the summer of 1962, following my sophomore year at Pitt. I never lost my enthusiasm for Pittsburgh sports.

"You've got to come on with me between periods," Prince said. "We'll talk about your plans."

This was a game, by the way, in which Prince drew criticism in a Pittsburgh suburban newspaper for the shoddy way in which he broadcasted a hockey game. He was out of his element, and often resorted to a play-by-play that went like this: "They've got it, now we've got it, oops, they've got it again, and — who was that? — someone shoots and scores." And that's no exaggeration.

Prince had me on between the second and third periods, as promised, and he talked about my return to Pittsburgh in the same tones one might reserve for General MacArthur's return to the Philippine Islands. Bob was always a booster. He liked to help young people get started in the business. He liked to help them move up in the world. He liked me and I was lucky to have a friend like Bob Prince. Pittsburgh was lucky to have a booster like Bob Prince. Joe "Screamer" Tucker, the voice of the Steelers back then, was like that, as were Tom Bender, Ed Conway, Red Donley, Hal Scott, Bill Burns and Jack Henry.

Within a year after my return to Pittsburgh, where I covered the Steelers when they won their fourth Super Bowl at the end of the 1979 season, I collaborated with local illustrator and publisher Marty Wolfson to do a book, *Pittsburgh: The Story of the City of Champions.* It chronicled all the successes in Pittsburgh during the decade of the '70s. It contained a foreword by Mayor Dick Caliguiri, whom I had first met when he was looking after his father's bowling alley in Hazelwood and I would go there to get scores for my sports section in *The Hazelwood Envoy.*

"Will it be too expensive for Joe Fan?"
— John Troan, Editor
The Pittsburgh Press

In doing my research on the book, I discovered that there was no longer a weekly sports luncheon in Pittsburgh, an event I looked forward to and often played hooky at Pitt to attend during my student days there. It was held at the Roosevelt Hotel in downtown Pittsburgh, where the Steelers offices and Art Rooney were ensconced at the time. Coaches and athletes from all the Pittsburgh teams would appear on the dais and discuss their respective situations.

It had been dropped, unbelievably, just prior to a period of the greatest sports successes in the city's history, including four Super

Curbstone Coaches meeting at Allegheny Club in 1981 featured, from left to right, Dan McCann of Pittsburgh Brewing Co. who was also football coach at Duquesne University; co-emcee Bob Prince, Pitt football coach Jackie Sherrill; Pittsburgh Brewing Co. president Bill Smith; *The Pittsburgh Press* editor John Troan; Penn State football coach Joe Paterno, and *Press* sports writer and co-emcee Jim O'Brien.

Curbstone Coaches lineup in 1981 included Dick Macino, promotion director of *The Pittsburgh Press;* Pittsburgh Brewing Co. president Bill Smith; Carnegie Mellon University football coach Chuck Klausing; Pittsburgh Steelers receiver Lynn Swann; Philadelphia 76ers star Julius "Dr. J" Erving, Duquesne University football coach Dan McCann, and sports editor Pat Livingston and writer Jim O'Brien of *The Pittsburgh Press.*

Bowl triumphs by the Steelers, two World Series titles by the Pirates in 1971 and 1979, a national football championship at Pitt in 1976, among other local achievements by the pro and college teams.

I mentioned this to officials at the Pittsburgh Brewing Company, notably Dan McCann and his boss, Bill Smith, and they picked up on my idea to resurrect the sports luncheons. They teamed up with John Troan, the editor of *The Press,* to promote a series of monthly luncheons at the Allegheny Club at Three Rivers Stadium.

The cost of the luncheon was set at $10 per plate, which gave Troan pause for thought. "Will it be too expensive for Joe Fan?" he asked.

It was called the Curbstone Coaches, a throwback to the name of the luncheons emceed by Chester L. Smith, the sports editor of *The Press* back in the '50s and '60s. Coincidentally enough, Alex DiCroce, who'd been the manager at the Roosevelt Hotel, was now managing the Allegheny Club.

No one had to tell him how to put on or host such a luncheon. It was an immediate hit and has played to sellout crowds ever since, into the late '90s.

I co-emceed that series of sports luncheons along with Bob Prince, who represented the Pittsburgh Brewing Company. He was a goodwill ambassador for them for years, hustling Iron City beer at sports banquets and smokers throughout the tri-state area. There was none better at such bantering than Bob Prince. He just had a way about him, a breezy style, that was so engaging, and he consistently charmed the crowd.

What I remember most about working with him for several years with the Curbstone Coaches was how exceptional he was at emceeing any event, and how generous he was in sharing the podium with a then young pup or upstart like me. We never stepped on each other's toes. It was my job to get all the information on the speakers, and Prince would just play off me. He didn't need notes. That luncheon series, by the way, was renamed the Coaches Corner in the early '90s.

I never tried to be like Bob Prince. He had his own act, and no one else could do it quite like him. I just took my cues from him and tried to stay out of his way. He was always kind, good-natured and so helpful. I have always tried to borrow the best of him, as well as Art Rooney, Frankie Gustine, Doc Carlson, Myron Cope, tremendous people and role models I was fortunate to meet as a young man. They were all great teachers.

That's why I was so excited when I decided to undertake this project to profile Bob Prince through the eyes and stories and photographs of the people who knew him best through the many years he promoted Pittsburgh and its sports teams and people like no other ambassador who has ever represented the city. His Pirates portrayed here are, for the most part, the ones who remained in Pittsburgh or kept their connections alive through the years.

Good Guys. . .

Bob Prince with Art Rooney

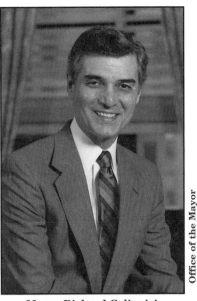

Mayor Richard Caliguiri

Bob Prince is flanked by Frankie Gustine and Red Donley in celebrity game at Forbes Field back in '60s. Anyone could learn a lot from these three individuals.

No matter how many people one talks to, all the stories do not surface. Some are selective in their story-telling, preferring understandably to put a positive spin on things. Bob Prince was a man of excesses. He drank too much and smoked too much, which was his undoing in the end, and he winked at a few women in his time. He couldn't help himself. He had that mischievous, madcap manner and a gleam in his eye that was only magnified by his dark-rimmed eyeglasses. He was full of himself. He made us smile and he made us growl. He taught Sunday school at his church, but he committed a few sins for setting his own rules on how to lead the good life. He was generous to a fault, and was an easy touch for everyone with a hard-luck story. He had a loose tongue before Michael Jordan was Michael Jordan, and it often slipped out the side, and he'd push it back in with the back of his hand. Some statements made their way out as well that he would have been better off not issuing.

He said some of the damndest things, made some unholy remarks, and insiders still quote some of the raunchy remarks he made at stag dinners or with the boys in the press room, but I'll help them retain their insider status by not repeating those remarks in this book. There's more than one book about Bob Prince, as there are about most people, and this is the one I chose to write.

My books are intended, by virtue of the stories and photographs, to spark your own memories, to take you on a trip down memory lane, not just to Forbes Field and Three Rivers Stadium, but also to your own home or backyard and the ballgames of your life, sitting on your dad's shoulders and feeling like a giant. Bob Prince shouldn't just remind you of your favorite Pirates, but of your father, mother, friends and neighbors, good times, bad times.

He always wore loud outfits to the Allegheny Club for the Curbstone Coaches gig and he never, even in the coldest days of October and November, wore socks. He always wore a smile and was glib and fun to be around, quick with a handshake, a sharp remark, and a pat on the back. That was the real beauty of Bob Prince.

While I was working on this book, I often had pictures of Prince positioned near my word processor so I could see him while I was writing about him, and I listened to tapes of him broadcasting Pirates games just to set the mood, for inspiration, for reminders of another era. Writing or reading a book like this is like squinting into the past. It provides airbrushed memories. Things get hectic in our lives and we like to look back to what we really believe were better times. We need some warm fuzzies from the past to deal with the demands of today. "Much of the appeal of nostalgia stems from a longing for a return to simpler times," stated a cover story in *Business Week*, March 23, 1998.

> **"All through junior high and high school, six years, every day, I found a word under my breakfast plate. When I came home I had to spell it, define it and use it in a sentence."**
> — Bob Prince

So the stories and photographs ought to open up memories of teenage years, for instance, and allow us to reinterpret those times. For the younger reader, hopefully, they will bring alive stories they heard their parents and grandparents offer while sitting in the stands at Three Rivers Stadium, or sitting on a porch listening to a Pirates' broadcast on the radio or TV. We tend to look back through rose-colored glasses. I still wear a pair of rose-colored sunglasses from time to time and the world really does look better through them. So this is a marriage of past and present, a history of warm memories, reconnecting us with our idealized past. Bob Prince was the announcer for what we recall as a Golden Age.

"I know how to fill the silence."

Bob Prince was known as a gabby guy and always boasted that he knew "how to fill the silence." It struck me, however, in listening to those tapes of baseball broadcasts by Prince & Co., that the games were done differently in those days than they are now.

Listening to a tape of a doubleheader with the Chicago Cubs he did on the final day at Forbes Field during the 1970 season, for example, I was struck by how curt his commentary really was. He often allowed the crowd noise to carry the excitement of the day.

His sidekick, Nellie King, didn't come in after every pitch with analysis, the way I remember Jim Rooker or Bob Walk doing in more recent times. King only came in, usually, during a pitching change or a break in the action, as the teams were changing positions on the field. So Prince had the mike most of the time, whether he was on radio or TV, exchanging the No. 1 slot with Jim "Possum" Woods, for instance, as he had done for so many years before.

He was with Woods the longest, 12 years (1958-1969) and also broadcasted Bucs' baseball with the help of Rosey Rowswell, who preceded him and was there 19 years (1936-1954), and for brief stints with Dick Bingham, Joe Tucker, Claude Haring, Paul Long, Don Hoak, Gene Osborne and, of course, King. Bucs baseball was on KDKA Radio continuously since 1955.

Prince explained the game, which women and young fans particularly liked, and the crusty know-it-alls swore about. He entertained most, annoyed some. He told you where the players were deployed, he painted a picture, and he explained strategy to set up the next pitch. He gave you the score, again and again, but he seldom read the p.r. notes and numbers and trivia that clutter broadcasts today. If he didn't have anything to say that would add to the event, he shut up.

Prince's opinion held forth on all aspects of the game. He spoke confidently. He and the crowd noise, and the vendors shouting "hot dog, hot dog" just below or above the broadcast booth, made you feel

37

like you were there. You could smell it. "The Bucs are trying to put the heat on here," he'd say. He'd tell a story, or pull something that happened ten or 15 years ago out of the air, detailing a sequence on an earlier era as if it happened yesterday, and he'd tag it by saying smugly, "What memories I have brought."

Indeed, what memories Bob Prince has brought.

Author Jim O'Brien is shown as young ballplayer in Pirates and Little League uniforms, respectively, batting against Butch Boyle in front of 5410 Sunnyside Street and fielding in backyard. Bob Prince and the Pirates made baseball fans out of many of us.

Betty Prince
The pillar behind Bob Prince

"She's deserving of sainthood."
— Ralph Kiner

T he P.A.A. was the perfect place to have lunch with Nellie King and Betty Prince. We went there, at the invitation of Betty, who was greeted enthusiastically by name — "Hello, Mrs. Prince" — by the valet in the parking lot, and the maître d´ and waiter in the grill room. This was definitely familiar territory for her and her family.

The ghost of Bob Prince, her late husband and King's one-time partner in the Pirates' broadcast booth, was still flitting about the familiar cherry-wood paneled grill room. Prince was still peeking his familiar long-necked head into every room in the rest of the stately gray building on Fifth Avenue, just across the street from the Cathedral of Learning on the University of Pittsburgh campus.

Bob Prince played the P.A.A. on many occasions. Oldtimers still tell Bob Prince stories.

"This was one of Bob's hangouts," said King.

"Bob certainly spent a good deal of time here," said Betty Prince. "He enjoyed this place. We got together here before and after the ballgames. Bob was very popular here."

The P.A.A., or Pittsburgh Athletic Association as it is formally known, was a much more popular place in those days. That's when the Steelers and Pirates were playing at Forbes Field, just two short blocks away, just past the old Schenley Hotel that became the William Pitt Student Union, and Frank Blandi's Park Schenley Restaurant. Bob belonged to a P.A.A. group called Saints and Sinners.

The Syria Mosque, where the Pittsburgh Symphony Orchestra and many concerts were featured, was located just behind the P.A.A. on Bigelow Boulevard back in those days. I saw Redd Foxx and The Drifters in a doubleheader there one night. The Mosque had been razed in a controversial change in the landscape in the early '90s. The Masonic Temple was still next door to the P.A.A. Prince was active in the Shriners for years. There's a story told that Prince fainted during an induction ceremony because he thought, while he was blind-folded, that someone had put a snake on his shoulders. It was a moist sausage, as it turned out. One of the Shriners had heard that Prince had a real fear of snakes.

Prior to my senior year at Pitt, in the summer of 1963, Bob Prince had taken me to lunch at the P.A.A., where I interviewed him for the introductory issue of *Pittsburgh Weekly Sports*, a tabloid newspaper that Beano Cook and I published for the next 4½ years. It was the first time I'd ever entered the hallowed halls of the P.A.A., a private club that was considered a citadel of the rich.

Now it was high noon, Thursday, March 19, 1998, and there were only a few other tables occupied in the room when Nellie, Betty and I broke bread together. IRS rules relating to deductions allowed for club membership and entertaining customers had changed, and the P.A.A. was having a tough time competing for new members with more contemporary health clubs throughout the city and suburbs. Many of the long-established private clubs were encountering difficulty in sustaining membership rolls. Jim Hefner, the vice-president and general manager of WTAE-TV, sat with two people at the nearest table. At the P.A.A., he may prefer to be called James R. Hefner III. Dr. Jack Freeman, who had been Chancellor Wesley Posvar's right-hand man when I worked at Pitt (1983-87), was with a colleague by the opposite wall.

Dr. Freeman was always supportive during my days as assistant athletic director and sports information director, and he asked me how I was doing. "I'm doing fine," I said. "I'm writing books and staying out of trouble."

The sun was shining brightly, and I was with Nellie King and Betty Prince at the P.A.A., so I figured I must be doing OK. I was also keeping good company in King and Prince. These are beautiful people. They have been around Pittsburgh a long time. They appreciate the place, its history and traditions. They are Pittsburgh boosters. They are fun to be with; they had the best insights into what made Bob Prince tick, and both were good story-tellers.

We had spent most of the morning taping a show called "Remembering The Gunner" at the studios of WQED/WQEX TV, about a half-mile east of the P.A.A. on Fifth Avenue. It was for an "Agewise" segment hosted by Eleanor Schano, who's been in the TV business from its beginning in Pittsburgh. She was in her 60s, looked splendid and had maintained her figure and enthusiasm. She was proud to have been the first local model, weather girl, and woman newscaster on the Pittsburgh TV scene, going back to WPTV (Channel 3), based in the Chamber of Commerce Building in 1952.

Eleanor Schano shared a TV studio or stage with Bob Prince on more than one occasion. After we had finished the taping, in fact, she was telling Betty Prince about a funny incident involving her husband many years earlier. Eleanor, svelte as ever and positively glimmering in a cream-colored suit, got on her hands and knees on the carpeted hallway to demonstrate how Bob Prince had crawled behind a table and grabbed her by the ankles with both hands as she was talking into a TV camera on a live newscast.

George L. Miles, Jr., the president and CEO of WQED-TV, happened to come down the hallway when Eleanor was crawling about. He had to wonder whether his bespectacled eyes were playing tricks on him. Eleanor had to explain her story all over again so her boss would understand her behavior, eliciting an encore laugh from her expanded audience.

Eleanor Schano, upper left, hosted "Agewise" show in April, 1998 on WQED/WQEX TV, featuring Jim O'Brien, Nellie King and Betty Prince to share their stories about legendary Pirates' broadcaster Bob Prince.

"How did you deal with being the butt of so many of his jokes?" Eleanor had asked Betty. "I remember him once saying he was critical of you before you went out together one night. He said he told you, 'Betty, your stockings are all wrinkled.' And he said you told him, 'Bob, I'm not wearing any stockings.'"

Betty laughed at that one, and responded, "That hurt. Because my legs were my best feature."

King had celebrated his 70th birthday only the Sunday before, March 15. Betty was 81. Her birthday is September 24. She had her hair cut and styled the previous day, two days before her regular Friday appointment. She looked terrific in a black outfit, a long black and white print scarf hung from her shoulders to midriff, and she wore black shoes and black stockings.

"You look wonderful!" exclaimed Eleanor Schano, her bright green eyes popping, when she first saw Betty Prince in a WQED/WQEX reception room.

"She says that like she's surprised," said Betty, always quick on the comeback.

"Jim writes in something I read that you said Bob was the most entertaining fellow you ever met," Eleanor said to Betty.

"Never a dull moment," said Betty. "I was not prepared for anyone quite like him. I was raised in a very conservative family."

"Bob wore all those loud clothes," said Eleanor. "Where did he get his clothes?"

"In Chicago mainly," said Betty. "There was a tailor there, and he had Bob's measurements. He'd go in and say I like that and that and that, and they'd make them up for him and ship them to him at our home. He bought some in Hong Kong."

"How did Bob deal with his firing by the Pirates?" Eleanor asked toward the end of the half-hour taped interview.

"Badly," said Betty, lowering her eyelids momentarily. "It took the life out of him. He retreated to the bedroom for three days right after. He had the drapes drawn in the bedroom and kept the door closed. He came out only to eat a little bit. I told him he couldn't hide that way. 'We can't live like this,' I said. 'You've got to go out.' And he said, 'I can't face the public. What am I going to say to people?' And I told him, 'You tell them you miss them, and that you enjoyed being the Voice of the Pirates all those years, and you appreciated their support. That's what you have to do.' And he snapped out of it."

Bob Prince had been broadcasting Pirates baseball from 1948 to 1975. His 28-year run was the longest by any announcer with one ball team in the country at the time. He was on the road, or out for the evening, a great deal of the time during that tenure, and Betty joined him most of the time at home games, and on special occasions on the road. Otherwise, her time was devoted to raising their two children, Nancy and Bob Jr., and being involved in many church and community activities. The Prince family lived in suburbs just south of the city, first in Mt. Lebanon and later in Upper St. Clair.

Betty had moved back to Mt. Lebanon a few years earlier, into an upscale two-story/three bedroom condominium called Woodridge. Her husband inherited money from his family. The Princes owned property in downtown Los Angeles that was leased for mall development, and was also used by Atlantic Richfield. Betty continues to draw a share of the money it continues to generate. Bob had an older brother, by nearly six years, named Seaton, who was deceased. She showed me a beautiful diamond ring she had received from Bob's Uncle Henry. She's secure in her retirement. She has a nice, comfortable place at Woodridge. That's where I had picked her up that morning. Then we called on King together, about a mile away.

As we drove down Seneca Drive, one street before James Place, where King had lived the last 28 years, Betty pointed out a red brick house to our left and said her husband's last secretary, Barbara Sirinek, still lived there. When King came out to my car, he brought Betty a framed photo showing the Pirates in their last game at Forbes Field as a gift. It contained a scorecard shared by King and Prince.

"Mr. King, not many people push me into the backseat," Betty said. Nellie laughed about that. There was no way he could have folded the legs on his 6-6 frame into a rear seat.

"I was at that game Haddix pitched."
— Betty Prince

As we emerged from the Fort Pitt Tunnels and took the Parkway East, we checked out Downtown Pittsburgh on our left and headed out to Oakland. Betty and Nellie took note of their surroundings, and it brought back stories from the past. We went up Forbes Avenue, saw the Cathedral of Learning in its splendor on the horizon, framed by buildings on both sides of the road.

As we passed the corner of Forbes and Bouquet — that's where you once got off the streetcar, and later buses, to go to the games at Forbes Field — more memories surfaced.

Nellie would remember something and that would spark a story by Betty. King was a catalyst for more Prince stories. What was scary was that Betty was telling Nellie stories that she hadn't shared with me in earlier extensive interviews at her home. I was driving and taking notes at the same time on a yellow legal pad on the seat between Nellie and me. No matter how many stories one gets from such exchanges there are always others that are not mentioned or uncovered. What else hadn't Betty told me, or shared with me? What did she leave out?

Betty was beautiful in that she smiled through most of her storytelling. She had a good mind, and often told stories in dialogue, a real blessing for a biographer. She had a great sense of humor, often acerbic — which helped her when Bob was at her side, ribbing her and everyone within earshot — and she carried a long needle in her handbag she was not afraid to poke into people who came up for consideration. Confidential stuff, though, as Betty wasn't about to upset anybody. She was critical of both Harry Caray and Vin Scully, two of the most famous baseball broadcasters of all time. She called Scully "pompous" because of something she once heard him saying about his professional status.

Nellie would mention something about a special day at the ballpark, as when one of his all-time favorites, Dale Long, hit a home run in his eighth consecutive game. It happened on May 28, 1956. Betty said she was there that day.

"We had a doubleheader rained out the day before," said King. "Long appeared on the Ed Sullivan Show on TV in New York that same night for a $2,500 fee and national recognition. Because of the rainout, there was a buildup in the papers about the record and over 30,000 fans turned out Monday night for a date with the Dodgers.

"Long teed off on Carl Erskine for his eighth home run in eight consecutive games. It went into the lower right field stands and the crowd went crazy. It was something to hear. It gave you goosebumps. The fans refused to allow the game to continue until Long came out of the dugout for two curtain calls. Branch Rickey said it was the first time he'd ever seen a ballplayer come out and tip his hat to the crowd like that. Today they do it if they hit a double in the second inning. Long was special; I really liked him."

"He was really a gentleman," added Betty. "He was tall, well-groomed, good-looking."

Then King recalled the Harvey Haddix 12-inning perfect game for the Pirates against the Braves in Milwaukee on May 26, 1959. After retiring 36 straight batters, Haddix was beaten in the 13th inning, 1-0, on a run-scoring hit by Joe Adcock. A muffed grounder by third baseman Don Hoak opened the gates for the Braves.

Haddix didn't think much of the game because he had lost it. He figured others had lost a game in similar fashion. Not so. You had to go back to 1884 to find anything close to it. That was pitcher Samuel J. Kimber of Brooklyn, who fired 10 perfect innings before a scoreless game was called because of darkness 75 years earlier.

"I was at that game Haddix pitched," said Betty. "I had tickets by the dugout. I was sitting with Sam Snead, the great golfer, and his young nephew, J.C. Snead, who later became a pretty good golfer on the pro tour. I have no idea what I was doing with them. Bob must've given them tickets."

Nellie mentioned how much attention the ballplayers got from fans, especially the young ladies, when he was playing for the Pirates in 1957. "We'd come out of the dressing room at Forbes Field and there would be groupies there. Our wives would be waiting for us. I had a sore arm and I knew I was done. My wife was pregnant with our first child and I knew my career was ending. I didn't know what we were going to do. One of these young women went up to my wife,

45

Bernadette, and she said, 'Wow, are you a ballplayer's wife? It must be wonderful to be married to a ballplayer.' And Bernadette shot back, 'Kid, it stinks!'"

"It brings back the memories."
— Betty Prince in Oakland

Betty was back in her home in Mt. Lebanon. She had enjoyed her outing in Oakland. "It brings back the memories," she said, "of my always having to meet Bob at the P.A.A.

"Bob would go out by himself in the afternoon, and he'd get a rubdown in the health club at the P.A.A. before I got there. We'd walk over to Forbes Field together. That's where I ate my dinner. I'd get two grilled hot dogs and a Coke inside the ballpark. We had our own seats, and I'd sit with different people from one game to the next. After Rosey Rowswell died, Bob bought his tickets from Hazel, or 'Gyp' as we called her, Rowswell. They had a son, Bill, who was born to Rosey's first wife who had died."

Mentioning Rosey Rowswell got Betty off on a tangent. "When Bob first started it was very different," she said. "Rosey never gave Bob the microphone. Rosey had some friends who felt Bob was trying to take Rosey's job away from him. Bob had a talk with Rosey and assured him that was not the case. They cleared the air. After that, Rosey treated Bob like a second son."

Then Betty got back on track about their day-of-the-ballgame routine at Forbes Field.

"After the game, I'd sit in the offices at Forbes Field till Bob came down," she said. "We'd go back across the street to the P.A.A. Our cars were parked there. Maybe we'd have a bite to eat there. Then we'd go home in two cars.

"One time, after a day game, I was coming down the Boulevard of the Allies, and I was sitting there, trying to make a left turn to go over the Liberty Bridge back when you could still do that. Now they have a loop that keeps the traffic moving better, and you circle around to the bridge.

"As I was sitting there in my car, Bob pulled up alongside me. He had a convertible with the top down. He had been driving behind me, protectively, and now he wanted to say something. He was acting like some teenager looking to pick up a date. He was playful like that. Then he pulled away and went across the bridge. Somebody came from behind him and pulled up alongside of me. 'Ma'am, is that man bothering you?' he asked me. I said, 'Yes, but he's my husband.'"

This story brought back to Betty how she met Bob in the first place. "Our first date was a blind date for me," she said. "He had seen me, and written a very formal letter to a teacher friend of mine, asking her to introduce us (see copy on facing page). So he had seen me. I hadn't seen him. We went out in late November of 1939.

THE PAUL REVERE LIFE INSURANCE COMPANY
WORCESTER, MASSACHUSETTS

Protecting the American Home

Gloomy Thursday, Nov 9, 1939

Mrs. Mi Wilson
Zelienople Hi School????   Subject: Re date with one B. Casey

Dearest Mi:

It pains me to the quick that I should have been delayed this long before succumbing to the erstwhile smiles of the said Miss Casey. She flashed me an "Ipana smile" last night and, if I had been looking directly at her, I would have been blinded by the dazzling repetoir that she carries around in her mouth. (I believe that I misspelled repertoir — check that for me). (Maybe it should be spelled — "repertoire").

Seriously, while I may sound girl-starved, it behooves me to say that I haven't seen a decent girl in ages since I have made this strange trek into Yankee land and now that I HAVE seen one what in heck are we going to do about it? My darling Aunt seems to be a bit backward re getting me a date, so I must call upon you, if I may attempt such a deal.

Will you please ask her if she would be so kind as to accompany me this evening to a show-a-dance-a bridge party-a coke date-or anything that she might care to do? Assure her of my literacy — and not my lunacy — but please don't attempt any sordid build-up other than I have the Good Housekeeping stamp of approval on me. At least I did as of 1938. Perhaps it has run out by this time.

You mentioned something about a dance Friday nite. If this can be arranged, I should love to attempt that also. However, I will be more than content if you can pull off this deal for me this evening. Call Marion and tell her of your success or failure and I shall wait with bated breath as to the outcome.

In closing, may I say that this is no more than I would do for you, should you ever wander into the sunny southland, where I so frequently hang out. With best regards, I am

Most assumingly yours,

Robert F. Prince

47

"We drove into Pittsburgh and went to a movie. It must have been at the Penn Theater or the Stanley Theater. The movie was 'Drums Along The Mohawk,' and it starred Claudette Colbert and Henry Fonda. Bob wanted to know if we could have another date the following weekend.

"I couldn't get together again as I already had a date. I told him I had an engagement to see a young man over the weekend. We were going to a movie and dinner one day and to church the next day. Bob said, 'You'd give somebody the weekend? Would you date me for a weekend?' I said I would. So the following weekend I went with him to a Pitt football game. They were playing Carnegie Tech.

"We had lunch at the Luna Cafe at the corner of Centre Avenue and Craig Street. He gave me his Phi Delta Theta fraternity pin that day. It was rather presumptuous of him. I still dated somebody else for a while. I was a teacher when I did that. I'd wear his pin, or part of it, under my blouse.

"It only took me a month and a half to succumb to his charm. I had to break my New Year's Eve date. I decided I liked Bob better."

"He was a sucker for his family."
— Betty Prince, on her husband

"I really didn't socialize much with the ballplayers and their wives. I was a lot older than them. I was never shunned or rejected by them, but we went our own way. The players were very friendly. I remember once we were playing the Yankees at Fort Lauderdale during spring training, and we were staying at a hotel there. Suddenly, someone had their arms wrapped around me from behind. I looked over my shoulder and it was Donn Clendenon. He was with Bob Veale.

"I liked Don Hoak. He was a rough character. You talk about being a competitor. Bob didn't call him 'Tiger' for nothing. We met his wife, the singer, Jill Corey, She was a sweet girl. Ted Kluszewski was another nice fellow."

When I asked Betty to name her personal favorites, her own Hall of Fame among the Pirates she met, she hesitated, and then listed them in this order: Bill Virdon, Dick Groat, Vernon Law and Willie Stargell.

When I asked Betty if there were two Bob Princes, the public one and the private at-home version, she nodded in agreement. "He was a sucker for his family," she said. "He was really a sucker for his two granddaughters. He wanted them there, at the ballpark. He wanted to know they were there, but he wanted me to keep them, because he didn't think they belonged anywhere near the press box. His grandson, Robert F. III, was born two months before Bob died. He had a chance to hold his grandson. He just turned 13 this month (March,

1998). Bob was excited about having a grandson, but he was just as pleased with Casey and Kimberly.

"When Bob was out in public, he was quite 'on.' At home, he was more relaxed, really relaxed. He loved to sit with his shoes off out on the back patio at our home in Upper St. Clair. It was 34 feet long and had a canvas awning over it. He liked to read while it was raining. He liked to hear the rain hitting the awning. He was real comfortable there.

"Bob was a showman in his first few years. He did everything he could to establish himself here. He was always out and about, making a name and reputation for himself. This one time we went to the old Nixon Restaurant, which is where the Alcoa Building is (by the William Penn Hotel). We were there for dinner. We were walking in, very proud with the children, and I turn around to say something to Bob and he's not there. He was at the first table just inside the door, talking to some people there. I went back and said to him, 'Can't you stay with us?' He said, 'They wanted me to meet their guests.' And I said, 'Can't you tell them you're with your family?' He said, 'These are my fans, dear.' I went back to our table. When Bob finally came over to us, he said, 'Honey, it's people like that who make up my audience. If I don't have that audience, I don't have this job.' That was that. After that, I never complained again.

"I was often asked what it was like to be the wife of a celebrity. I always said that when people recognized Bob and approached him when I was with him, they could care less about the wife. It didn't bother me. In a selfish way, it was very rewarding. I'd see people getting his autograph, and clamoring for his attention, and I could say to myself, 'He belongs to me. . .'

"Some people tell me the darndest stories about Bob doing this and that. They remember the strangest things. I don't know where they come up with some of their stories. Bob was wild, but not sexually. He was a bit of a prude. But, then again, I wasn't there, so what do I know? I just don't believe some of the stories. I think they've gotten their stories confused. Bob was no slouch as a drinker, but some of those stories are hard to believe.

"Initially, he couldn't stand the taste of liquor. He had to drink Coke or something with it. He started drinking to relax his stomach. He'd get a nervous stomach from time to time. Some doctor told him he could resume drinking something milder than he'd been drinking before he stopped for health reasons. That doctor didn't do him any favor. He would overdo it, though, when he was out at public functions. He never drank like that at home."

She felt that her husband deserved better treatment after his long years of loyal service in Pittsburgh.

"When Bob was taken into the Hall of Fame in Cooperstown, now that's quite an honor," began Betty. "I didn't say anything at the time, but not one single person from the Pirates' organization or KDKA was in attendance. Vera Clemente and her sons were there. Al Lopez and

Ralph Kiner, who had known us when they were with the Pirates, were present that day. But nobody from the Pirates or KDKA. That wasn't right." (Just for the record, Pirates p.r. assistant Sally O'Leary and her two sisters were there.)

Being at the P.A.A. earlier in the day brought another memory back for Betty Prince, as she relaxed in her living room. "Bob liked to go swimming there," she said. "The place was crowded all the time. It was always very, very busy back in those days.

"He took Warren Spahn and Lew Burdette there after a night game. They were crazy, fun crazy. He was taking them back to their hotel later in his station wagon. They were sitting on the top of the back of the car with their feet on the tailgate, yelling to people as they passed them on the way Downtown. They were hooting and hollering at the crowd on Fifth Avenue. Earlier, they had been tossing sugar packets at each other at the P.A.A. Can you picture that?

"When Bob first got into broadcasting, he got involved in other businesses as well. He was always looking for new opportunities. He was industrious; he was a hustler. He would do things to build up his name, all kinds of crazy stunts. He once laid on his back with a golf ball sitting on a tee in his mouth and let someone hit the golf ball."

Asked about her relationship with Bob Prince, she said, "You know you can tell when someone loves you. I always felt that way with Bob. They may disappear on you when they're out with you, but generally they're proud of you. He thought the work I did with the Presbyterian elderly was time well spent. He said, 'I take care of the young ones — the kids at Allegheny Valley School — and you take care of the old ones.' Bob helped get that school started, and was their prime fund-raiser for years. The Hillman family was very supportive. Bob pulled the money in. The proceeds from many of the events he was involved with went to Allegheny Valley School.

"Bob was always generous with his money. He said you have to spend some money to earn some money. He bought a new sport coat every year for John Hallahan, the Pirates' equipment manager. He looked after Radio Rich and his needs for years. He paid Sally O'Leary to look after his fan mail, making up for the money she'd lost by leaving her previous job to come and work for the Pirates. No one knew that. She had been working at Fuller Smith & Ross, an advertising agency, and Bob knew she was crazy for baseball, so he put in a good word for her with the Pirates. He paid for her vacation every year. She really helped Bob. Bob gave awards for diving at the St. Clair Country Club for years. He helped Earl Birdy Jr., the swim club manager, with his swimming program for the kids. Earl's still there and he'll tell you how much Bob helped him. Bob raised a lot of money for youth golf programs in the area, too. He never just lent his name to anything; he worked with them to make those things successful.

"He bought a microscope for Don Hennon when he was in medical school at Pitt. He bought clothes, and provided spending money, for Dick Leftridge when he was at West Virginia. Bob acted as his agent when he signed with the Steelers.

Bob Prince's parents, Frederick and Guyla Prince, as they appeared around 1950.

Cadet Fred Prince during West Point days. Bob's father was a football player for the Black Knights of the Hudson.

Bob at Fort Lewis, Washington in 1931

Bob's grandfather, George W. Prince, was an imposing figure.

Bob Prince, upon his return to the Pirates broadcast booth in 1985:

"This is a very emotional thing for me. I'm just delighted to return. Other than my family, you've given me back the only other thing I love in the world."

"There's a scholarship that's been established at Grove City College in the name of Betty and Bob Prince through Bob Prince Charities.

"He was able to be at ease with CEOs, and he was just as generous with his time with the guy who just came out of the mill, or the black man who stopped him on the street. Bob would stand for ten minutes talking to anyone who approached him. 'If he wants to talk to me, I'll talk to him,' he'd often tell me.

"I remember how he used to discreetly sneak some money to the bus boy at a restaurant. He'd tell me that the boy didn't get any of the tip he'd put on the bill. All I know is he never needed to say he needed more butter or cold water, as I recall.

"I remember one night in his last year, I was just sitting around at home, taking my time getting ready to go out. We were both about half-dressed. He came to me and said, 'How would you like to stay home?' I asked him if he thought we could do that. And he said, 'Yes.' So we stayed home. He liked to be home. He liked to relax like that. He'd say, 'This is great.'

"He often referred to me as 'Ol' Bess,' which was all right with me. My eyes used to just sparkle when I looked at him. He was a very tender man. He was easily hurt. He wanted everybody to like him, and he knew they didn't. It was important to be liked, and it wasn't because he thought he was important.

"When you talk day after day about the Pirates and the baseball games, he said there were hundreds of thousands of people listening to him. He said they become like your family. And you wanted your family to like you. He was glad when they liked him.

"One day he was doing a Penn State game. They had played here in Pittsburgh. We took his two spotters, Mickey Bergstein and Ernie Berkow, out to dinner afterward at the Ankara, a supper club on Rt. 51 near McKeesport. The restaurant was full of people who'd been to the game. Bob excused himself to go to the men's room. He walked by this one table, and he heard a man there telling his friend, 'There goes that so-and-so Bob Prince. He thinks he's great.' Bob stopped at the table on his way back from the bathroom, and he said, 'Excuse me, but I couldn't help but overhear the remarks you made about me when I passed your table. Tell me, did I ever offend you in any way? Did I ever personally hurt you?' Well, the man was flabbergasted. Bob talked to him awhile. 'I hate to think someone doesn't like me for any reason,' Bob told him. The man smiled and shook Bob's hand. 'You can count on me as a fan from now on,' he told Bob. Bob told us about the exchange when he came back to our table. He looked at us and winked, 'Well, I got another one.'

"He loved children. He'd be at the swimming pool at the country club, and he'd be showing children how to swim and how to dive."

Asked how her own children felt about their dad being so famous, she said, "My kids didn't like it at all. One of our friends, Bob

52

Keaney, once said to me, 'You don't realize how tough it is to be the son of Bob Prince in the city of Pittsburgh.' Bob said, 'The cruelest thing I think I asked you to do was to name our son Bob Prince Jr.' Nancy came home from Lincoln School crying because someone said her dad didn't know a thing about baseball. And Bob said to her, 'What does her daddy do for a living? He probably has a job where if he makes an error, he can probably erase it. I can't. So some people poke fun at me. You just be proud of your dad.'

"When young Bob was in ninth grade, he got all Ds on one of his report cards. The guidance counselor told me that when she asked him what his father did, something she asked all the students, he told her that his dad was an insurance salesman. He never let on that his father was the famous Pirates announcer."

"Underneath, Bob had an inferiority complex."
—Betty Prince

I had visited Betty Prince on October 22, 1997, the night of the fourth game of the 1997 World Series. The Miami Marlins were playing the Indians at Jacobs Field in Cleveland, and Betty had the game on her TV. "My God, it's snowing!" she said at one point.

The Marlins, who would go on to win the World Series, were managed by Jim Leyland, whose family was living in Mt. Lebanon, not far from Betty Prince's place.

Bob Uecker was one of the announcers. When his name was mentioned, Betty made a face like she had just bitten into a lemon and said, "My Bob always thought he was a buffoon. The NBC announcers aren't as good as the ABC announcers." From time to time, Betty would make observations like that. She was showing me scrapbooks that contained stories and photos about her late husband. Some of them had gotten stiff and brittle, and some of the edges had broken away. Betty smiled as she identified people in the pictures. She still got a kick out of "The Gunner." He could still make her laugh.

I asked Betty how she had gone to college when women didn't usually have that opportunity back in the '30s.

"My mother died when I was a junior in high school in 1933. I graduated in 1934. I was living with my father and older brother and younger sister. My aunt lived across the street and her sister was a few doors down. We lived in Sheraden, near Langley High School.

"My father wanted me to go to college. '34 wasn't long after the Depression. I thought I'd like to do secretarial work. I was going to go to Margaret Morrison at Carnegie Tech. My father, his name was John M. Casey, felt I should have dormitory life. I knew someone who went to Grove City. We went to visit Grove City. It was strict, but even in my day you had your fun. You had to go to chapel and stuff, but there were lots of activities. It was strict, but all the schools, except for the big universities, were strict back then."

53

As we looked at some photos of a young Bob Prince, a tall, spindly, handsome fellow with dark curly hair, I suggested that they had such different personalities. She was a cultured, refined conservative woman. "We were that far apart," she said, holding her hands wide apart, "but we got along great.

"I think Bob felt I was an important part of his life. Underneath, Bob had an inferiority complex. Oftentimes, someone who has that will act just the opposite to overcome it.

"Bob was — in spite of drinking and all that stuff — he was a bit of a prude. Basic principles were important to him. He'd skirt around, but there were certain things you didn't do. I think his father being in the military left its mark on Bob and his brother.

"There were two boys, Bob and his older brother, Seaton, and they were very patriotic. When you played the National Anthem you stood up and gave it proper respect, that's the way they were.

"Bob surprised some people by some of the things he did. Bruce Kison, a young pitcher for the Pirates, was scheduled to get married the day after the Pirates won the World Series in Baltimore in 1971. Bob arranged for Bruce and his best man, pitcher Bob Moose, to fly back to Pittsburgh in a private plane so they could keep the wedding date. Bob and I went on a world tour when he returned, two days after the Series was over. We'd never had a real honeymoon and we'd come into a little money. Bob made the plans in June, before anybody thought about playing in the World Series."

Betty said her husband was the broadcaster for Penn State football from 1950 or 1951 to 1961, and that he also did color for the Steelers with Joe Tucker at the same time.

"Dr. Rick Collins, who lives in Upper St. Clair, used to ride up to Penn State with Bob. They lived in our neighborhood and were close friends. Dr. Collins would read off lineups and stats as Bob drove there. By the time they got there, in 2½ hours, Bob knew everything.

"Joe L. Brown told him 'if you're going to be the Voice of the Pirates, you'll have to give up football.' That was OK with Bob because baseball was his first love anyhow. He kept his ties at Penn State. He'd been friendly with Rip Engle, and he remained so with his top assistant, Joe Paterno. He worked with Jerry Sandusky, one of the other coaches at Penn State, and helped get his golf outing underway in grand style. Bob really worked to make that successful."

Just then, Betty switched the TV to the game show Wheel of Fortune. "How much do you think Vanna White makes for turning those letters? And clapping. A lot, I'll bet."

She said that Jim Wright and his wife, Emily, at Westminster Presbyterian Church remembered how Bob had been at a banquet in Detroit one night and had gotten home late, yet he showed up the next morning to teach Sunday school at Westminster. Becky and Emil Narick said their son still remembered being taught Sunday School by Bob Prince.

Bob and Betty Prince, 1984

Betty at Grove City, 1935

Bob and Betty walking by Forbes Field, 1940

From the Prince family album.

Betty's father, John M. Casey

Betty
Prince

"Bob Keaney, who was heavily involved in the Sunday school, went into business with Bob, in Gunner's Beer Distributorship. I was president. Bob wasn't allowed to be, because of a conflict of interest. Neither of us ever touched a beer. Bob never drank any alcoholic beverages until he was 36 years old, but he sure made up for it.

"My big sister at Grove City got married. We went to a wedding reception at the Schenley Hotel. I was holding a glass of champagne in my hand. Bob said, 'What are you doing?' I said there was going to be a toast. He said, 'You can pretend.' My father was an elder and we weren't allowed to have a drop of alcohol in our house. That's the way I was raised.

"Bob always hustled. But he gave money away. All the money didn't come to the house. I took care of all the bills regarding our house and daily living. The country club bill came to me."

I remembered being with Prince one afternoon at St. Clair Country Club, when he chided the waiter, "Hey, don't keep putting down screwdrivers on my tab. Ol' Bess will be checking that. I don't want her to know how much I had to drink."

Asked where he got the gift to grab everyone in the room when he started talking, Betty observed, "He might have inherited some of it from his mother. She was plump, about 5-2 or 5-3, but when she entered a room pretty soon she was in the center of everything.

"Bob had a knack of seizing everyone's attention. He'd go around and talk to anybody. He treated everyone the same, like they were important, no matter their situation. When he talked to you, it always meant something. He was generous. He never denied us anything. I used to have to say we can't do this or that. He was not just giving things. He gave his time and money. He adored the granddaughters. He got to hold his grandson before he got real sick at the end. That was a highlight for him."

Bob and Betty Prince pose when he was the president of the St. Clair Country Club (1982-83).

Insiders
Princely stories

"He was a great tipper."
— George Burdell

Jack Berger,
Former Pirates Publicist

I started working for the Pirates in 1947, beginning in the minor league system, and was in Brunswick, Georgia when Branch Rickey offered me the position during the 1954 season to be the team's publicity director when Jimmy Long died. I didn't think I had the background for the job. I wasn't a writer; I wasn't a journalist. Rickey was perturbed with my hesitancy. 'I wouldn't have offered you the job if I didn't think you could handle it,' Rickey rumbled.

"My dad, who was also Jack Berger, was a sports cartoonist for *The Press*, and had played minor league ball. So I grew up with baseball. I was with the Pirates organization for 37 years, and handled the public relations work from 1954 to 1970. They have about 15 people doing what I was doing with one and then two assistants. Sally O'Leary was a real blessing when she came to work with me. She was a big help. But I did what they now call media relations, community relations, the speakers bureau and I was often the one who went out to speak at functions throughout the tri-state area. I did the game programs, releases, stats and sold some ads, and lined up some corporate sponsors, and hustled tickets. I never had time to get into trouble. It was a lot of fun.

"I never met anyone quite like Bob Prince. He was a perfectionist, no doubt about that. He was an expert in what he chose to do. He knew the game. He knew the rules as well as anybody in the game.

"He made a point to know the players, on a personal basis, not just the Pirates, but players throughout the league. He was just naturally colorful and, for the most part, he was well liked.

"He could be stubborn. But I always found him easy to work with. He'd give you a bunch of crap occasionally, but he was just pulling your leg. He'd do what you asked him to do. Bob was the best salesman we had, no doubt about it. He was our best ticket salesman, the best pitchman we ever had.

"One of the great promotions they have now is fireworks. I came up with the idea of doing it here. It would cost us about $6,000. We did things by committee; we'd have weekly staff meetings to make plans. Joe L. Brown and Joe O'Toole both rejected the idea. They didn't think it was worth the money. I knew it was a successful promotion in Cleveland; they were the only one doing it at the time. Bill Veeck was running their operation and he was a great promoter. They were the first ones to do Bat Day, too. We exchanged ideas at our league p.r. meetings, so I knew what was involved.

"I mentioned my idea to Prince. He said, 'I'll tell you what. I'll pay for it. You figure out what you would normally get for a crowd on the night we're going to do it. Then give me fifty percent of the gate over that.' I mentioned this at the next staff meeting, and they said, 'Hell no.' But that brought them around a little bit. They voted it in. It was a big success. Before you knew it, they were having two fireworks shows a year, then three, and now it's up to six. I thought it would be successful. Prince knew how to sell something, how to get people excited about something. He had a good promotional mind.

"One time a media person — I won't say who — was giving Joe Brown a hard time. I was there, watching. After awhile, I thought it had gone too far, and I was hot. I was ready to clobber the guy, and Prince grabbed me. He whispered in my ear, and calmed me down. I was ready to pummel the guy, but he told me I'd be out of baseball if I did something that stupid.

"I hope everyone knows how much he did for charity work. He really helped St. Anthony's School for Exceptional Children out in Oakmont in the early days. Later, he turned his attention to Allegheny Valley School for Exceptional Children. Bob had a big heart. He was always helping somebody get something accomplished."

* * *

George Burdell, Former masseur, Duquesne Club
North Huntingdon, Pa.

"This was in the early to mid-60s, and I was working in the health room at the Duquesne Club in downtown Pittsburgh. We're talking about the most exclusive club in the city, where all the CEOs and top executives belong. Bob Prince would come up there with Mr. Jim Daniell of U.S. Steel, who had been an All-America football player at Ohio State, and Mr. Walter Sapp and Mr. Willard Rockwell. Prince would be their guest.

"He liked to get a steam and a good rub. He was not any stringbean; he was built better than most people realized. He was a great tipper, that's what we remember best about Bob Prince. We'd say, 'Hey, Mr. Prince, why don't you join the club?' And he'd say, 'They're afraid I'll bring all my clown friends.' We wanted a great tipper like him to be a member of the club.

"I also remember that he was a pretty good ping-pong player, a real competitive fellow. While he was taking his steam and his rub, he ordered drinks for himself and the boys. We weren't allowed to drink while on duty, but he'd sneak us some drinks just the same. He was the greatest."

*   *   *

Alan Robinson, Associated Press sportswriter:

"I was 8 years old when the Pirates won the World Series in 1960, and that's when Bob Prince turned me into a baseball fan. I'm probably doing what I'm doing today because of Bob Prince. I was growing up in Sistersville, West Virginia, 47 miles south of Wheeling. It was once a boomtown in the oil business, and there are lots of mansions still there where the oil barons once lived. There were over a hundred millionaires in the town at one time. It was a big sports town. There were about 2,000 people who lived there, but there'd be 4,000 at the high school football game on Friday night. Ben Schwartzwalder, who played football at West Virginia University, had started his coaching career in Sistersville in 1926. His Syracuse University football team had won the national championship in 1959. Jerry West was the big star of the West Virginia University basketball team, which was one of the best in the country. I was into football and basketball before I liked baseball that much.

"Listening to Bob Prince on the radio did it. He was probably the No. 1 reason I got into this business. I had the best of all possible worlds in sports. I had Jack Fleming doing West Virginia football in the fall, West Virginia basketball in the winter, and Bob Prince doing baseball in the spring and summer. People don't realize it today, but back then, Fleming was one of the best basketball announcers in the country.

"Prince had me hooked as a listener. He was unique. No two broadcasts were the same. Today, I have a satellite dish and I can catch televised baseball games from all over the country, and all the announcers sound the same.

"Some people complained that Prince drifted from the action, and told too many stories. To me, that was the essence of Bob Prince. He was so entertaining. He kept you interested in the ballgame. After that great 1960 season, they weren't very good, except for 1966, but he still kept you interested in the Pirates.

"I used to set my alarm in the morning so I'd catch Prince doing Pirates reports on the Jack Bogut wake-up show.

"I didn't meet him until I was 19. That's when I was working in Wheeling in the '70s at *The Intelligencer*. It wasn't until 1982 that I got to know him. He was doing the Pirates' games on Home Sports Entertainment (HSE).

"When he was fired in 1975, I lost my interest in the Pirates for quite some time. I was working in Charleston, West Virginia when I saw the story about his firing on the Associated Press wire machine in our office. It was like seeing that your best friend had betrayed you. To me, he wasn't just the 'Voice of the Pirates,' he *was* the Pirates. After that, I wasn't interested in them. For a long time, I didn't go seeking them on the radio.

59

"Football was No. 1 and basketball was No. 2 for me. I'll still never forget that Friday night in 1985 when they brought him back to do a game against the Dodgers. The Pirates had a 9-run inning. He couldn't quite keep up with it, but there was an energy coming out of that booth that was unreal.

"To me, Bob Prince is right up there with Vin Scully, the Dodgers broadcaster. They are the only two announcers of all of them that I would tune in to listen to them and not the game. I love it when Vin Scully does the radio all by himself. I like it better when he's just playing to the Dodgers fans, and not playing to a national audience. That's Scully at his best.

"As for Prince, people either loved him or hated him. I had a ballgame on seven nights a week. I ran a softball league when I was 15. I organized games. I used to love to hear Prince doing the games late at night from the West Coast. When I was able to afford to go anywhere, the first place I went was to Dodger Stadium in Los Angeles. I had to see it for myself. I remembered Willie Stargell hitting home runs there. I remembered Koufax and Drysdale pitching in the '60s. Back then, California was on the other side of the world."

Winged Head

Alan Robinson
AP Sportswriter

Photos by Jim O'Brien

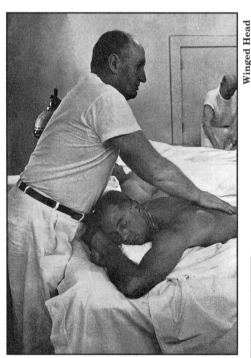

"The Gunner" gets a rubdown at P.A.A.

Jack Berger and Bob Friend met at Pirates'
1998 opener at Three Rivers Stadium.

Nellie King
Appreciates Prince more with passing years

"He could really broadcast a baseball game."

Nellie King waved something under my eyes like he was performing a magic trick, pulling multi-colored scarves or something from out of nowhere. It was a silver-plated money clip he had pulled out of his cream-colored slacks. He showed me how the bills, mostly $10s and $5s, were folded. Each bill was folded neatly in half, one atop the other, like cheese slices.

"That's the way Bob Prince kept his money," recalled King. "I've done it that way ever since he showed me his method. He said if you did it this way you wouldn't give anyone more money than you intended. One bill wouldn't get stuck inside another."

King clapped his hands together, the way he did after he told one of his favorite jokes or stories, flashed his protuberant pale blue eyes to emphasize his merriment, and flopped into a chair in his basement office like the Scarecrow in *The Wizard of Oz*.

The story brought Bob Prince to mind, and that was enough to tickle King. He still got a kick out of Bob Prince and recalling stories about the man with whom he shared the Pirates' broadcast booth for nine years (1967 through 1975). King was lanky, and all bones like Bob Prince, and a few inches taller at 6-6. King had pitched for the Pirates from 1954 to 1957, during the period when Prince replaced Rosey Rowswell as the principal Pirates broadcaster after Rowswell's retirement.

"Every time I fold money," said King, "I think of Bob Prince." The money clip itself dated King. Most men these days carry their paper money in their wallet. This was Wednesday, February 11, 1998 and King was just over a month away from his 70th birthday (March 15). "It's gone by so quickly," King sighed, alluding to the passage of time.

"Prince usually carried his money in hundred dollar and fifty dollar bills," King continued. "But he folded them carefully one atop the other, never inside one another."

This tale didn't seem to fit Prince's free-spending reputation. Prince was known for being generous and cavalier with his money, always eager to pick up dinner and luncheon tabs, and gifts for friends and needy causes, not a guy who was careful how he carried his money.

"He liked to pick up checks, that's for certain," recalled King. "I don't know if he needed to do it, or what. Like he wanted to do something for you. I've wondered about that. But some guys grab checks and they make you feel like you owe them something. I hated that attitude. You never had that feeling with Prince."

King said Prince never made more than $40,000 a year as the Pirates broadcaster, but that Prince had inherited money from his parents — as much as $750,000, according to King — and that he made more money than his base compensation in various enterprises and sidelines.

"Even when things were going bad for him," recalled King, "money never seemed to be a big issue."

King joined the broadcast team in 1967 as a decidedly junior partner to Prince and Jim Woods. "If Prince was the craziest and most untamed man in broadcasting," said King, "Woods was runner-up. They were both great on the air and the life of the party off the air."

King was low key under any conditions. King came from WHJB in Greensburg. "For the first year or so, I assumed kind of an obsequious role," said King. "I really didn't like myself very much."

"I work baseball in the winter,
I play baseball in the summer."
— Roberto Clemente

Nellie King can tell stories at the drop of a dollar bill or a familiar name. Nellie never tires of entertaining people. During a lengthy visit to his home in Mt. Lebanon in mid-winter, 1998, King swapped tales about Bob Prince, Jim Woods, Joe L. Brown, Branch Rickey, Dick Stuart — "he was crazy and the closest thing to Prince as ballplayers went" — Steve Blass, Dave Giusti, Bill Mazeroski, Dick Groat, Dale Long, Bill Virdon, ElRoy Face, Vernon Law, Willie Stargell, announcer Art McKennan, et al. Most of all he seemed to enjoy telling stories about Roberto Clemente.

"He was special in so many ways," said King. "I got to know him, and he was a proud man who meant more to the Pirates than most people can appreciate. He had a strong influence in the clubhouse and helped a lot of players find their way."

There were several framed photos of Clemente in King's expansive work area, including a prized one showing King interviewing "The Great One" in the Pirates' dugout at Three Rivers Stadium. My favorite showed King getting a warm hug from Mazeroski, another of his all-time favorites. It portrayed genuine affection, and told you a lot about both men and why they captured the hearts of Pirates' fans.

"Clemente tried to get Maz to stay for another season with the Pirates," King continued. "He invited Maz to join him in Puerto Rico for a few months to work himself into shape for another season. Maz

Spring training, 1957

Nellie and Bernadette King chat at Fort Myers, 1957.

Nellie King
Bucs' broadcaster

King interviews Roberto Clemente.

told him he couldn't fight his weight problem any longer. 'I've had so much trouble all these years with my weight,' Maz told him. 'My mother weighed over 300 pounds, and it's in my genes. I don't want to go through another spring training. It's been hell for me to try and hold my weight down.' Clemente took great pride in his off-season conditioning habits. He used to say, 'I work baseball in the winter; I play baseball in the summer.'"

King said Dale Long, an often overlooked figure in Pirates' baseball history, was one of the greatest leaders he had ever been around in baseball. To him, Maz had no peer as a second baseman, and that Maz and Groat, one of the most competitive people King ever came across, were sound and solid up the middle. "They made all the routine plays, and I mean all of them," said King. "They said Groat didn't have great range, but he was smart and he knew where to play the batters. I don't think Groat ever got over Joe Brown trading him to the Cardinals when Groat could still really play the game."

King remembers how Groat got hot one day while playing cards in the clubhouse, and backed away from the table in a huff. "You know he and Bill Virdon are the best of friends, but Virdon got on him that day. 'Hey, Groat, who the hell do you think you are?' Virdon hollered as Groat left the room. 'The great Dick Groat? Can't you lose at anything without taking the heat?' Virdon wouldn't take any guff from anybody."

He said Face felt he could strike out anyone, and his teammates felt the same way every time the gritty little guy took the mound. He thought Law and Blass were the best starting pitchers during his tenure as a ballplayer and broadcaster with the Pirates.

He thought Virdon was among the best defensive centerfielders in baseball, right up there with Willie Mays with the glove. He admired Virdon's virtues and loyalty as a man and pointed out, by the way, that Virdon was a strong, silent type not to be messed with. Virdon was close to Prince. "He was probably the most loyal man I ever met," disclosed King. "He had strong opinions and strong beliefs in what he was saying."

King kept offering opinions on Pirates from my youth, and it was like being back at Forbes Field for a weekend doubleheader. Asked what was the highlight of his own career pitching for the Pirates, King said it occurred in 1955 when he pitched seven innings of shutout ball against the Phillies to save a win for Vernon Law, and three days later when he shut out the Dodgers for six innings in relief, and was credited with the win.

"That's when I knew," said King, "I could pitch major league ball."

While he might have been able to pitch major league ball, he couldn't hit a major league ball. "I was 0-for-4 in the big leagues," he laughs. "0 for four seasons. I was 0-for-27 in four seasons."

King may have carried a money clip, but he was sitting in front of an Apple Computer, which he was using to write a planned book about his experiences with the Pirates, and to send E-mail to his friends and family. He might have been riding a fast ball toward 70, but he was utilizing the typing skills he'd learned in high school with state-of-the-art technology. His typing skills, he said, kept him out of Korea when he was in the military service, and helped him land his last job. I spotted the names of Dave Giusti and Sally O'Leary on his E-mail directory. Giusti was a good friend and O'Leary looked after the affairs of the Pirates' alumni from a home she shared with her sisters in Cranberry Township, though she had retired from the Pirates' public relations office staff two years earlier.

"Sally is a super human being; she was so loyal to Bob Prince who helped her get her start," King came back. "Dave Giusti is a guy I could count on if I needed something. We don't hang out together or anything like that, but he'd be there if I needed him."

It's impressive that many of the former Pirates do stay in touch with each other, comforting each other when there are health problems or deaths in the family, and saluting each other on good news, such as the birth of grandchildren.

King started out sitting at a table in his kitchen, where there was a picture of him with one of his golf teams at Duquesne University, and the cabinets were lined with pills and drugs of every possible prescription. It looked like a kiosk at Revco. King continued to coach the golf team at Duquesne, where he was the sports information director for 19 years before retiring in 1993, and to do analysis and color on basketball broadcasts for home games, though he hadn't been in the best health for several years.

"He's one of the nicest guys around."
— Huddie Kaufman, Tribune-Review

I had caught King in action a few days earlier when he and Ray Goss broadcast Duquesne's upset victory over Pitt's basketball team at the Civic Arena on WQED Radio. They were set up just down the press table from King's former teammate, Dick Groat, who was working in a similar role with Bill Hillgrove over WTAE Radio.

This was King's 24th year on Duquesne basketball broadcasts. Goss did his first broadcast 40 years earlier on the same student radio station. The Dukes' rich basketball history included a 50-year heritage of radio broadcasting. It began with Joe Tucker teaming up with Rege Cordic at courtside at Duquesne Gardens in Oakland. The first game on the air was a contest with Holy Cross on January 2, 1947.

King had been doing Duquesne games nearly as long as Prince did Pirates games, yet King was still more closely associated with the Pirates than he was with the Dukes in the minds of most local sports fans. He has been a most popular fellow, and respected by his colleagues, no matter where he was working.

65

Huddie Kaufman, a long-time sportswriter for the *Greensburg Tribune-Review,* who has known King since he became a broadcaster in Latrobe, and later Greensburg before he joined the Pirates' broadcast team, two years after he was finished as a ballplayer, put it best: "King will never enter the Hall of Fame unless he takes a motor trip to Cooperstown, New York. He will, however, go down in history around these parts as one of the nicest guys."

King once recommended Kaufman for the sports information director's job at Duquesne, which he ended up taking himself.

In Greensburg, King had succeeded Fran Fisher, who left to become the broadcaster for Penn State football.

King was to be honored at a dinner in late March by Myasthenia Gravis Association of Western Pennsylvania, who were giving him the Art Pallan Award (named for a KDKA deejay) for his service to community and human service agencies by donating his time and talent. Many of his former teammates, including Nellie Briles, Dave Giusti, Dick Groat, Kent Tekulve and Bob Friend, were in attendance.

King's credits also include involvement with the Mercy Hospital Heart Programs, helping out with the Boys and Girls Club of Western Pennsylvania, the Pirates Alumni Association, and he was inducted into the Western Chapter of the Pennsylvania Sports Hall of Fame.

"I played in the big leagues and I broadcast and everything else, that's great," said King. "That's a great personal satisfaction, but I did it because I liked to do it. That's why I was a success. I enjoy going out and speaking to groups about baseball; it is therapeutic."

You don't have to ask too many questions to get King to tell stories. He can't help himself. He's great company. It was difficult to comprehend that King was turning 70, though, to look at him and know he'd been having health problems, and to see that lineup of pill containers in his kitchen. Behind that bubbly personality and ready smile, he was really a Nervous Nellie, battling heart scares and roller coaster moods. Like Prince, he never fully recovered from his dismissal from the Pirates' broadcast team, though his life had been rich and rewarding in many ways in the interim.

Nellie could never put that behind him, or the fact that he came up a year or so short of qualifying for a major league baseball pension. It nagged at Nellie like a skin rash. In a sense, his Pirates' pension may have come in the form of a free education at Duquesne University for his wife and their three daughters — Laurie, Leslie and Amy — on a tuition-remission program for employees and their family. That had to be a savings of $150,000, and you'd have to earn over $200,000 before taxes to pay for that educational tab. After all, his stay with the Pirates led to landing his job at Duquesne.

There are many people on the Pittsburgh sports scene who dwell in the land of what-might-have-been, but that's natural in any walk of life. Many of us are guilty of that. Anyone who came by King through the years benefited from the association. They walked with a king, in so many ways, though Nellie never saw it that way. King couldn't shake the memories of his schooldays. When King was five, his father, Charles Vincent King, a mine foreman, died at age 52. His mother didn't have much money and three years later she sent the eight-year-old Nellie, the youngest of her five children, to the Hershey (Pa.) School for Boys. King confessed that a sense of abandonment stayed with him the rest of his life. Yet he has a reassuring manner about him that could calm others. And he was loyal to a fault. King was a complicated soul, more than met the eye, but he had always been a good man, and he felt blessed by his baseball involvement. He dreamed of becoming a big league ballplayer and he became one.

As a kid, he adored and kept clippings of the St. Louis Cardinals. Marty Marion, a spindly shortstop, was his favorite. He imitated Bob Feller in his pitching delivery until someone advised him to do it differently because he wasn't throwing as hard as Feller. He made $100 a month at Albany, Georgia, a farm team of the Cardinals, early in his pro career.

His first uniform was a hand-me-down from Enos Slaughter, one of the stars of the Cardinals. "'Can there be anything more than this?' I said at the time. I had to pinch myself," recalled King.

"Decisions that are made in your life, you don't know why they are made and how they happen, but God, I think that all things work together for reasons," continued King. "You don't see the plan right away, but there is something going on there and baseball was particularly that way."

We moved to his office in the basement of the home he and his wife, Bernadette, had shared for 28 years. Their three daughters were long gone, out on their own. There were two grandchildren, Amy Gayle and Julia Marie. Bernadette wasn't doing so well health-wise, either, and was lying across a chair and ottoman, a cream-colored afghan over her supine form. A woman was there to assist her with housekeeping and cooking.

"Howya doing, Bernadette?" I asked upon entering the family room.

"Don't ask," Bernadette came back. End of conversation.

Bernadette was the younger sister of Eddie Earl, the second baseman at one of King's early minor league teams. They were married October 10, 1953 at St. Joseph's Church in Newark. The morning after the wedding, Nellie picked up the *New York Times* and found out that the Pirates had purchased his contract.

He told his bride, "If I had known this was going to happen, I'd have married you a couple of years ago."

In 1954, he was on the Pirates' roster as a relief pitcher and he made his first appearance in the majors against the Dodgers at Ebbetts Field in Brooklyn on April 15. He came in at the bottom of the eighth inning. The first batter he faced was Duke Snider, a future Hall of Famer.

King can remember each pitch as if it were yesterday. Snider struck out trying to bunt, and King finished that inning unscathed. "I picked up every newspaper that I could get in New York," he said. "And I said, 'If you never pitch another game, that confirms it. You got the boxscore.' At that time, only 160 people were doing what I was doing."

He retired because of an arm injury at the end of the 1957 season. His overall record was 7-5 for four years. He wore No. 29 in a Pirates' uniform with pride. He still loved to get together with Pirates from the past.

King couldn't help from smiling wistfully at the memories. Things were better then; he was more optimistic.

"This has been the winter of our discontent," allowed King as we settled down again. "We've had a tough year with our health and other concerns." King confessed that he and Bernadette both suffered from depression now and then. He was a big fan of Prozac. "It helps, it really does," he said. "But I don't like taking too many drugs. Never have."

"He could just pick them out of the air."
— King on Prince's story-telling ability

Talking about Bob Prince seemed like a good antidote for whatever challenged King. King couldn't help but smile as he thought about his former sidekick in the Pirates' broadcast booth.

"My appreciation for him grows more each year," said King. "It's kinda odd. I was envious of the sonuvabitch in the beginning. He could walk into a room and dominate it, just by being there. 'How does he do it?' I used to ask myself. I was intimidated by him. He was so unique. He was so professional — he could really broadcast a baseball game — but he was so much more whenever he was with people, or whatever he was asked to do.

"He could do commercials like no one else. He could cut a 60-second commercial just like that." King snapped his long fingers for effect, and continued. "He seldom made a mistake. He had a great ability during a ballgame to bring back something, some story or incident, that was appropriate to the action on the field. He could just pick them out of the air."

King had the same gift. King's conversation was sprinkled with some magic names in Pittsburgh's rich history.

"Rege Cordic once told me that the secret of radio is getting past the microphone or the speaker," said King. "He said you've got to get through that radio and into the home of the listener. You're out there with the guy or gal, sitting right next to them and talking just to them.

"Vin Scully, the Dodgers' announcer, told me his approach to broadcasting a ballgame: 'I'm in my backyard, and I'm having a beer. There's a ballgame going on at the bottom of the hill beneath my home. I can see it, but my neighbor who's sitting in his backyard on the other side of a fence, can't see the game. I'm telling him what's going on, but I'm also talking to him about something else, just talking to him.' I think that's a good approach to take."

Cordic, of course, was a broadcasting icon as a creative morning drive time deejay at KDKA Radio when it ruled the airwaves and no one else was No. 2. He left Pittsburgh for Los Angeles. Scully started out with the Dodgers in Brooklyn, back in the halcyon days of Mel Allen and Red Barber and Russ Hodges in New York, and went to Los Angeles. They're all Hall of Famers, same as Prince. Nobody has ever been as big in Pittsburgh radio as Prince and Cordic.

"When I was on with Prince," recalled King, "our audience share at KDKA was astounding. This was before ballgames were on TV every night. You didn't have all the options you have today entertainment-wise. We were it!"

He also remembered something Red Barber used to say. "If you don't have anything to say, don't say anything."

Silence can be golden, offered King, especially if you let the murmur of the crowd carry the spirit of the moment.

"Prince would see a ball going out of the ballpark, and he'd say, as only he could say, 'You can kiss it goodbye.' And he'd let the crowd carry it.

"He was a stickler about giving the score. People are always coming into the game, he said, somebody new is tuning in, and Prince felt you couldn't give the score often enough. He said to give it every hitter and every time the count went to 3-and-2, simple things like that.

"The spontaneity of the guy was great; he did things so easily. I don't think he wanted an audience, he needed an audience. You either listened to him because you liked him or you listened to him because you hated him, a Howard Cosell kind of thing.

"Three guys in a radio or TV booth is the worst thing that has happened in sports broadcasting," continued King. "It doesn't work. You don't need three voices. Three makes for a bad marriage. Some guys think you have to fill all the available airtime."

King originally worked as the third man with Prince and Jim Woods in 1967, 1968 and 1969. When Woods left, he was replaced by Gene Osborne in 1970. "Prince and Osborne never hit it off," recalled King. "Osborne used to make an infield groundout in the first inning seem like a big deal. Where do you go from there? I don't like announcers who try to make it exciting by the way they say everything, screaming during routine plays. After Osborne left, it was just Bob and me. That's when I liked it best, and I thought the world of Jim Woods. He was a great baseball announcer.

69

"It's your job to make it interesting, not exciting. Every play is not exciting. That's not the way baseball works. One guy wrote me a letter complaining about Osborne. He said 'he makes a ground out to second sound like the second coming of Christ during the Normandy Invasion.'

"Prince knew how to do it. The kid in Prince never died. Blass is like that. He never lost that spontaneity. After 28 years, Prince still had that kid in him. I look back and think, damn, he was good. He started giving nicknames to players around 1954, Rowswell's last year, and he did it to have some fun with the guys.

"When he was sick and he came back to broadcast some games, it was sad. There could have been a better way to do it. He never had a chance to say goodbye.

"I've been fired in one form or another six times in my life. But losing the Pirates' job really shook me. I was 48 at the time. I was in a fog for six weeks after that. I didn't know what I was going to do. But it always worked out fine. The next door that opened was always better. When that door closes it looks like the end of the world. But it's the beginning of a new experience. My 19 years as the SID (Sports Information Director) at Duquesne were great.

"It's a business of people. It's who your relationships are with. The people you grew up with, made your mistakes with, had some success with. I think you remember where you started. If you know where your roots are, you don't get too far from them.

"The Pirates have had their ups and downs, too. They had money problems during last season and they had the lowest payroll in baseball. But they had an exciting season. Last year's team reminded me of the '56 Pirates. They got rid of the old guys, and we had a young team. We had Clemente, Groat, Maz, Skinner and Face, and Dale Long came here and was a leader. It changed everything."

King always makes sure anyone who talks to him about Prince knows that they didn't get off to the best of starts. Prince resented jocks coming into the broadcast booth, as King recalled.

"It was very intimidating," said King. "I wanted to belong. I played a boot-licking role. I didn't like myself for doing it. It takes two to play that role. The more obsequious I got, the more demanding he got."

Prince showed him up on the air a few times, until King called him on it after a broadcast, and told him he'd punch him in the nose the next time he ever repeated that stunt. "That," said King, "seemed to clear the air. After that, we got along fine. We were good friends. We had arguments and happy times, like anybody else."

King and Prince paired up during a period when the Pirates won four divisional titles and a World Series championship. Sometime in 1972, King recalls a special moment in the broadcast booth with Prince. "It was a very quiet, very poignant moment," said King. "You think of Bob Prince as being loud and dominating things, but this was a quiet, very private thing. It happened in September and we were

Nellie King, Radio Rich and Bob Prince at Three Rivers Stadium

Nellie King at 1997 Pirates Alumni golf outing

Bob Prince shares broadcast booth with Harold Arlin, who did the first baseball broadcast in the country at KDKA in 1921, Nellie King and Radio Rich.

Nellie King, Bobby DelGreco and ElRoy Face belly up to the bar at Myron Cope-Foge Fazio golf outing at Montour Heights C.C. for autistic children on June 16, 1997.

Nellie King and Ray Goss are long-time broadcast team for Duquesne University basketball games.

eight games out in front of the pack, and I thought we had the best team I'd ever seen. We broke for a commercial during a game broadcast and Bob leaned over to me and said, 'Nellie, what you are seeing is the halcyon days of Pirates baseball.' And I'll never forget that. He loved Pirates baseball."

"Who's number 54, Possum?"
— Bob Prince

"He didn't have an act," King said of Prince. "He was himself on and off the air. For all that ego, though, Bob was a pussycat underneath."

One of King's favorite stories about Prince happened in either 1960 or 1961 when King was living in Greensburg and working at WHJB Radio. King was sitting on the back porch listening to a late-season, totally meaningless game between the Pirates and St. Louis Cardinals at Forbes Field.

The Gunner was in the middle of one of those five-minute, rambling yarns of his when the Cards sent up a pinch hitter in the late innings. Prince didn't notice the hitter until the guy reached the batter's box.

"Bob asked his then sidekick Jim (Possum) Woods, 'Who's number 54, Possum?' There was a long pause and Woods finally said, 'I don't have a number 54. He's not on the sheet.'

"It was September, after teams brought up minor league prospects. Bob assumed number 54 was one of those kids."

At the same moment, King heard the muffled voice of the public address announcer, but couldn't make out — on the radio — what he said. The next voice belonged to Prince. 'Oh,' said Bob, 'the batter's Munge. Brad Munge. Bats left-handed.' He'd heard the p.a. announcer mention Munge's name and took his cue from that.

"To which Woods interjected, 'That guy looks like Grady Hatton.'

"Bob said, 'No, he's Munge. Brad Munge.' On the next pitch, the batter grounded the ball to second.

"Prince called the play, 'There's a roller to second. Mazeroski's up with it, over to first. Munge's out.'"

A second later, King nearly fell out of his porch chair when he heard the public address announcer, Art McKennan, say, clear as a bell, "Will Brad Munge of Charleroi please report to the security office. They've found your missing son.'"

"When Bob Prince was on top of his game, no one was better. Listen to the tape of Harvey Haddix's almost perfect game in 1959 and the way Prince's urgent call heightened the excitement of the moment."
— John Mehno, free-lance writer

"He's probably going to fire you."
— Leslie King

Nellie King can remember the day he was fired as the Pirates' No. 2 broadcaster like it was yesterday. The day was October 27, 1975.

"I had no idea they were dissatisfied with me. I knew that Prince had had his troubles with KDKA," related King. "I didn't know I was in trouble until Joe Brown called me and said that he wanted to meet with me before he went on a three-week vacation. At that time, I thought he wanted to speak to me about the speakers' bureau that I had been heading up for the ballclub.

"In this business, you can get pretty paranoid, so I thought I better check my contract, because I had a feeling that it was due to expire. I went down to my office and checked it and, sure enough, it was due to expire on November 1.

"It's kind of ironic in retrospect, but I remembered a poster I had seen in California that year that said, 'Just because you're paranoid doesn't mean that they're not out to get you.' I thought about it some more and I realized that in all the time I had known Joe Brown — and we had been pretty good friends — this was the first time he had ever invited me to his house. I had played for him in New Orleans, so we went back a way in our relationship.

"I knew that it was either going to be very good news or very bad. But I still didn't have any indication that they were dissatisfied with me. Before I left the house, my daughter, Leslie, asked me where I was going and I told her. She jokingly said, 'he's probably going to fire you,' and we laughed about that.

"I went over to Joe's house in Mt. Lebanon and he offered me a drink. I said I'd have an Iron City, and he said he didn't have an Iron, so I knew I was in trouble.

"Then he said, 'I have some bad news for you. You're not coming back as an announcer next year.' I couldn't believe it. I was really shook.

"He told me that Prince was having troubles with KDKA, and that he was probably going to go, too. Then he said that sometimes water splashes over onto other people. I said that was a helluva reason to lose a job.

"After that, there were some realizations. He said that, in their judgment, they didn't think I was capable of becoming the number one broadcaster. I said that I was hired to be the second broadcaster and I asked him what was wrong with being a very capable, qualified number two broadcaster. He said they wanted a younger guy who could eventually move into the number one job.

"Joe Brown told me that they sat around a table — the people from the Pirates, KDKA and the brewery, and they voted on it. He said they decided that I had only done a fair job, and that they could get somebody who could do it better. I asked him if he had voted that way, and he said he did.

"I told him I was sorry to hear that because I felt I had walked a lot of extra miles for the ballclub. I did pre-game and post-game shows for absurd prices ($35 a show), and he said, 'We'll make it up to you somehow.' I told him that he really disappointed me."

King thought that Tom Johnson, a Pittsburgh attorney who was part owner and vice president of the Pirates, was mainly responsible for his dismissal as well as Prince's.

"I just didn't fit in with that circle," said King. "I think Tom Johnson is the guy who did me in, and it was Joe Brown who had to fire the bullet because he was the general manager. I never shortchanged them and I never shortchanged the listener. I gave them 100 percent and I knew that I could broadcast baseball."

He said Brown offered him a job in the Pirates' public relations department at $18,000 a year, but he turned it down. His salary as the No. 2 man on the Pirates' broadcast team, according to King, was $28,000 that last year.

"I'm disappointed in you," King told Brown. "I'm not sure I want to work for the Pirates anymore."

Asked what he remembered about the effect of the firing on Prince, King winced and thought about that for a moment.

"It crushed him," King concluded. "So much so that his wife, Betty, told me that for three days afterward he would leave his bedroom only to eat.

"He went to Houston to do the Astros games and that didn't work. He came back to Pittsburgh and failed in a try at Penguins' hockey. He did different things to make a living, sports commentaries, commercials, a job with the Pittsburgh Brewing Company. He could do a lot of things.

"He developed mouth cancer and he died June 10, 1985. I heard him doing his last game, when they brought him back to work in the broadcast booth, and no one realized just how sick he was. I said to Bernadette, 'As painful as it is to hear him, he still has that something that is unique to Bob Prince.' He sounded tired, but that pixieish sense of humor was still there. He still had something different than anybody else. He was like Frank Sinatra singing a song. What he sang was not on the music sheet; it was coming from inside. He may have been 68 when he died, but he had about 100 years worth of living in those 68 years. He didn't get cheated.

"Bob Prince could get lazy. I remember one time he read Melvin Durslag's column (from the Los Angeles *Herald-Examiner*) on his show as if it were his own commentary. He must have figured no one in Pittsburgh was going to read a column in a Los Angeles newspaper.

"Everyone talks about Myron Cope and The Terrible Towel. But Prince came up with babushka power long before that. The Pirates didn't spend a penny on that promotion. Women got a free babushka just for showing up, and they had over 40,000 fans at Three Rivers, one of the biggest weekday crowds in 1972. I mean babushka power, what the hell was that all about? And the green weenie . . . c'mon. Only Prince could pull that off."

"I'm lookin' good, huh?"
— Nellie King

I attended a Pitt football press breakfast meeting at Pitt Stadium on Friday, August 8, 1997, prior to the Panthers departing Pittsburgh for the Pitt-Johnstown campus for pre-season training. Several in attendance expressed concern for Nellie King.

I did not know that King had been involved in an auto accident the day before as he was driving to Duquesne University from his home in Mt. Lebanon. He'd gotten dizzy while passing through the Fort Pitt Tunnels, and tried to pull off at the city end of the tunnel and struck a cement pillar.

I learned that he was in Mercy Hospital and I drove there after the Pitt get-together to see how King was coming along. He was registered under an alias, but I managed to contact him through the hospital's public relations office, and King gave permission for me to visit him.

It was a relief to see him. His head had a scratch on it, his nose was nicked, and he had a few stitches over his left eye. "It's good to see you," I said. "All things considered, you're looking good."

King cracked a smile. "Lookin' good, huh?" King came back, and I knew that I'd stumbled into a trap.

"Remember Pete Dimperio's story about lookin' good," continued King. "Pete said there are three stages in our lives. You're born . . . you're middle-aged . . . and then you're lookin' good." Here's King, recovering from another heart scare and an auto accident that left its marks on his elongated mask, yet it didn't keep him from being a clown. He couldn't help himself.

Now I really knew that King was recovering and that he'd be fine and able to go home in a few days.

He said he had played golf with friends on Wednesday, the day before his accident, and that he had felt fine.

He had suffered a heart attack while driving to work back on November 11, 1989, and had a few scares since then. It got him down, but he didn't want anyone to know it.

One funny story didn't satisfy King. He told me a joke about a boxer.

"This boxer is taking a real beating, and he's got one eye closed, then the other eye is closing.

"His cornerman tells him, 'He's not laying a glove on you.' He keeps telling him that, round after round, and the guy is getting hit left and right.

"'He's not laying a glove on you,' the cornerman keeps saying.

"'Then you better keep an eye on the referee,' the fighter complains to his cornerman, 'because some sonuvabitch in there is hitting me.'"

King said he knew how the boxer felt. He felt disoriented, and he had checked himself out in the mirror in his bathroom.

He related that he had been in Mercy Hospital back in 1989, when he had his first heart attack.

Dave Giusti, the former Pirates' fireman and a good friend of King, stopped in for a visit. He pulled up a chair at the foot of the bed. He told King he had just spent some time at Three Rivers Stadium and gone out to dinner with Bill Virdon, who was in town as a coach with the Houston Astros.

Checking out King's protruding feet at the bottom of the bed, Giusti got in a ribbing remark. "I'd recognize those feet anywhere," he said. Just as King can't help telling stories, Giusti gets a kick by ribbing whomever he meets.

As Giusti was talking to King, I could see a television set hanging from the ceiling on a distant wall, at the foot of the bed of the other patient with whom King was sharing a room.

Coincidentally enough, there was a Pat O'Brien movie showing on the screen. It brought back a family tale. I was born in Mercy Hospital on August 20, 1942. A nurse named Peg Shea took a liking to me and carried me throughout the maternity ward.

There was a movie starring Pat O'Brien that was popular at the time. It was called "Rockne of Notre Dame," and O'Brien played the part of Knute Rockne, the highly-successful and popular coach of the Fighting Irish. So Peg Shea started calling me "Pat" after Pat O'Brien. Peg Shea and my mother started corresponding with each other and continued to do so for 55 years. They went 50 years without seeing each other again, but got together when Shea returned to the city from Carlisle, Pa. to attend a reunion of the Mercy Hospital nurses at the Doubletree Hotel.

A nurse who identified herself as Sharon Howcroft came into the room, and asked Giusti and King if they could sign a few autographs for other people on the staff.

"He's a good patient," offered Nurse Howcroft of King. "Wish they were all like him."

King looked at Giusti, and said in a broadcast manner, "Dave Giusti was the saviour, the Fireman!"

"We know we shouldn't be bothering you like this," the nurse apologized to Giusti.

"Why do you think this is a problem for us to sign this?" asked Giusti. He gave her a few autographs, showed her and some other nurses his 1979 World Series ring, and suggested to Nurse Howcroft that she should get me to sign a few as well. "This guy writes books about the Pirates and all the Pittsburgh sports teams," said Giusti.

"I'm sorry," she said, "what's your name?"

I told her and she looked surprised. "Jim O'Brien," she repeated. "You're the sportswriter. I know your mother. I was her nurse."

About 12 years earlier, my mother, Mary O'Brien, had a long stay at Mercy Hospital, almost three months, and she nearly died. But she bounced back and surprised everyone. I told Nurse Howcroft she was still going strong at age 91.

"Yeah, I knew your mother," she said. "She was really sick. She had a great faith in God, I remember that. So you're a sportswriter. She talked about you all the time." So my mother was still making lasting friends of attending nurses.

It's a small world, I thought. After a while, Giusti gave his wristwatch a close look, and got up to leave. He went over and gave King a big hug and departed the room.

Giusti turned to Nurse Howcroft. "Make sure he eats his vegetables," he said in a parting note. "If he doesn't, scold him!"

Pittsburgh Pirates

Ronnie Kline gets congratulated after pitching six-hitter in 8-2 victory over the Cubs at Chicago's Wrigley Field on June 6, 1956 by three teammates who all hit home runs in the game (from left to right), Roberto Clemente, Dale Long and Frank Thomas.

"You know what I like about radio. It combines my words with your imagination."
— Eleanor Schano

Bob Prince teases Bill Mazeroski as he poses for picture with Ruth Marek of Belle Vernon at Forbes Field.

"Life is pure adventure, and the sooner we realize that, the quicker we will be able to treat life as art; to bring all our energies to each encounter, to remain flexible. We need to remember that we are created creative and can invent new scenarios as frequently as they are needed. Life seems to love the liver of it."
— Maya Angelou, from Wouldn't Take Nothing For My Journey Now

Pirates of the past
Memories from Maz & Co.

"Bob just fit in with our ballclub."
— Bob Veale

Bill Mazeroski, second baseman (1956-1972), Greensburg, Pa.

Bill and Milene Mazeroski were both sitting in the family room of their home in Greensburg when I visited them and played a tape of the ending of the seventh game of the 1960 World Series. Mazeroski smiled as he recognized that it was a re-created broadcast and post-game interview by Bob Prince.

"Bill, how's it feel to to be the hero of the World Series?" Prince asks Maz in the tape that was done after the fact. In truth, at the time Prince had no idea of how the 1960 World Series had ended, and brushed off Mazeroski, the first player to be pushed his way in the crazy clubhouse at Forbes Field following the game.

"I didn't think I remembered him talking to me like that after the game," said Mazeroski. "I was pushed toward Prince, and he asked me one question. He said, 'How's it feel to be on the world championship team?' I always wondered why he didn't ask me about the home run. I asked him a year later, 'Did you want Dick Stuart to hit the home run or me?' The truth is that, at the time, he didn't know who hit it.

"As a kid, you always dream of hitting the home run to win the World Series. It just happened to come true for me. A day doesn't go by during baseball season that someone doesn't come up and mention the home run to me. At least, it seems that way."

Mazeroski gets mentioned every year when it comes time for the Veterans Committee to choose candidates for the Baseball Hall of Fame, but so far he hasn't been picked. Maz doesn't grumble about this. He'd just as soon people wouldn't ask him how he feels about what they regard as a snub.

"What the hell does baseball owe us," he said. "We were just fortunate enough to get the chance to play. If I hadn't been a big league ballplayer I'd have been playing for some bar team and getting beer and spaghetti for doing it. I just enjoyed the game. A lot of people have dreams, but they don't get to live them. I'm one of the few who lived it to the hilt.

"I can remember walking down dirt roads and picking up a broom stick and hitting stones and pretending to be Babe Ruth and winning a World Series. Just about every kid who ever lived did that, or who lived on a dirt road and picked up stones. You just dream about being somebody."

At 3:36 p.m. on Thursday, Oct. 13, 1960, Bill Mazeroski, the leadoff hitter in the bottom of the ninth inning, made history by hitting a 1-0 pitch off Ralph Terry over the wall in left field at Forbes Field in a 10-9 victory over the New York Yankees. Fans, teammates and ushers mobbed Maz as he raced around the bases.

A magic moment...

Bill Mazeroski

Letter from David Mazeroski
Thoughts about his father

"I know what a great dad he is."

March 16, 1994

I have a little story I must tell you. Last October 13 (1993), on the anniversary of the seventh game of the '60 World Series, I took a walk before my 3 p.m. class at Pitt. It was a beautiful autumn day. The air was crisp and breezy and the leaves were changing. I walked by the remains of Forbes Field and wondered if it was a similar type of day thirty-three years earlier.

I saw a man sitting by the flagpole listening to a tape of the game. I walked over to a picnic table and sat for a few minutes. I tried to visualize a guy about my age stepping up to the plate with nerves of steel and hitting the most memorable and unselfish home run ever.

Then I thought about the same guy being my dad, and even though I wasn't alive to see him play, at least it is in my blood. Every time I drove down to school and winded my way around Roberto Clemente Drive, I pictured the infield of the old ballpark and would say to myself that this is where my dad worked. I am driving over my dad's footprints.

I never really remember my dad playing, but thanks to old films, a vivid imagination, and your book, **MAZ And The '60 Bucs**, I can picture in my mind the great game it was and the great player he was. Of course, I know firsthand what a great dad he is. Thanks again.

Sincerely,

David Mazeroski

Bob Veale, pitcher (1962-72), Birmingham, Alabama:

"I met Bob when I first came up. He took me to his home in Mt. Lebanon. He picked me up at the ballpark out in Oakland. It was snowy. There was snow all over the ground when we got to Mt. Lebanon. I said, 'Bob, I haven't seen that much cotton in my whole life.' That just ate him up. We sat down when we got to his home. Betty had cooked a meal. We sat around and talked. They'd call up during the course of the year to see how I was doing. He told me that everybody in Pittsburgh will be on you. He said, 'Carry yourself in a way you would like to be treated, to be respected.' He told me there were different social traps out there. He said you're going to be away from home and on your own, not knowing anybody, and you need to make the right kind of friends. As the years passed on, I saw a lot of them because of Bob's generous spirit.

"He was a great swimmer and diver, I know. I remember when he dove out of the window at the hotel in St. Louis. I thought he was going to kill himself. His skinny ass didn't even break the water. He wasn't crazy. He was daring, highly confident. If as many people had his confidence our world would be a better place. They said Columbus was crazy. They said Newton was crazy. They said a lot of great inventors were crazy. Bob just fit in with our ballclub. A lot of us were a little crazy. Like Barnum & Bailey said, you find a sucker every day. When he dove into the pool, it was like he was taking candy from a baby. He was always dressed up, and he was the picture of sartorial elegance. He was very loquacious. He adopted the whole ballclub. He got us involved in investments. I remember he recommended Mylan Pharmaceuticals, and some of the guys, like Maz, made money on that. Maz was the first one in. I was the last one in. I'm glad he included me."

Frank Thomas, outfielder/infielder (1951-58), Pittsburgh:

"Bob Prince was the best announcer the Pirates ever had. He sold the Pirates more than anything else. I remember one time we were playing softball. And I was playing barehanded, catching everybody's hardest throw. Bob happened to be there, and saw me. He got a kick out of that; he mentioned it on the air a lot. I didn't have much conversation with Bob through the years I played so I don't have any personal stories I can think of. Why? I have no idea. I was never close to Bob. I guess Groat and Virdon were as close to him as anybody on the ballclub. I know Spahn and Burdette from the Braves used to tease Prince a lot; they'd throw his shoes up on the batting cage, have a lot of fun with him.

"Bob was a fan No. 1 and an announcer No. 2. He wouldn't ever say anything bad about a ballplayer. He always said nice things about a ballplayer. I saw other radio announcers who would rip you.

If you said something off the record to Bob, it stayed that way. That wasn't always the case with some guys. You had to know who you were dealing with. I remember one time I was out of the ballgame, sitting in the clubhouse, listening to the game on the radio, and he still had me at third base.

"Things are going fine with me. I just got back from a vacation in Florida. I'm getting ready to go to Ringold, Georgia and Charleston, South Carolina to play in some celebrity golf tournaments. I play in one for Jim Kelly, the former Bills quarterback, at Charleston every year. I play in about 20-to-25 golf tournaments like that a year. I used to play in all the old timers' baseball games, but they quit having them. They couldn't get sponsors anymore and I guess it costs too much money. I've gone to some Fantasy Camps.

"We had eight children and now we've got 12 grandchildren, nine girls and three boys. We have a league of our own with the girls. I'm the manager and my wife, Dolores, is the coach. We live in a two-story, five-bedroom house in Ross Township, and we like living in Pittsburgh. It's our hometown. I started taking my baseball pension at 52. Dolores and I both collect Social Security. I consider myself fortunate to have a good family. Three of them graduated from college. We have a priest in the family.

"I see where Jack Butler is going to receive the Bob Prince Award at the Catholic Youth Association dinner. Jack went to the seminary with me. We were both going to be priests. I left and went into major league baseball and he went to college and ended up playing defensive back for the Pittsburgh Steelers. He was a great ballplayer. I'm happy for him. It's nice to see a local guy get his due.

"Hometown boys don't get recognized much in this town. When I came back here to play after I was traded I received a standing ovation, but that was about it. On Opening Day this year, the Pirates had Mario Lemieux of the Penguins throw out the first ball. That upset my wife. She said we have all these hometown guys still here, like me, Bob Purkey, Dick Groat, Tony Bartirome and Bobby DelGreco, and none of us has ever been asked to throw out the first ball.

"Oh well, I'm enjoying my life, enjoying retirement. We stay busy and we travel a lot, and enjoy our kids and their kids. I'll be 69 in June. I'm active with the Pirates Alumni. Nellie Briles is doing a bang-up job running that. If it weren't for him and Sally O'Leary, who still looks after the alumni, I wouldn't do all the things I do. It was nice to see her get that ('Pride of the Pirates') award on Opening Day."

> *"There was the radio voice first. It was the next best thing to being there yourself. And there was the awareness it might have been better than being there because that voice coupled baseball with the rich drama of the mind's eye. For 28 years, there were the Pittsburgh Pirates and Bob Prince, and to owe allegiance to one was to swear fealty to the other."*
> —Dick Shippy,
> *Akron Beacon-Journal*

ElRoy Face, pitcher (1953, 1955-1968), North Versailles, Pa.:

"Jack Hernon, who covered our club for the *Post-Gazette*, gave me my nickname 'The Baron of the Bullpen,' but Bob Prince picked up on it and made it stick. People still call me that when they see me. Bob was a good friend. I always got along fine with him. No problems. He was just one of the guys. He was all for the Pirates. He wasn't just close to the Pirates. He was also friends with Matthews, Spahn and Burdette from the Braves, Musial from the Cardinals, and other guys like that. He was partial to them, too. I thought it was a shame when he was let go. He was a good announcer and he didn't deserve it. But I didn't know all the details behind it. I didn't know the reason for it. I went to a lot of banquets with him. He was a great emcee. After we won the 1960 World Series, he emceed the show that Hal Smith and I had playing our guitars and singing at the Holiday House. The Gunner was always rooting for us, on and off the air. I retired from Mayview State Mental Hospital, where I had worked as a carpenter, in 1990. I play golf in those celebrity golf outings about 20-to-30 times a year. I enjoy seeing the guys. I'm still living in the same apartment in North Versailles, in the same unit as Charley Feeney, who covered our club all those years for the *Post-Gazette*. He's like Bob Prince. Just a good guy, just a good friend of mine."

Fred Hayes

They are Pirates forever: ElRoy Face, Willie Stargell and Frank Thomas. They attended All-Star Game luncheon at the wall at Forbes Field in June of 1994.

Willie Stargell
"Pops" to the young Pirates

"He took three good swings every day."
— Stargell on Prince

W illie Stargell was sitting between the Pirates past and the Pirates future. Stargell was leaning back in his cushioned chair, as he likes to do when he's talking to someone, relating stories about his travels with Bob Prince and the Pirates, smiling warmly with every twice-told tale.

"He took three good swings every day," Stargell summarized the man who was Bob Prince. "He lived life to the fullest."

The same could be said of Stargell as well, though he was never a character of Prince proportions. Stargell's style was more laidback, calmer, but no one brought more gusto to the game than he did when he waved that bat in a windmill manner and lashed into a fast ball at the knees.

"Let's spread some chicken on The Hill with Will," Prince would cry from time to time when Stargell strode to the plate with the Pirates needing some fireworks. Anyone who placed an order at Stargell's All-Pro Chicken outlet in Pittsburgh's Hill district would get their meal for free if Stargell hit a home run, so the place was often packed during Pirates games because of the special promotion.

The Pirates never had a more positive influence in the clubhouse, on the bench or on the field than Wilver Dornell Stargell. He and Prince were great ambassadors for the Bucs and baseball.

I didn't think Stargell looked or sounded very good during my visit. His face looked swollen, his eyes sunken, and he did not speak with his usual enthusiasm or smile much. Something seemed wrong. I was told two months later that he was sick, that his kidneys were shot, and that he was undergoing dialysis treatments twice a week.

No one in Pirates' history hit more home runs (475), had more RBI (1,540) or extra-base hits (953) than Stargell or made as many friends for the ballclub. Not Kiner, not Clemente, not Wagner, not the Waners. For the record, however, Kiner had bigger clout at the box office.

"You can kiss it goodbye!" Prince often shouted when Stargell launched a shot into the upper seats. "How sweet it is!"

"Pops" compiled a remarkable 21-year career with the Pirates, became the 17th player elected to the Baseball Hall of Fame in his first year of eligibility (in 1988) and had his number (8) retired.

Stargell was in his corner office in the Pirates' complex at Three Rivers Stadium in early March, 1998. He had turned 56 on March 6. There were framed photographs and portraits of some of his favorites on the wall to his right, including Roberto Clemente, Bob Moose, Steve

Blass, Manny Sanguillen, Dock Ellis, et al, and a large chart of prospects in the Pirates' organization on the wall to his left.

Clemente's last game with the Pirates was in the 1972 playoffs with the Reds in Cincinnati. That's the game where Moose threw a wild pitch that enabled George Foster to score from third with the winning run that allowed the Reds, and not the Pirates, to advance to the World Series.

Clemente was killed in an airplane crash the last day of the year, and Moose was killed in an automobile crash in October of 1976. Moose, the pride of Export, Pa., who had pitched a no-hitter for the Pirates, was driving while drunk and went off the road and struck a tree. The pictures brought bittersweet memories to Stargell who loved them both.

Some of Stargell's most-respected rivals were pictured as well, people like pitcher Bob Gibson of the Cardinals and catcher Johnny Bench of the Reds, both Hall of Famers. It was Bench who hit an opposite field home run off relief pitcher Dave Giusti to tie the game at 2-2 in the ninth inning of that deciding game in the 1972 NL play-offs. But he belonged up there on Willie's Wall of Fame.

Stargell's schedule for the day I was visiting with him included going to lunch later on with his youngest daughter, Kellie, who works at PNC. "Girls love to do things like that with their dad," said Stargell. Kellie was living in Edgewood. Stargell had four daughters and one son.

There were books and sports magazines everywhere in his office. The magazine on the top of one pile, *Sports Illustrated*, caught my eye because it featured coverboy Curtis Martin of the New England Patriots. His mother was from Donora and had lived in my hometown of Hazelwood. Martin was an NFL star who got his start in Squirrel Hill at Taylor Allderdice High and the University of Pittsburgh.

Those were my schools as well, and Stargell was a contemporary of mine. I remember him coming to visit Clemente and his family at the Pennley Park apartments in East Liberty where Kathie and I were also living in 1967 and 1968 in the first years of our marriage. So I felt at home in Stargell's company. He was always cooperative and generous with his time.

Stargell was starting his second season as a special assistant to general manager Cam Bonifay, checking out and working with young talent in the minor leagues. Willie had a way with young players. They listened when he spoke. Willie always spoke softly and carried a big stick, as was once said of Teddy Roosevelt. Stargell didn't need to swivel to survey the best of the Pirates' past and future.

Only Clemente was held in higher esteem than Prince by Stargell. Both remarkable men left their mark on a young man from Oklahoma who was trying to find his way in the big leagues when he first reported to the Pirates back in 1962.

Willie Stargell squeezes his pal, Bob Prince, at special night at Three Rivers Stadium.

Bob Prince bows before Willie Stargell in 1967 clubhouse scene. Other Pirates pictured (left to right) are Jim Pagliaroni, Tommie Sisk, coach Johnny Pesky, Pete Mikkelsen and ElRoy Face.

Stargell had returned to the Pirates' organization only the year before after being away too long. He had been working for the Atlanta Braves. He'd first gone there as a coach on the staff of Chuck Tanner in 1986. There was a controversy when Stargell refused to permit the Pirates to hold a night in his honor at Three Rivers Stadium. Through his agent, he had asked for a $10,000 fee. He got knocked in the newspapers for being greedy and ungrateful. There was new management for the most part, they saw Stargell as an asset to the ballclub and he liked their style and offer. Stargell was seeing more eye-to-eye with the current executives.

Atlanta wasn't Stargell's town. That's where Henry Aaron did his thing. Stargell should be enjoyed by Bucs' fans. They've always had a love affair with this warm-hearted giant of a man.

Stargell had been one of the biggest attractions a month earlier when he was among Bucs' alumni signing autographs at Piratefest '98 at the Carnegie Science Center, nearby on the city's north shore.

When Stargell strolls from his office to the water fountain, the lunch room or the bathroom at Three Rivers, he walks by portraits and photos of Clemente, Kiner, Wagner, Mazeroski, Murtaugh and Groat, recognizable faces who mean something to him, people he's met and shared good times with, people who have written the history of baseball in Pittsburgh. There are photos of Forbes Field and Three Rivers Stadium, where he had so many glorious moments. This is where he belongs.

"He was the city of Pittsburgh's No. 1 son."
— Stargell on Prince

"Something I found hard to accept was the firing of The Gunner and his partner Nellie King," said Stargell. "The city was shocked. Bob's life was thrown into total disarray. He never felt it coming. The reason given for his release, which I found to be incredible, was that his ratings had slipped. He was the city of Pittsburgh's No. 1 son. He was loved by everybody in the organization and in the stands.

"We as players enjoyed The Gunner's stories and antics. He was a constant flow of motion. He dressed to be absurd. He usually wore bright summery colors, with a $500 pair of Gucci shoes and no socks. And he was a brave man not to wear socks with his ugly ankles. 'It's gauche to wear socks with Gucci,' he used to tell me.

"No announcer could ever be a bigger hype for Pirate baseball than The Gunner. He invented the Green Weenie, a green plastic hot-dog-shaped object he'd lead the fans in shaking at the opposition. Such behavior was supposed to spur bad luck for Pirate opponents. He'd draw thousands of women to the games with his Ladies Nights. And he thrilled the fans with his 'babushka power.' Pirate fans loved Bob and he loved being their announcer."

Stargell worked with Prince and Steve Blass doing Pirates' games on Home Sports Entertainment (HSE) in 1983, after he retired with 21 years service to the club. It was a short-lived experiment, but it was fun while it lasted. It was the beginning of a new career for Blass, if not Stargell.

"It was an outstanding experience," said Stargell, "because Bob went out of his way to help us. He prepped us on things. As the first game approached, I kept waiting for someone to tell us what to do. The day of the broadcast, I just felt real empty. I didn't know what to do. Bob got us together and briefed us on what we were expected to do. It made all the difference in the world. He corrected us from time to time, but he never put us down. He never embarrassed us. He never felt threatened by us.

"What I learned from that . . . the real reason for Bob being like that was because he was secure within himself. How he dealt with people. He knew what his capabilities were; he never doubted himself.

"He said to me, 'Whoever you are, just be whoever you are.' I didn't understand what he meant, at first, but he thought you should be yourself at all times. He lived by that code, for sure. Bob was the best example of a guy who was true to himself.

"I screwed up one night. I said something that didn't come off the way I meant it. It sounded dirty. Bob started cracking up. He was in stitches. I couldn't talk. I tried to clean it up. Bob had always told us that when you make a mistake you just keep on talking. Don't give people a chance to think about what you just said.

"Another time, we're playing the Astros. Phil Garner was no longer with us. He was playing for the Astros. He was in their dugout and was hooked up for a post-game interview. I asked Bob if I could talk to Phil before we went on the air. I asked him if it wouldn't go out on the air. Bob assured me that we had a direct line to the dugout, that I could talk to him privately for a few minutes. So I started talking to Phil like I used to talk to him in our locker room. I was talking trash to him, saying some stuff that wasn't for public consumption. He called me 'Boy,' which he knew I hated. He said I was a token in the booth. We went on like that for awhile before we did the regular interview. When I got off the elevator afterward at the Allegheny Club, people started applauding. They said it was the best interview all night. Yep, they heard the whole thing. Bob set me up for that. Bob rigged that whole thing. He knew."

> *Going to war...*
> *On a Major League Baseball tour of South Vietnam, Bob Prince raised eyebrows as well as morale. "He actually started telling the brass how to run the war," said Willie Stargell. "We nicknamed him General Westmoreland."*

"Let's play chicken
on The Hill with Will."
— Bob Prince

There was that night in Houston when the Pirates and Astros went into extra innings in the second game of a doubleheader. Stargell stepped to the plate and Prince, anxious to get the game over with, promised free chicken at Willie's All-Pro Chicken in The Hill district if Willie would hit a home run. It was as if Prince had sprinkled Stargell with magic dust.

Prince related the story this way: "I said, 'Let's play Chicken on the Hill with Will, and send The Gunner the bill,' and he hit that (blessed) ball out of sight."

Within minutes, there was mayhem in The Hill, with fans rushing to the All-Pro Chicken outlet Stargell owned along with Brady Keys, a former Steelers' defensive back who started the business and became a local entrepreneur.

Willie warmed to the story with a smile. "It was July 3rd, and we had played a doubleheader and were into extra innings in the second game. We were all tired and frustrated. Bob was on the radio, talking about chicken on The Hill. I hit a home run, right on cue. People just poured out of their houses to get some free chicken.

"It turned into a real mess. There was a traffic jam outside our place, I was told. Police had to be called to control the situation. We were closing and we had run out of chicken. My manager's name was Larry, and he didn't know what was going on. He didn't know if there was a riot or whether they were coming to rob him. Here comes this swarm of people. He didn't know what was going on. He didn't know what to do. He called Brady and Brady said, 'Yeah, honor it. Give them certificates to come back for chicken.' We gave out $1,800 worth of coupons. At 7 a.m. the next day, I got a call telling me what happened. The actual bill came to about $800 or $900, and Bob wrote out a check to cover it. He was good for his word."

There were other amusing experiences Stargell had shared with Prince. Like the time they visited Vietnam after the 1971 season on a USO promotional tour with some other American baseball stars.

"After he had a few toddies, he wasn't afraid to say anything," said Stargell. "We weren't allowed out at night in the war zone. One night General Abrams had us over to his place for dinner. We had a wonderful time. Bob was talking; he was never lost for words. The next thing I knew he had suggestions for how to end the war.

"He actually started telling the brass how to run the war. After that, we nicknamed him 'General Westmoreland.'

"We did a radio spot in Vietnam. Jim 'Mudcat' Grant of the Pirates, Merv Rettenmund of the Orioles, Eddie Watt and Phil Niekro of the Braves, and Bob Prince. Bob took great pride in his ability to cut a commercial on one take. So he started getting on us about how

90

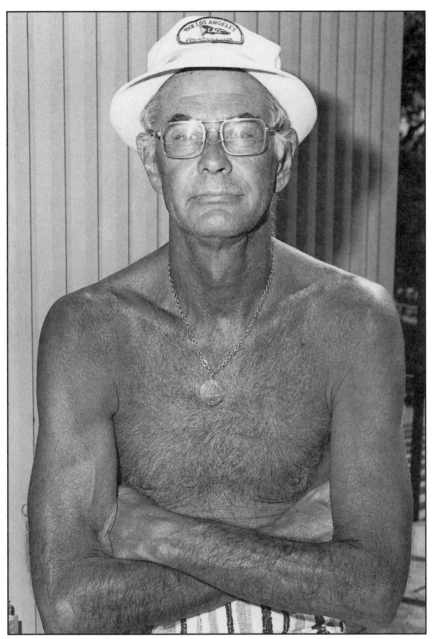

Bob Prince bares his chest at spring training.

"Giusti steps off the mound...Man, the adrenalin's makin' my sweat buds pop. I haven't had a drink in three months...I might just nudge a little one."
— Bob Prince, calling the ninth inning
of Game Three of the 1971 National League
Championship Series.

we were sure to screw up things. 'You donkeys are going to hold me up. We'll be there all night.' Once we got there, though, all the ballplayers did their bit on the first take and then it was Bob's turn. He couldn't say the name of this one city in Vietnam. It was Toewa — To-ee-wah. He was tongue-tied. We were there forever, one take after another. We really got on him about that. And he was supposed to be the professional announcer.

"When we were in Vietnam, I got to really know him. I was with him night and day for 18 days.

"The Gunner and I formed a tight relationship on that trip. We almost crashed in a helicopter soon after we got there. It was late November and we got caught in a monsoon. The rain was so thick the pilot couldn't see the ground. We both kissed the ground when the helicopter was landed safely."

Stargell also remembers visiting a hospital in Vietnam and seeing a soldier who had been burned over his entire body. "I was so shocked I began to get sick," he recalled. "I ran out of the tent and threw up. Then I began to cry.

"Bob followed me outside. Though I wasn't a drinking man at the time, the Gunner lifted me off the ground and pulled me into the nearest bar. We quickly proceeded to down a fifth of whiskey to calm our nerves."

Stargell saw a quadruple amputee who smiled as he approached him. He'll never forget that as well.

His Vietnam experience changed his mind about heroes. "To these soldiers, I was special and I was a hero because I could hit a little white ball a long way. Most had dreamed of being ballplayers just as I had.

"After seeing them, I didn't think of myself as a hero anymore. A hero is a person who gives his life to save others. Heroes are also doctors, surgeons, scientists and biologists who give their entire lives to curing a disease or keeping us alive."

If you've gone to war with someone and come away unscathed, as Stargell and Prince did in a way, you tend to remain loyal to such an individual. That's why Stargell showed up at a demonstration at Point Park when fans staged a civic protest over the firing of Bob Prince and Nellie King.

"I'd grown so fond of him over the years," said Stargell. "I knew deep down inside what a legitimate booster of the Pirates he'd always been. I knew how hard it hit him. It took a lot out of him."

"He was just real."

Bob Prince often got laughs at the expense of black athletes at all-white male stag dinners in Pittsburgh. He certainly got a lot of laughs at the expense of the physically gifted Manny Sanguillen. At the same time, no one extended himself more to make young black ballplayers get acquainted with the right people in Pittsburgh. Prince played to his audience, right or wrong, but he personally seemed to enjoy a wonderful rapport with players of all colors and creeds. "He was truly color-blind," noted Nellie King, who was the same way.

Pete Dimperio, another popular after-dinner speaker on the Western Pennsylvania rubber-chicken circuit, was like that, too. He'd tell funny but unflattering stories about his players. Dimperio had great success with a nearly all-black football team that dominated the City League for years when he was at Westinghouse High School. His critics in the black community didn't care for what they viewed as a two-faced approach and exploitation of black athletes. Dimperio's defense was that his actions and record spoke for themselves as far as racial relations were concerned.

Prince and Dimperio were two of the favorites for the annual "Sports Night" dinner at the Thompson Run Athletic Association in West Mifflin. Prince served as the toastmaster for 23 consecutive years, and a memorial award has been given in his honor ever since.

Prince never took Stargell, or any other black ballplayers, to that infamous dinner, but he did take him just about every place else. And Prince was a regular at sports banquets throughout the tri-state area. It wasn't the first place in his experience with the Pirates that Stargell wasn't welcome. Stargell joined the Pirates in the early '60s when the team still had to arrange for separate housing for the black ballplayers during their spring stay in Florida.

"When I first came up, he had a lot of charitable events which he worked with and helped get organized," recalled Stargell. "He took a lot of the veterans with him. For some reason, he saw fit to take me along."

I asked Stargell how Prince was, in his personal opinion, in regard to his interaction with black ballplayers.

"Prince treated everybody the same," said Stargell. "That's the way I saw it, anyhow. He got on all of us. He could say something about us, in reference to our color, and get away with it. We knew where he was coming from. He'd do anything for a laugh, at anyone's expense. That's the way we took it.

"It's easy to tell who's for real and who isn't. It's vibes you get. It's based on a number of things. It's not what a person says. It's how they say it. And their actions. Somebody else could say the same thing and upset you. If it wasn't coming from Bob Prince you'd read it differently. He felt comfortable enough with certain guys. He could say some things.

"I liked Jim Woods. I liked Nellie King. But they were all different types of individuals."

Prince was known to bring blacks to his home, Willie Mays and Willie McCovey of the Giants are two examples that come to mind. Prince once took Olympic great Jessie Owens to a supper club and the

St. Clair Country Club in his community, much to the chagrin of some of his more conservative acquaintances. Prince never cared what anyone said to him in protest of such nervy man-about-town tours. Stargell said he had never been to Prince's home.

"One time we had to go to the dinner in his car," recalled Stargell. "Bob was doing the driving. I was in the back seat with somebody else. Bob was definitely exceeding the speed limit and he kept turning around and talking to us. He was crossing over the medial line. We were winding up on the other side of the road. It was scary. I said to myself and to Bob I'd never ride with him again."

Stargell said that Prince was a vital part of the Pirates team, who contributed to a close, yet loose, clubhouse atmosphere.

"He came by the locker room and spent time with us," said Stargell. "He was always there, always entertaining us. I liked him a lot."

He had heard about some of Prince's zany antics, such as the swan dive he took into the swimming pool from a third-story window at the Chase Hotel in St. Louis. That was before Stargell joined the Pirates.

"He told me about the St. Louis incident," recalled Stargell. "It didn't surprise me, though, to hear that he'd done that."

Was Prince in a special category as far as all the people he knew from his playing days? "I don't know how to say that," responded Stargell. "That put him out there. Clemente was No. 1. He meant so much to me. But Bob wasn't far behind. Everybody got along with Bob."

He admired Clemente for many reasons, not only for his all-around ability, his leadership abilities, his concern about others, but he also appreciated how difficult it must have been for the so-proud Spanish-speaking Clemente to have coped with the difficulties of communicating in a country where he wasn't always properly understood.

"It's hard to put a finger on it. If I went to play in Puerto Rico every summer, would my life have been different? Would it be different for all of us? Where you're not understood as well?"

Stargell was checking the clock to make sure he kept his luncheon date with his daughter. While he told good stories, Stargell didn't sound good. He said he had a sinus problem. He sounded nasal and he was blowing his nose. His eyes were watery. He lacked his usual vitality. I didn't know at the time that he was ill.

It took a while for Stargell to find his way when he first came to the Pirates and to Pittsburgh. Prince helped. He told him how to act and what to say, how to win friends and influence people. Stargell did not always say what was on his mind, what was in his oft-wounded heart early in his career.

"That would have been suicidal," said Stargell. "I never had a chance to say what I thought about some things, good or bad, my way. The same was true with Clemente until the very end of his career here.

"I like to take full responsibility for what I did, good or bad. I'm happy where I am. I'm comfortable. The new people want me to be a part of the Pirates and of Pittsburgh.

"I'm very proud of what I've been able to sit back and look at. I was proud to play in the big leagues. And I was up here at a great time when there were a lot of great players, great role models for me and anyone else who wanted to play baseball the way I did. I didn't ever feel I couldn't compete with them, no matter how good they were. I thought my play should speak for me. I wanted to be a baseball player when I was a child. I knew that then. When I came up and looked around at some of the great players, I respected them but I never felt like I didn't belong.

"I knew that I was good enough. It was like a thirst, to be a big league ballplayer. I'd look around and see the players, and who was doing well. I never felt I had to take a backseat to any of them. I wanted to find out what I could do. Each day I go to the ballpark I expect to learn something and I do."

"I greet each day with an open heart."
— Willie Stargell

Anyone seeking to learn more about this man is urged to look for *Willie Stargell: An Autobiography* at your local library. It is no longer available at bookstores. Written with Tom Bird (Harper & Row, Publishers, 1984), it's worthwhile, an easy read, offering insights into Stargell's upbringing, his ballplaying exploits and the Pirates at large.

A sampling: Stargell was born in Earlsboro, Oklahoma, 16 miles southeast of Shawnee, the birthplace of Jim Thorpe, regarded as the greatest all-around athlete of his day. Stargell had some Seminole blood in his background, and lived in an American-Indian community as a child. He always felt like an outcast.

His family moved to a housing project in Alameda, California and he remembers that as an 11-year-old on a train traveling westward he was swinging a stick at an imaginary baseball and hitting home runs in the big leagues. He always dreamed of becoming a ballplayer.

Bird befriended him when Bird was working in the Pirates' publicity office, and Stargell shared a lot of his most personal thoughts on many subjects because he was obviously comfortable with his co-author.

Stargell grew up admiring Stan Musial, for instance, and later became Roberto Clemente's biggest fan and one of his closest friends on the Pirates. "I loved to watch Roberto," he said. Stargell was a link and a confidant of two of the club's most talented and temperamental stars of two different periods in Pirates history, Clemente and Dave Parker.

Stargell got along with everybody. Dock Ellis was one of his disciples, difficult with others but tight with Stargell who appreciated his competitive juices and independent ways. Stargell thought Ellis and Parker were both dedicated to winning at all costs. Most of these teammates, he felt, were misunderstood and misrepresented by the media. I never had any problems with Parker, but was put off by Ellis' attitude when I attempted to interview him.

It sickened Stargell that some of the sportswriters who had chronicled Clemente in such a negative manner most of his 18-year career with the Pirates turned to sympathetic eulogies after Clemente died in an airplane crash on New Year's Eve, 1972. In fairness, there were sportswriters who wrote honestly and fairly about Clemente from the start, but Stargell sees it through his own dark eyes.

"His death left me totally depressed and confused," said Stargell. "I cried like a baby."

He remembers the fans booing Clemente when he came onto the field for the 1969 opener because of a feud he was engaged in with the media who accused him of being out for himself. "No one wanted to win more than Roberto," insisted Stargell. Revisionist history would have young fans believing that Clemente was idolized by most Pirates' fans of that era.

While Stargell had his differences with the media, he masked his true feelings most of the time. He subscribed to Dr. Martin Luther King's passive resistance theories.

"I utilize the smile as my weapon instead of a rifle," said Stargell in his autobiography.

"I greet each person and each day with an open heart. I've always been a slave to my heart. I believe that my open-heart philosophy is the key to my popularity. I live and accept all people for what they are. I never expect them to live up to my expectations, only their own.

"There's nothing I love more than the closeness of my friends and family, a smile as I pass someone on the street."

Stargell said his tastes were simple. "Clothes hanging on the line in a backyard turns me on," he said.

He remembers how thrilled he was to emerge from the Fort Pitt Tunnels the first time, when Bob Veale drove him here in a dilapidated Studebaker to report to the Pirates at Forbes Field back in 1962. The Pittsburgh skyline, Stargell insists, is a scene that still excites him.

"The magic of the city and its people have never left me," Stargell told Bird.

He said Clemente, Tanner, Danny Murtaugh and Bill Mazeroski were among his most influential teachers.

He said Murtaugh was the perfect manager because he was patient and allowed a rookie to find his way without putting too much pressure on him. He said, "Maz taught me the value of patience and consistency."

He said Mazeroski was always smiling, always happy to be wearing a Pirates uniform, never too high or too low.

"He taught us to be consistent and to worry more about loving the game than losing a game," said Stargell. "He showed us that love is the key to success. Maz loved playing baseball."

Maz retired at the end of the '72 season, and Stargell felt strangely alone without Clemente and Maz on his side.

Stargell remembered how excited the Pirates were to move from Forbes Field to Three Rivers Stadium. It sounds strange hearing this now because of the Bucs' eagerness to exit Three Rivers in favor of a new ballpark.

"Moving in there was wonderful for us at the time," said Stargell. "We'd been freed of all the traditions of Forbes Field. We were writing our own record book. We all loved playing there. We felt so free."

When the Pirates move to a new ballpark, of course, they will leave behind a stadium that has markers indicating where Stargell's most epic home runs landed. The first three and four of the first five upper deck home runs at Three Rivers were all launched by Stargell

Some skeptics have suggested that the Pirates "Family" couldn't have been as tight-knit as promoted, but Stargell smiles at those of little faith and says, "Our feelings for one another were as genuine as the sunset."

In another chapter in the Stargell/Bird book, the Pirates' premier slugger says, "Baseball has always been a reflection of life. Like life, it adjusts itself to trends, fads, wars, depression and disasters. Like life, it survives everything.

"I'm still the same old loving guy who awakes every morning with a gleam in his eye and lives his life for all the beauty it has to offer. I'm still the smiling project kid."

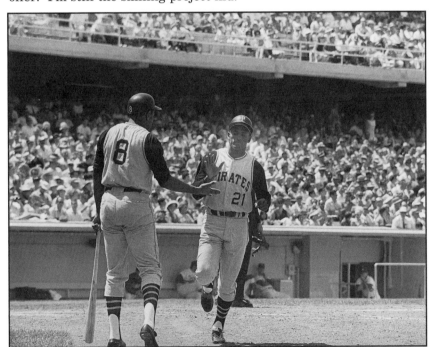

Street & Smith's Baseball Yearbook

Willie Stargell slaps hands with Roberto Clemente after he hit a home run.

A man for all seasons
Sunday school teacher,
car salesman, etc.

"He was a heckuva good guy."
— Ron Livingston, Sr.

Bob Prince taught Sunday school for years at our church, and he was quite popular. There are a lot of adult members today who still tell stories about Prince that they remember from being in his class in their childhood. He came in one day and got the kids to sit down on the floor and had them sitting in a circle. He tossed a $100 bill onto the floor in the center of the ring. He asked each of them what they would do if they found that $100 bill. After each of them told him what they would do, he scolded them, saying, 'Each of you told me how you'd spend this money to buy things for yourself. None of you told me what you would do for someone else with this money. Don't you think you ought to be more generous with your money, that you ought to be more charitable? That you ought to think of someone besides yourself?' He had made his point. It stayed with them. Most of them had never seen a $100 bill before.

"A couple of other memories come back to me regarding Bob Prince. A neighbor who lived directly behind the Prince home died suddenly of a heart attack. Bob was there immediately (ahead of me). He dealt with the situation with a truly pastoral touch. I cannot recall specific words or acts, but I was acutely aware of the compassion and good sense with which he dealt with the widow.

"I recall that he did not hold missionaries in high respect. This attitude rose, I understand, from his background as an Army brat. He was not a saint, mind you, he had his faults. But he always meant well.

"Oh, yes, one other. He invited the church staff, particularly the secretaries, to dinner and ball game at the (then new) stadium. He was aware of the critical importance of the secretaries to the operation of his church."

—Rev. John H. Galbreath,
Founding Pastor,
Westminster Presbyterian Church
Now retired in Black Mountain, N.C.

* * *

"My late wife Becky taught Sunday school at Westminster Presbyterian Church when Bob Prince would pinch-hit on occasion. Our son Kirk was in Bob's class. He said Mr. Prince was always asking them questions. He said Mr. Prince said he didn't have the answers. He just wanted to challenge them."

— Judge Emil E. Narick
Upper St. Clair, Pa.

"I was at this dinky airport in Tucson, Arizona back in 1962. The Yankees had just beaten the Giants in the World Series. There's a small bar and as I approach it, there's this wild sports coat that catches my eye. It pulled my eyes to the individual wearing it. It was Bob Prince. 'What are you doing here?' I asked him. He said he was there to visit his daughter, who was a student at the University of Arizona. 'You're from Pittsburgh,' Prince said to me. 'Pull up a stool.' I told him, 'You don't remember me, but I used to put gas in your car at my father's service station on Cochran Road in Mt. Lebanon back in the '40s.' Of course, he said he remembered me.

"He talked about the World Series and how it ended. Ralph Terry was pitching for the Yankees, just as he had in the '60 World Series. This game came down to the 9th inning, too. Terry was trying to protect a 1-0 lead. There were two outs and Felipe Alou was on third base, and Willie Mays was on second base. Mays had doubled to deepest right, trying to hit a home run. Then Willie McCovey came up. Orlando Cepeda was on deck. He hit a hard line drive chest-high right at Bobby Richardson, the Yankees' second baseman. It was like a rocket. 'They won by a gnat's eyelash,' said Prince. 'McCovey could have hit that ball between first and second, or out of the park just as easily and the Giants would have won the World Series. Ralph Terry was pitching for the Yankees, and he could have been the goat just like he was against the Pirates in the '60 Series. Instead, he was a hero. He won the MVP Award. Some Pirates' fans have forgotten that. Who better to discuss the World Series with than Bob Prince, huh? I was having some problem with my airline ticket because a flight had been canceled. 'Here, I'll get it fixed for you,' Prince said, pulling out his credit cards. Prince had these credit cards in a plastic foldout that was nearly as tall as he was when he unfurled them. He had cards for everything. He belonged to all these crazy clubs and organizations. One of them was called the Southern Nevada and Northern Arizona Mortuary Association, and it had all these CEOs and politicians as members. They played golf and raised money.

"We drank our way to Pittsburgh, and you'd have thought we were life-long friends. I'm an engineer and I was able to fix a cigarette lighter he had, so he could smoke. You could smoke on the airplanes back then. Then I was his friend. When he found out we went to the same church (Westminster Presbyterian Church in Upper St. Clair), he told me there were two things that bugged him at church. 'I think missionaries should just do what they can do to help when they're in a foreign country, but they shouldn't try to push religion on them. And I wish, when I came to church, people would forget I was the Pirates' broadcaster. I get tired of people asking me which way is the wind blowing.' Bob's wife, Betty, met him at the airport. He said, 'Betty, I want you to meet my ol' buddy.' He really knew how to build your ego."

— Ken Ball,
Bridgeville, Pa.

"When I was the pastor at Westminster Presbyterian Church, Bob knew I was a big fan of the Cardinals, having grown up in St. Louis. So he gave me a Cardinals jacket that Stan Musial had given him. I still put it on when I'm feeling sentimental and am sitting out on the porch on a cool evening."

— Rev. Laird Stuart,
San Francisco, California

*   *   *

"Twice I went with Bob Prince to the Brockway Glass outing at the Waldorf-Astoria in New York, and it was a first class affair all the way. We rode in limousines and private jets. I remember Prince sat down in the company president's seat on the private plane, got himself some vodka and orange juice and made himself right at home. He also did something for my mother that I won't ever forget. My mother lost her eyesight to glaucoma when I was 8 years old. She had been a Pirates' fan for a long time, going back to the days when Jack Craddock and Rosey Rowswell were the announcers. She could still type because she had been a secretary and used the proper touch typing method. She sent a type-written letter along with a birthday card to Prince because they shared the same birthday — July 1. After that, he'd call her on her birthday from all over the country. And he'd mention her birthday during the broadcast of the baseball game. That's my story of Bob Prince, a nice story. He was a heckuva good guy."

— Ron Livingston, Sr.
Pittsburgh, Pa.

*   *   *

"I used to do some part-time work for Bud Behling's automobile dealership in Bridgeville (BBL Leasing, Inc.) after I first retired, and Bob Prince did some promotional work for them. Chrysler-Plymouth was one of his main sponsors. I remember I was there one day, and a salesman was trying to wrap up a sale and Prince came in and he started telling the customer why it was a good buy. He helped close the sale. What a salesman he was! He was a cocky individual, but a good guy just the same. He was always nice to all the mechanics, and he took care of everybody. He'd slip them a $5 bill now and then. I played nine holes of golf once with Bud Behling and Prince at the St. Clair Country Club. Prince was a lot of fun. I can tell you this: he was a well-constructed guy. People thought he was skinny, but he was muscular. I know because he played bare-chested. He was a lefty, and he could hit the ball a mile. But you never knew where he was going to hit it."

— Baldo Iorio,
Heidelberg, Pa.

100

Bob Prince was a left-handed terror on the golf course.

"Bob Prince brought Jesse Owens, the great Olympic hero, to Gammons Restaurant out in the South Hills. Guys at the bar started grumbling about Prince bringing a black guy there, only they put it in a different way. Prince read them the riot act. He wouldn't back down on stuff like that. He also took Owens golfing at the stuffy St. Clair Country Club the next day. And he told those guys he was doing just that."
— Jim "Bear" Howey,
Homestead, Pa.

"I was a classmate and teammate of Bob Prince as a senior at Schenley High School in 1933. He was a very good swimmer and won more than his share of medals. I have scrapbooks from those days that show him winning a lot of races, especially in the 50-yard and 100-yard freestyle and relay events. I have a team photo in which he's the only one wearing a topcoat. He was not feeling well when we took the picture. I worked for the federal government and taught labor relations classes as a part-time teacher at Pitt for many years, so I kept track of Prince. Bob lived in the Royal York Apartments which was a very exclusive address at the time we were at Schenley. It was owned by the McSorley family. Unless you were appropriately dressed, you couldn't go in the front door. So our gang usually went through the garage when Bob took us to his place. I remember, at his suggestion, we once went to a meet with a heavily-favored Carrick team by riding in a hearse. Bob thought that might scare them. But they still beat us. He was a character. One time we were at the Irene Kaufman Settlement and Mrs. Teller, the wife of the director, was coming through the locker rooms. She hollered out to let us know she was coming through. We all ran into the showers, but Bob just stood there in the nude and faced her when she came in. He told her, 'Hey, you shouldn't be here.' He was always a fun-loving guy. He went to Stanford University after he was at Pitt. So the Pitt football team is out in Pasadena, California to play in the Rose Bowl. Bob showed up at the hotel where Pitt was staying, and he was wearing a Pitt varsity sweater. He went to the hotel bar and was drinking there in his Pitt shirt, attracting a lot of sportswriters. Jock Sutherland found out about it, and approached Prince and told him he had no business wearing that sweater. Prince told Sutherland he had earned the sweater fair and square as a varsity swimmer at Pitt. Sutherland was fuming, but Prince didn't care. He told the sportswriters that Sutherland was a lousy coach. He was something."

— Hyman Richman,
Pittsburgh, Pa.

Bob Prince, the tall fellow in the topcoat, wasn't feeling too good when this picture was taken of his Schenley High School swimming team in 1933. Teammate Hyman Richman, third from right in same rear row, offered this photo and some reminiscences about Prince, the Spartans' top sprinter.

Chuck Tanner
Baseball Ambassador

"Bob Prince was everybody's friend."

C huck Tanner can talk baseball with the best of them. Tanner's enthusiasm for the game, for every breath he draws, for his wife and family as well as everyone he has ever met, is contagious. Anyone who spends time with Tanner at Three Rivers Stadium has a good day.

This is truly a blessed man, who knows it, and feels charged to motivate any man or woman who walks his way. He considers himself, for example, lucky to have befriended somebody like Bob Prince. Tanner is thankful for the satisfying life he's led, and a seat behind home plate where he can sit and socialize with friends and fans, and watch his favorite sport. Talking about baseball is Tanner's second favorite pastime.

At the same time, he's no pushover. He can hold his own in any debate, whether it's about baseball or politics.

This was in late July, 1997, and Tanner had just turned 68, but he looked at least ten years younger. Keeping company with the likes of Tanner, or Prince, or one of their mutual favorites, Art Rooney Sr., has always been special and made sportswriting a pretty nice way to make a living. Imagine how great it would be to sit in the midst of those guys in the bleachers at a baseball game. Heaven, huh?

Charles William Tanner was born on the 4th of July in 1929. He always preferred to think his birth set off fireworks and not the stock market crash which set off The Great Depression.

Tanner can be found at Three Rivers for just about every Pirates' game, getting paid in recent summers to scout talent and file reports for the Milwaukee Brewers. One of his favorite former players, Phil Garner, was managing the Brewers.

Tanner broke into the major leagues in 1955 at Milwaukee, with the old Braves. He hit a home run in his first at bat in the big leagues, and he's had a love affair with the game ever since. He played in the big leagues for eight seasons, had a career .261 batting average, 21 home runs and 105 RBI. To hear him, he never had a bad day in baseball.

"I thought I had it made even when I didn't have it made," Tanner was fond of saying.

The sun, even in Pittsburgh where it's scarce, bleaches his light brown hair blond by mid-summer, and forces his bright blue eyes to squint as he stares out onto the field at Three Rivers. The wrinkles in his handsome fieldhand's face extend every smile to his ears.

Tanner has time for everyone and he's always been that way. He's a good listener, too, and makes you feel like you're telling him the best stories he's ever heard. I first met him in 1972, when he was managing the White Sox and I was covering baseball for *The New York Post*. After eight years of managing in the minors, Tanner got his break with the White Sox in 1970.

I approached Tanner in the clubhouse at old Comiskey Park to talk to him about his star player, Richie Allen, or Dick Allen as he adamantly demanded everyone call him at that time. By any name, Allen could be difficult, for opposing pitchers and for members of the press, no matter their affiliation. He was recalcitrant, moody, gunshy from being wounded once too often by critical commentary.

I first met Allen in 1963, just before my senior year at the University of Pittsburgh, when I was working as a summer intern with the late *Philadelphia Evening Bulletin*. Allen was in his rookie season with the Philadelphia Phillies. He would gain a reputation as a difficult young man during his long stay with the Phillies.

To Tanner, Allen was an altar boy, not a bad boy. "That's one of his favorite players," pointed out Sally O'Leary, who loved Tanner's positive attitude when she was working in the Pirates' publicity office. Tanner liked everybody in baseball. He especially liked power hitters who came from Western Pennsylvania, as he had done.

Allen was from Wampum, where he and his brothers added to the storied basketball success established there by Coach L. Butler Hennon and his son, Don Hennon, who went on to become an All-American in the late '50s and then a medical student at Pitt. Wampum is close to Ellwood City, near New Castle, Tanner's hometown, where he maintained a residence during his entire baseball career. Tanner first lived and went to school in Shenango, on the outskirts of New Castle, which is located about 50 miles north of Pittsburgh.

Tanner never forgot where he came from, or his humble beginnings, because he never left his roots for long. He returned home every winter because that's where he belonged.

"He's been a friend for a long time," noted Nellie King. "We first went up against each other in 1954 in the old Southern Association. He was playing for Whitlow Wyatt at Atlanta, and I was with New Orleans when Joe L. Brown was the general manager and Danny Murtaugh was the manager. Chuck's the same guy today as he was then. He's such a competitive fellow, yet I never saw him when he wasn't smiling. He's good people."

Prince on passing time...
When somebody hit a home run off the Pirates, Bob Prince might say, "We're hurtin' big. Call a doctor." As he explained, "What the heck, if you're getting beat 11-2 in the third inning, you're better off talking about things people want to hear. A lot of times when we're getting our brains beat out, I'll start reminiscing about Willie Mays or something and I won't even tell you about the game."

Jim O'Brien

Chuck Tanner takes break during Pirates Alumni golf outing July, 1997 at Churchill C.C.

Pittsburgh Pirates

Chuck Tanner and his team bow heads in respect at Three Rivers in June of 1985 when announcement is made that Bob Prince has died.

"When you were born, you cried and the world rejoiced. Live your life in such a manner that when you die the world cries and you rejoice."
— Old Indian Saying

"We love each other."
— Willie Stargell

I certainly had Tanner's attention that afternoon in Chicago after I told him I was from Pittsburgh. I can still remember how friendly he was, how generous he was with his time. Sparky Anderson was like that, too. That wasn't the case with some managers. Herman Franks, Leo Durocher and Billy Martin could ruin your day in a hurry. Tanner rattled off the names of some mutual friends, such as Frankie Gustine and Ralph Kiner, Pirates' broadcaster Bob Prince and sportswriters such as Al Abrams, Les Biederman and Jack Hernon.

"Bob Prince was everybody's friend," Tanner said. "He was a great salesman for baseball." It took one to know one.

Tanner talked to me at length that day about Allen, extolling his virtues.

Tanner was one of the best ambassadors of baseball in Chicago at the time. The Cubs claimed Ernie Banks, known as "Mr. Cub," and "Mr. Sunshine," and fond of saying, "It's a good day for two." With Banks, every day was a good day for a doubleheader. Banks might have been even more upbeat than Tanner, though that's hard to believe.

Harry Caray was working there, too. Caray, who died in February of 1998, broadcasted the ballgames for the White Sox and the Cubs in Chicago. When he stood up and sang "Take Me Out To The Ballgame" during the seventh inning stretch, you can bet that Tanner was humming along with him. No matter where Tanner was working that day.

Chicago is a great baseball town, whether you're watching the White Sox at the old or the new Comiskey Park or the Cubs at wonderful old Wrigley Field. It's Chuck Tanner's kind of town. Then again, Tanner thought it couldn't get any better when he was managing Quad Cities in Davenport, Iowa.

Tanner's friend and boyhood hero, Frankie Gustine, ironically enough, grew up in Chicago and died in Davenport. Gustine had a successful career playing for the Pirates and owned and operated a popular restaurant in Oakland for over 30 years. He's one of the best people I ever met in my life, and I was thrilled to be chosen by his family as an honorary pallbearer at his funeral.

The White Sox were Tanner's first major league managing assignment. He was with them from 1970 to 1975. He later managed the Oakland A's for Charles O. Finley for one scary summer, then the Pirates and the Atlanta Braves. Altogether, he managed in the major leagues for 19 years, and compiled a 1,352-1,381 record.

"At six-one and 200 pounds, he was a powerful man with thick arms that indicated enormous strength," wrote Bob Smizik in *The Pittsburgh Pirates — An Illustrated History*. "In his days as a minor league manager, Tanner was known to grab players by their collars

106

and lift them off the ground. It was an impressive way of getting across his message. He needed no such tactics on the team he inherited (in Pittsburgh)."

He was best known in Pittsburgh for directing the Pirates to a World Series victory over the Baltimore Orioles in 1979. His never-say-die approach and constant upbeat attitude were never more apparent than during that Series as the Bucs came back from a three games-to-one deficit to win the championship. That was easily the most satisfying achievement of Tanner's baseball career.

His ballclubs were colorful, free-spirited and confident. Tanner wanted them to enjoy being in the big leagues. The players understood where he was coming from, what he expected of them, and he communicated with them in a folksy manner.

Tanner doesn't forget much. He mentioned that he still had a clipping of an article I had written about his mother after she died during the 1979 World Series. "That was special to me," said Tanner.

His mother died on the morning of the fifth game.

Tanner decided to stay with the Bucs and they rallied to win the next three games and the championship. "It took a hell of a lot for this man to do what he did," Willie Stargell said after the fifth game. "This man walked extremely tall today."

Playing to the beat of the popular song, "We Are Family," by Sister Sledge, the Pirates had wiped out the Cincinnati Reds in three straight games in a best-of-five series for the pennant, and required seven games to become world champions.

The team became known as The Family, with Tanner and Stargell sharing the surrogate father role.

"I wish I could explain to everybody what a real close family all of us on this ballclub are," said Stargell after the Pirates clinched the division. "We love each other. I'm just so happy, not only for myself, but for all of the guys."

After the Pirates won the World Series, Stargell said,"Chuck was at the heart of our team's craziness. All of us respected and loved Chuck dearly."

Stargell and Tanner thought along the same lines, and shared a personal warmth that was welcomed by most everyone in the clubhouse. Tanner got along beautifully with Dave Parker, deemed difficult by others. Parker responded by being particularly kind and thoughtful to Tanner's wife and family.

"I'll always be a Pirate," said Tanner when he received the "Pride of the Pirates Award" from the ballclub in 1995. "I played for the Braves, Cubs, Indians and Angels, but this is my home — my backyard. Once a Pirate, always a Pirate.

"It all comes down to one thing: a lot of pride. I'm proud of the fact that we were able to accomplish the top of the mountain while I was here and do the job for the fans. I hope it goes that way again."

His Pollyanna ways were turned against him in his last years with the Pirates, in 1984 and 1985, when he painted a positive picture of the Pirates even though some of their star players were messing with drugs and playing below their abilities. Tanner insisted he didn't know of any such criminal activity in the clubhouse. Tanner continued to look at the world through rose-colored glasses, and he was mocked for it, and blamed for letting the ballteam get away from him.

Some of the sportswriters who criticized Tanner were surprised that Tanner kept talking to them in a kindly manner, and never — even years later — held a grudge against them.

It simply wasn't Tanner's style.

"Pirates fans suffered through a series of disappointments in the 1980s," wrote Smizik, the city's most outspoken sportswriter. "From Chuck Tanner they expected good managing, strict discipline and continued winning.

"Tanner remained a competent manager, but discipline within the team dissolved. Tanner treated his men like men, and they acted like unruly boys. Players he trusted betrayed him."

One of those who really let him down was Dave Parker, though Tanner never publicly expressed that disappointment.

Tanner managed the Bucs for eight seasons — from 1977 till 1985. He succeeded Danny Murtaugh and gave way to Jim Leyland. Smizik had been one of his toughest critics.

When Smizik wrote a history of the Pirates, however, Tanner came to the first signing session at a Downtown department store to help the promotion. "I always liked Bob, even though we had differences at the end," said Tanner, when I asked him to join other former Pirates for the promotion. "I'm happy to be there for him." Smizik always liked Tanner, too, but was flabbergasted that Tanner took the time to travel to town from New Castle on his behalf, considering his critical reviews of Tanner in his latter days with the Pirates.

That largesse was typical Tanner. His enthusiasm and receptiveness to players, media and fans made him one of the game's most popular managers.

"Bob Prince was my best friend."
— Chuck Tanner

Tanner was a visitor to the press box at Three Rivers Stadium before a game with the Astros in July of 1997, and I had a chance to talk with him.

"I could work in baseball another 50 years and I couldn't pay back what I've gotten out of it," he said.

Tanner didn't turn many heads during his playing days in the major leagues. He was mostly a reserve outfielder from 1955 to 1962. When he did do something noteworthy, Prince would pick it off the wire and pass it along to "all those wonderful baseball fans up in New Castle."

Tanner made his mark as a manager, but he had to pay his dues to get back to the big leagues.

"I spent eight years managing in the minors, away from my family, but I still felt like I had it made," said Tanner.

"When I was in ninth grade, we had one pipe and running water installed in our house. When I graduated from high school, I still had to use the outhouse in our backyard.

"We didn't get electricity in our house until I was in 10th grade. We had little lamps you lit at night before we got electricity. We got all our heat from a pot-bellied stove.

"I went to school at Shenango, just on the edge of New Castle. I went to Shenango High School, which competed in sports on a Class B level. I went to work pretty early. I helped my grandfather get the hay. He made his own wagon. We'd load that wagon and then we pitched it up into the loft. It was real work, believe me. We didn't get our muscles by lifting weights, the way they do today.

"I liked the people in New Castle, that's why I never moved. They never got too big for their boots. You can't change from the way you were brought up. That was ingrained in me by my parents. This is where I want to live.

"My father was like his father. He only knew one way to work, and that was with everything he had. He didn't express it, as far as preaching about a good work ethic. He just did it. He worked hard. We saw what he was doing. It wasn't hard work, but we worked hard. We did whatever it took to get the job done.

"My mother and father didn't have many rules for my two brothers and me. We just had to do what was right when we were kids, that's all."

Sometimes Tanner thought his players would do the same, but some betrayed him for believing they were adults.

During his schooldays in Shenango, Tanner also gained an appreciation for Bob Prince and Rosey Rowswell.

"I can say this," said Tanner. "Bob Prince was everybody's friend. He was one of my best friends. He made everybody feel that way, that you were special.

"That's the best way. What do you do for a best friend? Bob Prince was my best friend. He had a flair about him. Those loud jackets. He did so much out of the kindness of his heart. You'd ask him, 'Are you going to play in my golf tournament.' He'd say, 'Yeah, I'll play. You're my friend.' He was a magic man. No matter what charity he was connected with, he got everybody to come together.

"Listening to him on the radio was a treat. I still have memories of that. I was playing pro ball in 1948 when he broke in with the Pirates as an apprentice to Rosey Rowswell. Our season would end earlier than the major league schedule. I'd come home. What did I do? I listened to the Pirates ballgames on the radio.

"The first year I listened to him, I thought he was different. You listened to him and he drew you to him. He was a legend in the game of baseball.

"They had a night here for me when I was playing for the Cubs. All my friends and fans came down from New Castle. He emceed it. They didn't usually do that. My mom and dad were here, my two kids, Mark and Gary, and my wife, Babs. Bob introduced my whole family. He took the time. He didn't have to come out on the field.

"I always thought you should treat everybody the way you wanted people to treat your mother. That's the way Bob Prince treated everybody."

Somehow another of Tanner's all-time good guys got into the conversation. That was Art Rooney Sr.

"He was like Prince in the way he got along with people, and the way he made a fuss over you," said Tanner. "He made you want to be like him. That was something. So matter of fact about what he did. No big deal. Art Rooney was so great.

"One time he came into my office and I was down in the mouth, and he said, 'Chuck, you're the best manager I've ever seen in this ballpark.' His brother, the priest (Father Silas Rooney), would come in with him from time to time. He was a terrific person, too."

While Tanner got along with most media types, he didn't always enjoy the kid gloves' treatment afforded Art Rooney.

"They (the media) didn't know what I was all about," said Tanner, thoughtfully, and choosing his words more carefully as he continued.

"They wrote that 'Chuck's always positive . . . even when he shouldn't be.' Yes, I was always positive and I protected my players. I always said something good about them. I didn't rip a guy publicly. When I fined a guy it never got in the paper. They (the media) didn't like the idea that everything was OK. I told guys in our clubhouse I didn't want things we talked about getting out. 'This is our personal business here,' I said. 'We're a family.' And a lot of people didn't like that.

"Every kid on my team had a mother and a father, and I didn't want them thinking anything bad about their boys.

"If I had to get a point across to a player, I was confident I could do it. I respected them and I expected them to respect me. Some of these guys might have wondered what they could get away with. Some of them were warned by the veterans. 'Don't go into a room with him by yourself because he's going to come out and you're not,' they said.

"I wasn't looking to fight anyone, though. That's not the way to manage a ballteam, or to lead any kind of group."

"I met a garbageman who serviced Bob Prince's place and he said Bob was always leaving him big tips."
— Mary Hughes
Upper St. Clair, Pa.

"Some people have a 30-hour day everyday."
— Chuck Tanner

Tanner was asked whether it's realistic to be as optimistic as he always appeared to be, like he didn't have a problem in the world. That's not the real world.

"When you wake up, everybody has a problem," responded Tanner. "The way to do it is to assess the situation. How you handle that problem is the critical thing. I want to make every day the best day of my life. There's always something good out there. I wish more writers would take that approach.

"There are some people out there, negative-thinking people, who make me realize my way is the right way to live. They'll say things like, 'It's too hot today.' Just negative thoughts. When you're in school, when you're around somebody who's always negative, you've got to get away from them. They'll make you miserable. They'll drag you down.

"The approach you have to life can determine the outcome of a lot of things. If I ran a business, the people I'd go to first would be the sales people. They make work for everyone else. They keep working, keep producing.

"I believe the key to managing a baseball team is recognizing who your key people are. I let people like Stargell, Parker, Tekulve and Madlock have more freedom. I let them know they were stars. The rest of the guys took their cues from them.

"That's the way I did it. Others might do it differently. It doesn't matter what they say or what people think. If they ask me, 'How did you do?' I can say, 'We went to the top of the mountain.' It worked."

With that remark, Tanner turned his hand over and proudly displayed the ring he and the Pirates picked up for winning the World Series in 1979.

"I learned a long time ago that the size of your funeral is going to depend on the weather, so don't get too cocky," said Tanner, not to appear to be boasting about his success. "My way works for me. And I'm happy.

"Bob Prince had his own approach. He'd always kid around. When I was managing in Chicago or in Oakland, I'd see him in the winter. He'd be with Al Abrams. He'd say, 'Chuck, you're going to manage as long as you want to. You can communicate with people.' He made me feel better.

"I know one thing. There were about three or four teams that had better players than us the year we won it all, but we had the best team.

"Cincinnati had about six guys who could go to the Hall of Fame. We swept them. Baltimore had the best players. They scouted us for a month. Lenny Yochim scouted them in the playoffs. When Lenny was going to give our team his scouting report on the Orioles, I told him, 'When you talk to them, don't make it too long.' We made it simple.

"I always give credit to my coaches that year. They had a lot to do with our success. I had Harvey Haddix, Bob Skinner, Joe Lonnett and Al Monchak. We had a team. We made some trades. Getting Bill Madlock, getting Tim Foli, getting Phil Garner. It all came together. The team that was assembled was a good team. It wasn't exceptional. But the team never got credit for what it accomplished. There were at least three teams better than us, but we won it all.

"My perception always was to keep what we had to say behind closed doors in the clubhouse right there in the clubhouse. What transpired in the old days stayed in the clubhouse. The writers were like part of the team. They just covered the game. And they left the other stuff alone.

"The world is completely different today; everything is high-tech. The rules are different. Or there are no rules. Everything's a big story."

Tanner talked about a number of subjects and would bounce back and forth between topics, like he was playing rounders, or pepper ball.

"Frankie Gustine . . . he was just the nicest guy in the world. I felt privileged any time I was around him. He's a Mr. Rooney type. You're lucky when you have people like that on your side. The way he did it was not a bad way to live. In the end, it doesn't matter who you were, but it matters how you treated other people.

"I saw him for the first time in 1943 or 1944, and I was so excited. When the Pirates went to spring training in those days, my grandfather always bought *The Sun-Telegraph*. Frank Gustine was my favorite Pirate and I read everything about him. Writers liked Gustine and wrote a lot about him.

"Ralph Kiner used to say he could hit two home runs and a double in a game, but Gustine would get the headline if he went 1-for-4 with a single. He was special to me, that's for sure. He was a big league player, and he was the first player I ever saw. He started out hitting .450 or something every season, and as the summer wore on he tailed off to .270.

"I'd lie on the floor in my grandmother's house, and read the paper. I just loved Frankie Gustine. I liked Carl Hubbell and Mel Ott; they were left-handed like me. I liked Johnny Rizzo, Ralph Kiner, Al Lopez, Vince DiMaggio.

"I loved it all. Later on, when Prince came on the scene, he gave all the Pirates nicknames. If he gave them a nickname it was their nickname the rest of their careers. Whatever Prince said was the greatest.

"I love it. I love the game. I was on the bench with Phil Garner a few weeks back. I'm really into the game. The guys were kidding me about my intensity. People don't know how I manage to keep enthused about baseball."

Jim Leyland had left the Pirates at the end of the 1996 season to manage the Miami Marlins. His team was doing well in the standings, and would go on to win the World Series.

"Jim's a good guy," said Tanner. "I'm happy for him. I'm happy for Gene Lamont. I'm happy for the Pirates. They just keep rolling down the highway. I'm happy for Phil Garner; he's a great manager.

"Garner was great for our team when he was here. We had guys who became better ballplayers because of our attitude. Little things make big things happen. I have 1,352 victories as a manager. They can't take that away from me. My teams won seven games in the playoffs and World Series. Not many guys can say that. It doesn't matter what anyone says to the contrary.

"If you feel good about yourself, that's what matters.

"Some people have a 30-hour day every day. Remember Johnny Sain? What a great pitching coach he was. I remember Sain saying, 'Always keep your friends close to you. So you know what you're doing.' I like to spend time with my friends. But I'm also happy when I'm by myself. I'm in a zone. Maybe it's from being out in the public all my life. I've been living on the road by myself since 1959. I've been married for 38 years. My wife, Barbara, made it possible. I never had to make a meal for the kids. I went away for six years as a manager in the minors. We didn't have any money. She told me, 'I'll take care of the kids. You want to be a manager, go ahead.'

"I've been in baseball for 47 years. She made it possible. I never had a problem. I went to the ballpark. I never did anything but go to the ballpark. Stan Musial told me when I was a rookie, 'You know, Chuck, I grew up not far from where you grew up.' That meant a lot to me. We were both proud of our western Pennsylvania roots."

Sally O'Leary and Nellie King had both spoken over the telephone to Chuck Tanner during spring training, 1998. Tanner was in Sarasota, Florida. "He didn't sound his usual chipper self," said O'Leary. That was understandable. His wife, Barbara, had heart problems. She had undergone surgery twice, to insert a pacemaker, and then for bypass surgery. She had suffered a stroke after that and broke her wrist. Tanner had been scheduled to be the main speaker at an all-sports banquet at Robert Morris College in late March, but begged off after getting his good friend Dick Groat to pinch-hit for him.

> *Prince played favorites...*
> *During a game, Bob Prince rarely if ever said "Pittsburgh" or "Pirates" — it was always "we," "us" or "our." "We'll be home all next week" meant the Pirates were playing a home stand. "The Pirates belong to the tri-state area (Western Pennsylvania, West Virginia and Ohio)," Prince said, "and I belong to the Pirates. We play favorites here."*

Where have you gone, Mrs. Robison?
Reminiscences of The Gunner

"It was really a memorable day."

Baseball and life were more simple back in the '50s. The best evidence of that is a tale told by Rich Pollak of Oakdale about a special day with Bob Prince and Ralph Kiner in June of 1951.

It's about the time that Prince and Kiner came to the North Braddock home of his mother-in-law, Mrs. Elizabeth Robison, to personally cook a steak dinner for her family.

"Bob Prince is on the radio and he's raising money for the Roselia Foundling Home, and, out of the blue, he says that anybody who calls in and makes a pledge in the next hour will be eligible for a special drawing," recalled Pollak.

"Prince says, 'Me and Ralph Kiner will come and cook a steak dinner at your home. Of course, Kiner doesn't know anything about this, but he'll go along with it, I'm sure.'"

At the time, Kiner was on his way to winning the National League home run title for the fifth time in seven consecutive seasons, still a league record.

"He found out I was a meat cutter, and he told me that I should bring some big steaks," continued Pollak, "and that he'd pay me for them. It would be easier that way. Kiner and his wife, Nancy Chafee, the tennis star, and Bob Prince all came to my mother-in-law's house.

"They all pitched in in the kitchen. Nancy went up to my mother-in-law's bedroom to freshen up. Kids came to our front porch from all over the neighborhood, and Kiner signed autographs for all of them. He was so down to earth.

"Then they took us Downtown to the Copa Club for an evening of drinks. They both had to go somewhere else at ten o'clock and they told us we could stay as long as we wanted and that he'd sign for everything in advance. We stayed till about midnight, and Prince picked up the entire tab. It was really a memorable day."

* * *

Letter from a Carnegie Mellon football player:

"I was a senior offensive lineman on the football team at Carnegie Mellon University in 1979. Our coach, Chuck Klausing, called a meeting one day during our two-a-day practice drills before school started. He introduced us to Bob Prince, who was going to be our play-by-play announcer on WIXY Radio in McKeesport. Two years earlier, Nellie King had been our play-by-play announcer for two seasons.

House calls. . .

Bob Prince and Ralph Kiner, at left, pay a visit to North Braddock home in June of 1951 to cook a steak dinner for Elizabeth Robison (holding baby Colleen Pollak), Leonard Robison and George Eber of the Variety Club.

"Prince regaled our whole team with stories for a half hour. He told us a story about when he was doing Penn State football and Rosey Grier was on the team. He said the team was traveling on a train through the midwest when it made a stop. Grier was roused from his sleep, and he said, 'Where are we now?' Someone said they were in Indianapolis. And Grier said, 'Why don't we get off and play Navy while we're here.' He had us going.

"I went up to him after he was done and introduced myself to him. I called him Mr. Prince. He said, 'Mr. Prince is my dad. You call me Bob.' I mentioned to him that I had heard him doing the Pirates' games on the radio and that he often passed along greetings to fans for one reason or another, a birthday, anniversary or hospital stay. I asked him if he could say something to my grandparents, Mr. and Mrs. Albert Sparks of 84, Pa. They would tape the games for me and I would listen to them the following week. Prince told me not to worry, he'd take care of it.

"In the first game, we ran a play across my side of the line. Prince said, 'That hole was opened by No. 64, Mark Price of Carmichaels. I'll bet his grandparents, Mr. and Mrs. Albert Sparks of 84, Pa. are real proud of him.' When I got the tape of the game the next week, I could hear my grandmother talking over Prince's voice. She said, 'Albert, did you hear that? That man just said hello to us on the radio.'

"I went to Washington, Pa. the next year to see CMU play W&J there. One of my teammates was injured and was watching the game from the press box. He was serving as a spotter for Prince. I went in to say hello to him. I saw Prince. 'Hello, Mr. Prince,' I said. And he said, 'I told you last year not to call me Mr. Prince. Howya doing, Mark?'

I said, 'You remember me?' He said, 'Of course. How are your grandparents doing?' Of the tens of thousands of people he met, I couldn't get over him remembering me like that.

"Another Bob Prince story that comes to mind: CMU was playing in a semifinal playoff round at Ithaca, N.Y. We lost, 15-6. What I remember is that the game was played in the densest fog. Prince couldn't see what was going on.

"Prince was sitting next to Gerry Mancini, the offensive coordinator at CMU. You couldn't see the field from the press box, and we're talking about a high school-sized stadium. Mancini was on the phone with Coach Klausing on the sideline. Klausing would tell Mancini what the down-and-yardage situation was, and what had just happened. Mancini would relay the information to Prince, and then Prince told the listeners what happened.

"He was one play behind the actual game. He was recreating the game the way he once did baseball games from the Western Union ticker-tape, recreating the action. And Prince got real creative.

"In the game before that, in the first round of the playoffs, we're playing the University of Minnesota at Morris, and we beat them in double overtime. Prince came into our locker room after the game, and shook everybody's hand. He said, 'It was the most exciting game I have ever broadcast, and I'm including the 1960 World Series.'"

— Mark Rice, engineer with Duquesne Light Co., Beaver, Pa.

* * *

"My father had a riding academy at Roslyn Farms for 27 years. The parkway took out our house and four barns. Bob Prince came up there one day, as he often did, to ride the horses. It was cold and he borrowed an old flannel coat that belonged to my father. It was dirty and it stunk. We didn't want Prince wearing it. He said, 'If it's good enough for your dad, then it's good enough for me.'

"My dad had a polo team up there. Prince apparently fancied himself quite the polo player. So he got into a scrimmage with my dad's team. He caught a polo mallet right in the mouth. This woman picked splinters out of his mouth. He got hit in the upper lip and I think he ended up with scar tissue. I'm told that's why his mouth was crooked.

"I was 11 or 12 at the time, back in the late '30s. My brother, Michael, was six years older so I called him in Columbus before I called you to verify my recollections. He and my other brother, John, were there that day, just fooling around.

"We had pictures of Prince from that day, but we lost them all in a fire that destroyed our house in 1974. Everything went."

— Bill Laurick, Hickory, Pa.

* * *

"I was living in Sheraden and I was the batboy for my dad's team in the East Suburban League. I was 12 years old and it was 48 years ago. Our team was winning and it started to rain. My dad wanted to get in the 4½ innings needed to make the game count so he instructed his batters to strike out to hurry the game. One of our players, who hadn't had a hit earlier, hit the ball and I wasn't expecting that and the ball struck me in the eye. I lost my eye as a result. I was in the hospital listening to the Pirates' game on the radio when I heard Bob Prince give his regards 'to little Jimmy Clark who is recovering from surgery at West Penn Hospital.' I'll never forget that."

— Jim Clark, Carnegie

"Pittsburgh is a conservative town. You don't overwhelm this place. A lot of people thought I was an S.O.B. — and I was."
— Bob Prince

117

"I was at Presbyterian University one day (June 10, 1985) visiting my wife, Helen, who was being treated for cancer. I had just come from the Veterans Hospital where my son Danny was undergoing treatment. Dr. Bernard Fisher, the famous cancer doctor, was overseeing Helen's treatment, as part of a test group. Someone mentioned that Bob Prince had just died in the hospital. A pallor went over the whole place. It was eerie. Everyone there was so sad."

— Bill Priatko,
North Huntingdon, Pa.

* * *

"I was supposed to sing at the memorial service for Bob Prince at Westminster Presbyterian Church. I was determined to do it even though I was in the late stages of pregnancy. I was really pregnant. I wanted to do it for Bob's wife, Betty, whom I adored, and I wanted to do it because so many people from the Pirates would be there. One of my dreams was to sing the National Anthem at a Pirates' game. So I was thinking 'it ain't over till the fat lady sings.' But David had other ideas. He came early and I was in the hospital instead of our church. Evonne Wunderlich sang instead. I always know how long it's been since Bob Prince died — it was 13 years ago — because of David's birthday. I was once a student in Bob's Sunday School class. It was well attended because he told the best stories. He sent everyone in the class a postcard from Florida. We treasured them."

— Mary Hughes, Upper St. Clair

* * *

"Growing up in Pittsburgh in the '40s and '50s meant that you loved the Pittsburgh Pirates, good or bad and, unfortunately during this period, they were mostly bad. But Bob Prince kept them interesting and kept their fans loyal. Everyone in my family was a fan, including my older brother, mother and my aunt who lived with us. It was very common for us to sit on our front porch on Norma Street in Crafton and listen to Bob Prince broadcast the ballgames.

"One special night stands out in my memory. It was in (May 26) 1959 and the Pirates were in Milwaukee to play the Braves. It turned out to be one of the most extraordinary games in baseball history. It was the night Harvey Haddix pitched a perfect game for 12 innings, and then lost, 1-0, in the 13th inning. It may have been the greatest pitching performance ever. My brother, mother, aunt and I sat on our porch drinking iced tea and listening to Bob Prince describe every pitch. It was a wonderful time to be with this wonderful family. These are the kind of great memories I have of growing up in Pittsburgh with the Pirates of old and Bob Prince."

— Ron Temple,
Upper St. Clair, Pa.

118

Bob Prince is flanked by Ted Williams, an All-Star representing Boston Red Sox, and Pirates manager Billy Meyer.

Bob Prince signs baseballs and game programs for young fans at Forbes Field. Otto Milk is one of sponsors on back of program.

Jack Bogut
Bogie, My Boy

"Prince was always coloring
outside the lines."

A steaming cup of black coffee and Jack Bogut for breakfast was still a good way to start the day. Bogut had been doing an afternoon gig from 3 to 7 p.m. on WJAS Radio for six months when we met to talk about Bob Prince.

Bogut was now with a station that appealed to the 40-and-over pack, played "the music of your life," and he felt comfortable with the older crowd it attracted. After all, he would be celebrating his 62nd birthday the following week and was now one of them.

The lineup at WJAS included Jack Wheeler, "Chilly Billy" Cardille and Bogut, all crusty broadcasting figures on the Pittsburgh scene. They enjoyed calling Cardille an "ace between two Jacks." Wheeler would say that Bogut was now "with the rest of us old geezers."

They had all stood the test of time and remained popular with the senior crowd and some of their kids, and magnets in the market-place.

"Allegheny County has the oldest population of any county in the country," said Bogut. "We have surpassed Dade County, Florida, in that respect. So there are plenty of people who like the music we play and the stories we share."

Bogut had been off the local airwaves for 2½ years before WJAS offered him a comeback opportunity. He had been missed by the loyal fans he had acquired during a 15-year stint at KDKA Radio (1968-1983), a five year tenure (1983-88) at WTAE and five more years (1989-94) at WSHH.

This was early February, 1998, and Bogut and I were talking across a table at Elby's Restaurant in Mt. Lebanon, less than a mile from the condominium townhouse he shared with his wife, Joni, in an upscale complex called Woodridge. Betty Prince, the wife of Bob Prince, and some players from the Penguins lived in the same community. Bogut bumped into Betty from time to time, and admired her dearly.

"Betty has to be eligible for sainthood," observed Bogut. "Prince was out in the community, and he supported a lot of great causes. Prince would support anything you asked him to. He helped somehow. He was on the road a lot with the Pirates and the demands of broadcasting baseball. Plus, he emceed every sports banquet from here to Altoona and Timbuktu. He must have never been home."

Bogut had worked with Prince at KDKA for several years and recalled him with great glee, saying Prince was always a gentleman

**Jack Bogut bats and pitches
at Pirates promotion
at Three Rivers Stadium.**

**Pirates announcing team in 1970 featured this threesome: Nellie King, Bob
Prince and Gene Osborne.**

around his wife, Joni, and their children. "Prince had problems with management, which I understood," said Bogut, dismissing a report by a colleague that he and Prince had, at times, been at odds. "That's simply not so," said Bogut. "I never had a cross word or any disagreement with Bob. I enjoyed him from start to finish."

Bogut had come out of Montana, of all places, to ultimately replace Rege Cordic as the No. 1 morning man on the No. 1 station in the tri-state area. He had never met anyone in Montana to match Prince.

"Bob was an event looking for a place to happen," said Bogut as only he can. Bogut and Bob Prince were as big as they came in local broadcasting circles. If there were a Hall of Fame for same, they'd both be shoo-ins.

When he cut out on KDKA in favor of the biggest bucks ever paid a deejay in Pittsburgh, possibly as high as $400,000 a year, Bogut learned that KDKA's 50,000 watt station had contributed mightily to his popularity and ratings. Bogut went back to those KDKA days when he and Prince, Art Pallan, Bob Trow and Ed Schaughency ruled the airwaves.

"I was doing my drive time morning show on KDKA Radio, and Bob was supposed to call in each day at 20 after 7 with a report on the Pirates," began Bogut. "We took great pride in being the originating station on the Pirates' radio network, and we liked to brag about it. Having Bob Prince give a first-hand report at prime drive time the morning after the game was a real plus.

"Bob didn't always call when he was scheduled to, but overall he was pretty dependable. One day, he didn't call at the appointed time. But he calls me later on the hotline, and tells me he wants to come on the air to tell everyone why he wasn't on the show earlier when he was supposed to call.

"I didn't know what the hell he had in mind, but I was always game when it came to Bob Prince. So he comes on the air, and he starts off...

" 'Bogie, my boy, I'm calling you from New York, and I'm sorry I didn't get to you sooner. Let me tell you and our listeners why I'm late with this report. Westinghouse put me up in a cheap hotel here, which won't come as any surprise to you. You know how they like to save a buck. It's a real flea-bitten joint.

" 'I don't have a telephone in my room. So I went out in the hallway awhile ago to call you when I was supposed to. I was in my undershorts so, of course, I didn't have a wallet with me. No sooner did I get outside my door in the hallway when the only breeze that has blown through this hellhole all day comes along and blows my door shut.

" 'I don't have my room key, of course. So I'm stuck in the hallway in my undershorts. I knocked on one of the doors and a woman answered and soon as she saw me in my undershorts she slammed her door and — thank God — called the manager.

"'So the manager came up and wanted to know what I was doing in the hallway in my undershorts. I explained my predicament, and he let me back in my room. So I put on some slacks and got a dime from my pants pockets so I could call you collect. So now I'm talking to you on the phone with my report on the Pirates. Bogie, my boy, you ready to go now?'"

Bogut's story provides some insight into why Prince often pushed the envelope with his superiors at KDKA and the parent Westinghouse Inc. folks. He was irreverent and he would say anything, which appealed to many of the people who tuned in, especially those who would have loved to tell off their bosses as Prince often did. "Prince said things people loved to hear," added Bogut.

Another time, Prince called Bogut when he wasn't expecting it. "Gunner, where are you?" Bogut asked him.

"I'm in the bathtub," replied Prince, who then dunked the telephone in the tub to make his point.

"You never knew what he was going to do."

Bogut was always big on schmaltz. He said things on his radio show such as, "Outside of my wife and family, I can't think of anyone I'd rather spend time with than you." He was the opposite of Prince. He didn't rattle any cages.

And Pittsburghers bought into Bogut's easy-does-it manner and his homespun stories in a big way. Like Prince, he was a master storyteller. He continued to do commercials and be a spokesman for several companies around town, even when he didn't have his own radio show.

"Prince could tell one story after another, and you never knew what he was going to say," recalled Bogut. "He was the originator of the premise that it was better to ask for forgiveness than for remission. He constantly ran outside the fence; he was constantly testing the system. He was always coloring outside the lines.

"People outside the mold like him set the pace. He was the consummate broadcaster. You never knew what he was going to do. Bob had to be influenced by Rosey Rowswell with the stuff he did like 'Open the window, Aunt Minnie, here she comes!' Rowswell had some gimmicks, and Prince became a part of them. Rosey was fairly well disciplined. Prince was not.

"Prince connected with Pirates' fans on an emotional level. He could touch the lowest possible denominator without offending the highest. He'd give you the green weenie. C'mon, the green weenie!

"We all like the pie in the face routine, as long as it's not our face. Prince tossed a lot of pies in his time.

"He'd come away from a meeting with management where they told him to stick to the baseball, and quit wandering off into storyland. He'd tell them, 'I'm going to try and be good about this, and do what you said.' The next ballgame he'd be telling a story.

"He gave it to management every chance he got, right on the air! Like everyone would love to. He did this wherever there were people making rules. We were active at the St. Clair Country Club for years, and Prince was the best known member of the club. He'd wear the required jacket or sport coat, but he'd wear his Gucci loafers without socks. He was always scolding me, telling me I didn't have to wear socks in the clubhouse. He'd have a skimpy little bathing suit, a sheer bathing suit, and he'd have a pullover polo shirt.

"Everytime he came over to where we were sitting, or whatever, I felt like a loaded cannon was coming over. You never knew what he was going to say. When Joni or the kids were with me, he'd never say anything off color. Otherwise, it was open season on everyone, including me. It was like a short fuse, and you never knew how fast things would blow up. The guy had enormous presence. When Prince walked into a room, you didn't have to turn around to know it was him. You knew somebody was there. Heads turned.

"He was mercurial. He'd be in the middle of a conversation with your table or group, then he'd wrap up the story and he'd be gone. He was off to another table. When someone is gone, we tend to look back selectively. Tommy Edwards has a song, 'It's Only The Good Times We Remember.' It's the flip-side of 'The Morning Side of the Mountain.' Bob Prince was not a treat all the time. There were times he created serious problems for everyone.

"Prince told me one time when I had him on my show sometime after he'd been let go, 'I deserved it. They should have fired me a few years ago. They told me they weren't happy with how I was doing the broadcasts.'"

Bogut identified the people Prince had spoken to when he learned of his dismissal. They were Joe L. Brown, the general manager of the Pirates; Bill Hartman, the general manager of KDKA Radio, and Ed Wallis, a vice-president with Westinghouse.

"They said, 'Bob, we're thinking of letting you go. You insist on talking about everything but baseball. We've told you about this before.' And Bob said, 'Baseball is everything to me. Don't do this to me. I promise you I'll be better next year.' They gave him another chance, and he did it again. They called him in and they went through the same thing all over again. They fired him. He said, 'I realize I lied to you twice. I'll write a letter of resignation and say what you've told me as my reason for dismissal, and I'll sign it, and you can invoke it any time you want to. You can release it.' Bill Hartman said 'No. You'll have us by the plums.' And Nellie King got caught in the crossfire. He lost his job at the same time. Prince always insisted on doing it his way, and this time it cost him dearly."

Lanny Frattare
Pays Prince proper respect

"He reached out to help me.
He liked to give."

A gas log fire was burning brightly in a huge red brick fireplace, and a mug of black fresh-brewed coffee was within reach on an end table. I hope heaven is like that. The family room in the spacious three-year-old home of Liz and Lanny Frattare offered a comfortable setting for a conversation on a challenging winter's day.

Lanny was looking back on his 22 years as a broadcaster of Pirates' games, looking ahead to joining the ball team in Bradenton, Florida in a few weeks for spring training for the 1998 season, and he liked the view from where he sat in a thick-cushioned rust-colored chair in the center of the room.

Talking about baseball and Bob Prince helped warm an otherwise cold early February day when an overnight snow covered the ground outside the Frattares' two-story colonial home in Tall Trees. This is one of the newer neighborhoods in Upper St. Clair, a suburban community nine miles south of Pittsburgh and Three Rivers Stadium. Sunlight reflected off the snow and lit the room naturally.

This meeting was a modern day version of the old hot stove league, when ball fans might gather in a country store to talk baseball and while away a gray winter's day. All we needed were blankets across our laps to settle in for the afternoon.

Frattare looked successful and relatively at peace with himself and his situation — a good facade for a sensitive sort who frets about so many aspects of his public position and is a constant worrier — and he was good company who provided some stories and insights of an admired figure in his life. One could also learn a lot about Lanny Frattare, a learned fellow who does his best to keep everyone happy. He was wearing blue jeans, a yellow shirt, a casual look except for his furrowed brow.

Frattare had turned 50 — hard to believe — but retained his boyish good looks, the sparkle in his eyes and a friendly smile. By all appearances, in an inviting setting right out of *Better Homes & Gardens* magazine, he looked like a man who had it made.

I'd scheduled this visit a week or so earlier and told Lanny what I was looking for, personal reflections on his own experiences with Bob Prince and how his predecessor as "The Voice of The Pirates" had impacted his life and career. True to form, Frattare had taken notes on important moments with Prince, and lessons learned from "The Gunner" that got him off to a good start as a Pirates' broadcaster and still served him in good stead. Frattare was ready for this interview.

Frattare prides himself on his preparation, on doing his homework. He steels himself for every Pirates' broadcast by reviewing his scorecards, statistics, game day notes, and all sorts of stuff he culls and retains from voluminous reading and research. He showed me file cabinets in a storage room in his basement that contain the scorecards from every game — over 3,200 by last count — he has broadcasted about the Bucs. "It's a great reference file," said Frattare. He has all those scorecards filed by opposing team.

Frattare's critics complain that he offers too much information during his broadcasts, numbers and trivia not of interest to the average fan, but suffice to say that Prince had his share of critics as well. Many thought Prince didn't stick to the facts enough, and too often wandered away from the game into story-telling. Such criticism goes with the territory.

Frattare also collects quotes in a booklet he carries with him. His nicely-appointed home office has one wall unit full of history books, mostly about American presidents, especially John F. Kennedy, his favorite, while the other is stocked with baseball books. He cherishes several framed prints of different views of The White House. And family photos and montages complete the walldressing. His gameroom wall is graced by many plaques and awards he has received through the years.

One of the most cherished is a plaque showing the Pittsburgh skyline at night. It's the Bob Prince Memorial Award honoring his broadcasting career and community service, which he was presented at the 1996 Sports Night at the Thompson Club in West Mifflin. Prince served as the emcee at that storied dinner for over 20 years.

One of the quotes in Frattare's journal comes from Luke 12:48 in the King James version of the Bible, and was invoked in a talk by JFK: "For unto whomsoever much is given, of him shall be much required: and to him whom men have committed much, of him they will ask more." It suits Frattare fine. "I sincerely believe that we all have to give back," he said.

There's lots of good stuff to be found in Frattare's home. His voluminous files, reference books and pride in being prepared to go to work all point up how different Frattare is from Prince, a mentor of sorts when Frattare first came to Pittsburgh. Prince was the greatest of extemporaneous or off-the-cuff orators and raconteurs.

Prince would have winged it all the way, as he always did, relying on his inborn story-telling ability, his gift for gab, his sense of self and a compelling presence to spellbind and entertain a listener and capture a room, no matter its dimensions. Prince was confident he could hold your interest.

My meeting with Frattare was a one-on-one interview, with no one else present for the most part, which is the way Frattare and I prefer to conduct such exchanges. Prince preferred an audience, an entourage that was as reliable as canned laughter to provide the proper responses to his often outrageous and ribald remarks in such an away-from-the-ballpark and broadcast booth setting.

Pirates broadcasting team for 1998 included, left to right, Lanny Frattare, Bob Walk, Steve Blass and Greg Brown.

A youthful Lanny Frattare pauses during Pirates broadcast in his early years in broadcasting booth at Three Rivers Stadium.

Lanny's lovely wife, Liz, a perky brunette, had greeted me, moved an end table up close to a well-cushioned chair where I was sitting so I'd have a place to set my coffee. Then she left to take the family's two black labradors, Fitzgerald and Calvin (named after American presidents), for a walk on the winding snow-covered streets. Guido, the black and white cat, remained in the room and roamed freely, crossing and slithering through Lanny's lap as well as mine from time to time.

There was a large studio portrait of the Frattares' two children, 23-year-old David and 16-year-old Megan, over the mantel, and an abundance of books and family photographs that made it evident the Frattares really lived there. David was at work — he was a criminal investigator for the state attorney general working out of an office in Greensburg — and Megan was at school. She was a sophomore at nearby Upper St. Clair High School. David had a bachelor's degree in sociology, with a criminology emphasis, from John Carroll University in Cleveland. He was planning to get married in November.

There's a framed photo in Lanny's home office that shows an overhead view of the crowd at President Clinton's inauguration and it has an arrow on it pointing to where Lanny and his son, David, were sitting. It was a special time they shared.

"You've got to let the Bob Prince thing rest."
— Mark Sauer, Former Pirates' president

Lanny looked studious, his blue eyes framed by eyeglasses, his close-cropped hair dark and shiny with freshly-applied grooming gel, as he consulted his notes and reflected gladly on one of his all-time favorite subjects, Pittsburgh sports icon Bob Prince.

"I vividly remember the first time I met him," allowed Lanny for openers. "It was 1974. I had just finished my first year as play-by-play announcer for the Pirates' Triple A affiliate in Charleston, West Virginia.

"Our minor league season ended in September, and I had been invited by Bill Guilfoile, the Pirates' public relations man at the time, to come up to Pittsburgh and sit in the press box and meet the media, to see how things were done in the big leagues during the team's stretch run.

"I stayed at the home of Steve and Karen Blass, whom I had gotten to know because Steve had come to Charleston that season in the hope of straightening out his pitching problems. He had gone from being a World Series hero to a guy who couldn't get the ball over the plate for a strike in any league.

"I went to the ballpark with Steve, so we got there an hour before the ballgame began. Nellie King was doing a pre-game show, interviewing a guest, and for the longest time there was no sign of Bob. As it got closer and closer to gametime, I was amazed that there was still no Bob.

"Nellie introduced the starting lineup, introduced the National Anthem, and finally said, 'And, now, here's the Voice of the Pirates, Bob Prince.' Bob came through the door of the broadcast booth as Nellie was introducing him, picked up the headset and put it on, and was off and running. Bob didn't miss a beat. I figured that Nellie knew Bob well enough that he could get started without him, and know he'd be there for the first pitch."

I mentioned to Frattare that I had heard similar stories from several sources about Prince appearing at the last second to do five-minute sports commentaries, basketball and hockey games, or other kinds of broadcasts or commercials, making many in his supporting cast nervous. ("Here's the first pitch and here's Bob!" King claimed he said on more than one occasion.) Prince never sweated the small stuff.

"I've heard that," offered Frattare. "But that was the first time I'd ever seen it with my own eyes."

"There's another example," I suggested, "of something you could never do."

"You're right," said Frattare. "I could never do that."

Prince did the Pirates' games for 28 years, succeeding Rosey Rowswell, with whom he worked as a sidekick for the first six years of his storied Pirates' career. Prince presided over the Pirates' broadcast booth for 22 years after the death of Rowswell. Altogether, his tenure lasted from 1948 to 1975. Rowswell broadcasted Pirates' baseball for 18 years. Prince is better remembered by this generation of Pirates' fans.

"I could never be Bob Prince and neither could anyone else," said Frattare. "Our styles are so dramatically different, but our philosophies are so similar in defining our role as 'The Voice of the Pirates.' We got to that goal differently, that's all.

"In many people's hearts, including my own, and taking nothing away from Rosey Rowswell, the true 'Voice of the Pirates' was and always will be Bob Prince."

I mentioned to Frattare that I had heard him speak at banquets and church assemblies and felt he may have mentioned Bob Prince before he had to, or more than he had to, perhaps to beat any oldtime Pirates' fans in the audience to the punch.

At this stage of his career, I felt Frattare didn't need to apologize for replacing Prince as the Pirates' primary announcer. It must have sounded familiar to Frattare. He wagged his handsome head, and smiled knowingly.

"Mark Sauer, when he was president of the Pirates and a dear friend of mine, said to me once, 'You've got to let the Bob Prince thing rest.' But I've always been grateful to Bob for his help and encouragement when I really needed it, and for setting such high standards for a baseball broadcaster in this city. I've never tried to imitate him, or fill his shoes. That would have been stupid, and a disaster.

"To a large extent, whatever success I've had in Pittsburgh I've had because of Bob's guidance. It was always most amazing to me that, as one of two guys who replaced him, he reached out to help me.

"I was 28 years old when I came here, a young kid in the business, but Bob treated me so well right from the start. He liked to give. Some of the sharing and caring he gave me he also gave to others among the media, young writers on the beat, other young or inexperienced broadcasters. I soaked it up, and was grateful for his guidance.

"I knew I could do baseball when I came here. Bob helped me define the job in a broader sense. Being the 'Voice of the Pirates' is a 12-months of the year position. It's not just being behind the microphone at Pirates' games. It's getting out to meet the people.

"That wasn't easy in the early days. At the time there were a lot of people that really didn't want me out there. But I got out, made a lot of appearances, and really got to know Pirate fans. It was really beneficial and it's something I really enjoy doing to this day.

"I make many appearances on behalf of the Pirates on a year-round basis. I do big banquets and small club gatherings, wherever Pirates' fans can be found. I'd rather be out working on behalf of the ballclub than sitting around the offices at Three Rivers in the off-season. I like to do things for the community, fund-raising activities, anything to help people who need help.

"If I do 60 appearances in the winter, I will get paid a fee or honorarium for maybe three of them. But, the way I see it, I get paid by the Pirates for the other 57 because it's my job. That's the way I learned to do it from Bob, and from my dad. Much of what I am as a person is from my dad.

"Once, on one of the occasions when I was honored by the Vectors Club at one of their annual awards dinners . . . They had videotaped me in advance, and I said, 'Bob Prince was like a father to me.' As soon as I heard it during the dinner, I felt embarrassed. My father was in the audience that night. I went to him right after the dinner and apologized for how the remark might have come off. I had a good father and he influenced me in all the right ways. I never needed anyone else to fill that role."

Frattare credits his father for being the man who most shaped his life. "He was the one who taught me what was the right thing to do, and not to worry about things you can't control," said Frattare. "He taught me to respect other people, and how to talk properly to people."

It was a big loss to Lanny when his father died in November of 1996.

"I have been fortunate in my lifetime to have been surrounded by individuals like my dad, like Jim Leyland and Willie Stargell, Bob Prince and Kent Tekulve," said Frattare. "I have learned from all of

Pittsburgh Pirates

Bob Prince at work in broadcast booth

"I've always had a great respect for The Gunner. When I was one of the two guys who replaced Bob and Nellie King, Bob cared enough about me to help me. He gave me valuable advice and he was always there for me in those early troubled years. Not only was he a great broadcaster but he was a caring man who gave a lot to his community. I could never be another Bob Prince. But, fortunately, a lot of things he believed in, I believe in. I will never let the memory of Bob Prince be erased from Pittsburgh Pirate baseball. Bob will always be the Voice of the Pirates."
— Lanny Frattare,
   upon receiving Bob Prince Memorial Award at Thompson Run A.A. Sports Night, April 1996.

them. There are about ten to twelve people who've had a serious impact on my life that I'll always carry with me."

"What are God's plans for us?"
— Liz Frattare

Frattare takes his role as a father and husband quite seriously. He and Liz have long been associated with many school-related programs during David's and Megan's student days. The four of them were all in the kitchen when I visited them a second time within a week.

A terrible thing had happened in Upper St. Clair only the night before my first visit to the Frattares' home, just three days earlier. A 16-year-old junior at the high school, Ellie Batz, had lost control of an automobile while driving north on Route 19, went off the road, hit an embankment and turned over her car. Emergency crews had to cut the roof of the car away to remove her body. She died soon after at Allegheny General Hospital from head injuries suffered in the accident.

It was a stretch of road where other Upper St. Clair schoolkids had been killed or injured in auto accidents through the years. Memories of those calamities remained fresh in the minds of parents who were living in the community at the time. They were every parent's worst nightmare.

The young girl had been the student director in staging the school's musical, "Brigadoon," which was in rehearsal for a March run. Megan was in the chorus for the show. Lanny and Liz usually helped out painting scenery or doing some sort of behind-the-scenes support activity for the annual musicals.

"Megan was upset last night when we heard about the accident," said Liz. "She said she had spoken to Ellie in the last mods (periods) of the day. She had a lot of questions. It's difficult for everyone to deal with. What are God's plans for us? How do you explain that to a young girl?"

"Silence is an uncomfortable thing for a lot of announcers."
— Lanny Frattare

"I try to prioritize my responsibilities as a baseball broadcaster," said Lanny Frattare. "I want to call the play-by-play in a clear, concise, accurate fashion. That's always been my No. 1 priority.

"I think I can tell stories, but I avoid getting into stories because I don't want to interfere with play-by-play. I don't like to have guests, no matter how famous, in the booth during the game. It's a distraction, and I can't focus on the game as well as I want to. I've never been big on doing an interview while the game is going on, but some producers want to do that. They think it adds to the package.

"I like to do them before or after the game, or during rain delays. Then I can concentrate on my guest, look you eye-to-eye and listen to what you have to say. I think the key to a good interview is listening."

Frattare has a formula for what works best for him.

"I begin each broadcast by saying, 'Hi, friends.' To me, after all these years, they are my friends. Prince gave me some advice when I first arrived. He said, 'Don't be continually telling people what your name is. If you're good enough, they'll get to know you. If you're bad, you don't want them to know who you are.' The way I see it, I don't have to reintroduce myself to them. They know me by now."

The 1997 season was the second one in which Frattare called the action exclusively on radio broadcasts. He and Jim Rooker were taken off the TV games during the 1996 season. He was not sure what the plans were for the coming season, but he ended up doing both.

"I prefer to do radio," said Frattare, though it was pretty obvious the year before that he was miffed by being removed from the telecasts, and wounded by some of the unkind comments publicly stated by Bill Craig, an executive for a local sports cable network, KBL, later Fox Sports. Craig was never a fan of Frattare's broadcasting style, and belittled him in a bush league manner. Craig had since been removed from the mix himself, which had to give Frattare some satisfaction, though he chose not to discuss it. To his credit, that's Frattare's style as well.

"At this point in my career," Frattare continued, "I know what makes a good broadcast. I'm not sure I know what makes a good telecast. My ideas are often in conflict with what others think in that regard.

"I realized early in my career that sometimes it's best to be quiet, when you're on the air and even more so when you're off the air. Let them hear the crowd murmur; sometimes that's enough to carry the moment. Silence is an uncomfortable thing for a lot of announcers."

Lanny looked down at the notes he'd made about Prince's impact on his career, and checked off another on his list.

"I remember my first spring training with the Pirates, back in 1976," offered Frattare. "I was walking along the beach, going by where Bob and Betty Prince were renting a condominium on Anna Maria Island in Bradenton.

"Bob wasn't the Pirates' broadcaster anymore, but he and Betty were staying there. He invited me up and we talked for quite awhile. He started telling me about getting to know Pittsburgh and making public appearances, making the job more than just being behind the mike.

"The one thing he told me was to go out and meet Pirate fans. He told me it was important that I get to know the people listening to the broadcasts and it was important for them to get to know me.

"Bob tried to pass along some of his old wild plaid sports coats to me," offered Frattare with a winning smile, "but I resisted the idea."

I had seen Frattare mixing with fans for three straight days that previous weekend when the team held its Piratefest '98 at the Carnegie Science Center. Over 21,000 fans filled the building in that span, and Frattare touched base with most of them in one manner or another. There were photos of Bob Prince and Pirates of the past on sale at one of the stands.

Frattare said Prince suggested to him in his rookie year with the Bucs that he needed to find a way to distinguish himself.

"He told me I should come up with a home run call. I thought a number of ways to call it, but I didn't want it to seem like it was planned. I wanted it to come naturally."

Eventually, Frattare came across a signature phrase that he uses after every Pirates' triumph. "And there was N-O-O-O-O doubt about it." That phrase has become synonymous with Frattare. "It was a way to pay tribute to Bob without being a direct steal," explained Frattare, "because Bob always ended victories with 'We had 'em all the way.' "

Frattare's home run call, of course, is "Go ball, get outta here!"

I mentioned to Frattare that Milo Hamilton, who replaced Prince as the primary Pirates' broadcaster, complained to me about Prince hanging around after his dismissal, and constantly sniping at Hamilton, and telling his fans he'd be back in the booth before they knew it. Hamilton felt that Prince should have moved on, and that he hurt Hamilton's chances of blending in because of how he handled it.

Hamilton's stay in Pittsburgh was short-lived and so was that of his replacement, Dave Martin. Frattare hung in there and in 1988 he was officially designated the No. 1 announcer by the ballclub.

"Because people know of our close friendship with Jim Leyland, I was asked to approach Jim a few times this past year about appearing at dinners around Pittsburgh, and Jim declined, even though he would have had a good time and been among friends. 'This is Gene Lamont's town now,' he told me. One of Jimmy's strongest philosophies is 'turn the page.' That's not always easy to do.

"I have often thought that if the day comes I get fired or decided to step down that I would hope I'm offered an opportunity to thank a lot of people, and to properly say goodbye. I always thought it was impressive that Bill Virdon showed up at the press conferences when he was fired or replaced. Bill was a strong enough person, and sure enough about himself, to be there. Yet he was not someone who sought the spotlight.

"I would hope, whenever it's time to leave the booth, that I would be remembered for my enthusiasm, love of the game, and preparation. I would hope that these are the things that would stand out to Pirates' fans."

Greg Brown and Bob Walk were added to the broadcast team in 1994 when Jim Rooker and Kent Derdivanis were replaced. Rooker was with the Pirates' broadcast team for 13 years. "I thought he was one of the best baseball analysts I'd known in the business," said Frattare. "I learned a lot of baseball from him and, hopefully, I helped him when he got started. He said some things about me when he left, but I will always cherish the relationship we had through the years. I still consider him a friend, but I don't think he sees me in that way anymore."

The Pirates were preparing as we spoke to open their training camp in Bradenton, and Frattare was looking forward to going to Florida.

"I'm always excited about going to spring training," said Frattare, "and I am again this year. I like what I'm doing. There are things behind the scenes that detract from the job, but that's true for anyone.

"We're always trying to grow. Hopefully, we're getting better at what we're doing. The plus about 1997 for me was that I was able to concentrate on doing play-by-play on the radio, to focus on that medium, and dedicate myself to KDKA Radio and the Pirates radio network. The negative was I was pulled away from my partners. Our roles were defined in an awkward way. I made up my mind early on that I was best suited for radio broadcasts, so this is no comedown, as far as I'm concerned.

"Having followed Bob Prince to the broadcasting booth, there were many years when I was evaluating whether I could do some of the things he did. I finally came to grips with the realization that I could be on the air what I was in person.

"I used to be asked why I would want to come to this city and try to replace Bob Prince. But I was never really cast in that role. I had been preparing myself for a long time to do this job, and there was no guarantee I would get another chance to be a baseball announcer. The outpouring of love toward Bob has often been perceived as something that had to be a negative for me, and it wasn't.

"I always thought it said a lot about this job and this city that, after all these years, when you're not there anymore, they miss you. That was a neat thing to know."

"I learned a lot from Steve Blass."

Rochester, New York is 270 miles from Pittsburgh, and Frattare traveled some interesting roads to get from there to here.

Al Frattare, his father, used to listen to Pirates' broadcasts over KDKA Radio, picking up its powerful 50,000 watts signal. There was clearer transmission when the Pirates were playing on the West Coast and it was later in the night when fewer stations were on the air.

At age 10, Lanny started pretending he was an announcer doing the Yankees' games. Al bought him a good tape recorder for Christmas, encouraging him to chase his dream. "We were not a wealthy family, and I knew what a sizable investment that was for my dad," said Frattare.

In 1974, Blass was pitching for the Charleston Charlies, trying to recapture the magic that had mysteriously departed him a few years after he had been a World Series hero. Frattare was Charleston's play-by-play broadcaster, and the two struck up a friendship.

"I learned a lot from Steve Blass," Frattare said in an earlier interview. "No matter what he was going through, he always said how fortunate he felt he had been to have enjoyed a major league career and to have pitched in a World Series.

"Every minor league town that we went to, the press kept wanting to talk about his situation, and he was always so accommodating and so professional. Watching him deal with his adversity in such a top shelf way really taught me a lot."

After he'd come out of a game, Blass often good-naturedly joined Frattare in the broadcast booth to discuss the Charlies' games. "He always had a good sense of humor," recalled Frattare.

"Just a dream come true."
— Lanny Frattare
on Pirates' job

Lanny Frattare's favorite pastimes are playing golf, presidential history and music. He does charitable work for the Cystic Fibrosis Foundation, Goodwill Industries and Bob Prince Charities. He hosts a celebrity golf tournament at St. Clair Country Club each July for the benefit of the Parent and Child Guidance Center. A foundation in his father's memory has been established in conjunction with that annual outing.

Frattare's father and brother both played baseball, and Lanny got involved as a scorekeeper. He was never as adept at playing ball as his father and brother. He followed the Rochester Red Wings, and he got the notion early in his life that the broadcast booth was the best seat in the house. "And I've found out that it is," allowed Lanny.

He earned a degree in communications at Ithaca (N.Y.) College. His beginnings in the business were humble and a bit out of character, to say the least.

His first job back home was introducing the entertainment at the Pussycat Lounge. "It was a topless bar, a go-go club," recalled Frattare with a flushed look. "I had auditioned for a job doing radio commercials and came away with this offer. I was surprised my dad gave me permission to do it. That's how I got my start as a professional announcer."

That led to deejay jobs at local radio stations. Frattare's first job in baseball was doing play-by-play for the Geneva, New York baseball team in the Class A New York-Penn League. From there, he went to Charleston, West Virginia in the Pirates' farm system.

He still regards getting the Pirates' job as "just a dream come true." He wasn't able to see it in such a light in the early days because he and Milo Hamilton had a tough act to follow.

"Things got really bad at times those first couple of years," recalled Frattare in an earlier interview. "A lot of people were highly critical of Milo and myself. A lot of fans had a hard time accepting us.

"I'll be forever grateful to Bob Prince. The fact that he always believed in me and encouraged me when things were at their lowest really kept me going in those early years."

"I think of him a lot"

"There will never be another 'Voice of the Pirates' as that title will always belong to Bob Prince," Frattare told an early morning gathering at a media seminar at Westminster Presbyterian Church in Upper St. Clair, where Prince lived when he was doing the Pirates broadcasts. Bob and Betty Prince were church members.

"I wouldn't be here today if it weren't for 'The Gunner' helping me," he said. "He taught me about the importance of getting out and getting to know the people in the community, and of giving back.

"I think of him a lot. I hope he looks down and approves of the way I conduct myself, and the way I broadcast Pirates baseball.

"Bob Prince taught me some rules. For instance, he said when you go from radio to television think about shutting up right away.

"I don't think you can give the score too much. Bob Prince said to give the score every time a new batter comes up, and every time the count is three-and-two. And if you think you haven't given the score enough then give the score again."

Prince was the most popular toastmaster for sports dinners and public gatherings in the history of Pittsburgh. He had a loosey-goosey style, a flair about him that came naturally, and there will never be another one like him. He was often outrageous, and always unforgettable.

Prince also told a lot of saucy stories and off-color jokes, and Frattare wouldn't touch such blue material at any price. It's simply not his style.

> *"Our son, John, once asked Bob Prince why he never wore any socks. Bob told him, 'Son, I've earned that right.'"*
> —Joni Bogut,
> wife of deejay Jack Bogut

137

"I've been blessed to have a great family and by being able to make a living at something I've always wanted to do in a city and region that I truly love. I feel that I'm a fortunate man."

During Frattare's two seasons at Charleston, he came back to Three Rivers Stadium at the end of the season after the Charlies had completed their schedule.

"I was keeping score in the press box that first night, and Bob Prince came up to me, and asked me if I would like to do a half-inning on the air," recalled Frattare. "I was shocked. The next day I went to the ballpark early and I was talking to the ushers and so forth, and I was amazed at how many knew I'd been on the radio the night before. 'So you're the kid who was on with Prince last night?' they'd say. Bob asked me if I wanted to do a half-inning again the second night. But Mudcat Grant showed up in the press box that night, and went on with Bob, and I didn't get on the air that night. A year later, Bob invited me to come on with him again and call some play-by-play."

That was a telling anecdote about Prince because it pointed up how he was always trying to help young people get started, and how he was always boosting promising young people in the media business. Prince was popular and felt secure about his own position. Many people in his business would have feared giving a young talent an opening for fear that the youngster might steal their job.

"Bob and Nellie both told me they were interested in having me come in as a third announcer the next year," recalled Frattare. "That's when Bob got fired. I thought my chances of coming to Pittsburgh were over. I figured my career was over with his firing. And I didn't know if I was coming back to Charleston for the 1976 season.

"After Bob was fired, he called me in Rochester about every ten days to tell me what was going on regarding his replacement. He cared enough to do that. He might have been calling some other young announcers as well, but I was impressed with his personal concern for me. He was the most caring and giving individual I ever met, with the exception of my father.

"The Pirates brought in Milo Hamilton as the No. 1 announcer to replace Bob. And I came in as the No. 2 announcer; I think I was sort of a compromise choice for that slot, from all that I later heard about the situation. John Steigerwald went to Charleston and replaced me.

"I was amazed when I went around the league and learned of how many people had been touched by Bob's generosity. Whether it was the host of the press room — Bob was notorious for giving big tips wherever he went — and I was amazed at how many charities he had helped in one way or another. Milo Hamilton and I were the broadcasting team through the 1979 season. But Milo had an impossible situation trying to replace Bob. Nobody could have done it."

Asked about his most emotional moment as a Pirates' broadcaster, Frattare said, "It had to be in 1985 when the Pirates brought Bob Prince back to join the broadcast team. We were playing Los

Angeles at Three Rivers Stadium. When they introduced him to the crowd and he stood up, the electricity in the ballpark was unbelievable. He took over the play-by-play at the start of the fourth inning and the Pirates responded by scoring nine runs that inning. It gave everyone chills.

"That whole period was wonderful, yet awkward. I had been talking to KDKA for a long time about bringing Bob back to the broadcast booth. Some cynics said we were doing it to capitalize on his dying. We had no idea, from what the doctors had told us, that he'd get sick and die so soon after he came back.

"The thing that struck me most when I first came to Pittsburgh was people told me they grew up to develop a love for baseball because of Bob Prince. I wanted to develop a new generation of Pirate fans, and he passed the torch to me.

"I think I've succeeded. There's a whole new generation of fans who never listened to the Pirates on the radio.

"Last October, after we were out of it, I sat on that porch out there and listened to CBS radio broadcasts of the playoffs and the World Series. There's no better place in the world than right out there. We have a fish pond out back in the summer. I have a flagpole — I love the American flag — and we have a spotlight shining on it. I love to sit on that porch, listen to baseball games, and soak up the whole scene. We have good neighbors here and sometimes they'll come over. We'll throw some steaks on the grill. They all kid me in this house because I'll come through here and say, 'Cmon, gang, let's go sit on the back porch together.' I guess I'm just a corny guy."

Jim O'Brien

Lanny Frattare has statistics and notes at the ready in broadcast booth at Three Rivers Stadium in the spring of 1998.

Insiders
They worked with Prince

*"I never saw a figure
so respected and revered."*
— Bill Hillgrove

John Steigerwald, KDKA-TV sportscaster, Pittsburgh:

My mother and four of her sisters used to baby-sit Bob Prince's kids on Shady Drive West in Mt. Lebanon. They looked after Nancy and Bob Prince Jr. My mother used to tell us stories about seeing Bob wearing shorts and cowboy boots around the house. That gave me kind of an intro to him.

"When he was in the hospital in the '70s, my aunt, Dori Haller, told him about me. He asked me to send him a tape of my baseball play-by-play work. I sent along one of my scorecards. He critiqued the tape for me. He also said that someday he wanted to teach me how to do a boxscore properly.

"I replaced Lanny Frattare as the play-by-play broadcaster for the Charleston Charlies, the Pirates' Triple A team, when Frattare and Milo Hamilton replaced Prince and Nellie King in the Pirates' broadcast booth.

"When I'd run into Prince, he'd mention my mother, Katherine, and the Hatch sisters. There were five of them, all living in Mt. Lebanon.

"He's the reason I'm doing what I'm doing. I wanted to be a baseball announcer. I loved baseball. I used to come to games, bring binoculars, and watch Bob Prince during the game.

"As I got older and went off to college, my friends and I were really big on Bob Prince. Because he was such a Pittsburgh guy, so different from anybody I'd ever heard, a real good guy. Everyone else sounded the same, but Prince was Prince.

"One of the things I learned from Prince, that as much as he talked, he also knew when to get out of the way. Ray Scott always let the action carry itself on TV. Prince had great timing; he knew when to shut up and when to talk. There's a difference in how you do that home and away, because you're going to have crowd noise to carry the moment when the team is playing at home. On the road, the noise won't be there.

"I have tapes of ten or twelve announcers, and there's such a lack of personality. They all have the same phony radio announcing voices.

"I no longer yearn to be a baseball announcer. When I was 25, I was the same age as the players. I enjoyed being with them. At 40, it wouldn't have appealed to me. I came up to Pittsburgh in 1976

Jim O'Brien

Sportscasters Alby Oxenreiter, George Von Benko and John Steigerwald were all young admirers of Bob Prince, pictured in background by the bar of the media lounge at Three Rivers Stadium.

John Longo, WCNS Radio in Latrobe

Author Jim O'Brien joins Bill Hillgrove and Fran Fisher at WCNS Radio promotion at St. Vincent College in Latrobe in summer of 1997.

On sports talk shows...
"If you can't hang it out for three hours, you better hang it up."
— Bob Prince

when I was the play-by-play broadcaster for Charleston. We had Omar Moreno and Steve Nicosia on our team and they'd be Pirates before long. I thought I'd come to Three Rivers Stadium and hang around the park. I spotted Milo Hamilton in the press box, taking a break when someone else was on the air. You remember the stories about how Prince put Lanny Frattare on the air for a few innings when he'd come up from Charleston and it helped him eventually get the job. Well, I wasn't looking for that, but I did think that Milo might have some time for me, that he might want to know about some of the Pirates' prospects, and how they were doing. I introduced myself to Milo, and told him who I was and what I was doing. He shook my hand and said, 'Nice to see you.' That was the end of the conversation. It was like he was saying, 'I'm watching the game. Go away.' So I never cared much for Milo Hamilton after that.

"I talked to Jack Buck once about Bob Prince, and he had tears in his eyes when he was talking about Bob Prince. This was shortly after Bob died.

"The most enjoyable thing I've ever done in this job was in 1991 when I covered the Penguins when they won their first Stanley Cup. Covering the Super Bowls was right up there, too.

"But one of the best times I ever had was when Billy Hillgrove and I worked with Bob Prince at the 1979 World Series. We were doing special reports from a house we had rented right behind the wall at the stadium in Baltimore, and we were staying at a hotel in town.

"To me, to be sitting in a car, riding through Baltimore, going to the World Series, riding with The Gunner . . . How can you beat that? When we were in a hotel room, he'd order food for everybody. He'd just pick up the menu, and order a few sandwiches, some shrimp, different kinds of drinks, Cokes and lemonade. I've never done anything like that. There was something to suit everyone. He always picked up the tab for everything."

* * *

Bill Hillgrove, WTAE Radio and TV, Pittsburgh:

"My dad's name was Bill, and my son's name is Bill. We're not that creative with names in the Hillgrove family. My dad was an electrician, and he could fix radios and TVs. He rigged a wireless mike that would shoot the signal through an FM radio so I could pretend to be a sports announcer and the sound would come out of the radio. That's how I got started.

"I was taught by the Sisters of Charity, and I got a part on a weekly radio show sponsored by the Pittsburgh Catholic Diocese. I played the part of a 13-year-old brat, which I was. And the bug bit me. I have to thank my dad for that.

"My mother told me to hit the books. She didn't want me loafing, or hanging out on Penn Avenue. A lot of those guys are now loafing in Western Pen. I have my mother to thank for that. I went to Duquesne University and I did sports and other shows on WDUQ, the student radio station. It was a great place to learn the business.

"As a kid, I liked to play at being a sports announcer. When the kids in the neighborhood would play games in the backyard, I'd attempt to describe what was going on.

"From where I grew up in Garfield, I could see the light stands at Forbes Field. You knew when the game was held up by rain because they'd dim a few of the stands. You could also see the top of the Cathedral of Learning. In our neighborhood, when the street lights came on, you went home. That was the rule. We'd listen to the games on the radio. That's when baseball was king in this town. We'd listen to Joe Tucker doing his 15 minutes of sports around dinner time. Hearing him was like dying and going to heaven.

"As a kid, I heard Bob Prince's voice on every porch I passed on a summer evening. He was so entertaining. The guy was very unique.

"I worked the 1979 World Series with John Steigerwald and Bob Prince. Bob and I were roommates, and he called me 'roomie' after that every time he saw me. I could write a whole book on what I can remember from those two weeks. He was simply fun to be around.

"We did one of the greatest television pieces that ever hit this town. Before Game 1, Prince said, 'I got an idea. Let's you and Steigy go down to poolside with our shorts on, and sit around and talk about the game.' There were big, wet snowflakes coming down, and we're all lying on lounge chairs, like we're sunning ourselves, sipping beer and talking about the game, totally ignoring the snow.

"It was just pure Prince. At no point was there ever a reference to the snow. It was wicked, too. I lost it twice and we had to do the tape about three times to get it right. He said to me before we went to the pool, 'Billy, you've got more weight than Steigy and me, so you'll probably be warmer. But let's do it!'

"That night we had a pre-game special. We're on the field when Bowie Kuhn, the commissioner, called off the opening game of the Series because of bad weather. There was a horde of reporters around Kuhn at home plate. Prince hollers over to him, 'Commissioner, we need you live . . . for ABC Sports in Pittsburgh!' And Kuhn calls back, 'Yes, Bob, I'll be right there.' We were the only TV station in the country to have the commissioner on live. Only someone with Bob Prince's personality could have pulled that off. No one else could have done that. All the officials, all the umpires, everybody in baseball knew Bob Prince. I never saw a figure so respected and revered.

"He acted like I was the most special person who ever came into his life. He remembered little things about you. You could learn a lot of people skills from him. He made everyone feel special.

"It was the same thing with Art Rooney. Here, I wasn't a hill of beans, but he knew I was Irish. He'd give you a shot every so often about that. He'd say, 'You going to the track. Hope you break even.' Stuff like that. Both of them met so many people, but they had time for everybody.

"Ed Conway was great, too. We worked together on Pitt football in 1970-73. He was the play-by-play guy and I did color. He tipped me off to some station developments that enabled me to stay on when he lost favor. That showed me the kind of guy he was. I had some great role models in Tucker, Prince, Conway and Ray Scott. The Gunner took a liking to me, and always made me feel special. He and Mr. Rooney could make you feel pretty special. Those guys were much less narcissistic than they (announcers and owners) are today.

"It would be impossible to be a Prince today. The times wouldn't allow it. The players are making more money and aren't interested in having fun. He'd be viewed differently today. That's the shame of it."

* * *

George Von Benko, Sportscaster, WASP Radio/Cox Interactive Sports Media

"I had scheduled Bob Prince for an appearance on my Sportsline talk show in Morgantown, West Virginia, on WAJR-AM during the 1980 baseball season. I didn't tell him that his old broadcast partner, Jim Woods, was going to be a surprise guest. When I brought 'Possum' into the conversation, I could barely get a word in as they took off with a series of stories.

"One of my favorite exchanges was a story concerning old Colts' Stadium in Houston where the Colt 45s played before moving into the Astrodome and becoming the Astros. When they played night games at Colts' Stadium they had a real problem with mosquitoes. The ground crew had to spray the field and the stands on a regular basis with bug spray. Prince and Woods would pay some youngsters who hung around the stadium to sit in the broadcast booth with them and swat mosquitoes.

"Prince commented that he could never understand why the mosquitoes would swarm all over him, but wouldn't bother Woods. Jim Woods' reply was they didn't bother him because his blood wasn't ninety proof like Prince's was.

"The show also proved to be very profitable for me. During one of the commercial breaks, Prince asked Woods if he had any extra cash to invest and proceeded to tell him to buy stock in Mylan Pharmaceuticals. I said 'Mylan, that is located right here in Morgantown.' Prince said that was right and told me to round up some cash and invest in their stock. It was one of the best moves I ever made. Mylan stock split twice within the next month. What a great stock tip from The Gunner."

144

Hall of Famer Joe DiMaggio joins Bob Prince.

Pittsburgh businessman Bud Stevenson with Bob Prince and Notre Dame football coach Ara Parseghian at a sports banquet in downtown hotel.

Bob Prince with football Hall of Famers, Harold "Red" Grange and Bobby Dodd.

*   *   *

Barbara Sirinek, Mt. Lebanon, Pa.
Prince's last secretary (1970-1976):

"It was a wonderful time. I worked a long time in a lot of places as a secretary and I still work a couple of days a week. I have a skill that few secretaries have anymore; I can take shorthand. And I've kept up with all the modern computers — taking classes at the adult education classes at Mt Lebanon High School — and I can use them as well. Bob was great. He got an office somehow on the fourth floor of Three Rivers Stadium, right next to the Stadium Authority offices. I don't know how he negotiated that deal, but we moved in during the fall of 1970, and I was there until they let him go in 1975. I stayed on with him, working out of my home, when he was working in Houston. I didn't like the idea of working at home by myself, so I went to work at a law firm when the baseball season was over.

"He always had the most modern, most innovative equipment to work with. He gave me absolute power to take care of business. It was a wonderful set-up. I ate lunch every day at the Allegheny Club, and we could watch the Steelers practice. That was nice. I had a parking space in the inner circle under the Stadium.

"We did a lot of work on the phone. He gave me a lot of independence. He was very kind and very nice. I had a good time. I liked doing what I was doing.

"I'm dating myself, but Danny Murtaugh and his wife, Kate, were classmates of mine at Chester (Pa.) High. I was able sometimes to take people down to the dugout to visit Danny and some of the ballplayers.

"I didn't know that much about baseball, so Bob had to explain a lot of things to me carefully. I'm still not a big sports fan.

"No, I'll never forget Bob Prince. He did a lot of good. He co-founded the Allegheny Valley School for kids who were retarded and had other problems. He set up golf tournaments to raise money for a lot of good causes.

"He got a lot of mail from fans, too, and he insisted on having everything acknowledged. It was more difficult in those days because you had to type every letter from scratch. Today, you could keep model letters in the system and alter them slightly to suit the occasion.

"I went on a trip to Italy last fall with my niece, and it was hosted by Bill Cardille and his wife. He told me he'd gotten a long letter from Bob after he was let go, explaining in detail what had happened. Bill thought I might have typed the letter. Bob was a big believer in written correspondence.

"He used to speak every year at the Thompson Run Club. I think it was a stag dinner. He had a 'joke' file. It only had the punch lines.

Every time he went out to talk, he asked me for the 'joke' file. I thought that was funny that he only had the punch lines."

I suggested to Ms. Sirinek that she wouldn't have wanted to read the rest of the jokes. "Probably not," she said. "Sometimes I'd sit in the back of the broadcast booth. Bob and Nellie would be in the front row, and Radio Rich would be there with them. This fellow named George, who worked at KDKA, would say, 'It's time. I can tell when Bob's getting hot.' And he'd tap Bob on the shoulder with a long pole, like an antenna. He'd say, 'OK, Gunner, you're off the air!' He'd turn off his mike, and then Bob would explode. Then George would give him the go-ahead to get back on the air. I thought that was funny."

* * *

Art Rooney Jr., Pittsburgh Steelers, Mt. Lebanon, Pa.

"Bob Prince always talked to you like he really knew you. He always made you feel kinda important. He had some of the same qualities my dad had in that regard. He made you feel good about yourself. But, like my dad, he could cut you down to size in a hurry, too.

"I remember this time I tagged along with my dad when the Steelers were playing the Redskins in Washington. We might have gone there on the train. The game was at Griffith Stadium, which was a dingy place. I was in my early 20s, fresh out of St. Vincent College, and I wasn't working for the Steelers or anything.

"Prince was working with Joe Tucker doing the broadcast of the game. He'd talk to you during the commercials when he wasn't involved. He'd just lean back and start talking to people. He pointed out Vice President Richard Nixon in the stands in front of the press box, and said he was going to get him for a halftime guest. He told me to stick around at the half and he'd introduce me to Nixon.

"I was waiting for awhile at halftime. They had real good hot dogs at the concession stands at Griffith Stadium. I wanted one. I had this problem; that was one of my weaknesses. So I left the press box to get me a hot dog. As I was returning to the press box, I saw Nixon coming out, waving to everyone.

"When I got in the press box, Prince hollered to me, 'Hey, wise guy, you didn't think I could do it; you didn't think I could pull it off.' He was bragging on himself, about what he'd just done. Later, he leaned back, and said, 'You big donkey, how many vice presidents have you ever met in your lifetime? You blew it.'"

> *"Memories are a gift from God. We're told that memories are God's way of giving us roses in December."*
> — From a sermon at the funeral service of Walter Doherty at St. Bernard's Church, Mt. Lebanon, Pa.

Fran Fisher, Penn State announcer,
State College, Pa.:

"I always had the highest regard for Bob Prince, and always got such a kick out of him. We still run into Penn State fans who talk about when Bob was the Penn State broadcaster. And Nellie King succeeded me in Greensburg when I left there in favor of Penn State football. I got Prince as emcee when Jerry Sandusky, the Penn State assistant coach, began a fund-raising golf tournament. Prince came out, and he said he wanted to help make it a real fund-raiser. And he did. They turned the corner when Prince started promoting it."

*   *   *

Murray Tucker, Son of Joe Tucker,
Jersey City, New Jersey:

"Dad really liked Bob and they worked together on football and hockey (Prince never did know anything about hockey, but he had a good time) as well as when my dad was third man on baseball. My dad used to fill in for Jack Craddock with Rosey Rowswell back in 1936, the year that KDKA Radio began broadcasting Pirates baseball. They did re-creations then, even for games at Forbes Field. Craddock was a preacher and he wouldn't do Sunday games. So my dad did the Sunday games. When Craddock left, my dad was interested in working as Rowswell's partner. But there was some anti-semitism that entered into the decision. Barney Dreyfuss, one of the owners of the ballclub, was Jewish and, unbelievably enough, he did not want a Jew doing the Pirates games on the radio. And Art Rooney, a devout Catholic, hires my dad to do Steeler games. The rest is history."

From speech President John F. Kennedy was to deliver in Dallas the day he was assassinated. It's included in a book of quotes kept by Lanny Frattare, Pirates' broadcaster:

"There will always be dissident voices heard in the land, expressing and finding fault but never favor, preaching gloom on every side and seeking influence without responsibility. We cannot expect that everyone will talk sense to the American people. But we can hope that fewer people will listen to nonsense."

Pittsburgh broadcasters, left to right, include Joe Tucker, Carl Dozer, Rosey Rowswell, Bob Prince and Pie Traynor.

Bob Prince, Joe Tucker and Foge Fazio

Steelers coach Chuck Noll, Pittsburgh Press Club manager Adolph Donadeo, Steelers owner Art Rooney and Joe Tucker talk in March, 1971.

Tucker with Pitt coach John Michelosen before 1956 Gator Bowl.

Pirates owner Bing Crosby chats with Tucker in clubhouse at Forbes Field.

Milo Hamilton
He couldn't replace Prince

"Bob's situation cost me a good friend."

Milo Hamilton was moving about his room at the Westin William Penn Hotel, putting everything in its proper place. Hamilton and the housekeeper had combined to give the room a meticulous look. His scorebook and stats notebook were laid out neatly atop a nearby desk.

Beside the books were pens of different colors — red, blue, green, black, yellow — and they were lined up next to each other, aligned the same length. They were laid out like those of a secretary on her first day on the job. The colors are keys in the Hamilton code of record-keeping. The numbers, notes and lines in his personal scorebook looked as if they had been done by a draftsman. Their precision was a point of pride to Hamilton. He couldn't hide a smile as he showed them to me.

The man who tried to replace Bob Prince in the Pirates' broadcast booth in 1976 couldn't pass up an opportunity to point up his dedicated work habits.

"I come back to my room after a game and go over all this, and update all my information," he explained. "I have stats and information that even our p.r. people don't have. I keep records the p.r. guys don't keep. I have my own stats, good stats, that I like to pass along during the game. It's got to fit; you can't force it. I still do my homework and preparation to broadcast a baseball game properly. And I have them at my fingertips for an appropriate time to use them during the next game. Or the next game."

Doing such homework certainly set him apart from Prince, who was more comfortable in simply showing up at the ballpark or arena, usually at the last minute, no matter the sport, and telling you what he saw, and tossing in a few stories to entertain you. Personally, I preferred good description and good stories to good stats. Hamilton showed me some examples of "good stats," but they failed to light a fire under my heart.

The late Luke Quay, the sports editor of *The Daily News* in McKeesport once described Hamilton as "a polished professional with a thorough knowledge of baseball and every team in the National League through long experience with the Atlanta Braves and other big league teams."

His shortcoming was that he didn't remind anyone of Bob Prince, in any respect. He didn't have a nickname. He was not a colorful character, or a man about town.

Milo Hamilton is a familiar face in media lounge at Three Rivers Stadium.

Hamilton has reunion with former partner Lanny Frattare in summer of 1997.

Milo Hamilton in 1976, when he became Bucs' broadcaster.

"*Baseball's time is seamless and invisible, a bubble within which players move at exactly the same pace and rhythms as all their predecessors. This is the way the game was played in our youth and in our father's youth and even back then — back in the country days — there must have been the same feeling that time could be stopped. Since baseball time is measured only in outs, all you have to do is succeed utterly; keep hitting, keep the rally alive, and you have defeated time. You remain forever young.*"

— Roger Angell,
The Interior Stadium

"I was never one to go out much after the game," said Hamilton. "I can't drink before I go to bed. I like to have a martini before dinner, and that's about it. I do my work right after the game. I retire as soon as I complete my paperwork these days. My idea of doing nothing would be to close the bar every night at the hotel where we're staying."

Hamilton was in town as the play-by-play announcer for the Houston Astros. They were in Pittsburgh to play four games in as many days. Hamilton knew his way about town, and had taken the Astros' coaching staff to lunch earlier at Poli's in Squirrel Hill. He was wearing a coat and tie, which would date him right away in the Pirates' press box, and was ready to go to work. It was about 4 o'clock, and he would be catching one of the buses taking the ballplayers from Grant Street to Stadium Circle.

"There used to be a hotel across the street from here," Hamilton said. "It was called the Carlton House. I used to have coffee there on occasion with Al Abrams, the sports editor of the *Post-Gazette*. He'd be there every day with a real cast of characters that he often mentioned in his notes column. Billy Conn, the boxer, would often come to join him."

The Westin William Penn Hotel is an old hotel in downtown Pittsburgh that's been refurbished to its original grandeur. Most of the rooms are small compared to more modern hotels, especially the ones in the nearby suburbs. After you have been on the road with a baseball team for a week or so, the walls start closing in on you. I didn't think Hamilton had much room to maneuver.

Hamilton seemed right at home, though, even though he was living out of a suitcase. He had his suitcase on an ottoman at the foot of his bed, and his shirts and shorts and stuff had been neatly packed, and he pulled a handkerchief out of the stack. He could have been a salesman on the road. Willy Loman came to mind, I'll admit.

I wondered what life on the road was like for Hamilton, how he enjoyed it after all these years. I covered baseball on a full-time basis only one year, 1972, splitting the summer between the Yankees and the Mets in New York, shifting teams at the All-Star Game break, which was part of the beauty of covering baseball in New York.

It was a great year and I enjoyed it immensely. I just knew I didn't want to do it for the rest of my life. Baseball writers, I thought, tended to know other baseball writers better than they knew their own wives and kids. I covered baseball games from time to time through the years, but only to spell someone else on the staff. I shifted to boxing and basketball and hockey and, later, football. I enjoyed them all. While I loved it early on, I tired of traveling and life on the road. It could be ruinous to one's health and marriage. I didn't want to be out on the road when my daughters were growing up.

For Hamilton, life on the road with a baseball team was something short of heaven. At age 69, though he hardly looked that old, Hamilton still enjoyed it. He was 48 when he came to the Pirates in 1976.

He beseeched fans then not to compare him to Bob Prince, the man he was replacing. "It would be foolish on my part to try to be Bob Prince. You could bring Mel Allen or Red Barber here and they wouldn't be Bob Prince. I have to be myself. I have my own style and approach to the game. I'll just try to do my job and hope everybody likes me," he said then.

Ray Scott, another legendary announcer from the area, had been mentioned as a possibility for the Bucs job. He said he wasn't interested because of his long friendship with Bob Prince. "And second, Bob Prince is a very tough act to follow," added Scott.

It was 21 years later, but Hamilton's voice was still strong, and as clear as can be. Whereas another ace announcer Jack Buck's voice had grown weaker, and often cracked while he was commenting on a baseball game, Hamilton still had healthy vocal chords.

Hamilton is in the Baseball Hall of Fame, inducted in 1992, so his track record is pretty remarkable, and he's pretty good at what he's been doing all his adult life. In Pittsburgh, however, Hamilton is most remembered as the guy who tried — and failed — to replace Bob Prince. Hamilton wore socks, played it straight, and simply couldn't fill Prince's Gucci loafers.

Hamilton had come to Pittsburgh from Atlanta, where he was best known for calling the shot when Henry Aaron broke Babe Ruth's career home run record of 714 home runs. He described Bucs' baseball for four years — 1976 to 1979 — and moved on after completing his initial contract.

Lanny Frattare was brought in from Charleston to work with Hamilton. Frattare stayed on when Hamilton hustled off to Chicago.

Prince had been more popular in Pittsburgh than either the Pirates or KDKA bosses realized. There was great resentment of his firing in many quarters. Prince was a tough act for Hamilton to follow. The fans, for the most part, never gave him a chance and refused to accept him. Many baseball people and some sportswriters felt Hamilton deserved better.

Hamilton talked about those days, the good and the bad times, as he tidied his room and got ready to go to Three Rivers Stadium. He was harsh in his criticism of Prince and Nellie King.

When I wrote a book about Roberto Clemente, his biggest critic among his former teammates was ElRoy Face. The gutty little relief pitcher expressed his views openly and honestly, not trying to say all the politically-correct things. Face didn't care for Clemente, that much was perfectly clear and, to his credit, he never denied that he offered any of the criticism of Clemente that appeared in *Remember Roberto*. As Hamilton put down Prince repeatedly in our conversation, the thought struck me that Milo Hamilton was going to be the ElRoy Face of the book on Bob Prince.

"You're not going to have Bob Prince. You're going to have baseball."
— Milo Hamilton

Milo Hamilton warmed quickly to talking about Bob Prince. "I think he was in the right town at the right time," he said, explaining Prince's popularity in Pittsburgh. "He became part of the folklore around here. He came in with Rosey Rowswell and he followed the guy with all that 'Aunt Minnie' stuff. He was great with the gimmicks. Prince was like a lot of guys in this business who — when it was a big game — he paid attention. When it wasn't, he rambled a bit.

"He could be a wonderful guy. He was a great guy to be around. You had a lot of fun with him. He was always willing to go to different places to have a good time. He was a great story-teller.

"He had a great thing going for him. One of the owners, Tom Johnson, was always coming to his rescue. Every time somebody wanted to fire him, Tom Johnson said he'd have a talk with Prince, and set him straight. Prince showed up in the afternoon under the weather and high people in high places would look after him.

"He was a genuine character. All the things you've heard about him are probably true, and not exaggerated. Everyone tells the story about the time he dived into the Chase Hotel pool from a third story window. If he miscalculated, he'd have been dead.

"He was a lot of fun in the press box, fun to be with. I knew people who went to high school with him, and they said he was always the same. He was a constant cut-up. He liked to exaggerate. He always had guys with him who got a kick out of his company. He always had a glass of orange juice in his hand.

"I was here for four years and I enjoyed Pittsburgh a lot. I enjoyed it before I worked here."

Thinking about Pittsburgh and the Pirates, Hamilton offered, "A lot of people think this is a football town because of the crowds at the Stadium. But if you trace the history of the Pirates' franchise it's pretty good. They've had a few Hall of Famers here.

"I've been coming here since 1954. That's how long I've been going to Poli's. I'm close to the family. Larry Poli, the late owner of the place, and I were close friends. We went bird-hunting together. Going hunting is my passion in the off-season. I'm close to the family.

"My wife, Arlene, is a big bridge player. She has a life master's rating, and she had a good group here. I liked the town. We lived in Cochran Hall, up behind The Colony Restaurant in Mt. Lebanon. We had a new condominium.

"Many of the media didn't want me here. Some people were terrific to me. Norm Vargo and Bob Smizik, to name two, were always great with me.

"The fans were good to me. I never had one bit of trouble with the fans. My message to them was 'You've got to listen to me for what I am and who I am, not for who I'm not. You're not going to have Bob Prince. You're going to have baseball. I can't tell you as many stories.'

"I made some friends here. When I go to the Allegheny Club they come up to me and tell me they enjoyed me when I was here. I couldn't control what was going on around me because of Prince's departure. I'll tell you who was one of my biggest boosters, an old baseball and football owner named Art Rooney. He told me, 'Don't you worry about all this stuff. You keep on doing what you're doing. You'll be fine.' Art Rooney came to a lot of games. He owned the Steelers, but he was quite a fan of all the sports. He'd been quite a baseball player.

"The people knew who I was. There were people who fought the idea of me doing the games. It wasn't the same for them. Like John Cigna of KDKA who didn't know a suicide squeeze from the foul pole, yet he was against me.

"Dave Ailes in Greensburg was another. He took it upon himself to wage a personal campaign against me. He said that I wasn't going to make it in this town. Vito Stellino at the *Post-Gazette* really attacked me personally. He wrote such scurrilous things about me. I understandably challenged him physically. While I enjoyed it here, I wasn't going to put up with the negativity of the Ailes and Stellinos of the world.

"I didn't have anything to prove when I came to Pittsburgh. I had already been broadcasting baseball for 20 years when I came here from Atlanta. When my contract was up, there was an opening in Chicago and I wanted it. Jack Brickhouse wasn't going to return. He told me that one day when we went to dinner at Poli's.

"We went to the World Series in 1979, my last year with the Pirates. When I interviewed Chuck Tanner — I loved that guy — I told him that was the last time I would interview him as the Pirates' announcer. I still have my World Series ring, and wear it proudly.

"I went to Chicago for five years. Two years after I got there, I'm paired with Harry Caray. There was no way I could co-exist with him, but I managed to do it for three years. But you can't work with someone you don't respect. I wasn't comfortable and didn't believe in his lifestyle. You take someone like Jack Buck, on the other hand. He's one of the finest people in the world.

"Caray liked to say that he was the chief reason the fans came out to the ballpark. I told him that we had an open date coming up on a Thursday. 'Let's announce that you'll be out here singing *Take Me Out To The Ballgame* at three o'clock, and see how many people show up.' He thought he was bigger than the game. Prince had a little bit of that in him, too.

"Chuck Tanner is a great person. I saw him last night at the ballpark. He was a great communicator. He'd say, 'Let's talk baseball.' What people didn't realize until he was gone was that he was for real. It wasn't a phony effervescence. It's just the way he was.

"Some people don't want to be happy. Mike Tyson and Albert Belle don't want to be happy. Chuck used to tell me, 'Don't worry about the stuff those guys say about you. They don't know you.' One of the persons who was caught in the middle was Lanny Frattare. After I left here, to his credit, he told me, 'I didn't realize what you had done for me, until you were gone.' I took all the criticism. I was the lead broadcaster when I left, and Lanny didn't have to field all the criticism aimed at me for trying to replace Prince.

"If I had any problems with Prince — hey, there are a lot of people fired in this business — is that he wouldn't go quietly in the night. He hung around and he was always putting me down behind my back. He was always telling people he'd be back before they knew it.

"If you're as good as you think you are you'd never be without work in baseball. He failed one year in Houston. He bombed on ABC television with the Game of the Week series.

"At the Dapper Dan Dinner, he told the audience I'd only be here for a year. 'I'll be back next year,' he told them. Meanwhile, I had a four-year contract He was going to smokers and banquets about the city and constantly sniping at me. I'd hear about it. He was on talk shows and he'd say something about coming back.

"He wouldn't give it up. He kept after me. When I got fired in Atlanta, I came here and got a job. Prince should have picked up and gone elsewhere. When it became apparent I couldn't get along with Caray, I moved on. I was doing Bulls basketball and DePaul basketball.

"Then I went to Houston and I've been there 13 years. I work for the ballclub. Houston's been great to me. Dallas Green got me my job in Houston. He called Al Rosen, who was the general manager of the Astros, and suggested he hire me. It wasn't my fault that things weren't right in Chicago. So I went and got another job. That's what Prince should have done when I came to Pittsburgh.

"His situation cost me a friend. We'd always gotten along great before I came to Pittsburgh to work. In fact, when I was let go by the Braves I called Bob to ask him to put in a good word for me with the Cardinals who had an opening. I had no idea I'd end up replacing him in Pittsburgh.

"If he wanted to have his problem with KDKA and the ballclub, that was his right and privilege, but he involved me in it. He went on every talk show and discussed my situation as well as his own. And Nellie King, all he had to do was shut up, and he might have been working with me. And I'll bet he's still whining.

"Prince fired himself. He just kept getting himself into trouble with his bosses. There was a little tyrant at KDKA named Ed Wallis. He said, 'Bob, you gotta start doing the games. You gotta shape up. We don't want to know what bar you were in last night.'

"The guy who was miffed the most with Bob was Joe L. Brown, who'd always been one of his biggest supporters. The Pirates and

KDKA and the brewery (Iron City) all told him he had to get back to broadcasting the ballgames. He took them on on the air right after their meeting.

"His attitude was 'they can't fire me. I'm bigger than the ball-club.' Now the guy (Tom Johnson) who saved him all those years finally threw in the towel.

"If Prince had gone in and said, 'Let's have lunch,' and told them he'd go along with the program, I think he'd have kept his job."

Four years after he was fired by KDKA and the Pirates, Prince was kinder in his comments than he had been earlier. "Milo and I have totally different styles, there's no doubt about that," he said, "but he was not a bad play-by-play man. I wouldn't have wanted to be in his shoes. Rosey Rowswell, my predecessor, broke me in gradually. I had been with him for six years before I took over so people just accepted me. Lord knows I learned just about everything from Rosey. He was a real institution around here. If for some reason, Rosey had been fired and I was asked to step in, my career in Pittsburgh would have ended after the next season. That's just the way it is in this business."

"We played in a pasture."

Milo Hamilton had paid his dues to become a major league baseball broadcaster.

"My first year in the big leagues was in 1953. I started in the business in 1950 at Davenport, Iowa. It was in the lower minors. Guys like Vernon Law, Harvey Kuenn and Jim Bunning all came through there. I was born and grew up in Fairfield, Iowa.

"A lot of broadcasters have been at it since they were 18. I wasn't sure what to do. I joined the Navy at the end of World War II, back in 1945. The war with Japan was still going on. I wanted to go like all red-blooded young men.

"Baseball was big where I came from. Growing up in the '30s, we had a one room schoolhouse, but every school had a baseball team. We played in a pasture, and it wasn't like the ballpark in 'Field of Dreams,' which was also in Iowa.

"As a little kid in Iowa in the '30s, I met Paul Waner and Lloyd Waner — Big Poison and Little Poison — who were stars with the Pirates. We played in the same pasture field where my dad had played. We played all day on Saturdays and Sundays. We chased cows into another pasture so we could play. When you slid into second base you had to slide through cow stuff before you found the real base.

"You had to wash your glove when you got home. They took up a collection in the seventh inning. People drove cars to get to the games. Growing up, I listened to Bob Elson doing the baseball games in Chicago. He was the second guy to go into the broadcast wing of the Hall of Fame, following Ford Frick. He was with WGN, which is still doing the games.

"There was also a guy named 'Dutch' Reagan re-creating the Cubs games on WHO in Des Moines. We know him better as Ronald Reagan, who became the president of the United States. The cigar stores in our town used to have Western Union tickers, too, and they posted the scores in their store window.

"I think it's an important assignment and responsibility to do baseball games on the radio or TV. People are letting you into their homes. I've always taken the approach that everybody listening is blind. So you're their eyes. It makes them feel like they're right there at the ballgame. When a guy goes up to the plate — click — you've got to give them a picture of that.

"I've had a good life. I've got a great family and I was lucky to land the wife I've had right from the start. A lot of guys have lost their wives in this business because of the time demands and time spent on the road. You have to have a wife who wants the life as much as you do and is a fan. Arlene is like that. She comes to every home game. She went to all the Little League games when my son, Mark, was playing. Our daughter, Patti Joy, liked to go to the games as well.

"We've been married for 45 years. I met her in the fall of 1951. Her name was Arlene Weiskopf and she was secretary to the football coach and athletic director at Davenport High School. I went there to talk to him. I talked to Arlene awhile and liked her right away. Her boss, 'Butch' Stolfa, said he had been thinking of trying to get us together. I told a friend Larry Edwards that day, 'Larry, I'm going to marry that girl.' I was doing sports on every level, at St. Ambrose College, at St. Ambrose Academy, at Davenport High School, and at the University of Iowa, about 55 miles away. I was doing about 100 basketball games a year and making about $55 a week, and was glad to get it.

"On our second date, I asked her to marry me. She said, 'Yeah.' It's been a great run."

Hamilton has had a variety of broadcasting experiences. He did football for 25 years, starting on the collegiate level at the University of Iowa with Forrest Evashevski. He was a play-by-play announcer for Georgia Tech when Bobby Dodd was coaching there, and did three years of Ohio State football when Woody Hayes was there, and University of Houston basketball when Guy Lewis was the coach. Those guys are all Hall of Famers.

Aaron's record home run call

Hamilton had time to think about what he ought to say when Henry Aaron hit his 715th home run to break Babe Ruth's career record. Many thoughts ran through Hamilton's mind.

"I don't think you can decide what you'll say ahead of time," he said. "The crowd and the action of the moment dictate your description.

"It was on my mind a lot, what I should say when Henry broke the record," he went on. "I thought about the obvious things, drawing the parallels between the two players, like both being 40 when they hit 714. I wondered if I should say something as he touched each of the bases. I guess I might have been rehearsing in the back of my mind without even knowing it."

Hamilton has had a voice in more historical moments in baseball history than most announcers because he has been at it since 1953, when he broke into the big leagues doing the St. Louis Browns in their last year of existence.

"It was my first season with the old Browns," he recalled. "I was doing the television and had only been there a week. Bobo Holloman pitched a no-hitter. The unusual thing about it was that he was sent to the minor leagues two weeks later and never pitched in the big leagues again."

When the Browns moved to Baltimore the next season, Hamilton stayed in St. Louis to work with the Cardinals, who had shared Sportsmens Park with the Browns. With the Cardinals that year, he described the doubleheader in which Stan "The Man" Musial — the pride of Donora, Pa. — set an all-time record by hitting five home runs in the two games.

Ironically, Hamilton was also on the mike 20 years later when Nate Colbert of the San Diego Padres equaled the Musial mark by hitting five home runs in a doubleheader at Atlanta Stadium. To add to the irony, Colbert, who grew up in St. Louis, had been in the stands at the doubleheader when Musial set the record.

Milo moved to Chicago to do the Cubs' games and, in 1955, he called the play-by-play of another no-hitter. "Sam Jones pitched the no-hitter for the Cubs against the Pirates," he said. "Jones was struggling to stay in the big leagues, and he walked the bases loaded in the ninth inning with a 4-0 lead. A home run not only would ruin the no-hitter, but it would also tie the game. Then, unbelievably, he struck out the side — Dick Groat, Roberto Clemente and Frank Thomas."

Hamilton didn't mention it, but Nellie King was pitching that day for the Pirates. King, of course, would later work with Bob Prince and Jim Woods in the Pirates' broadcast booth.

Hamilton was doing the Cubs in 1956 when Ernie Banks hit five grand slam home runs that season to set a big league record.

Hamilton covered another no-hitter while working with the White Sox, and three more while working for the Braves.

The night after I interviewed him, Hamilton covered another no-hitter. Francisco Cordova went nine innings and Ricardo Rincon came on to pitch the 10th inning as the Pirates beat the Astros on a three-run homer by Mark Smith.

It was the first no-hit game for the Pirates since John Candelaria accomplished that feat in August of 1976. Hamilton called that game, too. "The Dodgers threw a lefty that day so we started Bill Robinson instead of Rich Hebner," said Hamilton. "He put two runs on the board early. Candy worked his way through a lot of trouble and pitched a no-hitter."

He remembers broadcasting another magic home run in baseball history.

"I was doing the White Sox games, and they closed the season on a Saturday night, rather than a Sunday as they normally did," said Hamilton. "When the White Sox didn't play, we would recreate another game from the Western Union ticker. That day we did the game between the Yankees and the Red Sox when Roger Maris hit his 61st home run."

Hamilton said that even though the broadcast of the Maris home run was not live from the stadium, great lengths were taken to make it sound like the broadcast was coming right from the ballpark.

"We did so many games that way that we were really able to make it sound real," recalled Hamilton. "It was very dramatic; the homer had to be hit that day; and that gave us plenty of opportunity for drama in the re-creation.

"The Western Union ticker even recorded when Maris tipped his hat to the crowd and I passed it on to the listeners."

Lanny Frattare and Milo Hamilton had high hopes when they teamed up as Pirates' broadcasting team at spring training in 1976.

Bill Virdon
A Prince of a fellow

"He treated me as good
as you'd want to be treated."

This was the morning after one of the magic moments in Pirates baseball history. It was July 12, 1997. The night before pitchers Francisco Cordova and Ricardo Rincon, a righty-lefty parlay from Mexico, had combined to pitch a no-hitter against the Houston Astros. Cordova went nine innings and Rincon came in to close it out. Mark Smith hit a three-run homer to win it in the bottom of the tenth, and the crowd went crazy.

It was a fireworks night in more ways than advertised, and it was witnessed by a sellout crowd of 44,119. It was the first combined no-hitter in the club's history. It was the first no-hitter by a Pirates pitcher since John Candelaria shut out the Dodgers, 2-0, on August 9, 1976.

Jackie Robinson's No. 42 was retired at ceremonies that same sultry night in the Summer of '97 as it was throughout major league baseball that month. The win put the Pirates back in a first place tie with the Astros.

"It was as good a night as I've seen here," said Pirates manager Gene Lamont. Club owner Kevin McClatchy called it "the greatest night I've had in baseball."

Those who were there, or watched it on television, will never forget it. The Pirates were handing out posters to commemorate the event within a few weeks.

In the not-too-distant future there will be 441,000 fans who will swear they were there, as well as at Forbes Field the day Bill Mazeroski hit the home run to win the 1960 World Series. Virdon can honestly say he was at both history-making events.

Virdon was also a coach on the 1971 world champions and the manager in 1972 when the Pirates were but one out from having a shot at their second consecutive trip to the World Series.

My wife and I were playing bridge with neighborhood friends at their home the night of the combined no-hitter, and never turned on the TV. We didn't even know what happened till the next day. We missed out on all the fun while we were playing cards.

I had been at Three Rivers Stadium the night before the no-hitter victory by the Bucs, and the day after. The Bucs were bombed by the Astros on Thursday and Friday nights, by 7-0 and 10-0. I did get to see them beat the Astros, 5-3, on Sunday to split the four-game series. I missed a game that people who were there or watched it on TV will be talking about for years.

I recall listening to the post-game show on the radio returning home on Friday night, and hearing Bucs' broadcaster and former pitcher Bob Walk say, "Well, it wasn't the Pirates night. But tomorrow night it can be a whole different matter. That's the beauty of baseball."

"Sure, Bob, sure," I said to an empty car. And Walk was right.

That's one of the mystifying and compelling aspects of sports, especially baseball. You just never know when something special is going to occur. It could come in the season opener, or in the playoffs or in a championship series. More often than not, it happens when you least expect it — a no-hitter following two blow-out setbacks, for instance.

Roberto Clemente and Willie Stargell, Mario Lemieux and Jaromir Jagr, Terry Bradshaw and Franco Harris all had great moments in mid-season games that didn't gain the greatest attention. You just never know...

Bill Virdon saw all three games between the Pirates and Astros, as well as the Thursday night game that opened the four-game series. As a player or coach or manager, for the home team or the visitors, Virdon has seen more than his share of baseball. Altogether, in one manner or another, Virdon worked 25 years in the Pirates organization. Virdon was 66 and complaining of a balky back, but his enthusiasm for the game itself was still the same.

Virdon was there when Maz hit the home run leading off the bottom of the ninth inning to win the 1960 World Series, and had been a major figure in keeping the Pirates alive that special sunny afternoon and making Maz's heroics possible. It was Virdon who hit the ball that took a bad bounce into the Adam's apple of Yankees' shortstop Tony Kubek in a much-discussed sequence that kept a rally going.

Virdon was the lead-off hitter for the Pirates in that 1960 World Series, unless you're counting Billy Eckstein, who sang the National Anthem. Virdon drove downtown at 1:30 a.m. to join in the civic celebration with teammates Dick Groat and Bob Skinner and their wives. Those six returned to Forbes Field in the wee hours of the morning because Skinner's car was still parked nearby. They stood and stared at a silent Forbes Field the day after the joint had been shaken to its steel girders.

Such memories are still vivid for Virdon. He smiles that knowing smile of his when reminded of such details. Virdon was there for many magic moments in Pirates history and had a hand in many of them one way or another.

He had also been a close friend of Bob Prince, closer than most of the players as far as spending time with Prince away from the ballpark. At first glance, Virdon and Prince seem like an odd couple. Virdon has always been a conservative, virtuous, close-mouthed individual — just the opposite of Prince — but there's more than meets the eye with this guy.

The morning after...

Francisco Cordova was found running in the outfield the morning after he and Ricardo Rincon had combined to pitch a 10-inning no-hitter, the first of its kind in Pittsburgh baseball history. Cordova went the first nine innings in dramatic 3-0 victory over Houston Astros. The July 11, 1997 game was the highlight of the season. The 44,119 who were there won't ever forget it.

Photos by Jim O'Brien

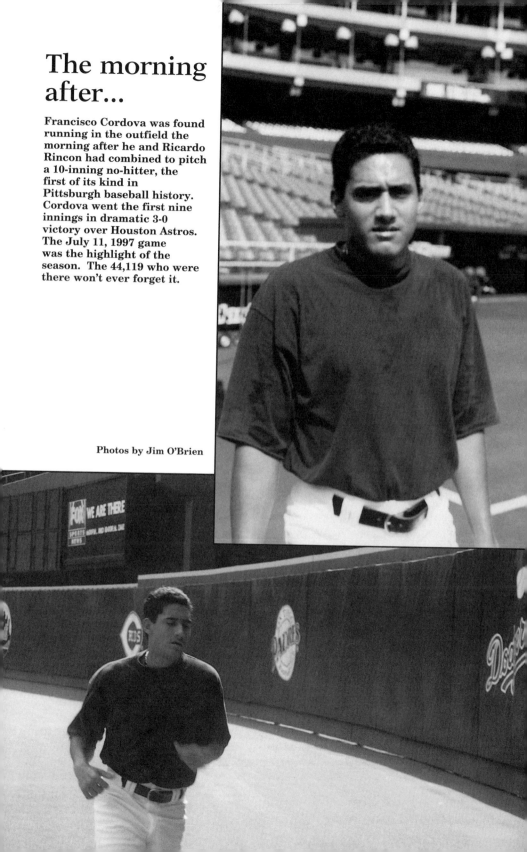

He was great at chasing after fly balls — patrolling the outfield next to Clemente for so many years — and throwing to the right base from center field at Forbes Field, one of the most spacious working areas in all of major league baseball. He could handle the bat well, too, especially early in his career. In 1956, the year he came from the Cardinals in exchange for Pittsburgh-born Bobby DelGreco, a defensive outfielder, and a left-handed pitcher named Dick Littlefield, Virdon led the Bucs with 170 hits and a .344 batting average.

Cardinals GM Frank Lane claimed it was the worst trade he ever made. It was one of Joe L. Brown's best trades.

Virdon was popular and employable and found a way to get paid to be around baseball in one capacity or another over an extended period.

Just when he thought he had left baseball behind him for good, one of his former players, Larry Dierker, called and asked him to help him when Dierker became manager of the Astros for the 1997 season.

"Larry Dierker was new and he needed somebody he could trust who knew his way around the league," explained Nellie King, one of Virdon's biggest boosters, when I broached the subject of Virdon with him during a meeting at his home.

I telephoned Virdon at the Westin William Penn Hotel in downtown Pittsburgh on Friday morning during the four-game series in July, 1997, to see if I could schedule an interview with him. I invited him to lunch, but he already had a commitment. He said Milo Hamilton, the Astros' broadcast announcer, was taking him and the other Astros' coaches to Poli's Restaurant in Squirrel Hill. It was Hamilton, coincidentally enough, who had such a hard time following Prince during a four-year stint after Prince was fired.

Hamilton was broadcasting the Cardinals games when Virdon broke into the big leagues in St. Louis back in 1955.

Virdon said we could talk before the game on Sunday. I checked the clubhouse when I arrived and was told I would find Virdon out on the field during the Astros' batting practice.

There were few fans in the stands when I walked out of the visitors' dugout onto the playing turf at Three Rivers. It seemed strange to be there the morning after, the quiet scene a far cry from the noisy activity the night before. I caught Cordova jogging alone on the clay-colored warning track in right field. I snapped some photographs of him and he even stopped and posed for me. I would have liked to have talked to him, but he spoke Spanish, and that language eluded me and was a source of constant frustration in my high school and college days.

It was great to see Cordova up close, though, the day after his great pitching performance. He still had a glow about him.

Later, sitting in the visitors' dugout, I spotted Virdon out on the field. He was positioned behind a protective screen at second base. There were Astros at bat and Astros in the field. The screen, about the same size as a screen door, was there so Virdon wouldn't get struck by a batted ball while he retrieved balls thrown in to him by the outfielders. The man who had worn No. 18 with the Pirates was now wearing No. 59 with the Astros.

Virdon moved quietly and efficiently about midfield, catching one or two hoppers, collecting balls that had been rolled his way, filling a bag with balls. When the bag was full, he carried it in and poured it into a large wire basket within reach of the batting practice pitcher. Then he'd fill up another bag with balls.

It seemed like a rather mundane task for a man of Virdon's stature. I not only remembered him as the Pirates' centerfielder, and later a manager and coach, but I also remembered him, from my days at the *New York Post* in the '70s, as the manager of the New York Yankees and later the Astros and Expos.

He's the answer to a trivia question: Who was the only manager of the Yankees never to manage a game at Yankee Stadium? He managed the team during the two year period that the Yankees played their home games at Shea Stadium, sharing it with the Mets, while Yankee Stadium underwent an extensive renovation. My Pittsburgh connection helped me as an ice-breaker with Virdon when I went out to Shea Stadium to interview him when I was on the baseball beat.

Two Pittsburgh-bred pitchers were with the Yankees in those days, "Sudden" Sam McDowell and George "Doc" Medich. Both later came to the Pirates.

Virdon did some stretching, spoke to some Astros, and gave me a "hi" sign to let me know he saw me, and would be in to see me in a few moments. Virdon had another visitor in former Pirates pitcher Dave Giusti in the same dugout later in the morning.

To me, an outsider who didn't understand the compelling hold baseball had on the people who worked in its environs, seeing Virdon collecting baseballs looked demeaning, somehow beneath his dignity. But that was my hangup. Virdon was merely doing his job, for which he was well paid.

Nellie King figured his old friend Virdon was making more than the average baseball coach, as much as a hundred thousand dollars, which is probably slightly better than high-seniority garbage collectors make in Pittsburgh.

"Virdon didn't think it was a demeaning job, I can assure you of that," claimed King in a later conversation.

There are a lot of pedestrian tasks associated with baseball, or any staged sports events for that matter, and someone has to do it. As Virdon views it, picking up baseballs on a sunny Sunday morning at Three Rivers Stadium beats most of the jobs he had as a young man in Missouri by a large margin.

Any baseball job was better than any job in the real world, as Virdon viewed it.

"Oh, yeah, I've done it a long time," Virdon said with a smile while flashing his bespectacled blue eyes when asked if he still enjoyed life on the road with a baseball team. "The last job I really had was driving a propane truck back in West Plains, Missouri, in the winter before I came to the big leagues. I also worked on an assembly line for Caterpillar in Peoria, Illinois. I once had a route for Coca-Cola in West Plains. Those were all pre-baseball jobs."

Virdon let that information sink in awhile. "This is better," he said. "Much better."

"I remember him diving out of the third floor..."
— Bill Virdon

The subject was Bob Prince, and Virdon warmed to the task quickly. He has never been a gabby guy, but you could tell right away that he enjoyed reflecting on Bob Prince.

"We had an outstanding relationship," said Virdon. "He treated me as good as you'd want to be treated. We went out sometimes, a couple of us, and we'd have a drink once in a while on the road.

"I remember him diving out of the third story on a dare bet of $20 (with Dick Stuart) when we were staying at the Chase Hotel in St. Louis. I didn't see it. I was in the hotel when it happened. The word got around fast. He was an experienced diver and college swimmer and he knew how far he could jump and still clear it. He knew what he was doing.

"He was always full of fun, always talking, always telling a story or a joke. He was fun to be around.

"He called me Quail. I came here in 1956 in May. For the rest of the year, I hit .340 and ended up at .319. Many of the hits I got were flares over the infield. Prince called them dying quails. He called me 'Quail' affectionately."

Virdon looks back on his days as a player with the Pirates with a great sense of pride, though the team records weren't always so hot. "Generally, they were all good years," he said. "We had good and bad clubs. We started out struggling."

The Pirates finished seventh in the first two seasons under Bobby Bragan, then second and then fourth in the first two full seasons under Danny Murtaugh. Then they won the World Series in 1960. They slumped to sixth the year after the World Series and eighth two years later. This only points up what a miracle year 1960 was.

"In 1958, we challenged for the pennant and started coming into our own," said Virdon. "In 1959, we dropped down a little bit. All my years, most of it under Murtaugh, I couldn't have asked for more. It was all fun and games. I don't remember any real adversity."

How did Prince play a part in that respect?

"He and Hoak got into it one night over something," recalled Virdon. "I was in the place. Hoak knocked him off the stool and pushed him. Hoak was like that, though. They'd been debating. Bob had his own ideas. Generally, he captured most of those arguments. He'd outlast everyone else. He was different. It was great that he was still there when we won the '71 world championship.

"His wife, Betty, is a saint. She put up with Bob all those years. Bob was good to her, but Bob was different. She looked after him pretty good. She and my wife are still close.

"He was something else, eccentric. Everyone loved him. It didn't seem to make any difference how much he had to drink. He was always in command. He was as big a booster of the Pirates as the team ever had.

"I played here ten years altogether, nine the first time and then I came back (in 1968) for one more. I coached four originally, then coached one more, then four more. I managed the team in 1972-73. That added up to 19 years. Then I worked for the organization for six more years altogether, for a total of 25 years."

Virdon was with Jim Leyland in the 1996 season, and then went to Houston when Leyland left for Miami. While he worked for the Pirates for 25 years, he never bought a home in Pittsburgh.

"I never planned it that way," said Virdon. "The reason I didn't move here to begin with was because of what happened to me when I was with St. Louis. After spending my first year there, I got traded to Pittsburgh and it made me think that I shouldn't sink roots anywhere. I couldn't count on staying. So I made my home in Missouri, and eventually moved to Springfield.

"It's worked out fine. Another reason I didn't move was because I never liked to be bothered in the wintertime. It was my way to get away from it. Somebody's always asking you to do something. My wife, Shirley, is in Houston at this time, so we're together. My family always joined me wherever I was staying after school let out.

"When the girls were in school when I first started, we'd take them out in the spring and bring them with us to spring training. We'd get a tutor for them and they'd do their schoolwork a couple hours a day. We spent a lot of time together. When spring training was over, they'd go back to Missouri until school was over. Then they'd join me in Pittsburgh.

"Prince introduced me to a lot of people in Pittsburgh. That helped, too.

"It was outstanding. I couldn't ask for a better city. The main thing was winning. I didn't have the good years some of the other guys had, but I was well accepted here."

Asked what he thought about the way people were responding to the present-day Pirates, Virdon said, "I think it's great. Last night was a great example. A full house for a great game. They have the fans on their side again. They're playing hard. That's a big factor as far as the fans are concerned. Pittsburgh fans have always appreciated good effort.

"Baseball will be better off in Pittsburgh if they have a new ballpark. I don't know what's right or wrong, as far as financing it, or the politics involved. If it keeps baseball in Pittsburgh it will be worth it."

"They (players) aren't afraid to work if you make them work."

Virdon thought he was finished with baseball after Leyland left to go to Miami.

"I had decided the year before I wasn't going to coach again," he said. "I like to go to spring training and work with the outfielders. Life on the road is more wearing when you get up there in age. I never planned on doing this again this year.

"Then I got a call from Tal Smith. He was president and general manager when I was managing at Houston, and he was an assistant to Gabe Paul when I was managing the Yankees in New York. Larry Dierker was the new manager in Houston. Tal told me Larry would like me to come coach with him. He thought I could help him. I knew Larry was a sharp guy. It was a good offer. And they had a chance to win. That helps. I decided to do it.

"Sometimes I feel 66. That feeling comes and goes. For the past month, I have had a bad back. I got it from hitting fungoes. Then one day it just hit me. For that month, I felt 66."

Virdon came into baseball with a different generation of ballplayers with a different set of rules. Different attitudes had chased good friends like Bill Mazeroski out of the game because he couldn't stomach some of the players.

While he knows exactly what Mazeroski's objections were about, he's been able to remain in the game, and deal with a different breed of ballplayers. He too grew weary of players who refused to perform because of minor injuries, of drug problems he didn't know about until it was too late, of players more concerned about dollar signs than bunt signs.

"It's different, no question," said Virdon. "I still have a problem with some players. In general, I don't care how much money they make. Players, in general, like to win and they aren't afraid to work if you make them work. They don't object when you put it on the line.

"The biggest difference is not the money. The baseball players are better than they've ever been, but ballclubs aren't close to what they were. You don't have depth. The talent is spread too thin.

"You don't have competition for starting jobs. They used to know if they didn't produce they wouldn't have their job. There are a lot of distractions today, and that comes with the money and the increased media demands. When I was playing, all you had to worry about was baseball. Every player today wants to do well. The feeling for the team isn't what it used to be, that's all.

"I don't think I had anybody work as hard as I worked when I was a player. The secret to playing the outfield is knowing where the ball is going, especially if you're looking at it while you're on the move.

"Andy Van Slyke was good at it. Clemente did it more naturally than I did. I had to work. I prided myself in knowing where to play in the outfield for different hitters. I tried to get better. I didn't sit on my laurels; I couldn't afford to. I'd shag flies from a fungo hitter for 25 to 30 minutes. I'd go out there and field the ball for as long as anybody would hit the ball to me.

"I'd ask the fungo hitter to move me around. Don't get me wrong, I didn't do that every day. But I did it often and I worked hard to improve my skills. I was fortunate in Forbes Field because I had all the room in the world to work. I didn't have to worry about fences.

"Clemente was easy to play with. He could catch it, wherever it went. I played with him ten straight years. I only ran into him one time, and that was during the '60 World Series. I caught the ball. The fans were so loud and boisterous, I couldn't hear him. I had the ball; I saw it all the way. I held onto it after we collided. The rule of thumb is that you should yield to the centerfielder. I never had to worry about balls to my left because Clemente could catch anything."

It was a mutual admiration society. "He makes everything look easy," Clemente once commented about Virdon.

"At Forbes Field, most of the seats were close to the field, close to the action," said Virdon. "Today, they don't feel a part of it like they did back then."

"It's like walking on a cloud."
— Bill Virdon

"I wanted to play the game ever since I was big enough to play. I always looked for a game. I liked to play any kind of ball, not just baseball. In fact, when I was younger, I played more football than I played baseball."

Virdon grew up in Michigan, and was a Detroit Tigers' fan in his youth. Hank Greenberg, the Tigers' home run hitting star who would finish up his career in Pittsburgh, was his boyhood favorite. Virdon said he listened to recreations of ticker-tape reports on games.

His family moved from Michigan to Missouri when he was in grade school.

He broke in with the Yankees in 1950. He was traded to the Cardinals in 1955 because the Yankees were set in centerfield with a well-muscled young man from Oklahoma named Mickey Mantle.

Virdon came to the Pirates in a trade on May 17, 1956. It was Joe L. Brown's first big trade. Brown liked the idea of having a left-handed batter who threw with his right hand playing centerfield. Virdon finished up with a .319 batting average, second best in the league.

When Larry Shepard became manager of the Pirates in 1968, he hired Virdon as a batting coach. Shepard gave way to Alex Grammas in the stretch run in 1969. Then Murtaugh came back from a heart problem that had sidelined him to resume managing. Murtaugh, in his third stint as manager of the Bucs, directed the team to divisional titles in 1970 and 1971, winning the World Series over the Orioles in Baltimore in 1971.

When Murtaugh had another health scare, Virdon became the manager of the Pirates for the 1972 season. Virdon directed the team to a third consecutive divisional title. The Pirates were 67-69 in the 1973 season when Virdon was replaced in favor of Murtaugh with 26 games remaining on the schedule. Brown didn't think anybody could manage like Murtaugh. And Danny directed the Bucs to two more back-to-back divisional crowns.

Virdon would manage another 11 years with three different teams in the major leagues. He managed in Pittsburgh in 1972 and 1973, the Yankees in 1974-75, the Astros from 1975 to 1982 and in Montreal in 1983 and was fired there during the 1984 season.

"I've done about everything I've wanted to do in baseball, although I missed a couple of times by an out or two of getting a team to the Series," he said, recalling the 1972 Pirates and the 1980 Astros, which lost out in the final game of the NL championship series.

"What I regret most about those teams were the players that were involved, the guys who never got another chance to go to the World Series. That was the tough part about it. I've been in baseball for a long time, but there's still no feeling like being in the playoffs or the World Series. It's like walking on a cloud."

Bill Virdon at 1997 autograph signing session

Fans remember "The Gunner"

"He taught me sports and sportsmanship."

When I was 14 and living in Brookline, about six of us went over to play for the Mt. Lebanon Wildcats. There were guys from Dormont on the team, too. It was a football team for kids 14 to 16 years old, and it was a first class organization. It was really a neat thing. They had the best equipment and their own team doctor.

"Ave and Jim Daniell were the coaches. They were brothers and had both been All-American football players as linemen at Pitt and Ohio State, respectively. Bob Prince was the athletic director, so to speak, and he got the money to pay the bills and he promoted the team.

"Most of the kids who played for the Wildcats were too small or too young to play for the high school team, but Prince was always telling people we were better than the Mt. Lebanon High School team. He loved stuff like that. I was younger than most of the guys and played tackle on the team. I would later be a back at South Hills High School before I went to Pitt.

"I remember, in particular, playing games on the North Side against the Perry Atoms, who were coached by Tom Foerster, who became the county commissioner, and playing in Braddock. Prince was always stirring up something on the sideline. We were supposed to be from Mt. Lebanon and we were the 'cake-eaters' and all that stuff, but we won more than our share of games against kids from tougher neighborhoods.

"Prince made a big deal about this, and he had a way of infuriating the fans and coaches from the other teams. Prince had an ability to agitate people pretty good. The crowds would really get on us, and Prince would be hollering back at them. Ave and Jim Daniell were big fellows and they would flank Prince and keep people from getting to him when we left the field. They protected him pretty good.

"I remember we played in the Porridge Bowl at Mt. Lebanon High School against a team from Cleveland. Jim Daniell, who had connections in Ohio and was an executive in the steel business, arranged the game. It seemed like a big deal at the time."

— Ralph Jelic, Mt. Lebanon, Pa.

* * *

"I can remember him driving a white Pontiac convertible and coming around helping out with the Mt. Lebanon Wildcats. I was on the team and I remember we played in the Porridge Bowl against a team from Ohio. I grew up in Brookline, but there were a bunch of us who went over to Mt. Lebanon because they had the best equipment. Prince took good care of us. We had the best uniforms money could buy. He'd take us up to his house once in a awhile for some snacks. He even got one of our games on the radio."

— Mel Lucas, South Park Twp., Pa.

* * *

"Bob Prince always had a special appreciation for his fans, right from the beginning. This was in the late '40s, before he got involved with a lot of stuff. He was on WJAS Radio, and he had a show called 'Bob Prince And His Case Of Sports,' which he did out of a studio at the Chamber of Commerce Building. I was one of four girls in their early teens who took a real liking to Bob. I was Marge Ciganik then and I lived on the North Side; I'm Marge Kennedy now. There was Kay Colleran from Oakland, and Bernie Andrasko (Stewart) from McKees Rocks and Dorothy Macey (Kirschner), who was also from the North Side. It was funny how we were from all over the city, yet we got together to get behind Bob.

"We started to go down to watch him do his show. We liked him a lot. We were his first fans. He also would go to WWSW at the Sherwyn Hotel, which is now the main building at Point Park College, and he and Rosey Rowswell would recreate games from ticker tape reports. That was interesting to see. You really had to have an imagination to do that.

"Every time Bob saw us out at Forbes Field he'd take us into the ballpark with him. He signed a photo of himself for me once and wrote, 'To Margie, who likes Ralph.' He hung out a lot with Ralph Kiner in those days. We weren't big fans of Ralph, really, but we told Bob we were because he liked him so much. We've never forgotten the way he treated us, and how much he appreciated his first fans."

— Marge Kennedy
Greensburg, Pa.

* * *

"A story told to me about Bob Prince: At the Allegheny Club prior to a night ball game, Bob was at the bar. He took a full shot glass and a bottle of Coke between his thumb and forefinger, put them to his lips and downed all but a little of the Coke in one swoosh."

— Bob Whalen,
Aliquippa, Pa.

"Dead air didn't used to be a crime. The pace of life was slower. People just liked to be sitting in the living room listening to the ballgame."
— Myron Cope, Sportscaster

This letter was written upon the death of Bob Prince:

"I was nine years old and he was the voice on the radio broadcasting a game I loved. I knew that voice and it denoted a certain order in life: that the Bucs win or lose, were our ball club; that local breweries made a beer for every sportsman in town and that summer was baseball. It was simple: You lived in Pittsburgh, loved the Pirates and 'The Gunner' was a friend. From April till season's end, that was the way it was.

"When Bob Prince was forced from the broadcast booth, baseball and I parted company. The game suddenly became slow, tedious, even a little predictable. Many of the players were no longer eager participants, but became 'professional athletes,' concerned with contracts and 'play-me-or-trade-me' demands. A trip to the stadium was now a measured task no longer worth the traffic and parking hassles. I didn't care anymore.

"Now Bob Prince is gone. At age 36, just as at age 9, I can still hear his voice. But now the Pirates are not my team, the local brewery advertises aerobic lite beer and football is a summer game. I am gonna miss ya, Gunner!"

— Martin P. Brocco
Upper St. Clair
June 18, 1985

* * *

"When I was 15 and he was 29, we lived in the same town. He taught me sports and sportsmanship. And if I looked like I was straying, we would end up at his apartment, bother his wife, eat ice cream, talk sports and peruse his scrap books.

"When I was 29 and he 43, we witnessed the greatest baseball game in Pittsburgh history. I saw it all; he missed the best part.

"When I was 40 and he 54, he and his friend Roberto thrilled me with their play and play-by-play.

"When I was 48 and he 62, we watched the greatest come-from-behind a Pittsburgh baseball team ever performed.

"When I was 54 and he 68, he left me.

"As we traveled through the years together, he always made me feel that I was 15 and he was 29. Until the day I die, I will think that I can turn on the radio and there will be that young friend of mine and his beloved Bucs."

— Benjamin J. Bain,
Marietta, Ohio

> **"I've gone from ticker tape (Western Union re-creations of road games) to satellite. That's how long I've been around."**
> **— Bob Prince**

"Our family met him in 1971. He didn't wear socks, I remember that. He showed us his World Series ring. He talked to us for some time. My brother was fascinated by him not wearing any socks."

— Rose Kerfoot,
Moon Township, Pa.

* * *

"We were in seventh and eighth grade back in the late '40s when we first started coming to Ladies Day. We'd take the streetcar to Forbes Field. You could get in for 50 cents in those days for a doubleheader. We'd take our lunch. We had a good team and we wanted to see Ralph Kiner hit some home runs. We're real fans. We'd go to Cleveland to see the Indians and Yankees play. We go back a long way with the Pirates. Our parents used to tell us stories. We loved Bob Prince."

— Helen Cepic Klassen,
Marilyn Schenck Thurn,
Pitcairn, Pa.

* * *

"As a kid, I lived up on The Bluff by Mercy Hospital. I sold newspapers at the hospital. That's where I met Honus Wagner and Frankie Frisch, when they were patients. Frisch had me bring in a chicken dinner for him that my mother cooked at home because he wasn't happy with the food there. I never got their autographs or anything. Later on, after I'd gotten out of Fifth Avenue High School, I was driving a truck for Pepsi-Cola, working for Chuck Mangold out of their McKees Rocks bottling plant. I was delivering Pepsi one day in 1955 up in the Hill District, and I stopped at the B&M Restaurant at the corner of Herron and Wylie Avenues. Roman Mejias and Roberto Clemente were sitting inside at a table. I introduced myself to both of them, and was talking to Clemente, who was in his first year here and didn't speak very good English. He was nice to me, though, and he gave me a pair of tickets for that night's ballgame at Forbes Field. I went and that's the night Vernon Law pitched 18 innings. (Law left the game with the score tied 1-1. He had given up nine hits, walked but three and struck out 12.) You'll never see that again. Oh, yeah, I got hell when I got home. My wife thought I had stopped somewhere on the way home and been out drinking. Bob Prince knew Mangold and he got his son, Bob Jr., a job when he was about 18 working in the bottling operation at Pepsi during the summer. One day I hollered over to him, 'Hey, Prince, your dad's on the radio,' and he responded by saying, 'To hell with him. Change the station.'"

— Bill Eckles,
Baldwin Twp., Pa.

Hall of Famer Frankie Frisch, the manager of the 1945 Pirates, demonstrates bunting motion for clubhouse gathering that included Spud Davis, cowboy movie star Roy Rogers, Bob Prince, Mort Cooper, Jake Flowers and Ken Gables.

PirateFest '98 faithful fans Helen Cepic Klassen and Marilyn Schenck Thurn remember when they used to take buses from Pitcairn to see Ralph Kiner and Pirates play at Forbes Field on Ladies Day games.

"For those of us old enough to remember him in the broadcast booth, Bob Prince's passing was an all-too-painful reminder that those carefree summers of our youth are gone forever.

"If you never heard him broadcast a baseball game, I can't possibly tell you how good he was — you had to be there. He enthralled us with stories even when the team was losing badly — and we kept the radio tuned to KDKA.

"When Ralph Kiner or Willie Stargell would hit a home run, his voice would explode with a 'Kiss it goodbye' as no other voice could. And — get this — he would croon 'we had 'em all-l-l-l the way' after a 17-inning nailbiter.

"Attendance problems? Prince could draw 40,000 with a wave of a babushka. He gave us a warm feeling with a simple 'hello' to his shut-in friends. And somehow, I'm not exactly sure how, he made us feel that Pittsburgh was sort of a small town, a community, and not just a place to store the suburbanites until they could escape at 5 o'clock.

"When Bob Prince died, not far from where Forbes Field used to stand, a piece of an era went with him. Smoke no longer spewed forth from our steel mills like it once did; the Jenkins Arcade was just a memory; and cars whizzed past the spot where Maz's home run left the park in 1960. Pittsburgh could console itself in the memory that not too long ago, a raspy-edged, velvety voice had you mesmerized and made us all feel like kids again.

"He lived life to the fullest. We should mourn for ourselves, and for a wonderful era that has passed away."

— Timothy Murray,
Malvern, Pa.

* * *

"The headline read, 'Bob Prince dies' and what a sad day that was in Pittsburgh sports history.

"Here we had Bob Prince's Bucs with the worst record in the major leagues. Then all of a sudden a month earlier hope sprung forth — not in another trade or a player, but in 'The Gunner' coming back to the Pirates' broadcast booth.

"Somehow those who loved and supported Bob felt that just his appearance and voice behind the ballclub would ignite a winning quality. Then he was gone again.

"Who else could have adequately replaced Rosey Rowswell? Being of an age to vividly remember Rosey and his impact on Pirates broadcasting, even when it was only a ticker tape play-by-play sent back to Pittsburgh from an away city where the Bucs were playing.

"Can one imagine trying to make this exciting? Well, those who remember know that Rosey Rowswell had that ability to keep you glued to his reports.

"His description of a home run was priceless. He would excitedly say, 'There goes a long deep drive to the outfield,' and then he would add, 'Open the window, Aunt Minnie — here it comes!' Then would come the sound of glass being smashed, and Rosey would come back with, 'She never made it.'

"Thankfully, for the Pirates organization, along came Bob Prince. And when one relates back, who else could have replaced Rosey in the eyes and ears of the fans?

"Like Rowswell, Bob had his own special expressions, like 'Bug on a rug' — 'kiss it goodbye' — 'bloop and a blast' — 'We had 'em all the way.'

"Bob was an exceptional M.C. at many social events in the tri-state area. He kept fans together from West Virginia, Eastern Ohio and even Cumberland, Maryland. It's difficult to evaluate his promotional success, but he undoubtedly was responsible for thousands of fans attending the ballyard.

"True, there were those who didn't appreciate Bob and his style of broadcasting, but they were a small minority and I would guess that many of them realized they were wrong a few years back after Bob was fired.

"Thankfully, Bob was brought back to the microphone for a few games before his death. He sounded so happy, like he had just arrived in heaven. God bless you, Bob Prince."

— Bob McVeigh,
Mars, Pa.

SRO crowd watched Pirates beat Cubs in doubleheader at Forbes Field on June 29, 1970.

177

Bob Prince Jr.
Chip off the old block

"I was always away somewhere"

Bob Prince Jr. looked perfect for the part. He had an impish, mischievous mug. He smiled whimsically as he talked about his life in the wings while his famous father held center stage wherever he went.

I had never met Bob Prince Jr. before, and I guess I expected him to look more like his dad, leaner, more angular. Instead, he looked and sounded more like his mother, Betty Prince, and bore a resemblance somewhere between a mature Leo Gorcey and a younger Jack Lemmon. Even so, there's a lot of the old man in his namesake.

He'd heard the Leo Gorcey look-alike line before, many times, he said. He agreed it fit, and it wasn't merely a mask. Gorcey was the gang-leader in the movie serial "The Bowery Boys," which Bob Jr. and I had enjoyed at our neighborhood theaters at Saturday matinees in our misspent youth.

The Bowery Boys were also called "The Dead-End Kids," and their mischief was mild, to say the least, compared to the crime and craziness of contemporary street gangs in the real world. Bob Prince Jr. and his father, for that matter, would have gotten along beautifully with the Bowery Boys.

Leo Gorcey and Huntz Hall portrayed hooligans who hung out with their pals in a drug store-soda fountain shop in New York City, driving shop owner Louie crazy with their short pockets and silly shenanigans. They also drove convertible clunkers, and got into all manner of mischief, or what was thought to be mischief in tamer times in the '40s and '50s. We'd mimic the Bowery Boys, or the Three Stooges, all the way home from the movie house, bumping and shoving each other.

His sister, Nancy, has watched "The Bowery Boys" on the American Movie Channel (AMC) cable outlet, and agrees that it's a good look-alike, in appearance and attitude.

"I wasn't a bad kid," Prince professed, "but I was a challenge for my parents. I liked to have a good time; I liked to have fun. I still do. I wasn't really that bad; I wasn't a ruffian; I never hurt anyone, and I didn't get into any real trouble."

His nickname was Beano. "Just like Beano Cook," he said with a smile.

He complains even today that his parents were always sending him away in his adolescent days. They were doing it for his own good, they insisted, to keep him out of trouble, so he would shape up. He's been away so long, it seems, that many prominent Pittsburgh sports people weren't aware that there was a Bob Prince Jr.

Jim O'Brien

Bob Prince Jr. relaxes in bed at his mother's home in Mt. Lebanon while recovering from hip replacement surgery in March, 1998. Overhead are portraits of him and sister Nancy from their childhood days.

Bomb scare...
        At an airport one summer, Bob Prince reassured Roberto Clemente about upcoming games against the Giants as they were boarding an airplane, saying, "Don't worry, we'll bomb 'em." A nervous stewardess called the security office. They called the FBI. And Prince was taken off the airplane and detained for questioning.

"There were times I wasn't sure, either," said the No. 1 and only son of the Pirates' popular broadcaster. "Since I didn't look anything like him, I thought maybe I was adopted. I'd go to the post office and check out the photos on the wall (the FBI's "Most Wanted" list) to see if anyone there looked like me, trying to find my real father."

Bob Jr. just peppers you with wisecracks like that, then laughs at length at his own lines. It's in the genes, his protests to the contrary. Anything for a laugh.

"My dad was on the road with the Pirates," he said, "and I was away, always away somewhere, while my mother looked after my sister Nancy and our dog at home. The dog was living a better life than I was."

"My dad was quite paranoid."
— Bob Prince Jr.

Since I had heard about him, and his personal struggles to establish his own identity, it was reassuring to see Bob Prince, Jr. in the flesh, or in pajamas, anyhow, when he was at his mother's place, recovering from hip-replacement surgery.

This was Monday, March 2, 1998, and Bob Jr. would be 54 in a month. I was only a year older, so we had a lot of common references. We were both the class clowns, eager to entertain everyone. We swapped stories. Our dads both drank and smoked too much, and were too often out of the house, entertaining everyone but their own family. Our dads died too soon, in their 60s, done in by too much booze and smoke, and we both wished we had a rain check to claim another day at the ballpark with them.

Bob Jr. was fun to talk to, a ready smile, a ready story. I liked him right from the start. He cracked me up with his constant complaints and funny remarks. Yes, there was a touch of self-pity and rancor, and he blamed that on his father as well. "My dad was quite paranoid," he said, "so I guess I got that from him, too."

There was a lot of his father in him, more than first met the eye. He liked to boast about the bad ol' days, his dad's great thirst and gift for the theatrical, his own penchant for sneaking off for a drink to lighten the day, and how they both tested his mother's mettle.

"Don't make this out to be an alcoholics' ward," he said, and laughed at his own line.

One of his father's co-workers, Jack Bogut, had said "Bob Prince was always coloring outside the lines," and "he was an event looking for a place to happen," and the son smiled at the familiar descriptions of his dapper dad.

"He knew everybody," said Prince. "He introduced me to Toots Shor at his saloon in New York, and just about everybody else who

180

crossed his path when I was along for the ride. He introduced me to Johnny Majors, to Billy Conn and to Joey Diven, and guys like Jack Cargo. I knew all the characters in the sports world. He knew the chairman of the board at every company, and he could call them to get their support for any fund-raiser he was involved with.

"He took me to three games at Penn State when he was broadcasting the games there. I met Joe Paterno. If he sees me, Paterno will still talk to me. I went to the Duquesne basketball games with my dad and I met the Ricketts brothers (Dick and Dave) and Sihugo Green.

"As an announcer, my dad was great in baseball, terrible in hockey and fair in football and basketball.

"He introduced me to Howard Cosell, and I talked to Cosell a few times. After Dad lost his job here, I thought of something Cosell had said earlier. Cosell told me my dad would never make it outside of Pittsburgh. 'He's a homer and it won't work in other towns,' Cosell said. He told me that, and he was right.

"I asked Cosell if he really smoked Kentucky Club tobacco, which he appeared in an ad for. 'I wouldn't smoke that crap if you paid me,' Cosell told me. Then again, my dad did all those commercials for years for beer companies in Pittsburgh, and he never drank beer. He couldn't stand the taste."

Bob Jr. had been living in Michigan for 14 years, 16 counting an earlier stint, with his third wife, Ellen, and their son, a 13-year-old named Bob Prince III. He was in his third marriage and, by his own account, his second childhood. He was normally at home in Clarkston, a community 30 miles southwest of Detroit. Earlier, he had lived in Grand Rapids and Troy.

His two daughters by his first marriage, to a hometown girl, were living in Venetia, just over the Washington County border not far from their grandmother's home. Kimberly Prince Bacchiochi, 33, was the mother of two boys, and Casey Prince, 31, was planning on getting married. Bob Jr. kept in touch with both of them. His second marriage lasted eight months and there were no children.

Once the ne'er-do-well son of the Pirates broadcaster, with a reputation as a habitual hell-raiser, Bob Jr. had cleaned up his act considerably, and was proud of himself and his family. "I loved my dad, and I miss him dearly," he said. "I didn't always. I hated him, at first, when he sent me away to school. When they closed the gates behind me, it really hurt me. But I got over that. He never hit me, to my knowledge. We had some great times together. I just wish we had spent more time together. He was kind to me. He helped me get jobs for a long time."

His head was propped up by two pillows as he sat up in the bed he had commandeered from his mother, bumping Betty Prince to a couch in the living room for a week. Bob Jr. was being treated like a Prince in his mother's comfortable townhouse in Woodridge, a pricey condominium complex in Mt. Lebanon, a suburb about eight miles south of Pittsburgh.

Bob had come back home to have hip replacement surgery eleven days earlier, February 20, at St. Clair Hospital. He had grown up, sort of, in Mt. Lebanon and later neighboring Upper St. Clair when his parents moved there during his high school years. Betty had come back to Mt. Lebanon after the house she and Bob shared in the Deerfield Manor section of Upper St. Clair became too much for her. Her husband remains a legend at the St. Clair Country Club, and grandfathers in both communities remember when they played sand-lot football as kids for the Mt. Lebanon Wildcats, a team sponsored and promoted by Bob Prince Sr. that always went first-cabin.

Betty could have slept in one of the beds in the guest rooms upstairs of her two-story unit, but then she wouldn't have been able to hear her son when he called for something. She was being a good mother, looking after her son hand and foot, as they say, as he recovered from his surgery. Betty was battling a lingering cold, and was coughing a lot. She sat on an ottoman at the bottom of the bed briefly, and Bob Jr. would frequently address her as "Mother" when he sought a second motion to confirm a fact or two.

"Where'd you get that outfit?" his mother asked him, shaking her head at the sight of her son when he sat on the edge of the bed at one point. Bob Jr. was wearing Carolina blue and white striped pajama bottoms, a black and gold print pajama top, a garish black and white large-sleeved silk robe, a combination that even his dad wouldn't have dared to wear. He waved his hands a lot when he talked, just like his dad.

When I called a few days later to ask if I could come back and shoot some more photographs of him and his mother, Bob Jr. asked, "Do you want me to wear that outfit I had on the other night?"

There were framed photographs of his family filling walls to his left, just past the crutches that were leaning against the wall between the bed and the nightstand. Some showed Bob Prince Sr. in his colorful sport jackets and signature lop-sided grin. One of them showed Bob Jr. and his sister, Nancy, sitting on cement steps in front of their childhood home — "that's my favorite photo of the kids," boasted Betty — and another showed a handsome Bob Prince Jr. in his dress uniform at Valley Forge Military Academy. "Doesn't he look like his grandfather in that one?" asked his mother, who said she says goodnight to her gallery upon retiring each evening, and good morning when she gets up. The grandfather had been a graduate of West Point and was a career military man. Bob Prince was rejected when he attempted to enter the military service because of a perforated ear drum.

Bob Jr. spent too much of his developmental years at military academies or prep schools to suit him — he spent more winters at Valley Forge than George Washington, and they were harsher winters than Washington experienced to believe Bob Jr. — and a misspent period at the University of Oklahoma before completing his extended college education at the University of Pittsburgh. Again, he was following a trail once taken by his father. "I think Dad went to more schools than I did," he said with a wink.

Bob Prince Jr. poses at Valley Forge Military Academy circa 1960. He wasn't permitted to watch final game of World Series.

Prince family checks out newspaper clippings in 1958. Nancy, nearly 16, her father Bob, brother Bob Jr., 14, and mother Betty were living in Mt. Lebanon at the time.

Every so often while he was reminiscing on the pleasantries of growing up in the Prince family, he would interject a complaint about being sent away too often to military schools and summer camps, all aimed at introducing discipline and regimen to his daily life. He admitted those days still haunted him somehow.

Bob Jr. had a new pal named Percodan on his nightstand. "This is good stuff," he said, "and it helps to take away the hurt in this hip." He patted his right hip. "The doctor tells me I'm going to have to replace the other one in a few years."

He rinsed down the prescribed pain-killer pill with Pepsi-Cola, requiring four gulps to get it down. "That'll help," he said.

His preferred drink was scotch and water, Dewar's and water, thank you. His father's was vodka and orange juice, a Screwdriver, when I was last with him at St. Clair Country Club.

"His original drink was Canadian Club straight, with a Coke chaser," said Bob Jr. "After he met Chuck Mangold, the major distributor for Pepsi-Cola in the Pittsburgh area, he switched to Pepsi as a chaser. After Dad had his heart attack, he had to quit smoking and drinking. But he talked his doctors into letting him drink again. The doctors told him he could drink mildly. 'Mildly' meant 50 drinks a day to my dad. That's when he switched to vodka and orange juice, or cranberry juice. That was milder."

Bob Jr. just couldn't help chortling over his recall.

He seems to have taken his cues for his rascal role in life from his father, only doing it with a different twist. He spent precious time with his father in his critical adolescent years. "He complains now, but he adored his dad," said his sister Nancy. Bob Jr. went on the road with his dad during cherished weeks with the Pirates and opposing players in the National League, and he was a first-hand witness to his father's misbehaving ways. It gave him an excuse, and still does, it seems, to do it dad's way. He sang a different song than Frank Sinatra, one of his father's favorites.

"I was an albatross for them."
— Bob Prince Jr.

Bob Prince Jr. spent a lot of time on the road in his work as a salesman of plastics for the bottling and toy industry, logging as many as 60,000 miles a year on behalf of Crest Polymers. The time sitting behind the wheel had contributed to the wear and tear on his hip bones.

When he was on the road with his dad and the Pirates, he had some of the most famous baby-sitters in the world of fun and games. One night it would be Bill Mazeroski. The next night it would be

Roberto Clemente. There were nights when he was looked after by the likes of Dick Groat, Bill Virdon, Ted Kluszewski, Dale Long and Jack Shepard, Pirates all.

"I liked Don Hoak, but I didn't get along with him too well," said Prince. "He was too tough."

He stayed with the Pirates players after the games while his father cavorted with Jim Woods, one of his partners in the Pirates' broadcast booth, sportswriters and some of the ballplayers. "Jim Woods was one of my favorites," he added. His dad liked to drink and talk the night away.

His father had great recuperative powers, though, and he would be up early the next day, and take his son out to the ballpark, wherever the Pirates might be playing.

So Bob Jr. got to spend time and mix with the likes of Stan Musial, Ernie Banks, Roberto Clemente, Willie Mays, Willie Stargell, Warren Spahn and Sandy Koufax, all Baseball Hall of Famers like his father, and they talked to him and gave him baseball instruction, none of which stuck much. Mental pictures of those players as they appeared in their heyday stay with him today. While in St. Louis, the young Prince even stayed at the home of Lillian and Stan Musial, close friends of his father who were originally from Donora, Pennsylvania.

"I should have married Musial's daughter, but that's another story," he offered as a throwaway line.

"Warren Spahn said I was the best Wiffle-Ball pitcher he'd ever seen," said Prince proudly.

"Ernie Banks said I'd never be an infielder because I looked up too much and didn't stay down with the ball.

"Roberto Clemente said I was the worst hitter he'd ever seen. I wasn't much of a ballplayer.

"When I was at Valley Forge, my father introduced me to Byron Saam, the Phillies long-time announcer, and he took me and my classmates to some games in Philadelphia. I'd spend two or three weeks every summer with my dad. We'd stay together at the Knickerbocker Hotel in Chicago or the Chase in St. Louis.

"The Pirate players were baby-sitting me while my dad was out foolin' around. Dad would go out with friends, and he'd assign Bill Mazeroski to watch me. Or sometimes it was Roberto Clemente. I was an albatross for them. They had to stay in while dad was out having a good time. I don't know how he got away with that.

"I especially liked Ted Kluszewski, 'Uncle Ted,' as I called him. He was big and strong and I always felt safe with him. The only player who wasn't nice to me, as I recall, was Dee Fondy of the Cubs. I was walking around with the players at Wrigley Field before a game there, and Fondy nearly took my head off with some fungo shots he sent my way on purpose. Maybe he didn't like the idea of me being there. Uncle Ted grabbed Fondy and bent him over the top of the dugout and told him not to ever do that to me again.

"All the other guys were great with me. I'd be out on the ballfield at 9 a.m. on the day of an afternoon game, shagging flies. People like Ernie Banks and Willie Mays would be trying to teach me how to play the game. Danny Murtaugh, the Pirates' manager, would spray chewing tobacco on my shoes in good fun. He was accurate as all hell with his spitting."

"Danny did that on purpose," interjected his mother. "He did that to everyone."

Bob Jr. smiled at his mother, and continued with his story-telling.

"I'd sit and play cards with Sandy Koufax," said Prince, picking up where he left off. "I remember doubleheaders with the Dodgers. Don Drysdale would pitch the first game, and Koufax the second game. The Pirates had their hands full on those days. Clemente didn't like to face Koufax."

In fairness, that hardly set Clemente apart from the pack from any of the sane souls in the National League.

"I liked it when I went to away games," Prince continued. "It was a thrill other children my age couldn't experience. Dick Stuart tried to teach me how to field ground balls, which was a joke."

"Dr. Strangeglove," interjected Betty Prince.

"Prince Jr. will never make it in the major leagues," said Ernie Banks, the Cubs' "Mr. Sunshine."

Prince said he traveled with his father each summer from the time he was 13 to 18 years old. "He'd say, 'We're going to Philly tomorrow. Get one of your friends.' And we'd drive off to Philly the next day. That's how I met so many players.

"Or he'd say, 'What are you doing tomorrow? We're playing the Cubs in a four-game series in Chicago. Let's go.'"

"I remember," Betty Prince offered, "meeting Dick Groat one day at the airport, and he pointed to young Bob and said, 'If I ever have a son, I hope he turns out like this boy.' And he and Barbara ended up having three daughters."

Bob Jr. mentioned some of the military schools he attended, and how he often went off to summer camp when the school session ended. "Most children got to come home," he said. "I got shipped away."

Betty Prince winced whenever her son said something like that. It was done for his own good, she thought at the time.

"I went from Mt. Lebanon Junior High to Valley Forge Military School without any notice," he recalled. "I always thought it was because I had bad grades — too many Cs and Ds — but my sister, Nancy, told me it was because I had gotten in with a bad crowd. I hung out with kids from Canonsburg rather than kids from Mt. Lebanon, and you know who the tougher kids were.

"I got no notice from anyone that I was going to Valley Forge Military Academy. My mother asked my dad for money to get me some new clothes. My dad said, 'I got him some new clothes.' It was my uniform for Valley Forge. That's how I found out I was going away to school.

"I was at Valley Forge in 1960 when the Pirates won the World Series. I wasn't doing K.P. or anything like that on the day of the seventh game, but I didn't get to watch the game on TV, either. I missed the whole thing. Typical military school stuff.

"I hated it. There was physical hazing. I got punched in the chest more than once to get my attention. It was not my idea to go to a military school. I was there for two years. Then I went to Mercersburg Military Academy for a year. But they didn't think I was Mercersburg material. Two of my classmates and friends who were allowed to stay both ended up being indicted for criminal behavior as adults.

"Somewhere in between, during the summer, I went to Culver Military Academy in Evansville, Indiana. They kept shuffling me away. I went to Upper St. Clair High School for one year, and graduated from there. I was too small to play most sports, but I wrestled.

"I could swim pretty good. My dad had been a really good swimmer. He held some swimming records at Schenley High, at Stanford and at Pitt. And at the P.A.A. He was a few seconds behind Johnny Weismuller, who was the best swimmer in the world at the time. He was close; he was that good. He also showed me how you had to break the water when you dived into it from high up, like he did that time when he dove into the water from the third floor of the Chase Hotel.

"Then, for college, they sent me to Oklahoma, one of the schools my dad attended. Dad said, 'You'll love it at Oklahoma.' Everyone else got to go to Grove City College, where my mom had gone, but I'm out in Oklahoma. And I'm in ROTC. I was in college for seven-and-a-half years and finally got my degree in liberal arts after one year at Pitt. I used to go across the street when I was a student at Pitt, and drink some shooters at the P.A.A. I'd put them on my dad's tab. What did you think? I remember my dad one day telling my mother, 'Are you sure he graduated from Pitt? I can't find his diploma. I don't know that he graduated.'

"My dad got me a job at U.S. Steel. I was at a meeting once where they mentioned that there was an opening in Grand Rapids. I said, 'I'll go. I've been away all my life; it's no big deal.' I got canned twice at U.S. Steel. The second time didn't count because everybody in my department was let go."

"My dad wasn't a pauper with me."
— Bob Prince Jr.

He still had friends in the area. He recalled getting together with writers like Pat Livingston, Tom Hritz and Myron Cope at the Living

Room at the border of Bethel Park and Upper St. Clair. Cope also caught his act a few times at Oakmont County Club. "Cope said he had played with a lot of bad golfers, but that I was the worst golfer he'd ever played with," said Prince, with more than a hint of pride.

Even though he wasn't a good golfer, he remained a non-resident member at Oakmont Country Club, and liked to entertain customers there. He told tales where he failed to obey a stop-play bell ringing when it began to rain. "I had one hole to play and I wanted to finish," he said, forgiving himself and laughing off the dressing-down he received from club officials for playing through.

During his recovery from hip replacement surgery, he left his mother's place one day to visit an ailing friend, who was feeling lonely. So he had a good soul, just like his parents. Wherever he goes, people insist on telling stories about his dad. He had a few of his own to offer: "My dad had big hands, and he could fix his fingers a certain way so that he could hold a shot glass of Canadian Club and a small glass of Coke or Pepsi, depending on who he was working for promotion-wise, and he could turn his hand a certain way so that he could drink his shot and chaser in the same motion. He'd put a napkin under his chin to catch the drips. He liked to show off that way. He never mixed them in the same glass.

"I used to like going to the P.A.A. with him. They'd have a Father-Son Night and we'd march from the P.A.A. over to Forbes Field. We'd come back after the game and have dinner, and then my dad would take me downstairs to the duckpin bowling lanes they had there. He'd go back upstairs and drink with his friends. We'd get home later than my mother thought we should have. And he'd tell my mother I was bowling with some young friends and he didn't want to break it up, that's why we were late. Meantime I was down there all alone. I was the only kid bowling by myself. He'd come and get me and he'd say, 'Did you have a nice time?'

"I miss my father, but then again I was never really around him, not for any real amount of time. He was around, but he wasn't around. He was around, but he was away. When I got older in life, in my 30s and 40s, he started telling me. 'You'll never have to worry. You'll never have to work. You'll have a good time.' He was going to leave me enough money, you see, so I'd have the good life. In the end, there was no reason for me to go to the reading of the will. There was nothing there for me."

When I told Bob Jr. I had heard his dad had inherited considerable money, he smiled. "My dad's father was a colonel in the Army," he said. "How much money could he have made? But we had an Uncle Hud and an Uncle George and they were in the oil business, and they owned some land in downtown Los Angeles. I think that's what my mother's living on. My dad and Ralph Kiner bought a local TV station and a restaurant and they went broke in 1955 with both of them. My dad and his money were soon parted.

"I think the most money my dad ever made was $460,000 a year, all things combined, and maybe $200,000 of that was from all his promotions and salary from the Pirates."

That's considerably higher than Nellie King contended that Prince made, or didn't make, during his last years with the Pirates. Betty Prince said her son's figures were way too high. "He never made that kind of money," she protested.

"He was always generous with me," said Bob Jr. "My mother would give me $10 to go somewhere, and he'd know that and he would still give me another $20. He always got me a car from one of the dealers he was representing. He used to take me to Larrimor's for shoes. He was never a pauper with me.

"After he got canned in the '70s, nobody could help me in this town. It was a good time for me to go somewhere else. People either loved him or hated him. There was no in between. But when he was gone from the Pirates' picture, he was gone.

"I have this picture in my mind of him that's always there. It was shortly after he lost his job and somebody shot this picture of him. He was standing on Grant Street. He was wearing a dark topcoat. He had his head down, and he was holding a cigarette in his hand. It was snowing a little. It was a black and white photo. He had like a depressing look on his face."

Ellen and husband, Bob Jr., flank Bob and Betty Prince in September, 1983.

From the Prince family album

Pirates of the past
They played with Prince

*"I can still hear him
talking about me."*
— Bob Purkey

Kent Tekulve, pitcher (1974-1985), Pittsburgh:

"Bob Prince brought a lot of good things to our ballclub. I was a 28-year-old rookie when I came to the ballclub. I was joining a veteran ballclub and that helped me a lot. They didn't have to say a lot; I watched the way they went about their business and followed their lead. Prince brought me along in a different way, and I didn't fully appreciate this until years later. We also had a veteran broadcasting team in Bob Prince and Nellie King. They knew how to handle a rookie. They knew how to guide me. They taught me how to deal with the media. Bob Prince genuinely loved his Pirates. He cared about how they were perceived and helped you along. Younger broadcasters could be more worried about themselves and their own interests. Prince was like a coach on the team, the way he led you through the p.r. aspects of being a big league ballplayer.

"He taught you not to stick your foot in your mouth. He never asked you the kind of questions that would get you into trouble. Guys get in trouble because they say the wrong things. They just want to cooperate with the media and they think they have to answer every question. Bob and Nellie never led you into traps.

"No. 1, Bob was a Pirates fan. He'd upset some of the players sometimes when he said 'we won,' and sometimes he'd say 'they didn't play so well tonight.' It was 'we' when we won, and 'they' when we lost. Players were sensitive to that sort of stuff. He did care, though. He was not a down-the-middle-of-the-road professional. You knew very quickly who he was rooting for.

"He wasn't just Bob Prince, the baseball broadcaster, either. He had a full plate as it was, with all his regular responsibilities. But he also had time for everything else. His community involvement was most impressive. When I first started my golf tournament (an annual event to raise funds for myasthenia gravis), he helped out. We had no clue what we were doing, and he took over the show.

"He knew how to raise money. He invented games we still use today. He said we had too many doorprizes and we weren't raising enough money. He told everyone in the room to write their name on a $20 bill and toss it into a box. It was a 50/50. We still do that today, almost in his honor.

"I turned 51 on March 5 (1998), and I'm finally really retired. I thought I had retired eight years ago after 15 years in the big leagues, but I've been broadcasting Phillies games the past seven years. I'm not doing that this year. I'm finally staying home. I hope Linda can stand having me home all the time after all those years on the road. I hope we don't drive each other crazy.

"I still hold the record for most relief appearances (1,050). Hoyt Wilhelm holds the record for all-time pitching appearances (1,070, with 1,018 in relief). Dennis Eckersly has a chance this year to break both of those records, and the amazing thing about it is he was a starting pitcher for his first ten years in the majors. I tell people my arm didn't give out, my legs gave out. It was all that walking in from the bullpen that did it to me.

"All I do now is play golf. And I visit my father as often as I can at Country Meadows. He was 80 this May 6, and he just learned this past year that he has leukemia. They seem to have his medication straightened away now, and he seems to be doing better. I am going to try and get this retirement thing right for a change."

(Kent Tekulve's father, Henry, died May 20, 1998.)

Nellie Briles, pitcher (1971-73), Pittsburgh:

"Bob Prince liked to say athletes all had short arms and deep pockets, and that they never pay for a damn thing. He liked to say that on the air, too. He threw money around with the best of them. So one time Maz and Gene Alley and myself invited Prince to join us for dinner. We took him to the East Pump Room at the Ambassador Hotel in Chicago. We ordered all the best stuff. We started out with all top shelf stuff. We had chateaubriand and lobster, the most expensive meals. We had a tremendous evening, laughing the whole time. When it was time for the bill, Bob called for the check. We had already told the waiter he was not to get the bill. 'I'll take the bill,' he cried out. 'I'm sorry,' the waiter told him, 'there's no bill.' He said, 'What do you mean there's no bill?' And the waiter said, 'These people will be paying for it.' Prince said, 'What the hell's going on?' He couldn't believe what he was hearing. I said, 'Bob, we just wanted you to know that there are guys with long arms and short pockets on this team.' And we laughed our asses off. That was a rare deal, I must admit. Gene Alley never paid for anything, and Maz wasn't much of a free-spender, either.

"I'll tell you about the first time I ever saw Bob Prince. I was pitching for the St. Louis Cardinals and we came into New York on a day off, and we were there one night right after the Pirates had played the Mets. They were flying out the next day. Our people went to Toots Shor's Restaurant, one of the most famous sports hangouts in the city.

"I'm introduced to Bob Prince. I was told he was a character much like our announcer, Harry Caray. He had his drinks lined up on the bar. He had five shooters in a row, Canadian Club straight, I was told. At the end he had a small shot glass of Coke. He said,

191

'Bottoms up,' and threw down all five shots and took a sip of the Coke. We were there for 5 hours and he never finished the Coke. I was impressed."

Bob Purkey, pitcher (1954-1957, 1966), Bethel Park, Pa.

"Bob Prince and I just had a great relationship. I can still hear him talking about me — whether I was pitching for the Pirates in Pittsburgh or for the Reds in Cincinnati. He always called me 'poetry in motion.' That was his description of me. I played in his golf tournament over ten years. I know that because I have one of those jackets he gave to the guys who played ten or more years. It's a blue blazer with all his famous expressions on patches all over it. I think I may have played in all his golf tournaments when I could.

"I thought he was a great guy; many people didn't. I thought he did a great job for Pittsburgh. I was disappointed with what happened to him. When he was let go, I rode in the parade in downtown Pittsburgh to show support for him. We wanted to show our appreciation for him and Nellie King. Bob had some faults. Who didn't?

"I was a Pittsburgh guy. I grew up on Mt. Washington. But Joe Brown did me a favor when he traded me to Cincinnati after the 1957 season. I was leaving the Rinky-Dinks, a team that had finished last or next-to-last for eight years. I was going to a team that had a chance to win. They had a good infield, and they'd just set a new National League record for most home runs by a team. They needed pitching. That's why they wanted me.

"So Joe Brown did me a big favor. Whenever I see him, at some banquet or something, he shakes his head, and says, 'Hey, Purk, you're still haunting me.' He said people still get on him for trading me, one of the worst trades he ever made. But he brought me back to Pittsburgh for my last year. There were never any hard feelings.

"I started my insurance business the day after I retired from baseball, back in October of 1966. I've been here ever since, for 31 years. I'll be 69 this July 14 (1998), but I feel good, and I'm still servicing my customers. I turned over management of the office to my long-time associate, Tom O'Malley Jr., but I'm still working. My wife Joan and I have been living in Bethel Park all this time. I love playing golf at the alumni outings. So I get to see my comrades about once a month, at least, during the summer months."

Ronnie Kline, pitcher (1952, 1955-1959, 1968-1969), Callery, Pa.:

"I'm moving up in the world. I'm now the mayor of Callery. I think we have 517 people in the community, which is near Mars and Evans

City in Butler County. I live on a street — Kline Avenue — that was named after me. Why would a guy ever want to leave a town that treated you so good? Bob Prince called me 'The Callery Pa. Hummer' and it has stayed with me all these years. He did so many favors for me through the years. He was a great friend of mine.

"One time, the coach of our high school football team, Lloyd Parks, went undefeated in the late 1960s, maybe 1968 or 1969. He asked me if I could get him a speaker for a dinner they were going to hold in our fire hall to honor the team. 'I can get Bob Prince,' I told him. He didn't believe me. I asked Bob if he could stop by and make an appearance that night. I didn't tell him he was going to be *the* speaker. He said, 'Sure, ol' Bess — that's what he called his wife, Betty — will be out.' Betty was living and teaching in Zelienople, not far from here, when they first met. They came to my place, which was about a quarter-mile from the fire hall. Betty stayed behind and talked with Dorothy, my wife, and Bob and I went out to go to the dinner. As we're getting into the car, I said, 'I just heard that our speaker didn't show up. Do you think you can handle it?' Prince said, 'Sure, that ain't no problem.' He sat down next to Lloyd Parks, and asked him questions. They went over the highlights of the season as they were eating dinner. When Prince started the show, he talked about the games like he had broadcasted all them through the season.

"One time, Dick Groat and I went with him and Al Abrams to the Dapper Dan Dinner they had every year in Cumberland, Maryland. Groat and I were in one car, and Prince was driving Abrams in the other. Prince kept bumping us from behind; he was going about 80 miles per hour. He was something. He came up here a few times and went with Friend, Lynch, Face and me to the Johnny Maier Masonic Lodge in Mars. We did a question-and-answer session there. We all belonged to different Masonic lodges.

"If you were a rookie, he'd take you out to dinner in each new city, and show you how to get around the town. He broke everybody in that way. He took care of the bills.

"I'm 66 now, and I've had some health problems in recent years, but I'm doing okay now. I had to give up smoking and drinking. The only Black Velvet I see now is my dog. I had to give up golf because my legs would give out on me. I can still do a little hunting. I still see Jim Lokhaiser, the old sports broadcaster, up in Butler and we have a good time. I miss The Gunner. He was great. I think he was the greatest they ever had. He did so much for the city of Pittsburgh."

Jim Pagliaroni, catcher (1963-67), Grass Valley, California:

"Don Schwall and I came in from Boston together, in a trade for Dick Stuart and Jack Lamabe. We beat the Mets this one game, and we go on with Ralph Kiner on 'Kiner's Korner' after the game. Bob Prince asked us to do this, so Don and I went on Kiner's post-game show together. We combed our hair down on our foreheads like the Beetles, and wrapped ourselves in bedsheets so we looked like we were wearing togas. We were carrying bunches of grapes from the clubhouse buffet. And we talked effeminately. Real swishy. Kiner couldn't talk when he saw us. He's in shock. Joe L. Brown was furious with us. Bob thought it was funny, though. He was a class act. He was the second best baseball broadcaster in the business, second only to Vin Scully. You couldn't beat Bob for having a good time.

"I was the player rep for five years and I asked Bob once why he was so descriptive and dramatic on the radio. He said, 'Jim, I learned a long time ago that you must think of the shut-in, or the person who can't see, and you have to paint a picture for them.'"

Don Schwall, pitcher (1963-66), Pittsburgh:

"I've been the president of Bob Prince Charities since 1986. Bob started it with his first golf tournament back in 1982 or 1983. We've raised about a half million dollars during that time. Our two main beneficiaries are the Allegheny Valley School for Exceptional Children and the Verland Foundation. I've been in the insurance and securities business for 30 years and this is my eighth year with Paine-Webber. I used to handle investments for Jim Woods and helped Bob in that respect, too. I liked a lot of things about Bob.

"I first met him when I came here in 1963 in a trade from the Boston Red Sox. We took to each other right away. I admired him because he didn't run down players on the air. He was strongly biased for the Pirates. He wouldn't criticize individual players like some broadcasters did. From the standpoint of persona — he just stood out. He was unique."

Gene Freese, infielder, (1955-58, 1964-65), Wheeling

Gene and George Freese were brothers from Wheeling, West Virginia, who both played infield for the Pirates in the mid-'50s. Gene played second base and George played third base. Gene played in the Pirates' Alumni annual golf outing at Churchill Valley Country Club in the summer of 1997, and shared a story about Bob Prince.

"Bob Prince and Jim Woods got tanked up in New York one night, which was not unusual," offered Freese. "When they came back to our hotel they told me they had tried to climb the Empire State Building. I said, 'Why'd you want to do that?' And Prince said, 'Because it was there!'"

Jim Pagliaroni

Don Schwall

Gene Freese

Ronnie Kline

Bob Robertson
The Maryland Strongboy

"Robby has a chance of being another Kiner."
— Larry Shepard

Baseball players are bigger and stronger today than ever before. Size-wise, they offer quite a dramatic contrast to the players of 20 and 30 years ago. In his day, for instance, Bob Robertson was considered a big guy. He was 6-1, 195 pounds when he reported to the Pirates as a rookie in 1967. That wouldn't turn too many heads these days. Those numbers hardly rival those of sluggers such as Mark McGwire, Mo Vaughn, Cecil Fielder and Frank Thomas.

Robert Eugene Robertson was a husky, hot-tempered redhead who could muscle the ball. Robertson was referred to in newspaper reports and baseball broadcasts as "a young Samson" and as "the Maryland strongboy," indeed, "the pride of Mt. Savage." His teammates thought he was always put out about one thing or another and often called him something else. He's matured, mellowed and old teammates are happy for the conversion.

He was one of those big kids who excelled in several sports in high school, like Terry Bradshaw, Willie Stargell, Dave Parker, Danny Marino, Joe Namath, Joe Montana, to name a few, and there were great expectations for him.

Most ballparks he played in during his high school and minor league days couldn't contain him. He set home run records wherever he went. He hit 130 home runs in five years in the minors. He got off to a great start in the majors.

Larry Shepard, one of his managers in his early years with the Pirates, said, "Robby has a chance of being another Kiner."

Such praise has stayed with Robertson. Some times it cheers him, sometimes it haunts him. He had some great days; they simply didn't last long enough.

"Bob Prince said I could hit a ball out of any park, including Yellowstone," recalled Robertson with a smile. He could also handle the glove. Stargell, who gave way to him at first base, said Robertson was the best fielder at the position in the league.

He could hit and field and throw the ball. He was on a team that had a lot of talented players. There was so much promise. They won three consecutive divisional championships (1970-72), plus a World Series in 1971. They won four division titles in a six-year span. It was a great period for Pirates baseball. Even so, it was thought that they could have done better. Especially Robertson. What went wrong?

Robertson was sitting at a table on the veranda at the Churchill Valley Country Club, just east of Pittsburgh and the Squirrel Hill Tunnels, having breakfast with his wife, Carolyn, prior to playing in

Bob Prince chats with Bob Robertson on Bucs' bench in early '70s.

Bob Robertson #7

Steve Blass (28) and Bob Robertson (7) celebrate final out of 1971 World Series.

a Pirates Alumni golf outing. This was July 21, 1997. Robertson was 50 and would be 51 on October 2.

The Robertsons would be married 30 years come February, 1998, and they were eyeballing each other like newlyweds as we spoke. In the case of Carolyn, she was looking at her Robby like she must have when he was the hometown hero back in Mt. Savage. They had the same look and coloring, as couples often do who've been together so long. To her, Bob Robertson was the best thing since Elvis Presley. And she absolutely adored Elvis Presley, and still mourns his passing.

Whatever Bob offered about his baseball or athletic career, Carolyn would come into the conversation with something that would enhance the tale. She was still proud of him. While he may not have lived up to everyone else's expectations through the years, Carolyn was still happy in his company. She nodded and smiled when her husband told familiar stories, and interjected a thought or two of her own.

"When you hit those high pop ups," Carolyn said, "Bob Prince would say the ball was in an elevator shaft."

Bob's blue eyes positively sparkled when he spoke about the best of times, and his eye lids lowered to half mast when he discussed the difficult times.

He had a roller coaster career in baseball and life after baseball. He was not always a day at the beach, so Carolyn had to be challenged from time to time. It was great to see them looking so good, so sunny on a bright morning, and pleased with the way their life was going. He had known hard times as a kid — the family still had an out house in the backyard when the scouts came calling on him — and he had known hard times in recent years, just finding a suitable job and paying his bills. Nowadays, Robertson boasts that he conducts free baseball clinics for the kids back home. "I thank them when they ask for an autograph."

"Bob has really come around in recent years," said Dave Giusti, one of his former teammates who was at the golf outing. "All the guys are so happy for him. He's really changed for the better, and grown up a great deal. Carolyn is great for him."

Other wives would show up later in the day and attend a post-golf dinner. Carolyn rode around in a golf cart with her husband. She wanted to enjoy the entire day at Churchill.

These days Bob liked to muscle golf balls, taking pride in how far he can hit 'em, and only wishes he had the know-how and touch to play the approach shots and putt like Bill Mazeroski. Most of the former Bucs who come to the alumni outings are more envious of Mazeroski's golf game than they are of his home run that won the 1960 World Series.

Robertson said he enjoyed golf and his grandchildren, Alexa Clair Sivic, born three years earlier, and Colton. "We finally got the first boy," said Bob. "He's the next major leaguer in the family."

The Robertsons had two daughters, Geneen, 27, and Julie, 22 at the time of our meeting. "We have two good kids," said Bob. Nodding toward Carolyn, he added, "She's responsible."

The Robertsons were sharing photographs of their grandchildren with anyone who asked about their family.

Robertson was wearing a white golf shirt with a black collar provided by the Pirates Alumni organization, and a black Tommy Armour Golf straw hat. He wouldn't remind anyone of Garth Brooks, but he did look a lot like a one-time home run phenom. His golf shirt was snug around his biceps.

At this golf outing, Robertson was still bigger than most of his contemporaries. They were from a different era. Oh, Nellie King towered over everyone on the greens at 6-6, but he was still so skinny, and Kent Tekulve was 6-4, but just as skinny at 180 pounds, so they didn't scare anyone.

I was always the smallest kid in my class in grade school and my first two years in high school. So I was amazed to discover at a reunion of the '60 Bucs at the Green Tree Marriott in 1990 that, at 5-8 1/2, I was bigger than Smoky Burgess, ElRoy Face and Harvey Haddix, some of the biggest heroes of my youth. Johnny Callison of the Phillies and Eddie Mathews of the Braves were both there, too. They were sluggers, yet they seemed as normal as the next-door neighbor in size. Maybe my perspective comes from spending so much time as a sportswriter with heavyweight boxers and basketball players.

Robertson turned out to be more like Dick Stuart, a bright meteor that flashes briefly across the sky. Robertson didn't have the staying power of Kiner, or Stuart for that matter. He wasn't quite the eccentric character that Stuart was, and he was a superior gloveman. "Don't compare me to Dick Stuart," Robertson says. He adds a glare just in case you weren't paying attention.

Robertson still looked like a guy you wouldn't want to annoy.

"I was scared to death."
— Bob Prince

Talking about Bob Prince prompted Robertson to share a story about one of his days on the road with the Pirates when he was pouting because he was sidelined by an injury.

"Richie Hebner was my roommate" Robertson said. "Things weren't going well for me in 1972. I started out at first base, but my knee blew out. Virdon was the manager. I showed up in the clubhouse one day with a bandage on my right hand. I'd cut my hand.

"Virdon saw me and stopped me. 'What happened to your hand?' he asked me.

"'I just got rid of a little frustration.' I told him."

Robertson still smiles at the memory of how he hurt his hand and how Prince had a bit part in his escapade, or tirade.

"We'd had an afternoon game, and I didn't play," Robertson said. "Me and Hebner had gone back to our hotel room. Hebner was lying on the bed. He was on the phone.

"I decided to pick up the end of my bed. I started picking it up and dropping it. I was having a little tantrum. I banged the bed against the wall a few times. I knocked over some stuff while I was at it. That's how I hurt my hand. Hebner pulled the covers over his head until I was finished.

"When I stopped, Hebner poked his head out from under the covers. 'You OK?' he asked me.

"'I'm fine now,' I told him.

"The next day the hotel manager comes in. He'd gotten complaints about noise coming from our room. He was taking note of the damage I'd done. The bill came to $250. I borrowed the money off Hebner. I didn't want Carolyn to know about it.

"That same morning Bob Prince came up to me. He said, 'What the hell was going on in your room yesterday? I was just ready to go to sleep when I heard all this banging on the wall. What was going on? I was scared to death!' Turns out Bob was in the next room when the bed hit the wall."

And you thought trashing rooms started with the NHL players who represented the U.S. in the 1998 Olympic Games in Nagano, Japan.

"I didn't hurt nobody but myself," Robertson said. "I may have damaged the bed and some lamps, and Prince's peaceful nap, but that was about it."

Things were coming apart for Robertson in 1972 in many ways. At 25, he was hindered by nagging injuries and he never regained the stroke that offered so much hope in his previous two major league seasons. He became a decent extra player, but never the home run king his early power and production suggested.

Nellie King recalled an incident that involved Roberto Clemente and Bob Robertson in the clubhouse after the disheartening 1972 playoff loss to the Reds in Cincinnati. The Reds' winning run came on a wild pitch by Bob Moose, which made it hurt even more. Robertson had been a hero for the Pirates a year earlier when they swept the Reds in the NL playoffs and beat the Orioles to win the World Series. This time Bill Virdon didn't even call on him as a batter in the series. (For the record, Willie Stargell was a disappointment as well. He had a hit in his first at-bat against the Reds and then went hitless in his next 16 plate appearances.)

"After the Pirates lost the game at Cincinnati," said King, "Clemente came into the clubhouse and told everyone to get their heads up and to carry themselves with some pride when the press came in. And they did.

"Afterward, when the writers had left the clubhouse, Clemente got into Robertson's face. He said, 'You let us down this year. You didn't work. You should've been in early every day. You should've been taking batting practice in the morning, and in the afternoon, and right before the game. You should've been working to get better.' He really let him have it. Robby really took it on the chin."

What a difference a year had made. Robertson's batting average tailed off to .193 in 1972. He had 12 home runs and 41 RBI. He would hit 30 home runs altogether in 1973 and 1974.

Despite getting chewed out after the 1972 playoffs by Clemente, Robertson enjoyed talking about Clemente just the same. "Robbie was a great guy, a great team person," he said. "You could always tell when Robbie came in the clubhouse. He'd be hollering for Tony Bartirome, our team trainer. He'd be hollering, 'Tony, my neck, my neck.' If he came in feeling poorly, he'd get about three hits. If he were jolly, he'd pop up or something.

"I played catch with him. He'd throw it underhand. I'd challenge him. We'd have a little accuracy contest. That was my mistake. He could put the ball there every time. When I was at first, I recall that twice he threw out baserunners who appeared to hit singles to right field. They might be a slow-running catcher or pitcher. We got a lot of guys who circled first base too far. Roberto was such a competitor, with his whole body, mind and soul.

"I learned from Bill Mazeroski about fielding ground balls. I learned from Clemente and Stargell. Willie taught me a relaxed stance. He and Maz were alike in that they never got too high or too low. I watched what my teammates were doing."

He has no bad feelings towards Clemente. He and Carolyn came back to Pittsburgh in May of 1998 to see the musical *¡Arriba! ¡Arriba!*, about Clemente's life story, and again a month later to participate in a Roberto Clemente Foundation golf outing.

"We were well-matched."
— Robertson on his
roommate, Richie Hebner

The year before, in 1971, in a championship series against San Francisco, the Bucs lost the first game. In the second game at Candlestick Park, Robertson hit three home runs and a double to drive in five runs and score four runs as the Pirates won 9-5 and went on to crush the Giants. Before that outburst, Robertson hadn't hit a home run since August 25. He hit another home run off Juan Marichal in the next game in Pittsburgh in a 2-1 victory for the Pirates.

These feats earned him a spot in the record books, for most home runs in a playoff game (three) and the most home runs (four) and the most assists (eight) by a first baseman in a championship series.

Then he hit two more home runs in the World Series to help the Pirates win the third and fifth games of a seven game series as the Pirates dethroned the Orioles as champions. He missed a bunt sign before he hit one of those home runs.

The Orioles had won three of the first four games and were hoping to close out the series in Pittsburgh. In that fifth game, however, Robertson gave his team an early boost by hitting a home run leading off the second inning against Dave McNally. The home club shut out the Orioles, 4-0, behind a sterling 2-hit pitching performance by Nellie Briles.

Robertson was signed as a third baseman. The Pirates had Hebner to play third, however, so Robertson became a first baseman. He worked hard at learning how to play his new position, and he became one of the best in the business. Even so, he had to share first base with Al Oliver. They were both 22, and both wanted to play full-time. Stargell was shifted back to left field. Danny Murtaugh had a hard time keeping everyone happy. He used the right-handed Robertson against left-handed pitchers, and the left-handed Oliver against right-handed pitchers. They hated being platooned.

Hebner, Oliver and Manny Sanguillen all came to the Pirates during this period. Robertson and Dave Cash established themselves at the same time. These newcomers joined with veterans Roberto Clemente, Matty Alou, Willie Stargell, Gene Alley, Bill Mazeroski, Fred Patek and Jose Pagan, plus pitchers Steve Blass, Bob Moose, Luke Walker, Dock Ellis, Bob Veale and Dave Giusti. In 1971, they added pitchers like Nellie Briles, Bob Johnson and Bruce Kison, and picked up some useful reserves like Vic Davalillo, Jackie Hernandez, Gene Clines and Milt May. There was depth everywhere.

Robertson roomed with Hebner, and they had adjoining stalls in the clubhouse. The Pittsburgh fans had a love-hate relationship with Hebner. As a hitter, they loved him. As a third baseman, they weren't quite as thrilled. "We were well-matched," Robertson said. "We got along great. Richie was a good guy. He did a lot for kids. He went to Children's Hospital on a weekly basis. He did it simply because he was a good-hearted guy."

"I always dreamed of playing for the Pirates."
— Bob Robertson

As a kid growing up like few others in Mt. Savage, the Pirates were always his favorite major league team. "Probably because they were sitting 90 miles away," he said, "and I went to a lot of games at Forbes Field." His boyhood idols were Roberto Clemente, Bill Mazeroski and Mickey Mantle. His Little League team was called the Pirates. He once hit a 320-foot home run when he was playing for the Little League Pirates, quite a poke for a pre-teen kid.

He traded his high school diploma for a Pirates contract in the spring of 1964. "I signed the same night I graduated," recalled Robertson. "It was about 2 a.m. when we fully agreed. I always dreamed of playing for the Pirates It was really quite a thrill to sign with them at the age of 17."

Just before he graduated from Mt. Savage High School, Robertson hit a reported 560-foot home run. As a 17-year-old at Salem, Virginia in the Appalachian League in 1964, he hit one farther than that. "It went over a house that was 120 feet beyond a 320-foot fence," Robertson said. "I really tied into that one."

Thinking back to those first days in the Bucs' organization, Robertson shook his head. "I'm 17 and I'd never been away from home," he said. "All of a sudden I'm going to Salem, Virginia and I had a hard time making the adjustment. I was scared to death."

At Asheville, in his third season in the minors, he bombarded the Class A Western Carolinas League. He set new marks with 32 home runs, 98 runs batted in and 258 total bases. He had a .287 batting average and was named the league's Player of the Year.

"I'm going to hit more than 61 home runs in one season."
— Bob Robertson

His rookie season with the Pirates was 1967. He was forced to sit out the 1968 season for a kidney operation. That was a lost year.

Soon after he reported to the Pirates, Robertson revealed to a reporter that his goal was to hit 500 home runs in his big league career.

Nellie King spotted the rookie bathing his left knee in a whirlpool tub. "Robby, you will never hit 500 sitting in there," said King.

Robertson did hit 53 home runs in his first two full seasons in the big leagues, and all things seemed possible. In only 390 at bats in 1970, he hit 27 home runs and drove in 82 runs. In 1971 he batted .271 and hit 26 home runs and drove in 72 runs. He hit a home run off the Padres' Steve Arlin that same 1971 season that landed in the top level seats in left field at Three Rivers Stadium. It was measured at 456 feet.

One day at the Pirates' spring training camp in Ft. Myers, Al Abrams, the sports editor and columnist of the *Pittsburgh Post-Gazette*, wrote that he overheard Robertson talking to himself in the batting cage.

"Some day I'm going to knock the hell out of that asterisk beside Roger Maris' name in the record book," Robertson was reported to have said. "I'm going to hit more than 61 home runs in one season."

At age 19, Robertson was mentioned in the same breath as Dick Stuart by someone who watched him closely at spring camp. "Don't compare me with him," Robertson advised Abrams.

"I couldn't believe I was right there with them."
— Bob Robertson

He still recalls how great it was just to talk to some of the people whom he spent time with while they were taking leads off first base. "People like Willie Mays, Willie McCovey, Hank Aaron, Tom Seaver, Mike Schmidt, Frank Robinson...they'd be there, right next to me, and I got a kick out of just being with them. I couldn't believe I was right there with them.

"Aaron would be there, for instance, and I'd say, 'Hey, Hammer, how ya doin'?' Talking to Richie Allen and Frank Robinson and Willie Mays, that was something."

He said Bob Gibson was the toughest pitcher he ever faced. "Especially in tough situations," added Robertson. "I swear his fast ball was five miles per hour faster, and his slider broke an extra five inches."

Just being on the same field as a Hall of Famer like Gibson gives Robertson a super feeling even today.

"Like a lot of kids, I had a boyhood dream of being a major league ballplayer. I remember listening to the radio and hearing about Roberto Clemente. Then one day we're running out on the field right next to each other. That's what it was about. He'd go to right and I'd stay at first. I dressed next to him in the clubhouse.

"That's probably why I work with kids today at the baseball clinics. I can see in their eyes how excited they are to work with a former major league ballplayer.

"That's why I always say that my biggest thrill in baseball was not the World Series ring, not the three home runs in the playoffs. It was just being able to put on a major league uniform."

That reminded me of a time when I was at a "Bucco Bash" in Greensburg in 1995. It was part of the "Pirates Caravan" in the winter, sponsored by WCNS Radio of nearby Latrobe. Bill Mazeroski was on stage with ElRoy Face, Nellie Briles, Steve Blass, Chuck Tanner and Jim Bibby. A fan asked them all to recall their greatest thrill in baseball.

Mazeroski, of all people, hesitated when it was his turn. "I know what you're thinking," said Mazeroski with a boyish smile. "The home run that won the World Series was something special, for sure, but my biggest thrill was the first time I put on a Pirates' uniform."

Stan Musial once said, "I still say the greatest thrill was in just pulling on the uniform and going out there to compete."

That remark tells you all you need to know about Pittsburgh's two favorite Polish ballplayers, Mazeroski and Musial, and why they have remained so popular with fans.

Robertson hasn't been forgotten in Pittsburgh. Early in 1998, he was inducted into the Western Chapter of the Pennsylvania Sports Hall of Fame at a dinner at the Sheraton at Warrendale.

He was seldom a happy camper.

Bob Robertson was co-captain of every one of his teams in high school. In basketball, he set nine school records while scoring 2,007 points in four years. In track & field, he set a school shot put record of 54 feet, 4 inches. In baseball, he was 10-0 as a pitcher, and he pitched a no-hit game in Pony League. He also played the guitar. He could do it all. He spent time with the U.S. Marines at Parris Island and Camp Lejeune. He could have been a poster boy for the Marines.

J. Suter Kegg, sports columnist for the *Cumberland Evening Times*, frequently came to Pittsburgh to write about Robertson.

Robertson won the Dapper Dan Award three times at a dinner in Cumberland, recognizing him as the top athlete in his home area. Brooks Robinson, the Hall of Fame third baseman for the Orioles, presented the award to him on one occasion. Bob Prince would emcee that dinner just about every year, and Danny Murtaugh was a frequent honored guest.

Robertson had his own Louisville Slugger, a Bob Robertson model, which he had on display in the home of his parents, Mr. and Mrs. Charles L. Robertson. He had a picture showing Muhammad Ali pointing a fist in the direction of his chin.

He was often disturbed about one thing or another, seldom a happy camper. He was disgruntled and complained a lot. Even his friends felt Robertson had a "red ass."

The Pirates released Robertson on March 30, 1977. He was with the Pirates organization from 1964 to 1976. He sued the Pirates when they released him. He said he suffered a back injury in spring training. He was awarded his full salary, $50,000, when he won his case.

Robertson underwent back surgery in 1977. He signed with Seattle and later he signed with Toronto. His medical resume included three knee operations, two for his back, and one kidney operation. He came up short of his promise.

He finished with 115 home runs for the Pirates, somewhat shy of his early goal of hitting 500 home runs.

"Mom, one of these days maybe I can get on that radio."

Robertson said there were 800 or so students in his school, from elementary on up. He said there were 93 in his graduating class.

His family lived in a row house that had no running water. There was an outhouse and inside there was a 5-gallon bucket for when it was too cold to go outdoors.

He recalls Joe Consoli, a scout for the Pirates, and Syd Thrift coming down to see him.

At one point in their conversation, Consoli said, "Hey, Bobby, I have to go to the bathroom."

Robertson was a little embarrassed, but he gave Consoli some simple directions. "Just follow the little path down by the creek...," he said.

"At banquets, they'd bring it up, about going to the bathroom outdoors at Bob Robertson's house. That's just the way it was for us. My family was doing the best it could.

"My dad worked for the state road commission," he continued. "He worked heavy equipment. He operated graders and back hoes. Hey, our old house has been designated a landmark by the local historical society. The late Cardinal Mooney was born in that same row.

"Baseball was my favorite sport. But I also liked basketball. My favorites there were Jerry West, Elgin Baylor, Oscar Robertson. I used to watch them on TV. Yeah, we had a TV. It was a black and white model. We had to put a plastic sheet over the screen to make it have color.

"I would get a big coffee can and a rubber ball and I could play my own basketball game right there in my kitchen. I'd pop the ball into the can. I'd try to emulate Elgin Baylor at halftime.

"What I really wanted to play was football, but our school was too small to field a team. I loved Johnny Unitas. He was my favorite football player."

Now Robertson and I had something in common. I confessed that my favorite football player was also Unitas, who had grown up in Pittsburgh and played for St. Justin in the Class B Catholic League, and later played sandlot football in Blooomfield for $7 a game before catching on with the Colts in Baltimore.

"I had a good arm," said Robertson. "I threw shot put in track. I still have the county record back home for an 8 pound shot. Some guy gave me a 12 pound shot when I was in 8th grade. I practiced with the heavier shot. I was putting it out there 40 feet. When I signed with the Pirates, my arm was strong from that shot put.

"When I was a kid I'd go to my grandmother's house in Cumberland a lot. When you turned on the radio you heard Bob Prince's voice. She'd have dinner for us. I remember hearing Bob talking about Virdon and Maz and Stargell and Clemente.

"One day, I said, 'Mom, one of these days maybe I can get on that radio.'

"Then my best friend took me to a game at Forbes Field. My friend's name was Ralph Wilson. I was about 15. I said, 'Ralph, you know, I'm going to play here one of these days.'

"We'd play at his house. They had running water. I'd go to the bathroom every chance I got. I'd press that level and marvel at what happened.

"My friend went on to college. I think he has three different degrees. He was a big kid, a left-hander. I got him a tryout with the Pirates, but his arm went bad.

"He was such a colorful announcer."
— Carolyn Robertson

"I didn't listen to baseball as a kid," said Bob's wife, Carolyn. "I'd go home when Bob was on the roadtrips. Bob Prince, to me, was the most colorful, excitable announcer. He always made me feel like I was at the game. I knew what my Bob was doing. Bob Prince never stopped talking; he told you everything that was going on. You always felt involved; he was such a colorful announcer. He was always so upbeat. I loved the way he dressed. His voice was so distant.

"He was caring. He'd say things on the air about personal aspects of the players. I had my last child at the beginning of the season. Bob Prince told everybody about it. He said Bob Robertson was the proud papa of another girl. I watched it from my hospital bed and it made me feel good. Jim Woods was a good announcer, too. Nellie was excellent. Two different styles. That made it a real good combination."

Her husband took his cue from Carolyn, and came back into the conversation by saying. "It's something you never ever forget."

Robertson said Prince was more than the Bucs' broadcaster, as he saw it.

"Bob Prince was a big part of our clubhouse," Robertson said. "He always stopped by. You always knew when he showed up. He said hello to everyone.

"He always remembered your friends. I could bring my friends in from back home. Two months later, my friends would come in, and he'd shake their hand and call them by name. I thought that was neat."

He glanced at Carolyn to capture her attention and continued. "So many memories are coming up," he said. "She was a big part of it all. She was a great baseball lady. She'd have the girls with her. So many pictures come to mind."

Carolyn said, "I always brought them. They weren't just going to the ballpark. They were going to their daddy's office."

"The fans are the most important people."

"We had yearly contracts. You went out and busted your butt. Every time up. If you did good, Joe Brown would give you a raise at the end of the year. If you didn't, he could take some money away.

"Today, as far as I'm concerned, the fans are the most important people. Not owners, not players, it's the fans. I always had a good rapport. The fans of Pittsburgh were always there. I had some injuries, but they were patient.

"I went back with the Houston Astros in 1989 and 1990. I had been a hitting instructor there for four years for Bob Watson."

One day Robertson got a long distance call from Houston. Carolyn called out to him in their home. "Hey, Robbie, Bob Watson has a job for you. He wants you to teach Jeff Bagwell how to play first base better."

The Astros had just gotten Bagwell from Boston. He could play either corner in the infield, like Robertson. "He's strong, a Little Hammer," said Robertson. "He was great to work with. He was a good student. What I don't like about baseball . . . some of these instructors. Kids have had success in Little League, Pony League, high school and college. Then some instructor wants to create a new athlete all in one year."

Jim O'Brien

Carolyn and Bob Robertson share breakfast table at Pirates Alumni Golf Outing at Churchill Country Club in July of 1997.

Ralph Kiner
Partner with Prince in disasters

*"No one else at the bar ever had to
touch their wallet when Bob was around."*

Bob Prince and Ralph Kiner were ahead of their time. They were enterprising young men, entrepreneurial types. Prince was the promoter and something of an agent for Kiner, and Prince kept coming to Kiner for the money they needed to make a killing. "Usually we were the ones who ended up getting killed," said Kiner. "But we had a great time and I wouldn't trade it for anything."

Talking to Kiner has always been a delightful experience, and when Prince is the subject of discussion Kiner couldn't be happier.

"I'll tell you something I'll never forget about Prince," said Kiner, swinging as hard as he could on the first pitch, hoping to hit a home run. "That's when Bob used to come early to Forbes Field and pitch batting practice for us. He was a real sight, believe me, with those pipestem legs of his. I also remember the day that Frankie Frisch hit a ball to Bob and broke his thumb."

The 1998 season was Kiner's 36th as a broadcaster with the New York Mets. He'd gotten his start with WIIC-TV (now WPXI-TV) doing a post-game show with Jim Woods when the Pirates were playing the New York Yankees in the 1960 World Series. It was Prince who promoted Kiner for the assignment. Kiner spent one season with the Chicago White Sox before joining the Mets in their inaugural season of 1962 along with the late Lindsey Nelson and Bob Murphy. "I still enjoy it," commented Kiner. "I've always loved being around the baseball scene."

Kiner was an icon from my youth, one of my first sports heroes. So it was still a thrill to talk to him for several hours at the Doubletree Hotel in downtown Pittsburgh. He was one of the first ballplayers I knew when I was learning how to play ball. When I mentioned to him that I had spent some time with "Bullet Bill" Dudley, a Pro Football Hall of Famer who had seen early service with the Steelers, I was surprised when Kiner said, "Hey, there's one of my contemporaries." I didn't think Kiner was quite as old as Dudley.

But, as Casey Stengel would say, you could look it up. Dudley and Kiner were both playing in Pittsburgh in 1946 — it was Kiner's rookie season in the big leagues and Dudley's last with the Steelers before he was traded to the Lions. Both were 74 in the summer of 1998. "I'll be 75 on October 27," said Kiner. "It's been quite a run, a great run. I've never missed a Mets' game in 35 years because of health problems; I've missed a few because I took days off, but that's it."

During the 1997 season, Kiner had to cut back his schedule, however, because of a bout with Bell's Palsy.

Kiner's countenance showed considerable mileage. His face was fuller, and more lined, than when he put fear into opposing pitchers during his days with the Pirates, Cubs and Indians. It was freshly sunburned as he had been out playing golf that day with Gil Lucas, a Pittsburgh-based executive with the Fox Sports cable channel, at the Alcoma Golf Club in Penn Hills.

Kiner was round-shouldered, but still a big man with big hands. He wore an open-collared light blue shirt, a plain gold necklace, and a gold bracelet, and white slacks. We sat on high stools at a small, circular table on a level just above the bar, and frequently checked out a nearby movie-size screen to catch some sports action or scores.

He smoked a cigar — he said he smokes about three a day — and he drank Monterey Cabernet Sauvignon, a red wine from his native California. Gin used to be his favorite drink, but he has cut back on that consumption considerably, he said, as a concession to his age.

As a kid, I considered Kiner the greatest. I was delivering the *Pittsburgh Post-Gazette* during his latter days with the Pirates, and I used to devour the daily sports section.

I was writing for *The New York Post*, and had been on the baseball beat with the Mets and the Yankees, when Kiner was voted into the Baseball Hall of Fame in 1975. I made a point to go to Cooperstown, New York, for his induction ceremonies, asking for the assignment at *The Post*, because he had always been such a favorite of mine. We first met in New York in 1970, and my Pittsburgh heritage gave me an advantage in hitting it off with him right away. Heck, I was one of his fans. I was always in Kiner's Korner.

"Prince and I were close friends."
— Ralph Kiner

Kiner is a candid individual when he does his baseball broadcasts. He calls them as he sees them, for the most part. He is one of the few honest men in America when it comes to Bill Mazeroski's heroic home run to lead off the bottom of the ninth inning in the final game of that 1960 World Series.

So many men, and women, insist they were at Forbes Field when it happened. "The park held about 37,000 people at best," said Kiner, "and at least 500,000 were there that day, if you believed everybody who says they were there.

"I was here for the seventh game of the World Series, but I never saw Mazeroski's home run. I was on my way to the TV station to do the post-game report. I never saw it. Neither did Bob Prince see it. He was outside the Yankees' clubhouse, figuring they were going to win it. They told him to go to the Pirates' clubhouse. That's where the winners would be.

Sports banquet gathering in 1948 listening to boxing champion Jersey Joe Walcott included, left to right at dais, Ralph Kiner, Post-Gazette sports editor Al Abrams, and Bob Prince.

Sports banquet speakers include, left to right front, Al Abrams, Ralph Kiner, Notre Dame football coach Frank Leahy, Bob Prince and, standing behind them, Pirates Hank Greenberg and Dixie Walker.

"After my show, I was part of the crowd that filled the city. It was the most unbelievable spontaneous scene or celebration I've ever seen. We were going to the LeMont Restaurant on Mt. Washington. We were going to have dinner with Bob and Betty Prince. It was usually about a 15 minute ride, but it took us an hour and a half to get there.

"Jim Blandi owned the LeMont; he still does. When I first met him, he ran a place called The Playhouse Restaurant. It was a private club at The Playhouse. It was the only place I could go in this town when I was playing ball where no one would bother me. His uncle, Frank Blandi, had the Park Schenley, a block from Forbes Field, and I'd go there when I came to town. I would go to Klein's and the Cork & Bottle once in a while, too. Some days we went to the Nixon, where they had a supper club. Jim Blandi's place on Mt. Washington was the first of the real glamour spots in this city, as restaurants go." (Jim Blandi died at age 72 on May 6, 1998.)

I mentioned that I heard about how Prince talked Kiner into investing in a restaurant in Oakland, near the corner of Craig Street and Centre Avenue. "It was called The Cameo," recalled Kiner. It could have been called The Black Hole of Calcutta, the way money went down the drain for Kiner and Prince in that ill-fated project.

"I got traded to the Cubs soon after we bought the restaurant, so I was almost never there," recalled Kiner. "Prince was around all the time. He was buying drinks for everybody, which is one of the reasons we quickly went out of business. That's why we didn't make any money. Prince and I were very close. We got that way through osmosis, I think. He was the announcer, and he sorta latched on to me. We had a close relationship. He'd come out to Palm Springs and stay with me on occasion during the winter months. He was one of the ushers at my first wedding. He was sort of an agent for me. We shared an office in the Oliver Building."

Kiner wasn't that close to many of the Pirates who played on the 1960 World Series team. "I was never that involved with that bunch," he said. "Dick Groat was my roommate when he was a rookie in 1952. I had played a little with Bob Friend, and Vernon Law had been with us in spring training in my last year in Pittsburgh. And I played with Murtaugh; that's about it."

I mentioned to Kiner that Groat had told me he always appreciated Kiner's kindnesses when it came to dining on the road with the Pirates. "Kiner would let you pick up a check for breakfast or lunch," said Groat, "so you wouldn't feel like he was carrying you, but he always grabbed the big check at dinner time. I admired him for that."

When he heard that story, Kiner shrugged. "I always felt I should do that," he said. "I was making a lot more money than those guys. The whole infield that year was making about $24,000 total. They were all making the minimum of $6,000 a season. Wally Westlake and Murry Dickson were the only guys making any decent money. The whole payroll had to be less than a quarter million."

Kiner could not remember most of his teammates by name, off the top of his graying head, but he mentioned Murtaugh, an infielder who would manage the 1960 Pirates to a pennant and World Series championship, and Dick Cole. He mentioned two young men who came out of Pittsburgh's Hill District to stick with the Pirates, notably Bobby DelGreco and Tony Bartirome.

"As a ballplayer, Murtaugh was a hard-nosed second baseman," said Kiner, "who could run with a body that didn't figure to be able to run. He was one of the most subtle pranksters I ever met. He could spit tobacco juice better than anybody. He could hit your shoes from 30 feet away. He had a lot of fun on the train rides. He would have been the last guy I'd have thought would be a good manager. He was an Irishman's Irishman."

What was Kiner's impression of Roberto Clemente?

"I had him on Kiner's Korner once after a game when he went four-for-four against the Mets. And all he did was complain that he had been hurting for five days. He had a reputation for complaining about various hurts and ailments, and never being satisfied. Joe Durso of *The New York Times* asked me to read and review Clemente's book. I got the impression he felt he was never appreciated. He felt he was a much better ballplayer than anybody else who played the game.

"Bob Prince was close to him, and liked him. In his own mind, Clemente thought he was the greatest player in the game. I don't know about that, but I thought he was right up there with guys like Stan Musial."

Musial has always been a favorite in Pittsburgh because he came from nearby Donora. What did Kiner think of Musial?

"Stan Musial was a good friend of mine," said Kiner. "Stan Musial was Frankie Gustine with a better batting average. He was a terrific guy. Stan Musial was one of the greatest hitters who ever played the game."

Kiner's memory of Groat, in particular, was a positive one. "I remember him being extremely polite, and a well-mannered kid who was scared to death when he first came to the big leagues from college," said Kiner. Groat, who grew up in Swissvale, just east of Pittsburgh, was signed by Branch Rickey after he had starred in baseball and basketball at Duke.

"Groat was extremely competitive as a ballplayer, and extremely confident," said Kiner. "He was smart as hell, and he picked up quickly on what he needed to know. He asked a lot of questions.

"I always took a lot of extra batting practice, and he asked to participate. In my last season, in my last series in Cincinnati, we had an off-day, and I wanted to go out to the ballpark and take some extra batting practice. I wasn't hitting the ball well, and I wanted to lead the league in home runs. Dick came out and pitched to me. I hit a home run the next night and ended up tied for the league lead at 37 home runs with Hank Sauer of Chicago.

"I held out the next year because Branch Rickey wanted to cut my salary the maximum 25 per cent. He'd have cut me more if he could have."

That's when Rickey made the famous remark when Kiner complained about having his salary cut after leading or tying for the lead in home runs for seven straight seasons. "We finished last with you," Rickey retorted, "and we can finish last without you."

Kiner felt he deserved a raise because, individually, he had always done more than his share for the Pirates. At the close of the 1997 season, Kiner's seven-year streak of home run leadership was still unmatched in either league. Even Babe Ruth, whom Kiner regards as the greatest baseball player of all time, never did it. Kiner hit 23 home runs to lead the league as a rookie. Over the next six years, he hit 51, 40, 54, 47, 42 and 37 home runs. Kiner's 301 home-runs for the Pirates was second in team history only to 475 by Willie Stargell, who played for the Pirates a team record 21 seasons, three times longer than Kiner. Consider this, however: Kiner hit a home-run 7.1 times per 100 at-bats, second only to Babe Ruth in baseball history. His slugging percentage (extra-base hit totals per at bat) with the Pirates was .567, the best by a right-handed hitter, and Stargell's was .532, the best by a left-handed hitter.

In his 1990 book, *The Pittsburgh Pirates — An Illustrated History*, sportswriter Bob Smizik wrote that Kiner was the only player in Pirates' history who was a bonafide drawing card. "Attendance figures show that neither Honus Wagner nor Pie Traynor nor Roberto Clemente had a significant impact on attendance," wrote Smizik. "During Stargell's best years attendance declined. But there never has been a Pirate who so excited the fans, made them buy tickets, and then stay in the seats like Kiner."

Frank Gustine, a three-time All-Star performer and later a popular Oakland restaurateur, roomed with Kiner when Kiner first came to the Pirates. "It was amazing," said Gustine, shortly before he died in 1991. "If Ralph batted in the eighth, it seemed like the whole place would get up and leave. But if there was a chance he could bat in the ninth, nobody left."

The 54 home runs Kiner hit in 1949 has not been surpassed since then in the National League, though Roger Maris did hit 61 for the Yankees in 1961.

The Pirates pulled in more than a million fans four straight years (1947-1950). The 1,517,021 they drew in 1948 held up as an attendance record until the 1960 season when the Pirates attracted a record 1,705,828. That stood up until 1988 when the Pirates drew 1,866,713 fans to Three Rivers Stadium.

"I was making $90,000 the year before (1952)," said Kiner. "There wasn't much in the way of endorsement money back then. I got $500 for being on a Wheaties box, and a case of Wheaties for every home run I hit.

Bob Prince talks to Ralph Kiner and Rosey Rowswell.

Prince chats with Jimmy Stewart, the pride of Indiana, Pa., at formal dinner program. Prince's daughter, Nancy, still remembers her dad introducing her to the Academy Award-winning movie actor.

Young Bob Prince interviews singing star Bing Crosby, a minority owner in the Pirates, as Danny Murtaugh looks on.

"My wife Nancy (Chaffee, a former tennis star) and I did a Chesterfield ad, though neither of us smoked, and we got $1,000 for that. The only guy who made any money in those days was Bob Feller. He was the big guy in endorsements."

"That was a weird World Series."

I asked Kiner for a critique on Billy Mazeroski. "We've met at some Old Timers' Day games," said Kiner. "I saw him play. He was the best doubleplay man I ever saw. Gerry Priddy was also pretty good at that, and Priddy came before Mazeroski."

Kiner said he has heard that Maz is a happy man, content with his lot in life, and doesn't require a great deal. "I think that's more important than having a lot of money," said Kiner. "I think Roger Maris was a lot like Maz. Maris never took advantage of having hit the 61 home runs to break Babe Ruth's record. He'd rather go fishing than to a sports banquet, or a business deal."

Why does Mazeroski's home run still have such a hold on people? When his home run is shown on the video screen of the scoreboard at Three Rivers Stadium it still draws strong and sustained cheering from the crowd.

"I've seen it a thousand times," came back Kiner, "and it has to be one of the greatest moments in sports. It sorta captures what baseball is all about. Plus, the Pirates hadn't been in a World Series for so long. It had been 33 years since the Yankees swept the Pirates in four straight with Babe Ruth and Lou Gehrig in their lineup. Revenge was a long time coming."

I asked Kiner what he thought of Mazeroski's situation in regard to the Hall of Fame. He had been eligible for 15 years, but never came close to getting enough votes to be inducted, and 1991 was his last year on the ballot. Then his fate was turned over to the Veterans Committee for annual consideration.

"I never gave that any thought, to be truthful," said Kiner. "Nobody's ever asked me that question before. He certainly shouldn't get into the Hall of Fame on that home run he hit. He was the best fielding second baseman, but he was never an outstanding hitter."

What if Mazeroski had played for the Yankees? "If Maz had hit that home run for the Yankees," said Kiner, "he'd be in the Hall of Fame."

Some of Kiner's critics believe he had an advantage in getting into the Hall of Fame himself because he was popular as a broadcaster with so many of the New York sports writers, and their number gave anybody associated with New York an edge in the voting.

"I think you should have to dominate the league in some category for a period of time in order to get into the Hall of Fame," said Kiner, defending what he did in a brief nine year career. "I don't think longevity should do it, either. To me, it's a mistake to think that just because a guy gets 3,000 hits you should be in the Hall of Fame."

I asked Kiner if Stengel ever spoke much about the 1960 World Series when he was managing the Mets. "Stengel said, 'I had the best players, and they beat us,'" recalled Kiner. "That was a weird World Series!"

It was one of the most incredible postseason encounters ever. The Yankees won Games No. 2, No. 3 and No. 6 by a combined score of 38-3. The Pirates used great pitching, defense and timely hitting to stretch the Series to a seventh game at Forbes Field (where the Pirates had lost two of three games). The Pirates took a 9-7 lead into the ninth — thanks to Hal Smith's three-run homerun in the eighth — but the Yankees came up with two runs in the top of the ninth to tie the game.

"Hal Smith should get more credit," Kiner said. "That was the play of the World Series."

Kiner volunteered an anecdote involving Mazeroski. "I didn't know him that well, but I remember something he did once that impressed the heck out of me," said Kiner. "When they were filming the movie version of 'The Odd Couple,' they wanted Roberto Clemente to hit into a triple play. They would pay him $1,000 to do it. He refused. So Maz said he would do it. On the first pitch, Maz hit it perfectly to the third baseman and he started a triple play. Usually, they'd have to film a sequence like that 10 or 12 times to get it right. But Maz did it in one take."

"He was always getting me into one deal or another."

When Kiner left Chicago in favor of New York, he was replaced as a White Sox broadcaster by Milo Hamilton. Yes, the same Milo Hamilton who replaced Bob Prince when Westinghouse officials got furious with Prince and bounced him from his post as the Pirates' principal broadcaster. It was a bad move that has been blamed on the Pirates, who merely went along with the wishes of the owners of KDKA.

Kiner said that Betty Prince was one of the few friends he retained in Pittsburgh from his playing days. "I see her from time to time," he said. "She is such a nice person. She's so reserved, and such a contrast to Bob. She deserves every medal in the world for being married to Bob.

"I'd stay at their home from time to time. I don't know how she put up with him. But he was Pittsburgh.

"He was always getting me into one deal or another. They were always sure things. We were going to clean up. I put up everything I had on more than one occasion in one of his financial schemes.

Invariably, we lost our ass. He always had something going. He was in oil wells, you name it. They all went dry. He had one idea after another and, finally, I said, 'Bob, go get somebody else to bankroll this one.'

"Bob was always loose with money. Even if he was hurting financially, and he was more than a few times in his life, he always picked up the tab. No one else at the bar ever had to touch their wallet when Bob was around."

While Kiner was sharing Bob Prince stories, I asked him what he thought of the decision to drop Prince from the Pirates' broadcast team before the 1976 season. Prince had been with the Pirates since 1948, and had been one of the most popular people in Pittsburgh, indeed, a local institution.

"I think it was the dumbest decision that they ever made," commented Kiner. "It wasn't the Pirates' decision. He rubbed some KDKA or Westinghouse executives the wrong way; Bob forgot that everybody has a boss. But the Pirates went along with the decision. It was stupid. He was Pittsburgh, and he was the man who put Pittsburgh into prominence in sports. He was a great front man. He was the best in the business. He was the greatest raconteur. He could tell wonderful stories all night. He was a legend in the business. He was one of those guys who come around once in a lifetime.

"Bob parlayed a raspy voice, baseball savvy, shameless partisanship, a delightful sense of humor and an eccentric personality to become a Pittsburgh institution. His charismatic yet brash demeanor, clever command of the language, entertaining gift of gab and appreciation of baseball humor made him the consummate professional.

"We did a lot of crazy things together. I'll tell you one, though I probably shouldn't; Betty probably never knew about this one. We were driving from my home in California to spring training in San Bernardino. It's about a 50 mile drive. I had a back road route to get there, a road that had no traffic. It was a two-lane highway. Prince is following me in his car. We're driving about 90 miles an hour. All of a sudden, Prince is right behind me, and he's tapping his front bumper up against my back bumper. He keeps doing it, and I can see him laughing like hell in the rear view window.

"I can see a guy a mile down the road coming out just as Bob is passing me, and the guy is heading our way. Bob's eyes are on me alone. I see this car coming up closer and closer. And Bob is going 90 miles an hour in the same lane as the guy coming at us. I thought they were going to smash head-on. Prince went around him on the dirt to the left of the guy. If that guy had panicked and veered off to the right, Prince would have been dead. He had a heart of gold, but he was fearless. And sometimes foolish."

Kiner's tale brought another Prince story to mind. How about the time that Prince made a bet with some fellow travelers on a Pirates' road trip and dove out of the third floor of the Chase Hotel in St. Louis into the hotel pool.

"I was at the Chase after that incident, and I went out by the pool to check it out, and have a look. He knew he could clear the cement and make it into the pool; he knew the angle because he had been on the swimming team at college."

"Do you think he had been drinking before he took his daredevil dive?" I asked Kiner.

"I heard he had two drinks; that was nothing," Kiner came back. "There were some wires stretching across the area; it's a good thing he didn't hit them. They'd have lit him up pretty good."

Jim O'Brien

Ralph Kiner signs balls in 1997 at Robert Morris College card show.

Did you know...
Ralph Kiner hit a home run every 14.1 times at bat, surpassed only by Babe Ruth, who homered on average one every 11.8 times at bat.

Stan Musial
Still the Man

He and Prince were pals

Stan Musial, the great St. Louis Cardinals Hall of Famer, hailed from Donora, and was always a close friend of Bob Prince. He often traveled to Pittsburgh to speak at banquets paying tribute to Prince.

"I couldn't miss this night," Musial said at a night in Prince's honor at Three Rivers Stadium. "Bob attended the first dinner ever held for me in Donora and he was also at the testimonial in my honor in St. Louis after I retired.

"I'll never forget his remarks when he came to St. Louis. Speakers were limited to two minutes because of the number of people on the program. But the time was cut to a minute as the evening wore on. It was late when Bob finally got to the dais and in typical Prince fashion, he declared.

"'Here's a man who has been at bat more than 10,000 times during his great career and has made more than 3,000 hits. Now, what else can I say? Oh, yes, he also made the most outs. I think it is ridiculous that we are gathered here to honor a man who made more than 7,000 outs.'

"End of speech.

"I also recall an incident involving a Prince broadcast in 1960, the year the Pirates won the National League pennant, then upset the New York Yankees in the World Series.

"I had beaten the Pirates two straight days on late-inning home runs, and I came up in a similar situation a third time. I didn't hear the broadcast, naturally, but friends told me how Bob described that third game situation.

"He said, 'Now, here's that man Musial again. You know what he did to us yesterday and you know what he did to us the day before. Tune in tomorrow to find out what he does to us today!'"

"What better way to make a living than to go out in the fresh air, what there is left of it, anyway, and get paid for playing a boy's game. My greatest thrill...I still say the greatest was in just pulling on the uniform and going out there to compete."
— Stan Musial
At his retirement dinner

Bob Prince interviews one of his favorites, Donora's Stan Musial, at Forbes Field.

Joe Gordon
A man for all seasons

"We always wanted to be sure it was the right thing to do."

Joe Gordon and Bob Prince had a lot in common. They shared a love and enthusiasm for baseball at large, the Pirates in particular, football and basketball and hockey, Art Rooney and Joe Tucker, Pittsburgh and its people and all things associated with the city, Radio Rich, sunshine and sartorial splendor.

Gordon was far more conservative than Prince when it came to clothes, but he believed in looking good and being properly attired for all occasions. He was certainly never a character in the same class as Prince. But he was a stellar sports figure, an always reliable behind-the-scenes individual who made things click, and he was respected by most of his peers. Like Prince, Gordon had his fans and his detractors. Like Prince, Gordon was a man for all seasons.

He was a mover and shaker, up to the standards of the Steelers when they won four Super Bowls in six seasons and were named the NFL's Team of the Decade during that glorious run of the '70s.

He thought himself lucky to have known and worked with Art Rooney, Dan Rooney and Chuck Noll, all Hall of Famers in his book.

He was a perfectionist, and demanding of those around him, and he could be sharp-tongued at times, bringing people up short, an ambassador and the best of company at other times. He could freeze you with a disapproving look. He could make you smile with some off-the-cuff remark. He'd crack up when he was trying to relate a funny story. Nobody promoted Pittsburgh more than Joe Gordon. He was proud of its past, dealt with the challenges of its present, and believed in and fought fiercely for its future.

His reprimands and pats-on-the-back were accepted with equanimity because they were genuine, and you had to respect the source of same. In his boyhood neighborhood, he was known as a kid with *chutzpah*. He lived by some of the Steelers' oft-mentioned mottos. He believed in doing it right and he would do whatever it takes to complete a task. In all respects, he was a winner.

"Before we made any decisions in the Steelers' front office, we always wanted to be sure it was the right thing to do, that it was the fair thing to do," said Gordon.

"And I've always believed that you should never lie. You can say you have no comment. But never lie. It can get you into real trouble."

Gordon grew up in South Oakland and then Squirrel Hill and was always running off to ballparks, stadiums and arenas to watch his favorite athletes and teams, listening to radio sports broadcasts, watching all televised events, devouring the daily newspapers. His boyhood enjoyment became his career.

Jim O'Brien

Steelers president Dan Rooney and Joe Gordon stand by portrait of the late Arthur J. Rooney, the founder and patriarch of the Pittsburgh Steelers. They were in the memorial library that was once the office of "The Chief" at Three Rivers Stadium.

Donna Rae

Long-time Steelers publicist Joe Gordon is toasted at retirement dinner by Dave Ailes, left, of the *Tribune-Review* and Ed Bouchette of the *Pittsburgh Post-Gazette*.

Bob Prince at Stan Musial's retirement dinner in St. Louis:
"I think it is ridiculous that we are gathered here to honor a man who made more than 7,000 outs."

Bob Prince, like Joe Tucker, was one of those people he always admired, first as a fan and then as someone who worked with them as a sports publicist for several Pittsburgh teams.

When the Civic Arena opened in 1961, Gordon became the public relations director for the Pittsburgh Rens in the short-lived American Basketball League from 1961 to 1962. That second season turned out to be a half-season before Abe Saperstein, the league founder, and the owners gave up the ghost. In that season, Gordon, at age 27, also served as the team's general manager. He was hailed in a national sports publication as the youngest to hold such a post in pro sports across America at that time.

The Rens were owned by Archie "Tex" Litman and his brother Eugene Litman, who now holds a minority interest in the Pirates. One of the ABL teams, the Cleveland Jets, was owned by shipping magnate George Steinbrenner. Steinbrenner once said he'd trade one of his ships to get Connie Hawkins, the star of the Rens and the ABL's MVP.

When the ABL folded, Gordon went to work for Steinbrenner for a few weeks in Cleveland, but figured that was going nowhere and returned to Pittsburgh. He was never paid for his services by Steinbrenner, the boss of the New York Yankees in recent years.

After that, he sold space for Yellow Pages for a year-and-a-half — "one of the best learning experiences of my life" — before becoming the publicist for the Pittsburgh Hornets of the American Hockey League for the 1964-65 season. He remained there until the Hornets gave way to the Penguins when the National Hockey League expanded for the 1967-68 season, doubling in size from six to 12 teams.

Dan Rooney hired him to work with and later supplant Ed Kiely in the public relations office of the Steelers in 1969. Kiely asked Roy Blount Jr. who his favorite interviews were for his book, *Three Bricks Shy of a Load*, about the Steelers of the '70s. Blount thought Ray Mansfield and Dwight White were the most interesting individuals he had interviewed for that book. Kiely always asks me the same question about my books on the Steelers, Pirates and Penguins. It surprised me, I must admit, when Gordon became one of my favorite interviews for this book. Gordon's life has been intertwined with Pittsburgh's sports history for more than half a century, and he had seldom taken the time to talk about himself.

He paid his dues. Gordon had worked with three pro sports teams in his hometown — basketball, hockey and football — and, ironically enough, never worked with the Pirates in his No. 1 love, baseball. "The Pirates talked to me on two occasions, but nothing ever came of it," said Gordon. "I thought it would be a great way for me to complete the cycle here."

Along the way, he went from being a fan of Bob Prince to someone who called on the popular Pittsburgh sports broadcaster from time to time, and always found him to be willing to help him in whatever he was attempting to promote. He learned from Prince how to get people to do things for a common good. Gordon was good at organizing fund-raisers such as the Ray Mansfield Memorial Golf event, named in honor of his old pal, "Ranger" Ray Mansfield, and no one was better at selling space in the game program.

Joe Gordon and I had a lot in common. He was eight years older, but we had shared many similar experiences and attended the same schools, walked some of the same streets and knew some of the same characters. We loved Art Rooney, Bob Prince and Joe Tucker, admired Al Abrams and Frankie Gustine. When we got together for this interview, we had both been married for 31 years. We both lost brothers around the same time in our lives. His brother, Mark, died at age 41 in 1978. My brother, Dan, died at age 43 in 1981. They were students at Allderdice at the same time. We missed them dearly. They'd come to mind when we were in certain places, attending certain kinds of events, and we wished they were there with us, at least for one more day. "This is the 20th anniversary of his death," said Gordon.

We both organized games in our neighborhoods, collected sports bubble gum cards, loved and saved our copies of *SPORT* magazine, the best sports magazine by far in those days, and later *Sports Illustrated*. We pored over the sports sections of the daily newspapers.

Gordon and I were both graduates of Taylor Allderdice High School and the University of Pittsburgh and admirers of Myron Cope who went the same route. We've attended a lot of the same sporting events through the years, made our way through the same streets and minefields of our youth, and worked together. We share many memories, the best of times and similar slings and arrows, ideas, ways and means to get things accomplished, and a gratitude for the entree we've enjoyed to some wonderful times in the history of Pittsburgh.

We both got a kick out of Cope and Beano Cook, both beloved eccentrics on the Pittsburgh sports scene. Gordon grew up in the same neighborhoods as the late Richard Caliguiri, also an Allderdice grad, and cared about the city in the same passionate manner. They had the same sort of street savvy, a way of working with people for a common purpose. He respected people like Caliguiri who could get things done, who had a vision for the city, and ignored the naysayers who wanted to keep things just the way they were.

When I first was getting established as a professional journalist in Pittsburgh, Gordon always gave me first-class treatment. At first, when Beano Cook and I were publishing *Pittsburgh Weekly Sports* on a shoestring, Gordon treated us as if we were with *The New York Times* or *The Sporting News*. So did Prince and Tucker, but that wasn't true with everyone in similar positions of power.

I've known Gordon for over 35 years, and admire and respect him and have learned a lot from him. It wasn't until he retired, however, at age 63 after 28 years of media relations, marketing and sales service to the Steelers, that he had time to *really* talk, and share some stories and sentiments that he had never offered before.

It struck me that Gordon was now the same age as my father was when he died, and that hardly seemed possible. Gordon looked so much younger than my dad, so much more spirited and vibrant. Our mutual friend Beano Cook, more recently an ESPN analyst and sports commentator, had lost a toe in surgery two weeks earlier, the result of diabetes. Talking about Beano's setback made us both more aware of our advanced years and the accompanying vulnerability.

Gordon looked so good, so relaxed, so bright-eyed. Those Jiminy Cricket eyes, dark and protuberant, have always arrested your attention. He has that gleam in his eyes I believe is critical in becoming successful in any pursuit. He had all the time I wanted, he was expansive in his remarks, smiled often, and seemed to be enjoying talking about his family and friends, co-workers, et al, and reflecting on his early impressions of Bob Prince and other Pittsburgh icons. Gordon looked like he was sunning himself on a beach, something he hopes to do more often in retirement.

Gordon came to work for the Steelers in 1969, joining the organization the same year that Chuck Noll was hired as the head coach by Dan Rooney. It was the beginning of a beautiful relationship for all concerned. Noll used to scold me whenever I wanted him to wax nostalgic about his early days with the Steelers while he was still coaching the club. He said there would be plenty of time to talk about those things when he retired. He was too busy looking ahead to look back.

The same was true with Gordon. It wasn't until he no longer was working at his usual frenetic pace that he was able to pull up a chair, lean back in it, and look back into his storied past serving several Pittsburgh sports teams and the local media that I was able to fully appreciate who he was, and what he was really all about.

I always thought Gordon must have had a sprinter's starting blocks at the foot of his bed the way he went about his work in such a mercurial fashion. It was often frustrating trying to get his full attention and quality time when he was going full blast. So it was a rare pleasure to sit and talk without being under the clock.

When the Steelers were winning four Super Bowls in six years in the '70s, the Steelers were regarded as having the best public relations operation in the National Football League. Joe Gordon, Dan Rooney and his late father, Arthur J. Rooney, were most responsible for that reputation. Noll was never the easiest interview in the league, but he was always accessible, and so were his Steelers. Art Rooney, Mr. Rooney or Chief or Prez, was everybody's surrogate grandfather, and out-of-town writers wondered why they didn't encounter more owners like him in their travels. He was a Godsend.

"Some of my favorite guys were Connie Hawkins, Art Rooney, Joe Greene, Red Sullivan — he was a fantastic guy, so far ahead of his time when he was coaching the Penguins at the beginning. Pete Rozelle and Joe Browne in the NFL office were my adult heroes," said Gordon. "I learned so much about p.r. from those two men."

Gordon showed me a letter he had received from Rozelle, the late commissioner, responding to a letter Gordon had sent him upon his retirement as head of the league. "When people ask me if I miss the job," replied Rozelle, "I reply not really except for some of the people. You and your boss would certainly rank at the top."

I asked Gordon where he got his philosophy from to do his job the way he did it.

"I got my philosophy," he said, "or the way I've worked, from my parents, the way they lived their lives. They treated everybody with respect. My mother was the most accommodating person; she smiled all the time. I got my father's stubbornness.

"There was never a mandate here about how we were to operate. It was just something that evolved. After I got started here and became comfortable, Dan and I got real close. It was truly like a family. Everyone who was here was your friend. Every time a tough decision came up, we'd ask the same question, 'Is it right?' Dan would say, 'Is it right?' They didn't want to do anything that was wrong."

I caught up with Gordon a half hour before the NFL draft began on Saturday, April 18, 1998. It was one of those days when Gordon normally would have been flitting about the Steelers' complex, checking with the coaches and scouts and Dan Rooney, then the media, and making sure everyone was on the same page, scolding someone for being out of line for some reason, praising someone for a job well done the week before. Service was his middle name.

Only the week before, however, the Steelers had hired Ron Wahl away from the University of Pittsburgh to become the team's media relations director. He was replacing Rob Boulware, who had worked the job the previous three seasons. Wahl was working the draft along with Ron Miller, who would be leaving the Steelers a few weeks later. Dave Lockett, a young man who had been working in the league office, had been hired to assist Wahl. He was there as well, getting acquainted with his new surroundings. Wahl and Lockett looked excited about their new challenge. Gordon welcomed them and introduced them to some insiders, but held back on offering any advice, lest it be unwelcome or unappreciated.

Wahl would be one of about six people who were now doing all the things Gordon did when he first came on board and through the early '70s as the Steelers were forging a revamped franchise that would become the envy of everyone in the league. It was the same with the Pirates, where many were now doing what Jack Berger had done in the team's halcyon days at Forbes Field. It was a different era, the multi-media and marketing demands were different. One person could no longer handle all the assignments and requests.

Gordon had given up his large office and moved into a smaller office. He had given up the only office with a window — cut out of the cinderblock wall only a few years earlier with a sliver view of the outdoors — in an office complex that could be easily mistaken for a bomb shelter of the '50s. Gordon was being retained as a consultant by Dan

Rooney, but Gordon didn't know how often he'd be coming into the office, or how much he'd be called upon as a consultant. Noll was also a consultant, but was seldom seen at the Steelers' offices. It was nice to remain on the payroll in any case.

The Steelers were now run by Dan Rooney, the boss of bosses, his oldest son, Art II, Tom Donahoe, the director of football operations, and Bill Cowher, the head coach.

Gordon was always a whirling dervish, a telephone constantly pressed to his ear, a pen in his hand jotting down "to do" notes, with an eye on the TV in his office, usually in recent years, tuned to the business news channel to see how his stocks were doing. CNBC and ESPN were his favorite channels. He always seemed to be doing three things at once, a pinball machine gone mad. I always thought it was best to call him on the telephone than to show up in front of his desk seeking his attention.

He brought the same intensity to his tasks as Bill Cowher & Co. Dan Rooney believed in having a lean and mean staff and expected an extended effort from everyone. Football was his only business, and what he knew best.

"Coming here was the greatest thing that ever happened to me," said Gordon. "It was fantastic. It determined the course of my later life. It couldn't have been a better situation. Noll came in and Danny was beginning to assert himself as the head of the organization. Art Jr. was extremely good at scouting players and writing reports in those days. The camaraderie was unbelievable here. I never saw a situation when everyone wasn't working for a common goal.

"But it got out of control. The money changed everything. The players deserve to share in the money, but it's changed the way everyone approaches the game. There's no loyalty on either side."

Through the years, Gordon made good money, especially in his latter years with the Steelers when he was generously rewarded for his fruitful and loyal service to the organization. He had saved and invested his money wisely. He had been married for 31 years to his wife, Babe, and she had worked as a secretary to the *Post-Gazette*'s Dapper Dan Charities for 23 of those years before retiring from those duties in 1986.

"We were married on June 2," said Gordon. "That was the same date that Lou Gehrig had died."

Together, he and Babe had done quite well.

They had no children of their own, but they were close to their nieces and nephews, and attentive, generous and proud of them through the years.

The Gordons were financially secure, and lived in a two bedroom apartment with a glorious view atop Mt. Washington. They could see the city's skyline and the stadium from their deck — fireworks were an in-your-face attraction — and Gordon couldn't wait until the new ballpark and stadium could be seen from there as well. "When we entertain visitors from other NFL cities at our place, they can't get over the view," said Gordon. Music filtered up from the I. C. Light Tent at Station Square just below their balcony on summer nights.

They enjoyed traveling and entertainment of all kinds, dining out, etc. They were regulars, for instance, for the banjo nights on Wednesdays at the James Tavern on the North Side. Both were approaching Joe's retirement with great concerns. He had always been so busy and so enthused about his work. He loved going to see the Pitt and Duquesne basketball games, the Pirates and Penguins. He was usually in the company of one of his pals, either Tom "Maniac" McDonough or Burt "Porky" Caplan, guys he'd grown up with in Oakland back in the '50s.

Joe and Babe both wondered what it would be like to see so much of each other during the day. As the wife of Mets' General Manager George Weiss once said upon hearing of his retirement plans, "I married you for better or worse, but not for lunch."

The environment of pro football and the Steelers' front office had all changed, different personalities, different demands, and Joe was no longer enjoying his job as he once had.

"When I got into this, 80 percent of my job concerned football and 20 percent concerned business," he explained. "Now it's the other way around: 80 percent business and 20 percent football. I liked it better the old way. The money has changed everything. But change is inevitable, I've always known that. Noll always preached about that. He was right.

"This is the right time for me to move along, to slow down perhaps, and to do some other things I've wanted to do. I have no regrets. It's just something I want to do, personally, because the business has changed, but more importantly, I have changed. It's time to move on."

"Bob Prince was bigger than life."
— Joe Gordon

It took us awhile to talk about Bob Prince, but Gordon almost gushed in reflecting on the Pirates' broadcaster and one of the city's most beloved sports commentators of another era.

"I think he was, in my mind, bigger than life," said Gordon. "He was one of the most remarkable people I've ever known. He was comfortable in every situation.

"He could emcee the raunchiest stag dinner one night, and the next morning deliver a thoughtful eulogy at a church.

"He epitomized what the Pirates were all about when baseball was king. People talk about John Facenda, who did all those NFL highlight films, as having such a great, authoritative voice. But Prince didn't have to take a back seat to Facenda. He had a great voice.

"He was totally without pretense. He was so accommodating when I came on the scene. He always made me feel special. If Prince was walking on one side of the street and he'd see you on the other side of the street, say Grant Street, he'd always holler out to you across the street. 'Hey, Joe, howya doin'?' He'd irritate you sometimes with some of his tactics, but that was Bob Prince, too.

"He was a real asset to this city, a true Pittsburgh icon. I have a thing about people who promote Pittsburgh. It's better, he believed that. Prince was always selling the town. I'm sure he had a lot of chances to leave, but he stuck around. He's one of the all-time guys I've ever come across in this town, like Art Rooney.

"I remember people like Prince and Joe Tucker and Ed Conway and Red Donley and how super they were to work with. These guys were available. You called and they answered the phone. You can't get the guys at the TV stations on the phone anymore — you have to leave a message —and sportswriters are never at the office anymore. They only go in to pick up their checks. Prince had a heart of gold. He had time for everyone. And he never just put his name on a board behind some charity. He went to work, and got the people and money to make it successful. I remember all the things he did for Radio Rich — the kindness and largesse he exhibited."

Mention of Radio Rich prompted me to ask Gordon to provide more insights into this character who was Radio Rich, another part of Pittsburgh's rich sports scene through the years, and how Prince and then Gordon himself had become guardians for Radio Rich.

Richard Gloucewski had been abandoned as a baby, left on a doorstep at a convent in Brookline, and raised by nuns. He loved sports and found a way to get into every sports event in Pittsburgh without a ticket. He became a go-fer, assisting in some manner or another all the broadcasters and sportswriters, keeping stats, spotting, providing out-of-town scores.

He was bald and didn't have any teeth for most of his adult life, and had that omnipresent pipe in a corner of his mouth, and looked like a first cousin of cartoon character Popeye the Sailor Man.

He always had a transistor radio at his ear, and he would provide scores and soundbites to passersby, most of whom had no idea what he was talking about, or wondered what relevance there was to Radio's latest report. . . "the Bullets are up by three points at the half." Radio Rich was ESPN before there was such a thing.

When he traveled with a team, Radio Rich always had a briefcase neatly packed with transistor radios and colored pens and enough packs of pipe tobacco to get through a football season let alone a weekend on the road. The packs of pipe tobacco were packed as neatly as stacks of dollar bills, like gangsters were always showing off in the movies. Radio Rich was a neat guy.

Radio Rich was a regular at Duquesne basketball games, all the hockey games, Steelers games and Pirates games, staying close to Prince in case he needed something.

Radio Rich is assisted in ice skating venture by Jack Riley, former general manager of the Pittsburgh Penguins, and Joe Gordon, the team's first publicist. Gordon's wife, Babe, is skating in the background at the team's 1987 holiday season party at the Civic Arena.

Joe Gordon receives the first Bob Prince Memorial Award in 1985 at the Thompson Run Athletic Association's annual Sports Night in West Mifflin from club officials, Jim Kenney, left, and Darrell Hess. Prince was the emcee at the dinner for 23 consecutive years. Hess has hosted and coordinated the dinner for 40 years.

Nellie King knew Radio Rich, too, having benefitted from his support services first as a Pirates' broadcaster and then as the sports information director at Duquesne University. "Bob Prince didn't adopt Radio Rich," recalled King. "It was really the other way around. Radio Rich just adopted Bob Prince. Radio was street smart and he knew how to get money from people. He'd drop less-than-subtle hints about his birthday coming up and what size sport coat he wore, stuff like that."

Prince provided Radio Rich with money to keep him going, to pay for his rent at the Downtown YMCA and later in his own apartment on the North Side. Joe Tucker used to pay Rich as well for services provided, as did some newspapermen.

Once Prince prodded Radio Rich into getting a set of dentures to fill that cavity in his face. After Radio Rich got his new set of crockery he complained to Prince that he needed a raise in his weekly stipend. "What do you need more money for?" protested Prince in reply.

"Now that I have teeth," responded Radio Rich, "I can eat steak."

Radio Rich died June 20, 1986. "He was the most innocent guy you'd ever want to meet. He'd call me at home at night, and tell me the Lakers had won, and Wilt had 34, and I'd ask him what did that have to do with the price of eggs in Pittsburgh, but that wouldn't keep him from calling the next night with more breaking news," said Gordon.

"He was a good guy. He didn't have a mean bone in his body. It's a tragedy that he died at such a young age (55). He didn't know what hit him. I'd taken him to Central Medical Pavilion for a checkup. He didn't understand what was wrong with him. It was cancer.

"I told him he'd be fine. He was so devastated. I'll never forget the day he died. We used to have to go up to Mercy Hospital, and I'd take him. I'd leave him off, and he'd have his treatment, and I'd pick him up in an hour, and take him back to his place.

"He was living on North Avenue at the time. He had a one-bedroom apartment; it was perfect for him. He had his own bathroom, stuff like that. Babe and I were supposed to go to Puerto Rico the following week, and I was trying to make preparations for him to be taken care of while we were away.

"I told Lynne Molyneaux at our office that if anything happens to Radio here's what you need to do. You can call me here, and here's what else you have to do. We had already made arrangements for him at a funeral home on Cedar Avenue. That night Babe and I went to Heinz Hall. I get home, and I got a call. He'd come out on the front steps of the house where he was living, and he just keeled over and died, right there.

"It was really a sad thing. He had no family or anybody, but it was a nice wake. Beano was there, and Nellie King was there. A bunch of guys Radio had worked with — when he was cleaning dishes at the Sheraton and at the Roosevelt — were there, too.

"He was unique. He was something special. Radio was probably the most loyal person I've ever known. Tell him something and tell him to keep it to himself, and it would die with him.

"He was washing dishes once at the Sheraton, which is where Point Park's main building is now, and Bill Burns, through the Chief, got him a job at the Roosevelt Hotel. Bill Burns was another one of his benefactors. Radio was slightly retarded, and he'd been raised in an orphanage. But he found a way to live a life in which he went to all the games, got the best seats, and had fun. The Rooneys, to their credit, took him to all four Super Bowls.

"A lot of people couldn't get tickets, and they wanted to know how the hell he managed to pull it off. They'd ask, 'How the hell did that dumb sonofabitch get on the Steelers' plane?' He'd be walking around the hotel like he owned the team, puffing on his pipe. . ."

Gordon grinned as he could picture Radio Rich putting on the ritz. "Babe and I would frequently take him to dinner, usually at Eat'n Park or some place like that. One night we took him to the Edison Hotel. We thought he'd get a kick out of the show. We sat down next to the stage where the girls came out and danced. He had a real aversion to women, we learned, especially nude or scantily-clad women like you had dancing at the Edison. He sat with his back to the stage, and we left after about 15 minutes. It was the damndest thing. We felt sorry for him.

"Bob Prince was his first true benefactor. Tucker slipped him money. I'm sure the Chief did the same, like he did for so many others. I think the Chief was paying the rent for a lot of the old guys who lived at the Roosevelt. Prince got him his teeth. Prince was good to him. Prince was a piece of work. He was a helluva guy. He was a great thing for this community. Tucker was fantastic in that same light. They made you feel special.

"If Prince was Radio's stepfather, then my wife was his stepmother," continued Gordon. "Every single holiday, Rich was at our house. He'd be drinking his Coca-Cola and smoking his pipe. My wife and her mother treated Radio like he was royalty. He sucked it up. My mother-in-law, Bubba Dzmura, would ask Babe or me, 'Is Radio coming?' She was the greatest cook in the world, and Radio was her biggest fan in that regard."

It goes without saying that Babe and Joe Gordon were good successors to Bob Prince as patron saints of Radio Rich.

"I hired Bob Prince to do p.r. work for us the day after he was fired by KDKA. He stayed on the payroll till the day he died. We went to Europe together. I loved his wonderful personality and his very enthusiastic attitude on life. I'm a little enthusiastic myself, so I appreciated that."
— Jack B. Piatt,
Millcraft Industries

As a child growing up with games all around him in South Oakland and later Squirrel Hill, Joe Gordon regarded Joe DiMaggio, Stan Musial and Ralph Kiner as his earliest sports heroes.

He lived on Parkview Avenue, not far from where Danny Marino and his family would live. Bruno Sammartino, who would become the greatest draw as a world wrestling champion, grew up in the same neighborhood. Dom Abbott, who made a fortune when he marketed women's wigs when that was first popular, and then became an entrepreneur by developing restaurants like Dingbats in the area, lived a block away from Gordon as he was growing up.

"My dad would get my brother Mark and I and we'd walk a half dozen blocks to get to Forbes Field. My dad's name was Manny, and he was a former minor league baseball player. He played infield in the old Mid-Atlantic Baseball League.

"He was a very modest and quiet guy. He was so interested in sports. He was always playing ball with us. He took us to Frick Park to that ballfield at Forbes and Braddock, and he'd hit fly balls to us. Mark was a year and a half younger. He became a dentist, and he always liked sports, too."

"We had a sister, Patti, who was a great gymnast and dancer. She was four years younger than me. We're very close, and we're very close to her children. And Mark's.

"The conversation at our dinner table was always sports. My mother, Sara, didn't go to the games, but whenever I'd come in the door, even in later years, she'd always say, 'Who won the game today?' She was very interested in the Steelers.

"My dad devoured the sports pages. When he owned his bar in Homestead, he had to close down at midnight. My brother and I would stay up because my dad would stop on the way home and he'd buy us fresh hot corned beef at Hebrew National, where Rhoda's is now (since sold and renamed Kazansky's), and he'd buy hot rye bread at Herman's Bakery at the corner of Forbes and Murray."

"Bob Prince began needling the players long before Howard Cosell ever saw a microphone. "He's in the twilight of a mediocre career," was his analysis of one pitcher. A batter lunges clumsily at a pitch, and Prince says, "He tomahawked that one. If he'd have hit it, he'd have scalped it."

That brought back a memory for me as well. "Wasn't there a pool hall upstairs of that bakery, or just around the corner?" I asked.

"Yeah, Ross's Pool Hall, right next to it."

Then Joe and I swapped stories about playing hooky from Allderdice and going to Ross's Pool Hall, or some other billiards parlor in Downtown Pittsburgh to play pool with friends instead of being in class.

I talked about how my buddies and I would play hooky and return to school for lunch, especially on Turkey Day when they offered three different kinds of turkey dishes at the school cafeteria — turkey on bisquits, turkey on mashed potatoes and turkey on rice.

"You could get lunch for 23 cents," gushed Gordon. "Imagine that. You could get two main dishes for eight cents apiece and a dessert for seven cents. And drink water with it." I think it cost me a little more, as I had to have milk, and maybe one other main course. But you couldn't beat the price. It was worth risking getting caught playing hooky by the teachers to reenter the school for lunch.

"My dad would bring the corned beef and rye home and we'd eat sandwiches after midnight. He'd stop and bring home the early Sunday edition of the Pittsburgh *Sun-Telegraph*. It had a great sports section.

"We read all three papers every day. Later, I started reading *The Sporting News*. We used to look up the box scores of the minor leagues to see how the Pirates' prospects were doing. We were really fans. I loved *SPORT* magazine. It was the best magazine for young sports fans. There wasn't any *Sports Illustrated* back then. That came later. My brother and I saved every issue of *SPORT* for about ten years. We saved baseball trading cards.

"When we moved, my mother threw out all our magazines and cards. We could have cried.

"I loved to read stories by Al Abrams and Les Biederman and Jack Sell. I listened to Joe Tucker doing his sports reports. He did three a night. He was the dean of local sports broadcasters back then. He was the nicest and most accommodating guy when I started out. When I was with the Rens, Joe was fantastic. Sid Berlin was the general manager at WWSW, and we were good friends.

"My dad owned and operated the Hi Lite Cafe on East 8th Avenue in Homestead, right up from the Homestead Business Machines, near McClure Street. It was right on the border that separates Homestead from Munhall. I was just there in that same block on Monday getting my Royal typewriter repaired. They had another Royal typewriter there they had cleaned up, and I bought it for $45."

Gordon pointed proudly to the Royal typewriter on the stand by his desk. I asked him why he didn't get a word processor or computer, and he just smiled and shrugged. "I don't know how to use one of those, and I don't want to be bothered with it now," he said. I told him it made writing easier, and more efficient, and that there were all kinds of benefits, but Gordon wasn't going to be convinced. Change was inevitable, but he didn't have to yield to everything new that was coming his way. It was his holdout.

"I had my other typewriter for 25 years, so this should last me as long as I need it."

Then he got back to talking about his family.

"I was about 10 when we moved from Oakland to Squirrel Hill. We moved early in the summer. My brother and I would walk back to our old neighborhood every day to play with our friends. We had gone to Holmes School and we liked playing in a lot next to it. There was another field behind Parkview Avenue close to the bridge and we played ball there, too. Sometimes we went down to the end of South Oakland and played at Frazier Field, overlooking the J&L (Jones & Laughlin Steel), which has been renamed Danny Marino Field. We played ball from dawn to dusk, no matter what the season was.

"We loved it. Living in Oakland was the greatest. We had nothing to compare it to at the time, but looking back I realize how special it was. Everything was there at our doorstep. We went to the Carnegie Museum and the library. We saw the dinosaur exhibition, which is still one of the greatest in the world. We'd go to the Nature Museum. Phipps Conservatory was there. The Schenley Oval. The park. Flagstaff Hill. Carnegie Tech. Pitt. You name it.

"We'd walk to the Pitt games. As kids, we'd get into the Pitt football games for 25 cents. One day, the Steelers were playing the Rams that night. On the way back from Pitt, Mark and I decided we'd sneak into Forbes Field for the football game, too. We hid out for four hours. We were freezing our asses off, but it was worth it. The Rams clobbered the Steelers that day."

He couldn't wait to see what Al Abrams and Joe Tucker would have to say about it the next day. "Joe was fantastic," said Gordon. "Everybody was in awe of Al Abrams. He was the man-about-town, the society writer as well as the sports writer. He knew everybody. And everybody had him on a pedestal. Everyone's dream was to be like Al Abrams.

"He went to all the big events. He went to all the boxing championship fights, the football championships before there was a Super Bowl, the World Series, the Kentucky Derby. He never missed a big event. He would spice up the bottom of the columns with mentions of his friends and all the characters he knew at all the hotels he frequented around town."

And Gordon kept busy, playing baseball, playing shortstop for every team that would give him a uniform.

He played for his neighborhood ballteam, the Squirrel Hill Bulldogs. "I was the manager, general manager, promoter and player," Gordon said with a grin.

"I played for the 31st Ward in Hays, for the Shady Side American Legion, Murdoch Chevrolet in Oakland. I played shortstop and sometimes second and third."

And in the mid-50s, he remembered that the Pirates had an infielder named Sid Gordon. "He was a right-handed hitter who hit home runs to right field," recalled Gordon. "He'd come from the New York Giants and they had that short porch in right field at the Polo Grounds so he learned to hit them out that way. Guys couldn't hit home runs to the opposite field in those days. Now they're so strong they can hit home runs to any field."

Gordon also played shortstop and lettered for three years on the Pitt baseball team. He showed me a letter of commendation that was written May 20, 1957 acknowledging his ballplaying at Pitt that had been sent to him over the signature of then Chancellor Dr. Edward H. Litchfield. The letter still meant a lot to Gordon. He kept such correspondence in his files.

The Pirates were playing the San Diego Padres at Three Rivers Stadium that same Saturday afternoon as the NFL Draft was going on. The Pitt baseball team was scheduled to play a doubleheader that same evening, a Big East encounter with Notre Dame on the same surface.

The Pitt baseball alumni were having a get-together there that day. Gordon had gotten notice of it, and had agreed to attend. He would be seeing some of his teammates from his playing days at Pitt.

A tripleheader and a draft all in the same day at Three Rivers. It was Joe Gordon's kind of day. He didn't have to concern himself with the media attending the draft — others would be looking after their needs and fielding their questions and complaints — so he could go watch some baseball games and talk to good friends.

Joe Gordon didn't have to worry. It looked like retirement would suit him just fine.

"I remember one game at St. Louis. I threw a forkball down and away and Musial hit it over the right field roof. And I think I'd been 21 innings without giving up a run and we lost the ballgame on that, a good pitch. After the game I'm sitting in my locker and Murtaugh — who had this dry sense of humor — comes in and slaps me on the back and says, 'Relief pitcher, my ass!' "
— ElRoy Face,
Former Pirates relief pitcher

Nancy Prince Thomas
"Dearest" and "Nanny"

"He was a Santa Claus dad."

Nancy Prince hated being the daughter of Bob Prince, but she loved her dad dearly. Since she has been married, to Ray Thomas, she still feels the same way.

To her, sharing her mother's sentiments, there were two Bob Princes: the public one and the private one. She much preferred the latter, the one who looked after and loved her and treated her like she was a princess. The one who called her "dearest" and "Nanny," and kissed and hugged her, whispered sweet things in her ear, took her special places and introduced her to all kinds of interesting people.

Bob Prince was something else.

"That's two people to me," she explained. "There's Bob Prince, the man who worked for the Pittsburgh Pirates for 28 years. That person I did not dwell on. I was a very shy, introverted girl in my younger years. I didn't want anybody bringing Bob Prince's name up to me. I refused to get to know anything about baseball. I didn't like people staring at me, pointing me out as Bob Prince's daughter, or making a big production out of it. There were times I came home from school crying because of something somebody had said about him.

"Bob Prince was another person. That wasn't my dad. Bob Prince was the announcer for the Pirates. My dad was somebody else. Maybe I did it to save my sanity.

"If somebody introduces me, even now, and says, 'This is Nancy Prince. Do you know who her father was?' Well, that really turns me off. When people tell me stories about him, especially some of the stories they choose to tell, or suggest that there had to be a lot of pros and cons to being his daughter, I'm sorry, but I don't show them any of Bob Prince's charm.

"It was especially hurtful when someone said mean things, like he didn't know anything about baseball, or that they didn't like him, or they didn't care for the way he broadcasted a ballgame. Why tell me that? Are you trying to make my day?

"On the other hand, he was a Santa Claus dad. He had the most compassionate eyes of any man I ever knew. He had very expressive eyes. My father's soul shone through his eyes. His sense of humor was bar none — sick and off-the-wall — and some of the absurd stories he would tell. . .

"He would tell me some stories you wouldn't believe. But he was constantly warning me to 'always be a lady, always conduct yourself like a lady, no matter how anybody else behaves around you.'

"I know he was no innocent. He had his fun, and was a bit of a playboy. I don't know if that's the right word or not. But he adored

Bob Prince, at age 26, with year-old daughter, Nancy, in Mt. Lebanon.

Nancy, at 4, with her Dad, then 29. Note the pocket handkerchief.

Betty Prince with daughter Nancy and her husband Ray Thomas after Sunday services at Westminster Presbyterian Church in Upper St. Clair.

my mother. He was a prude around my mother. He saw her in a different light. He respected her in every way. Men just have their own rules, which is not right or fair. I can see him doing some of the things people say in their stories about him. I never condemned him for that.

"To me, my father was fascinating."

Whereas Nancy Prince wasn't much of a sports fan in her youth, you wouldn't know that to see her now. Nancy Prince Thomas welcomed me at the door of her home wearing an official Steelers game jersey. It was a black one, with white numerals, No. 82, THIGPEN. "I loved that guy and now he's gone," she said. Ray had given her the jersey as a Christmas gift because he knew how much his wife liked Yancey Thigpen. One of my personal favorites among the Steelers of the Bill Cowher era, Thigpen had signed as a free agent for big bucks with the Nashville Oilers during the off-season.

"That hurts," said Nancy. I felt the same way, as did many Steelers fans.

Ray Thomas may have something to do with the makeover of Nancy Prince Thomas. Her husband of ten years is a big sports fan. The gameroom of their three-bedroom, split-entry home in Bethel Park has handsomely framed photographs, paintings and posters of sports subjects on all the paneled walls. There are paintings of popular Pittsburgh scenes throughout their home, and Nancy has a mini-version of her mother's Wall of Fame family photographs around the mirror of their bedroom.

Her favorite rendering of her father, showing him in an Octoberfest costume, complete with a tyrolean hat and suspenders holding up his shorts, is in the gameroom, right next to a Roberto Clemente portrait. "I just love the expression on his face in this one," she said of her father's portrait.

On the mantel, there was a beautifully-matted scorecard from the Pirates' last game at Forbes Field, the second game of a double-header against the Chicago Cubs, on June 28, 1970. The Bucs won both games. The scorecard was kept by Bob Prince and Nellie King. It had been given as a gift by King to Betty Prince when we spent a day together a few weeks earlier.

Her husband had cut out full-page newspaper posters of Bill Cowher and some of their favorite Steelers and needed to frame them as well. They were laying flat on the bar.

"Ray got me interested in the Steelers," said Nancy, "and now I'm a real bonafide fan. I don't understand everything about football, but I like the game. I love Bill Cowher. I think he's the greatest. I always preferred football. How about baseball? Is this going in the book? I watch an occasional baseball game, but I always thought it was too slow."

Her husband has a degree in mechanical engineering from Pitt, and works as a building supervisor with a federally-funded program called Renewal, Inc., in downtown Pittsburgh. He trains men who have been in trouble or difficulty for one reason or another, and require rehabilitation and manual training to help them become contributing citizens.

The Thomases have a shih-tzu dog named Ling Li, a close-cropped blond who is the best behaved dog I'd been around in years. They got her from Animal Friends seven years earlier. Ling Li was lying on the living room carpet near where Nancy and I were sitting and talking. Ling Li has the biggest most expressive eyes. There's a lot of compassion in those eyes, just like Nancy had said about her dad. "I know that," she said. "She's a sweet dog."

"I know how much he cared."

Nancy Prince Thomas was talking animatedly to me across the dining room table, showing me some family photos, especially those of her father, Bob Prince, which she had dug out in advance of my visit to her home on Wednesday, April 8, 1998. Her salt 'n pepper hair was close cut, and bangs fell over her forehead. She takes pride in resembling her father, though she has some of her mother's characteristics as well. And she's her brother's sister, for sure. We were the same age — 55 — and graduated from high school the same year — 1960 — so our references and memories were mutual ones.

We share fond memories of Bob Prince. "My stories will be different from what others are telling you," she promised, and she kept her word.

"Sometimes I'll find a postcard he sent me," she said. "Seeing his handwriting can bring tears to my eyes. If I hear his voice on TV or the radio, which has happened a lot lately, it has the same effect. After all these years, it still has the same effect on me. I can talk about him for hours, then suddenly something will click in, and the tears come.

"The greatest gift he gave me," she continued about her father, "was meeting people from all walks of life. It could be a homeless person in the street or movie stars like Cary Grant and Jimmy Stewart. He treated them all the same. My father taught me how to like people. He didn't kowtow to a person, no matter their position, and he never looked down on anyone. He had a variety of friends and I was introduced to many of them.

"I was 18 and I accompanied my father to Indiana, Pa., and we were visiting the neighbors of Jimmy Stewart. Mr. Stewart was there at the time, and I met him and talked to him.

"When I was working in Los Angeles, in Century City in Beverly Hills, sometimes my dad would call me when the Pirates were going to be playing in San Diego, Los Angeles and San Francisco. If any of those games fell on a long weekend, I'd join him. Maybe my roommate would accompany me.

"I was out there for six years. I was 27 when I moved there and 32 when I came back here. It was August of 1970 and I had just moved to LA. I went to Dodgers Stadium and went up, with my roommate, to sit in a private box. I sat down next to Cary Grant. He was close to 80 and he was stunning. He was married to Dyan Cannon at the time and they had a five-year-old daughter, Jennifer. Cary Grant talked to me about his daughter. When I first turned to him, he said, 'I'm glad to meet you, Nancy. I'm Cary Grant.' When I could breathe again, I talked to him. He said, 'You must be proud of your father.' I told Cary Grant I didn't like being raised in the public eye. He said, 'I hope you're not ashamed of anything your father ever did.' I told him I'd try. Then we watched the game.

"When I was in San Diego, I was there for the weekend. I was sitting with players out by the pool. They were like older brothers to me. All of a sudden we hear this booming voice coming from the balcony overhead, 'Men, just remember one thing. She's my child.' They all laughed and I was embarrassed. Sure, it was Dad."

Nancy also remembers her dad calling her on the telephone one time, after he'd been taken off a Pirates charter and turned over to FBI authorities because he had mentioned the word 'bomb' while boarding the plane. "'I just wanted to tell you about something before you read about it in the newspapers,'" he told me.

"I was by his bedside at Presbyterian University Hospital in his last days. I saw my father die. It was the most peaceful death I ever saw because he'd gone into a coma. Bob Jr. didn't make it in time, but he tried.

"Even though I was there, I've never accepted his death. I was the only one in the family who didn't cry much. His hair was snow white and fluffed up, and he looked like an angel. One of the doctors told me to look up at this box, or monitor, above his bed and said that when all those numbers reach zero 'your father will be gone.' I thought, sure, that's the dumbest thing I ever heard of. My dad's not going to die.

"It was a moving time. I'm glad I went to the hospital. He looked beautiful. It was the best he ever looked. After his death, for about four or five months, my mother and I were going to all these award presentations in his honor. We were there, but we weren't there. I am very emotional, like my father, an extreme sentimentalist. I know how much he cared about me.

"I'll tell you a story that shows you the extremes he went to in order to protect me from harm. When I was a student at the University of Arizona in Tucson, there had been some robberies and murders on campus, and my father was concerned about my safety.

"My birthday was November 14, and I was going to turn 21. I wanted to spend this special birthday in Las Vegas. I wanted to fly to Las Vegas with my college roommate. I wanted to show my own I.D. card and be legal. I told my dad about what I was doing, and he said it would be a memorable way to spend my birthday. He told me to be careful. We stayed at a hotel on the Strip. We had a ball. Harry James and Nat 'King' Cole were playing there, and I had met them both through my dad when I went to a junior college in upstate New York. I had met Harry James and his wife, Betty Grable.

"Years later, I was at the Georgetown Inn up on Mt. Washington with my dad, and he started laughing in the middle of a conversation. I asked him what he was laughing about. He said, 'Do you remember that time you and your roommate went to Las Vegas on your birthday?' Of course, I remembered.

"The more he talked, I started remembering how everywhere we went in Las Vegas, these three guys showed up at every place. My girlfriend and I had noticed them. Hey, there are those guys again. It turns out my father had called the owner of the Stardust, where we were staying, and arranged to have three bodyguards tail us everywhere. All of a sudden it all made sense."

I particularly liked that story because it sounded like something I might do. My two daughters think I don't give them enough credit for being able to look after themselves. They roll their eyes when I am giving them directives about what to do when they're away from home on vacation. See, I told them about this Bob Prince story, that's what dads do.

"I could do no wrong."

I asked Nancy if she and her brother, Bob Jr., knew then how much their father truly cared about them.

"I don't know if my brother did, but I was the apple of my dad's eye," she responded. "I could do no wrong. My brother wasn't sure how my father felt about him because he wasn't as demonstrative with him. My dad came from a military background and the men gave each other handshakes, not hugs. So my brother didn't know. He wasn't sure my dad loved him. But my brother adored his dad.

"I told you I would tell you the story about the teddy bear, too. When I was living in LA, we went to see my mother's aunt, Marian Van Dyke. We were having lunch at a place in Century City, just talking, and my aunt told us this story. She said my dad had been shy as a child.

"She said he never talked about his problems, but that as a little boy he used to take a teddy bear into a closet and tell the teddy bear about his problems. My father's face turned fuchsia. After hearing that story, I bought a teddy bear for him the following Father's Day, so he could tell his troubles to his teddy bear."

Nancy explained some of the pictures placed between, identified family relatives I didn't know. I told her I loved some of the photos of her father as a young man. "My mother likes those, too," she said. "He was too much of a zoot suiter for me in some of those. As he got older, I thought he was handsome and distinguished. He did a lot of sweet things for me.

"He gushed all over me, like he did my mother. My brother didn't get the hugs and kisses we did, and he looked upon going away to those military schools as a punishment, rather than as something aimed at helping him.

"I didn't always feel good about myself, either. But I do now. I'm a complete winner. I have many friends and many things. I feel very blessed. I think I came into my own at 35. I didn't get married until I was 45 because I just didn't think marriage was for me, for whatever reasons.

"I finally put all the negative stuff behind me. The fans don't mean it, but when you're in the public eye they think they own you. I'd be having a private breakfast with my father, and someone would come up and start talking to him. They'd butt right in, completely ignore me, never excuse themselves or anything. My father told me to be grateful that people would come up to him like that.

"But I didn't see it that way, not back then. Today, I may see it a little differently. I don't care what anybody thinks of Bob Prince. That's not my father.

"My father took me everywhere. He was a lover of people. Now people fascinate me, too. He's given me that gift. My mother is good with people, too, even though she was shy and reserved herself most of her life.

"She never lived in his shadow. They both had tremendous strengths. I used to say my mother was the June Cleaver from the 'Leave It To Beaver' TV series. My mom is very shy herself, and she always said I met people a lot easier than she did. Everyone feels comfortable with my mother. My girl friends went to her to tell her their problems. She's a genuinely good person.

"My brother got the gift of gab from our father. He's a great salesman. For a long while, my brother shied away from being mentioned in the same breath as our dad. My brother was extremely proud of our father. He idolized him. My father didn't know how to handle that.

"I loved my dad. He reminded me — and my mother won't believe this because I never said it — of Robert Browning, the English poet. My father had a very gentle side. That picture downstairs shows the gentle, compassionate side of my father.

"A lot of stories told me about my father aren't pretty, but my memories of him show him as a beautiful man, a devoted father, and someone I miss a great deal to this day."

A few days after I visited Nancy Prince, on Easter Sunday, 1998, she had flowers on the altar of Westminster Presbyterian Church for "my dad." Her mother also had ordered flowers in memory of her husband. Bob Prince never had bigger fans.

"There's the guy I married," said Betty Prince when she saw the photo below of her husband, Bob, back in early '40s. Daughter Nancy spoke of his sensitive eyes. "My father's soul shone through his eyes," she said. Sounds like an Eric Clapton song . . .

Photos from the Prince family album

Steve Blass
A sentimental guy

*"He was important.
He was a presence."*

Steve Blass was on the brink of the greatest moment in his major league baseball pitching career. There was one more inning to go in the seventh game of the 1971 World Series, and he was holding on to a 2-1 lead against the Orioles at Memorial Stadium in Baltimore.

Blass was, understandably, a bit nervous. The Pirates were batting in the top of the ninth, and he was pacing the dugout. "The dugout wasn't big enough for me to pace," recalled Blass. "So I walked down the hallway, and I went into our clubhouse. I was just trying to kill time before I went out to get the last three outs."

As Blass walked into the visitors' clubhouse, he saw Bob Prince, the Pirates announcer, standing there. Blass said he was startled to see him.

"What the hell are you doing here?" Blass asked Prince.

"Me?" Prince responded. "What the hell are you doing here? You're not done yet!"

Blass went out and completed the task. There are some famous photographs showing him and his catcher, Manny Sanguillen, leaping into the air simultaneously. There's another view of the same sequence, only Bob Robertson, the first baseman, is leaping alongside Blass in that one. Blass never jumped higher in his life.

"That was my biggest moment in baseball," said Blass.

"We'd won the World Series. I was the winning pitcher in the deciding game. That's the stuff you dream about as a kid. Hitting a home run to win the World Series — as Maz did in 1960 — or throwing the final pitch to close it out, as I did."

He'd gone nine innings and had tossed a 4-hitter. The Pirates had put themselves in a bad position by losing the first two games of the Series, but Blass was the stopper, winning the third game on a 3-hit, 5-1 victory. So he'd gone the distance twice and was the winning pitcher in two of the four victories over the Orioles.

Back in 1960, Prince was in the Pirates' clubhouse in the late going and wasn't aware that Maz had been the hero of the seventh game. Prince had learned his lesson. He was fully aware that Blass was the hero this time. He knew he wanted to interview Blass.

Prince was also there in the worst of times for Blass. In 1973, when Blass baffled everybody in baseball, plus psychiatrists, psychologists, astrologists and fortune tellers, when he suddenly couldn't find the strike zone. He'd had his best year in baseball the year before,

posting a 19-8 record in 1972, but he was out of baseball a year later, in 1974, when the Bucs finally had to give up on him. Blass, at 33, was finished as a major league ballplayer.

"Bob was one of the people who was behind me during my worst days in baseball," said Blass. "There were several people who stood by me, and were so supportive, but none more than Bob Prince."

There were other special moments with Prince that Blass talked about during a lengthy interview at his home on Thursday morning, May 7, 1998. Blass lived less than a mile from my home. He suggested we go out on the back patio to talk. He offered a cup of coffee — warning me that it might be a little wicked because he'd been up bright and early and thought the coffee pot might have been on the burner too long. It's easy to relax and get comfortable in the company of Steve Blass. His wife, Karen, came out to say hello, and to bid Steve goodbye as she went off to keep an appointment.

"I guess it's better to interview somebody at their home rather than the clubhouse," said Blass. "The clubhouse belongs to the players. You feel more free here, I guess, to talk."

He had made some notes about Prince, and he consulted them as he told me some more stories.

"When I was pitching well," began Blass. "My father would go out at night and drive around in his car to a certain spot in Falls Village, where we lived in Connecticut. He could get KDKA Radio and hear my games. At the end of the season, my dad would send Prince an invoice to cover the cost for one car battery and a six-pack of beer. Prince loved that.

"When I first came up, I made a few public appearances with Bob. I wasn't very good. He gave me some great advice about public appearances. He said, 'You're not going to change the world; you're a baseball player. Just make sure you have a tight close to your talk. Don't stumble around at the end, finish up neat and tidy. That's what they'll remember best.' I still follow his advice. I don't think I'm that good as a public speaker, but I have a nice, tight close.

"When I came up as a rookie in 1964, I was driving to the ballpark that first day. I was reviewing in my mind all the people I needed to know when I got there, like the front-office officials, the manager, the coaches, the players and Bob Prince. You had to know Bob Prince, too. He was important. He was a presence. You also had to check in with him. They used to say that Bob Prince was as much at ease in a boardroom as he was in a barroom. He could mix with everybody, the corporate executives and the regular fans."

> *"Part of how you get along with people is not how they are. It's how you are."*
> — Steve Blass,
> Pirate broadcaster

"He knew I could do it."
— Blass on Prince

In 1983, Blass began his broadcasting career working alongside Prince for Home Sports Entertainment (HSE), a short-lived local cable venture. He said Jim Rooker had recommended him when they were looking for another analyst.

"They put me in with Prince," recalled Blass. "In the fifth inning of the first game I worked with him, Diz Bellows, who looked after the media room, brought him two screwdrivers and slipped them under the table. I didn't know drinking during the game was taboo. I thought it was just a fact of life and that Bob knew what he was doing. It seemed like a good idea to me, so I told Diz, 'I'll have two myself.' But I couldn't handle it as well as Bob. By the eighth inning, I was starting to slur my words. So I decided that wasn't such a good idea.

"About midway through that season, one game between the fifth and sixth innings, Bob got out of his seat and started to walk away. 'Where ya going?' I asked. He said, 'You've got it, lad.' So I was on my own. He didn't do that until he thought I was ready. He'd brought me along to the point where I could do it on my own. He knew I could do it.

"We had a 'cough button' that you could press when you had to cough or burp, or if you wanted to say something as an aside to each other and didn't want it going out on the air. But they could hear you in the control truck. This one game, Bob hits the 'cough button' and screams, 'If you show me one more replay of a simple single, I'm going to come down and rip your blanking heads off! What more can I say about it?' I was shocked. I didn't think you could talk to the producer that way. And that's not exactly what Bob said. He was a little saltier than that, as was his custom.

"I remember another time he arranged to have Bruce Kison flown back to Pittsburgh to keep a wedding date, the day after we'd won the World Series in Baltimore. Kison had made the date, not realizing we might still be playing that late in the season.

"He arranged to have Jack Piatt of Milcraft Industries provide his company jet airplane to get Kison and Bob Moose, who was his best man, back to Pittsburgh in time for the wedding. I don't know how Prince arranged to have a helicopter waiting in the parking lot outside the clubhouse at Memorial Stadium to take Bruce and Bob to the airport in Baltimore.

"Kison came up to me in the clubhouse after the game and thanked me for making it quick. That game was over in 2:09. I don't think he even said, 'Nice game,' after I'd gone the distance. I had just pitched the whole game of the last game of the World Series, and all Bruce is thinking about is getting back to Pittsburgh in time to hear the wedding bells.

"You know that Roberto Clemente gave Prince one of his silver Louisville Slugger bats he was given for winning a batting title in 1961. Clemente really cared about Prince.

"I've got another story about Prince making special flying arrangements. This time it was to make sure he and I kept our own broadcasting commitment. He and I played in Andy Russell's golf tournament for Children's Hospital at Laurel Valley on a game day.

"I called Bob the day before the golf outing, and I said I didn't think I could go. I told him, 'We're not going to get back on time.' Tee-off time in Latrobe was 1 p.m., and game time was 7:35 p.m. There was no way we could get back in time, if we were driving.

"'Don't worry, Lad,' Prince told me. He always called me Lad. 'You just meet me at the ballpark tomorrow at 10:30.' He had a state police helicopter in the parking lot that took us to Laurel Valley. After we played golf, we returned to Pittsburgh in the same helicopter. It was waiting for us in the first fairway. We landed at 7:28 in the parking lot at Three Rivers Stadium. I don't know how he did it.

"Bob had his coat and tie on as we got off the helicopter. He gets to the mike with a moment to spare, and he says, 'Good evening, Pirate fans, this is Bob Prince. As I was discussing with Joe Smith around the batting cage tonight...'

"I got him during a commercial break right after the opening, and I said, 'Damn, Bob, you had them thinking we've been here since noon today.' Bob looked at me and laughed out of the corner of his mouth, as he always did. And he said, 'Hey, I can give them seven minutes standing on my head!'

"Another time, we played in a charity golf tournament held by Bob Robertson down in Cumberland, Maryland. Bob was doing commercials for Subaru at the time, and it was a compact car. It was called the Subaru Brat. We got there and we had a drink, then 40 more, and Bob asked me to drive back.

"Prince said, 'Lad, just set the wheels on each side of the white stripe on the highway, and put your foot on the pedal and get us back to Pittsburgh as fast as possible. 'How's this plan, Lad? We're going to load up the Brat, and get out of here.' And off we went."

Blass, as well as former broadcast cohort Jim Rooker, both had been stopped by police for exceeding the speed limits. "I learned my lesson," said Blass. "I still drink, but I don't drink and drive anymore. I've grown up in that respect."

This reminded me of another story someone had told me. I can't find my notes to get the name of the fellow who shared the story, but I remember his tale.

"Bob Prince and Dick Groat had a speaking engagement at a banquet in Irwin and they stopped afterward for a few drinks at the Jacktown Inn," related the man, who said he was a drummer in a local band. "Groat left early and Bob was pretty much in the bag by the time he left.

"I told him I'd be glad to drive him to his home in Upper St. Clair, that my brother would follow us in my car. And I'd come back with my brother. Prince leaned back against his car, and chuckled. 'Lad, I appreciate you looking out for the ol' Gunner, but I'll get home just fine, thank you.' Then Prince made a request. 'Do me a favor, Lad, and just point me in the direction of Pittsburgh. That's all I need.'"

"Bob was always generous with the gift of his time."

Blass, hale and hearty at 56, remembered his early days with the Pirates and Prince. He was wearing a ballcap and a light beard — he hadn't shaved yet because he had a ballgame to go to later that night at Three Rivers Stadium — and looked his usual affable self as he sat on a chair on his backyard patio.

"I used to enjoy doing interviews with him as a player," he said of Prince. "I'd get real animated, and Prince liked that. I told him once that my folks were listening to the game back on Belden Street in Falls Village.

"After that, when I was doing well, he'd say, 'There's bedlam back on Belden Street. . .' I used to have my family come down from Connecticut when we were in New York to play the Mets. He always had time to say hello, or have a drink in the hotel bar, or a visit in the lobby. He was their connection with the Pirates. I always appreciated him doing that.

"My old theory is that the only gift a lot of us have is time. And Bob was always generous with the gift of his time. He had time for everyone.

"From a personal standpoint, he was an important figure. He was fun to be around. He was a bright man. He taught me a lot. I learned a lot from him.

"Joe L. Brown was like that, too. He was like a baseball father figure to me. There was no draft then. I was signed, almost reluctantly. I went to the rookie league, and there was no hubbub about me, but Joe always had time for me and took an interest in me. I weighed about 155 pounds. He'd slip me $20 from time to time when he saw me. He'd say, 'Get some milkshakes.' He stayed with me. He had time for me.

"To this day, I think the world of Joe Brown. The real test was when I was going bad. He stuck with me."

I mentioned that Dave Giusti had said something similar about Brown, how he helped him when he was in a slump.

"It was a different era then; there were relationships, not just business dealings like you have today."

Blass said he had begun taking his baseball pension when he was 46. "I needed it then," he said. "If I knew I was going to get into broadcasting and stay with it, I wouldn't have taken it. Now it's like a bonus."

He said he and Karen had paid off the 25-year mortgage on their home, a two-story brick home in Upper St. Clair, in August of 1997. They had moved into the house in June of 1972. "I've had only one wife and one house," boasted Blass. They live a half-block away from Dave and Ginny Giusti, two of their dearest friends.

"My younger son has just moved back into the neighborhood," said Blass. Chris, 32, is married to Lisa and they had a four-year-old daughter named Megan. "It's nice to have them so close," he added.

Their older son, David, 33, is divorced, but was readying to get remarried. He lived in his dad's hometown of Falls Village, as did his two children, Nichole, 11, and Jacob, 7.

He said that when Bob and Betty Prince lived in Upper St. Clair, they used to call on occasion and invite them and the children over to go swimming in the Prince's backyard pool. "I remember us going there once for a New Year's party, and Wes Posvar, the Pitt chancellor, was there, and so was John Michelosen, the former Pitt football coach," he said. "They knew we lived in the community, and they'd include us in some of their social events."

Blass has been in Pittsburgh long enough to appreciate some of its history. When he sat in on the combined no-hitter by Francisco Cordova and Ricardo Rincon the previous summer, it was the fourth that he had witnessed. He saw three previous no-hitters, one by Bob Gibson of the Cardinals in Pittsburgh, by Bob Moose in New York, by Dock Ellis in San Diego.

I had been at Three Rivers two nights earlier when the Pirates played the St. Louis Cardinals in the first of a two-game series. Mark McGwire, the strongboy firstbaseman for the Cardinals, attracted most of the pre-game interest as he lofted one ball after another into the left field stands during batting practice. Some fans believed that he had the best chance, along with Donora-born Ken Griffey of the Seattle Mariners, to break Roger Maris' record of 61 home runs.

McGwire wouldn't give interviews about the subject of his home run situation. "I'd rather talk to him about him allocating a million dollars of his salary for abused kids in St. Louis," said Blass. "That would be more interesting to me."

There were some big guys in the visitors dugout, however, who drew some attention as well. Three of the stalwarts of the Pirates' 1979 World Series team were enjoying a reunion. Judging by their boisterous behavior, and warm exchanges, the "We Are Family" theme song of Sister Sledge was still appropriate.

Steve Blass and Greg Brown are always reminded of the heritage of Pirates' broadcasting going back to Bob Prince and Rosey Rowswell.

Family Reunion at Pirates-St. Louis Cardinals game on May 5, 1998 includes, left to right, Willie Stargell, John Candelaria and Dave Parker, Cards' hitting instructor. They were all big factors in Pirates' 1979 World Series triumph.

Dave Parker, who was now a batting instructor for the Cardinals (and a changed man, we were told), was chatting enthusiastically with Willie Stargell, now working with minor league prospects on behalf of the Bucs, and John Candelaria, who lived in suburban Pittsburgh. All had put on extra pounds since their playing days. "I can relate to that," said Blass.

I happened to be in the media room when the Fox Sports telecast showed a scene taped prior to the game, with Stargell, Parker and Candelaria chatting away. Blass was the voice over. He mentioned how Stargell had hit .400 in that 1979 World Series, after having a disappointing 1971 World Series, how Parker had hit .345, and how Candelaria had been a big part of the Pirates' success that season.

The last individual to pitch a no-hitter for the Pirates was Candelaria, who did it in a 2-0 victory over the Dodgers on August 9, 1970.

"I was still playing when Candy came up," said Blass, "and I once gave him a ride to the beach from Pirate City. He was looking for a ride. That was during my heyday, and he always reminded me of how much that gesture meant to him at the time. He always was good with me when I needed interviews after I got this job.

"I always got along with him. And I got along with Parker. And everyone got along with Stargell."

The same, of course, could be said of Steve Blass. "Part of how you get along with people," offered Blass in a bit of dime store philosophy, "is not how they are. It's how you are. If you're nice to people, they're usually nice to you."

Just as I was about to depart the Blass home, I asked Steve if we could go upstairs to his den. I had been there several times, but I wanted to make sure what was there. I knew there were some pictures of Prince on the walls.

There was much more and as Blass spoke about the background on each of the pictures and mementos, I was glad we had taken the time to review the room. It reminded me of the time I was ready to depart the home of Suzie and Sam Narron in Middlesex, North Carolina, and they asked if I wanted to see their attic. It was like going into a mini museum of baseball, with bats wielded by the likes of Musial, Clemente, Frisch, Ruth, and Hornsby on display, wonderful photographs of the champion Cardinals — "The Gas House Gang" — and the Brooklyn Dodgers that Roger Kahn had chronicled in his great baseball book, *The Boys of Summer*.

Blass has been an interesting baseball figure who grabbed the attention of another wonderful baseball biographer, Roger Angell of the *New Yorker*, and it was easy to appreciate the attraction. Blass is a big-hearted, sentimental, soft-spoken, easy talker who's known some wonderful highs and some depressing disappointments in his playing career.

He pointed out a cartoon of Bob Prince that had a message from the man himself. It read, "To Steve, We've been through a lot together, but you have made it easy for me to ride out the storms."

Blass said, "The irony of that is that he wrote it when I was going through my personal hell, trying to regain my pitching form in my final two seasons. He just turned it around. That's so typical of him."

There was a note from Nellie King, alluding to their relationship. There was a plaque that Stargell had made for some special people in the organization. He had a personal note on the plaque to Blass. "When I think of you," wrote Willie with a dark felt-tip pen, "I think of so many good and wonderful things. I'll always have a special feeling about you."

There were autographed photos of Babe Ruth and Roberto Clemente. There were pictures of all the people Blass had worked with in the broadcast booth, Lanny Frattare, Bob Walk, Jim Rooker, Kent Derdivanis, John Sanders and Greg Brown.

There was a photo of Bob Blass hugging his son. "That's when he jumped off the top of the dugout and came out when I was being interviewed after I'd won the third game in the 1971 World Series," said Steve. There were photos showing Steve and his dad on the mound at Three Rivers Stadium. "That was taken the day after the All-Star Game here in 1994," said Blass. "He called me a few days before he came here for that game. He was 74 at the time, and he said, 'Steve, it's been a long time since we had a catch. And I'm getting up there. Do you think we can do it one more time?' And the ground crew took the cover off the mound for me the day after the All-Star Game and we had our catch."

How can you not like a guy who tells you stories like that? Blass said he was three months old when his father went off to fight in World War II and that he was three years old when his father returned home. He showed me photos of his mother and dad, as they appeared on their 50th anniversary, and as she appeared as a high school senior. His parents had been married for 57 years.

There were signed baseballs and mugs and lapel pins and press passes, and photos showing Steve with his sons, when they were toddlers wearing Pirates uniforms with their dad's number — 28 — on them. Then he showed me his scorecards that he runs off on a copying machine every so often. They are the kind of scorecards that Bob Prince used. "Lanny introduced Nellie King in our broadcast booth when he was interviewing him last week," said Blass. "Nellie noted that I'm still using Bob's scoring system."

Then Blass showed me a special ballpoint pen that had a blue tip at one end and a red tip at the other. "Bob told me to use the red pen for offense, so I could check the scoring fast late in the game, or after the game. It's still a good system. I still buy them in a stationery store Downtown that Bob told me about. So his hand is still on every scorecard I keep."

255

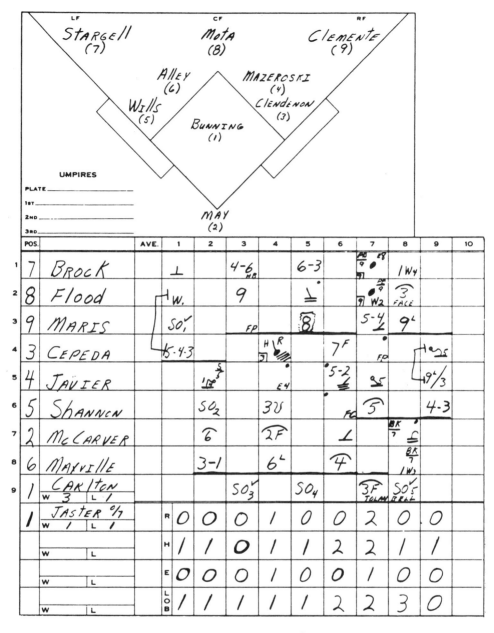

Field positions

- LF: STARGELL (7)
- CF: MOTA (8)
- RF: CLEMENTE (9)
- Alley (6)
- MAZEROSKI (4)
- Wills (5)
- CLENDENON (3)
- BUNNING (1)
- MAY (2)

UMPIRES

PLATE _____
1ST _____
2ND _____
3RD _____

	POS.		AVE.	1	2	3	4	5	6	7	8	9	10
1	7	BROCK		⊥		4-6 HB		6-3		AB/9 K8 9	1W4		
2	8	FLOOD		W.	9		⊥		9 W2	3 FACE		
3	9	MARIS		SO✓		FP	8		5-4 ⊥	9L		
4	3	CEPEDA		6-4-3		H/R 3		7F	FP	9S	
5	4	JAVIER			1B S/S	E4	5-2	9S	9✓/3		
6	5	SHANNON			SO2	3U		FC	5	4-3	
7	2	McCARVER			6	2F	⊥		BK/7 £		
8	6	MAXVILLE			3-1	6L	4		BK/7 1W3		
9	1	CARLTON W 3 L 1				SO3✓	SO4		3F TOLAN BALL	SO5✓		
	1	JASTER 0/7 W 1 L 1	R	0	0	0	1	0	0	2	0	0	
		W L	H	1	1	0	1	1	2	2	1	1	
		W L	E	0	0	0	1	0	0	1	0	0	
		W L	LOB	1	1	1	1	1	2	2	3	0	

Out Short To First —————— 6/3
Popped to First —————— /3\
Fouled to Catcher —————— 2F\
Called Third Strike —————— SO
Swinging Third Strike —————— SO✓
Base On Balls —————— W
Intentional Walk —————— IW
Lined Out To Left —————— 7L
Hit Batsman —————— HB
Error Shortstop —————— E6

The secret to easy scoring is to learn the numerical system as follows:

Pitcher	- 1	Short	- 6
Catcher	- 2	Left	- 7
First	- 3	Center	- 8
Second	- 4	Right	- 9
Third	- 5		

Secondly, in your score card squares place all the plays involving outs right in the middle of the square.

The fun in scoring is to do it in such a way that you can look at your card months later and still vividly recall what happened on every play. My system eliminates memory work because I have worked out a series of symbols that paint a picture of every detail.

Just one other thing -- look at your square and consider the lower right corner as first base -- upper right is second -- etc.

On hits and runs scored and runs batted in it is important you follow the course of the runner around the base.

Was the hit a line drive? A Bloop? An infield single? Well let me show you the various symbols and once you master these you'll be able to chart the games with ease. By the way you can settle a lot of arguments with my system because you can tell exactly what happened on every play.

Courtesy of <OODLAND>

Passed Ball	PB
Wild Pitch	WP
Run Scored	●
Sacrifice Bunt Pitcher/First	SB-1-3
Third-Second-First Double Play	5-4-3
Force Play	FP
Fielder's Choice	FC
Balk	BK
Interference	IN

Steve and Karen Blass collecting sea shells on beach during spring training with Dusty, 4, and Chris, 4, when Steve was a young Pirate.

Glory Days . . .

Steve Blass is mobbed after winning 7th Game of 1971 World Series.

Photos courtesy of Pittsburgh Pirates

Manny Sanguillen and Steve Blass celebrate distance-going 2-1 victory over Baltimore Orioles in the 1971 World Series finale.

Mt. Lebanon Wildcats
Prince's favorite team

"It was a wonderful experience."

Pete Mervosh has much memorabilia from his playing days in sports. He has a lot of game programs, lineups, newspaper clippings, etc., from his days with the Mt. Lebanon Wildcats. Bob Prince was listed as the athletic director of the sponsoring Mt. Lebanon Athletic Association. The group, founded in 1942, fielded three football teams in different age divisions, and several baseball teams. Walter Willoughby was the trainer.

Mervosh made his way to Mt. Lebanon in the mid-'40s from his boyhood home on East Carson Street on the South Side. His father moved the family to Dormont for one year, and then to Mt. Lebanon in Pete's freshman year.

As a 15-year-old sophomore, Pete played tackle for the Wildcats, which he described as "a wonderful experience."

The Mt. Lebanon Wildcats won the Dapper Dan Junior Football Conference by winning all six games and outscored their opponents, 165-18, in 1946. The year before, they went 10-0, and outscored the opposition, 249-30.

Some of the big games were officiated by NFL refs, including Sammy Weiss and Yans Wallace.

One of the newspaper clippings in a scrapbook kept by the Mervosh family was an advance story that makes one smile over the prose. The story read like this, which gives you a hint of how sports were written in those days:

"Philosophers opine the best way to get into trouble is downhill, but Walter (Charley Young Zivic) Affif's Washington Social Club will cross the railroad tracks and hike up the South Hills slopes tomorrow afternoon, to collide with the Mt. Lebanon Wildcats in a football fracas that probably will decide the champion of the Dapper Dan Junior Conference.

"Affif, a professional pugilist who adopted the name of his ring tutor, Fritzi Zivic, will send his youthful team from the Hill district, against the upper crust, headed by John Lucas, a bank vice president.

"Affif does the coaching for Washington, while the Wildcats are blessed with at least a half dozen outstanding mentors, and no fewer than four team physicians."

Mt. Lebanon won that contest, 28-12, in the most closely-contested game of the season.

There were several entries from the North Side in the Dapper Dan Conference, including the Perry Atoms, coached by Tom Foerster, who later became the county commissioner, the Sheffield Apaches from Manchester, the Rooney Steelers and North Side Apaches.

Other teams were the Homestead Navy Blues, St. Mary's Lyceum, Universal Scarlets, Greenfield Midgets and Holy Name Lyceum. They also played games against the Brushton Merchants, East Liberty Cadets and the Brentwood Cardinals.

The Wildcat Kittens, a younger team, even had Fritzi Zivic's son, Fritz, in the lineup, as well as Hunter Caffee and Don Mosites, who would make their mark in the local business world in later years.

In a 1946 issue of a magazine called *Huddle*, edited by Eddie Beachler and Eddie Cooper of Mt. Lebanon and Jack Henry of Bethel Park, there's an article under the byline of Bob Prince.

"Nowhere in the country is there an association the equal of this Mt. Lebanon group," wrote Prince, then a WJAS Radio sports broadcaster and not yet associated with the Pirates. "And nowhere in the country is there another juvenile football team the equal of the Wildcats.

"In three years of play, they have won every game and every title that came along. Save for one occasion when they stepped out of their class and tackled Kiski Prep. They lost, 13-0, but had the edge in statistics.

"These are youngsters not old enough to play on a good high school team, but instead of loafing on the street corner to wait their chance, they are out learning how to play. Their uniforms are tops. No college in the country can boast finer equipment.

"Everybody wants to play and beat the Wildcats. They think that because the kids hail from so-called 'Mortgage Hill,' they're nothing but a bunch of sissies parading up and down the field.

"Visiting teams playing the 'Cats for the first time can't understand how any boy dressed in fancy blue satin pants, gold silk jerseys, blue plastic headgears — and sporting a half-dozen coaches, two physicians and a team trainer — can play rock-em, sock-em football."

Prince sure knew how to win friends and influence people from the inner-city of Pittsburgh. Is it any wonder the inner-city kids hated "those cake-eaters" so much after reading that sort of hyperbole. It was, in truth, a feeder system for Mt. Lebanon High School football, though there were "ringers" on the teams from neighboring communities.

There were kids from Upper St. Clair, Bethel Park, Dormont and Brookline on the ballclubs fielded by Mt. Lebanon.

The coaches included Dick Ewalt, former Penn State halfback; Ave Daniell, All-America tackle at Pitt in 1936; Jim Daniell, his brother who was an All-American lineman at Ohio State and had played for the NFL Cleveland Browns; Dick Hoel, another Pitt star from the early '30s; Vic Maitland, Little All-America fullback at Hobart; Bill Reese, former star end for Mt. Lebanon; and Ken Maxey, fullback from Mt. Lebanon.

"It was great and exciting to play for a team that had those kind of coaches," recalled Mervosh, retired in Lower Burrell, after a long career as a guidance counselor at Highlands High School, a merger of Har-Brack and Tarentum.

"My most memorable experience was of a game we played in 1946 against the Rooney Steelers. Mr. Rooney brought along the NFL officials who had worked his game with the Eagles the night before. I know that Walter 'Monk' Ketchell and Carl Reble were some of the officials; I can't remember the rest.

"Dr. Jock Sutherland, the Steelers' coach, came with Mr. Rooney. Ave Daniell had played for Dr. Sutherland at Pitt (1934-1936), and he told us before the game he didn't want to be embarrassed in front of his old football coach. We were using the same single-wing system Sutherland used at Pitt and with the Steelers. We won the game, and afterward Dr. Sutherland came into our dressing room.

"He was the biggest name in Pittsburgh football, mind you. To have him talk to us in the dressing room under the swimming pool at Mt. Lebanon was something special. I was in awe of him. He told us, 'If my team would execute that offense that efficiently we'd never lose.' I'll never forget that. To see Mr. Rooney and Dr. Sutherland was something else."

Prince teamed up with Al Abrams and the Dapper Dan Club and the Jaycees to sponsor a high school all-star game at Forbes Field in 1948 and 1949.

Among the players who participated in the 1949 game were future college standouts Rudy Celigoi Jr. of Scott High, Gene Gedman of Duquesne, Merle DeLuca of Penn High, Lloyd Colteryahn of Brentwood, Dick Modzelewski of Har-Brack, Tony Romantino of Donora, Ed Kraynack of Connellsville. Gedman, Colteryahn and Modzelewski went on to play in the NFL.

"He was a flashy guy."

Another good friend of mine, Ed Harmon, was a chum and teammate of Pete Mervosh on the baseball team, and briefly with the football team, fielded by the Mt. Lebanon Athletic Association. Harmon started out helping his father build homes in the South Hills, and later was a top executive with Ryan Homes for 18 years (1963-1980) before forming his own company, F.E. Harmon Construction, Inc., which builds custom homes. He worked for Ed Ryan, a larger-than-life success story. At 67, Harmon was still building beautiful homes with the same pride his dad instilled in him.

Bob Prince, in his own way, was like Ed Ryan, a larger-than-life success story, someone who could get other people to do things. That was mostly good, sometimes bad.

"I remember after the word got out about Prince doing that dive from the third floor into the swimming pool of the Chase Hotel in St. Louis that guys I knew in business would have a few too many drinks at a party and want to do the same thing," said Harmon. "And they did. It's a wonder a few of them didn't break their necks."

Harmon has better memories of Prince being a more positive influence, and having fun with the young athletes in Mt. Lebanon, where Prince was living at the time. Harmon later played baseball at Mt. Lebanon High and Grove City College, and credited his early experience with the Wildcats for giving him an edge.

"He was a flashy guy," Harmon said of Prince. "He drove flashy cars and dressed in a flashy manner. I came over from Upper St. Clair, which was mostly farm country in those days (the mid-'40s), and I'd never seen anything like him. He wore bright shorts and shirts. He wore loose clothes when it wasn't the style. I was never in awe of him, or anyone else, but I always admired his flair.

"He played golf and I didn't know anybody who played golf. He teed it up, right there on the baseball field, while we were practicing, and just whaled away at the ball. In a way, I wanted to grow up and be able to do the things Bob Prince could do: belong to a country club and play golf.

"As I perceived back in 1946, Prince was an inspirational, confident, flashy, quick-witted, funny guy.

"It's funny what you remember. Our baseball manager was Jerry Tjoflat, and Art Long was one of the coaches. To get a better batting eye, we used axes to cut up trees near the backstop at the ballfield along Cedar Boulevard.

"Our uniforms were bright orange and yellow with dark blue piping. They were two-way stretch uniforms, and we had home and away versions. This was big time, especially for us 'poor boys' from the sticks. Prince might have picked those colors.

"As we practiced, Bob Prince would show up. He drove a Chrysler convertible with running boards below the doors and vinyl side trim. While we were practicing, he would hit golf balls from right center field to where the Little League field is below the Mt. Lebanon Park Swimming Pool.

"He also hit us infield practice and pitched batting practice to us, along with scooping balls at first base. He wore a first baseman's mitt, and he did everything with a little extra flair, turning the glove over just so, stuff like that. He was quite good, but he was also quite a showman.

"He was always giving us some sort of a motivational speech or tidbits about baseball or sports in general. Our coaches were all like that. They had fun with us, and they kept us loose, which I think was important.

"His best ever talk was delivered many years later to the Sunday School class at Westminster Presbyterian Church. That was in 1972, and it was entitled 'One Iota More' — the importance of giving that extra effort, which usually makes the difference between winning and losing. Our boys, Doug and Tom, were there and they were mesmerized by Prince, and what he had to say. They were all on the edge of their seats.

262

"Back when I was playing, there were two baseball teams in the Mt. Lebanon Athletic Association. One was a team made up mostly of sophomores and juniors in high school and the 'B' team made up of mostly freshmen. Pete Mervosh and I were on that team. Pete was important to me because he became sorta my body guard when I first got there. We didn't have our own high school in Upper St. Clair back then. Some guys from Mt. Lebanon were giving me a hard time because I was from Upper St. Clair. Pete was one of the biggest guys and he took a liking to me and looked after me. I'm forever grateful.

"One game sticks out in my mind. It was our annual July 4th game against the 'A' team. They had hard-throwing Phil Sweet pitching against us. I remember hitting a double after being beaned by one of Phil's high fast balls on my previous at-bat.

"The team came mostly from Mt. Lebanon, but some of the best ballplayers were from Bethel Park, Upper St. Clair, Brookline and Dormont, which shows Mt. Lebanon was smart to bring in some outsiders. A few years later, Dormont won a high school football title with its stars all having played previously for the Mt. Lebanon Wildcats. Our baseball team had good support from Mr. Prince, Mr. Lucas — his son, Dave, went on to play at Penn State — Mr. Long, Mr. Tjoflat and my dad, Ferl Harmon, who seldom missed a weekend or twilight game of mine, though he had a demanding schedule as a homebuilder.

"Prince also added some color to the scene. I still have the program from the banquet they held for the football and baseball teams (on February 27, 1947, at the Mt. Lebanon Women's Club). It was the fourth annual banquet, according to the cover of the program. Prince was the toastmaster, and Judge Sammy Weiss, who was also an NFL official, delivered a talk. Al Abrams, the sports editor and columnist of the *Post-Gazette,* presented the Dapper Dan Trophy. Phil Grabowski, a sportswriter from the *Sun-Telegraph*, was there, too.

"They showed highlights of the 1946 season, courtesy of John McGreevy of the Harris Amusement Company. Everything was always first class. Flowers, everything. It was always that way."

Jim O'Brien

Wildcats alumni Ed Harmon and Pete Mervosh show off memorabilia from Mt. Lebanon ball-playing days during reunion in May, 1998.

Dave Giusti
True grit

"Those years were the best of my life."

G inny Giusti gave her husband, Dave, all the right numbers he needed to negotiate a new contract each year. No one was better prepared to prove his value to Joe L. Brown, the no-nonsense general manager of the Bucs, than Dave Giusti.

"Joe was always impressed with the wealth of information I had at my fingertips," said Giusti (pronounced Just-tee). "I could back up all my claims." It helped Giusti become the first $100,000 relief pitcher in baseball history in 1974. He was making $80,000 in 1973.

Throughout her husband's 15-year career as a pitcher in the major leagues, Ginny went to most of the home games and kept an ambitious scorecard. When Dave was pitching on the road, Ginny listened to Bob Prince's pitch-by-pitch account of the contest, and kept track of each pitch — balls and strikes — and how he fared in each challenge. She had a complete record of his pitching performances going back to 1965.

"I liked working with numbers, and I was well organized," said Ginny, "and Dave liked the information I provided him. He said it also helped him be more aware of what he was doing, and how he was most effective."

Ginny, a sweet slim woman with a quick smile, has always brought out the best in her husband. They were happy in each other's company, that was most apparent by their light-hearted exchanges and teasing, after nearly 35 years together.

They first met when she — then Virginia Lee Frykman (that's Swedish) — was a freshman at Syracuse University, and Dave was working on his master's degree in physical education.

They both laughed when I showed them a photograph in which Dave is sitting next to Bob Prince on the Pirates' bench. Dave was sporting sideburns about six inches long and three inches wide in the style of that period. "Can you believe that?" he asked.

David John Giusti, Jr., who was born November 27, 1939, in Seneca Falls, New York, just outside of Syracuse, has a gruff exterior, and remains competitive in everything he does, even in conversation. Giusti never met an argument or debate he didn't like.

Ginny and Dave sat at a dining room table on a Monday evening, April 6, 1998, in their pin-neat home in Upper St. Clair, a suburb nine miles south of Pittsburgh, and talked about the topsy-turvy life they have shared. They bought the home after Dave came to the Pirates in the fall of 1969. It's the only home they have ever owned.

They had moved 27 times in his first seven years in pro baseball, going back to their days in Oklahoma City and Syracuse, thus their

Bob Prince and Dave Giusti talk during spring training in 1971.

Dave and Ginny Giusti check out photo at top at dining room table in their Upper St. Clair home during visit on April 6, 1998.

hesitancy to sink roots. Giusti and Dave Ricketts, a catcher and former Duquesne University basketball player, came to the Pirates in exchange for Carl Taylor and Frank Vanzin in a trade orchestrated by Joe L. Brown. Roberto Clemente had urged Brown to get Giusti. He was a 5-11, 190 pound right-handed pitcher who was paired with Steve Blass as roommates.

When he was 37, Giusti was traded from the Pirates to the Oakland A's in 1977 along with Doc Medich in a package that landed Phil Garner, a big contributor in the Bucs' 1979 World Series winning team. Giusti finished 1977 with the Chicago Cubs. That was it.

Their home, a three-bedroom tri-level, tells you a lot about the Giustis. From the street, it looks small, at least by comparison to most homes in the affluent community. Looks are deceiving. It's spacious inside and immaculate, as is the surrounding yard, including a steep-sloped backyard which ends where the woods begin. Dave and Ginny keep a garden and flower beds, prune shrubs and trees out there.

He likes to cook and make great salads and is as comfortable in the kitchen as he once was in the bullpen. He remembers his mother and grandmother cooking, and he comes by it naturally. He is proud of his Italian heritage, loves to find and talk to old Italians. His dark eyebrows and eyes positively dance as he discusses gardening, cooking and golfing, his favorite activities these days, and Ginny and their two daughters. He talks softer when Ginny is at the table. He and Ginny were both looking forward to becoming grandparents for the first time in August of 1998.

Dave draws a sizable pension from major league baseball, another from American Express, where he worked for 12 years before retiring in 1994. Ginny shares a position with a friend as a receptionist at a local doctor's office. "I love my job," she said, "and I look forward to going to work." They will both be eligible for Social Security. The Giustis have got it made, but they wear the mantle modestly.

"We've always been conservative; that's the way we were raised," said Dave.

"We didn't think it was important to spend money on fancy things," said Ginny. "That's just gingerbread. It's not what our family, or being happy, was all about."

Such sensible folks are hard to come by in the suburbs, especially among well-paid modern-day athletes. Their good friends, Steve Blass and Kent Tekulve, who live in the same community, come from the same stock, and have always lived beneath their means, and paid their dues and participated in PTA and community activities.

"There are a lot of people worse off than us," said Giusti. "It was instilled in us that it was not important to have worldly goods. You were to take care of yourself, your health and your kids. We never changed.

"We do a lot more things now than we ever did. We're very satisfied with our neighborhood and environment. It's a friendly street. We do a lot of things together. We've banded together to get some things accomplished, to protect our neighborhood, to assist someone who needed some help.

"We have a lot in common with our neighbors. That's why we've been comfortable in staying here."

There are two automobiles in the driveway. The Cadillac is Dave's. "I always wanted to drive a Cadillac, and I finally made it," said Dave. It's a 1993 Cadillac, which he bought secondhand. Ginny drives a 1994 Oldsmobile, also bought secondhand. "Secondhand, that's the only way to go," the Giustis agreed.

"You should see Dave driving his Cadillac," said Ginny. "He leans back, with a cigar in his mouth, and he looks like a Mafia boss."

"Ah, come on," Dave begged to differ.

Their daughters, Laura, 33, and Cynthia, 29, grew up in that home and now have their own places. Laura has a Ph.D. in clinical psychology, having gone to Miami of Ohio, Kansas and Brown. She works in a hospital in Providence, Rhode Island. Cynthia Redmond has a master's in education from Penn State University. She had been teaching in Penn Hills, but was now working as a nanny, taking care of a neighbor's children. She was married, living in Castle Shannon, and expecting a child in August.

The Giustis live about a half-mile from my home, and I have played platform tennis with Dave as a partner in several club competitions around Pittsburgh. Unlike some of his other teammates, I never take Giusti for granted. I never forget that Giusti was one of the best relief pitchers in baseball, certainly in Pirates' history, right up there with ElRoy Face and Kent Tekulve. He is a gutsy, gritty competitor. Playing paddle tennis, he loves to cut the ball and make it drop dead just over the net, an offshoot of his pitcher's approach to any game, no doubt. It always annoys the opposition, which gives Giusti great satisfaction. It's great to be paired in any kind of competition with somebody who has pitched in World Series pressure. We were down 5-2 in a match once at the Fox Chapel Racquet Club and I goaded Giusti, taking Ginny's place at pulling the best out of him, and we rallied to win, 7-5. "If I had been your catcher," I told Dave after our win, "you'd be in the Hall of Fame today." Our paddle playing friends still recall that comment with chuckles.

I get on Giusti's case when he carps about the difficulties of life as a big league ballplayer. I remind him that the life he led was a dream job to most people, and better than working in the mills, the mines, McDonald's, or working on the railroad. Everything's relative.

Dr. Donald Goldstein, an Upper St. Clair resident and history professor at Pitt who writes books about World War II, told me only a week earlier that if he weren't a teacher and writer, he would want to be a baseball player. "Not a football player, a baseball player," Goldstein said for emphasis, releasing his best Walter Matthau smile. "It's the best life."

This was the eve of the Pirates' 1998 home opener at Three Rivers Stadium, and there was no better way to get in the proper mood for the new baseball season than to discuss his career, and his relationship with Bob Prince, with Dave and Ginny Giusti at their home.

For three years, anyhow, from 1970 to 1972, Giusti was as good as it gets as a closer coming in from the bullpen to preserve a Pirates' victory. In the tradition of Joe Page, Jim Konstanty, Hoyt Wilhelm and ElRoy Face, Giusti was a tireless relief pitcher, who took pride in always being physically and mentally ready to save a victory for the Pirates. His arrival in Pittsburgh not coincidentally began a streak of division titles for the team. He had been a starting pitcher with the Houston Astros and St. Louis Cardinals, but was not effective in that role with the Pirates so Danny Murtaugh turned him into a relief pitcher. He routinely gave Giusti the ball to protect a 1-run lead in the 9th. Who else?

"He is the cavalry charging over the hill just as the Indians are about to massacre the settlers," wrote Bob Smizik in *The Pittsburgh Press*. Smizik also said Giusti was the Pirate the team could least afford to lose and was, indeed, the most valuable man on the club.

"When he is right, there is no finer line of defense," wrote Phil Musick in the same sheet.

Giusti won Fireman of the Year honors from *The Sporting News* in 1971, a World Series-winning season for the Pirates, finished runner-up the year before, and fourth the year after. So he was second, first and fourth among relief pitchers in that three-year period. He won or saved 70 of 186 victories (38 percent) for the 1970 and 1971 Eastern Division champions.

During that 1971 season, Giusti also notched saves in each of the Pirates' wins over the San Francisco Giants in the National League Championship Series and added another save in the fourth game of the World Series, feats which didn't even figure into the Fireman of the Year voting. In seven appearances against the Giants and Orioles, Giusti pitched a total of $10\frac{2}{3}$ innings while yielding just four hits. You could look it up, or Ginny can get you the numbers.

He was picked for the All-Star Game in 1973 for the first time in 11 years. He was upset with Murtaugh for failing to name him to the team a year earlier when he had a chance to do so, and Giusti felt he was deserving.

"Murtaugh was good for me, and extended my career," said Giusti, "but I could never understand why he didn't look after me when he was managing the All-Star team in 1972. Yes, I was miffed about that." Giusti, according to newspaper clippings in his file in the Pirates' offices, also had a falling-out with Red Schoendienst, his manager in St. Louis.

Giusti could get huffy and stormy, had a bad temper, and wasn't afraid to express his opinions. You always knew where Giusti was coming from.

Bob Prince relaxes before filming KDKA TV interview with Danny Murtaugh at spring training in the early '70s.

"Why certainly I'd like to have that fellow who hit a home run every time at bat, who strikes out every opposing batter when he's pitching, who throws strikes to any base or plate when he's playing outfield, and who's always thinking about two innings ahead just what he'll do to baffle the other team. Any manager would want a guy like that playing for him.
The only trouble is to get him to put down his cup of beer and come down out of the stands and do those things."
— Danny Murtaugh, 1974,
Pirates manager

When he completed his pitching career, Giusti owned a National League record for saves in a career (133) and also established a Pirates mark with 30 saves in 1971, which still stands. Tekulve eventually had 158 saves to pass his career mark. Prior to its recognition as an official statistic, Face had 188 saves.

"Without question, winning the World Series was the highlight of my career," said Giusti. "And the most memorable player has to be Roberto Clemente. One of the things I can always say about my career was that I had an opportunity to play with one of the most approachable superstars ever.

"Steve Blass and I had so much fun with Roberto. We were always pulling pranks on him. If you didn't know better, you would think we were having some awful fights in those days. But those years were the best of my life."

Giusti experienced some enormous highs and lows in his baseball career. He pitched a one-hitter during his Houston days. "The next guy hit into a double play, and I faced the minimum of 27 batters," recalled Giusti. "I threw only 84 pitches. We beat Juan Marichal and the Giants, 3-0, on national TV. That was 1966; I thought I was going to be a star."

When Giusti was in Houston, GM Paul Richards criticized him "for being too much of a thinker." Even Ginny said he had a habit of pacing, worrying about what he was going to be doing.

"For a long time, because Dave was always playing baseball, we never had a summer vacation. We went to the beach this one time. Dave was so relaxed. I saw him, and I thought, 'There's the guy I married.'"

Giusti grins when people talk about his peaceful side. He was always lucky to have people to pull him back from highs and lows. He credited Joe L. Brown with being a big booster when he'd hit bad spells during his stay in Pittsburgh. "There'd be lulls," recalled Giusti, "and Joe and Danny were both patient when that happened."

He remembers great moments like striking out Willie Mays of the Giants with the bases loaded in a battle of division leaders — "It was late in Mays' career and I got him on a fastball," — and he remembers, in April of 1976, how he was pounded in a 17-1 Mets' victory over the Pirates. He was ripped for 11 hits and 10 runs — seven earned — during the last four innings. Giusti grimaced at the reminder.

> *"I love to play this game of baseball. I love putting on the uniform."*
> — Stan Musial,
> St. Louis Cardinals,
> SPORT, 1963

"It was like someone just took your insides and pulled them out of you."

The lowest point of his professional career remains in the gut of Ginny and Dave Giusti. It happened at the end of the 1972 season, when Dave's good friend Nellie King says the Pirates had the best team he'd ever seen in his nine years as sidekick to Bob Prince in the Pirates' broadcast booth.

Danny Murtaugh had retired as manager once again, giving way to Bill Virdon for that 1972 season. The Pirates led the majors in batting average with a .274 mark. No other team was close. The 1972 Pirates tied a major league record with nine players having more than 100 hits. The pitching staff had a combined ERA of 2.81, second only to the Los Angeles Dodgers in the National League. The Pirates won the division title by 11 games over the Chicago Cubs.

The Pirates and Cincinnati Reds split the first four games in the best-of-five National League championship series. It was October 11 and Steve Blass opposed Don Gullett, as they had in the opener, which Blass won. Blass pitched into the eighth inning this time and was leading 3-2 when he was relieved. With right-handed hitting Johnny Bench to lead off the ninth inning, Virdon brought in Giusti, his ace right-handed reliever. Ramon Hernandez was the Pirates' left-handed relief pitcher at that time.

On a 1-2 pitch to Bench, Giusti threw a palm ball, a changeup that came in eye-high. Bench got the best of it, the ball dropping into the right field seats to tie the score. It shook Giusti, and he gave up successive hits to the next two batters, Tony Perez and Dennis Menke. Giusti gave way to Bob Moose. Moose got off to a good start. He was able to retire Cesar Geronimo and Darrel Chaney with no further scoring, but a runner had advanced to third base. With pinch-hitter Hal McRae at bat, Moose uncorked a wild pitch that hit the corner of the plate and skipped past catcher Manny Sanguillen and pinch runner George Foster raced home from third to give the Reds the National League pennant. It was a heart-breaking loss for the Bucs.

"I thought I had him all set up," Dave Giusti said of Johnny Bench. "I think he double-clutched to connect on that fourth pitch. I thought I fooled him. I think he hit two home runs to right all year.

"I just lost it after that. I was like a 15-year-old kid throwing the ball out there. I had been so hyped. The adrenaline was flowing. When Bench hit that ball, it was like someone just took your insides and pulled them out of you. I just lost it. I kept throwing one pitch after another, not really thinking about what I was doing."

Ginny Giusti was sitting in the stands at Riverfront Stadium in Cincinnati with Karen Blass, the wife of Steve Blass. They have lived about five houses away from the Giustis for 26 years, and have remained the best of friends.

"Karen Blass used to wear hats and look great in them," recalled Ginny. "But I don't look good in hats. When Dave came into the game in that difficult situation, Karen took her hat off and put it on me. So I could hide, I guess, because she knew I'd be nervous. It was just awful, awful, going back to the hotel, still hearing the crowd screaming down below. It was just a nightmare. That's why I always feel sorry for a team that loses a championship series in the other team's city.

"No one was blaming Dave for the defeat. Bob Moose had a wild pitch, but it was always a team loss."

They mentioned that when the team got back to Pittsburgh that night, many of the players, including Clemente, went to the home of pitcher Bob Johnson in Upper St. Clair to let off steam. They had no idea that was the last time most of them would ever see Clemente. He was killed in an airplane crash in his native Puerto Rico on New Year's Eve, 1972. The Giustis were at the Blasses in the early hours of the morning when they got the telephone call from Joe L. Brown about Clemente's tragic death. Moose was killed in an auto accident on October 9, 1976. The handsome kid from Export, Pennsylvania was driving while drunk and went off the road and slammed into a tree.

"So it's tough to feel sorry for yourself about what happened that day in Cincinnati," said Giusti. "We came out of that a lot better off than a lot of people."

I covered baseball on a full-time basis that 1972 season, and I was in Cincinnati covering the National League playoffs for *The New York Post*. The beauty of covering baseball in New York was that you switched sides at the All-Star Game break. So I covered the Mets in the National League the first half of the season, then the Yankees in the American League the second half.

I had asked for the assignment to cover the hometown Pirates against the Reds in the National League Championship Series. I should have known better. I had spent the entire spring training session in St. Petersburg trying to get to know Mets' manager Gil Hodges. He was a tight-lipped giant of a man who had been a standout first baseman for the Dodgers during their best days in Brooklyn. Toward the end of camp, I felt comfortable in his company. The Mets were opening the season in Pittsburgh, and I received permission to depart St. Petersburg to go to Pittsburgh a few days before the Mets broke camp. When I arrived at my in-laws' driveway in White Oak, my mother-in-law came out to tell me that Gil Hodges had died of a heart attack earlier that day. Yogi Berra became the manager.

Those were the Mets of Tom Seaver and Jerry Koosman, Tommy Agee and Cleon Jones, Bud Harrelson and Ron Swoboda, Jerry Groat and Ed Kranepool. They had been the Miracle Mets in 1969. They traded a wild right-handed fireballer named Nolan Ryan in 1972 to the California Angels for a washed-up infielder named Jim Fregosi. Rusty Staub came to the team from Montreal. The Mets obtained Willie Mays from the San Francisco Giants during the season.

I wrote a column about how dumb it was to bring Mays back to New York when he was over the hill — it was too late — and annoyed my boss, sports editor Ike Gellis, who thought my premise was heresy. You didn't say bad things about Willie Mays in New York, even if he was a Hall of Fame pain in the butt. I still think I was right.

I remember how badly I felt at the beginning of the season when I learned that Hodges had died in St. Petersburg, especially when I, as the beatman, was in Pittsburgh. I remember how badly I felt at the end of the season, in Cincinnati, when the Pittsburgh Pirates had lost in the worst possible way. It was the worst way to lose a championship series until the Pirates lost the seventh game to the Atlanta Braves in 1992.

"I felt as if we were friends."
— Ginny Giusti on Bob Prince

Ginny Giusti hesitated when I first asked her what she thought of Bob Prince. She smiled. "Tell him what happened," Dave interjected. "Tell him the truth."

Ginny wasn't sure she should. "Bob was a friend," she began. "He had us and the Blasses out to restaurants; we were guests at his home. I felt as if we were friends. That's why I was so upset when he said some things about the players when they were struggling with some union issues with ownership. Dave was the Pirates' player rep, and represented them to the National League. This was before free agency when players were battling for a fair share of the profits. During a game, Bob Prince started talking about the players' demands, and how he had a hard time relating to their complaints. He said he couldn't understand why baseball players felt they deserved more money and more rights. He said the steelworkers put their lives on the line every day, and could fall into a blast furnace and die in their workplace, and that the baseball players had it made.

"Dave was spearheading a drive for the ballplayers to gain some rights. It was a scary time. Baseball was making big money and the ballplayers simply wanted their fair share. When the Pirates came home from the road trip, I went out to the airport to meet Dave. I saw Prince approaching, and I looked the other way. I avoided his glance as I just didn't want to talk to him.

"I got a telephone call from Nellie King later in the day, and he asked me if I was upset with Bob Prince. He told me I should call Bob and tell him what was on my mind. I didn't want to, but I did. With a very shaky voice, I told him I didn't think he should take the owners' side so strongly, that he should think about the ballplayers, too.

"Back then, they owned you. You had nothing to say about where you played, and not much about what you were paid. They

273

often had a take-it or leave-it attitude. We were just looking for our fair share, and the key word is 'fair,' as far as we were concerned. That's what we were looking for.

"Bob was very gracious about it. He did go on the air and he said a player's wife had spoken to him, and complained about the point of view he had expressed concerning this player-owner problem. He didn't use my name. But I appreciated him telling the other side of the story. He handled it nicely."

To which Dave added, "Back in 1965, I was making $7,000 a year for pitching in the big leagues. So we didn't always make big money." (Everything's relative, back in 1965, I was making $4,000 a year as a corporal in the U.S. Army. In 1969, I was the highest-paid sportswriter on the staff of *The Miami News* at $10,400 a year. Bob Smizik recalled that in 1965, his first year out of college, he was making $5,000 a year as an elementary school teacher in Pittsburgh.)

Giusti said he made more money with American Express, as a corporate sales manager in Pittsburgh, peddling travel-related services, than he did even at the end of his career in baseball. "I made more money in less time than I had in baseball," recalled Giusti.

"In 1982, just when I got a job with American Express, cable TV was just coming around the corner. Bob Prince was available and they hooked Steve Blass and me up with him to do some games on the schedule. I found out about this on Wednesday and we did our first game on Saturday. I have no background for the job. I'm a little hesitant, because I have a new job and I don't want to jeopardize that in any way. It rained during that first game we did, and there was a total of an hour and a half delay.

"Prince started talking to me about pitching, and he has me demonstrating how to throw the palm ball. I must have talked about how to hold the ball to throw a palm ball for about 15 minutes. I was very apprehensive; I felt lost.

"Prince seemed to be enjoying himself. It was his time to shine. He loved that stuff. He could talk forever. How we got through that day together I'll never know. But I knew right then and there I didn't want to become a full-time baseball broadcaster. I just can't talk that freely and easily. That's not me.

"The American Express deal was great for me. I knew some people and could get in the front door at some big companies. I was selling them something they didn't have and needed that related to travel and entertainment. I had some previous sales experience. I had worked for Jack Piatt at Millcraft Industries, and called on people at mills throughout the area, from 1978 through 1981. So I knew I could sell."

Piatt was also a good friend of Bob Prince. Giusti gave some thought to Bob Prince prior to my visit, and had made some notes on a yellow legal pad. "Somehow my mom and dad would get some of the games on KDKA Radio at their home in Syracuse," said Giusti. "They would get better reception if my dad would go out and turn on the car radio. I know Steve Blass's dad did the same thing in Connecticut. The bottom line is that I once mentioned it to Bob. Every so often, when he was doing a game, he'd mention Mr. and Mrs. G up in Syracuse, and say he hoped they were listening to the game over the car radio. My dad heard that, and it meant a great deal to everyone in our family. Prince would do little things like that.

"Another thing that came to my mind was how obsessive he could be about his job. He had such great abilities in marketing and promotion. I feel he could have been a marketing whiz in the corporate world. Of course, he might not have lasted very long. He wanted to do things his way.

"I remember a period when I swear he was trying to change my name. He found out that the Italian people pronounce my name differently. They say 'Jue-stee.' One of my daughters was in Italy last year and they told her that her name was pronounced that way over there. There's a big Italian community in Providence, where my older daughter lives, and they say it's 'Jue-stee.' So Prince started calling me 'Jue-stee' on the air. He did that for six weeks, before I begged him to go back to calling me 'Just-tee,' like he had been before."

Giusti first heard about Prince when he was playing for the Astros and Cardinals. "We stayed at the Chase Hotel in St. Louis and we heard about him diving off the third floor into the swimming pool," said Giusti. "We'd say, 'Who is this guy?'

"When I first came to Pittsburgh, I helped sell season tickets during the offseason. I went to some banquets with Bob Prince. I couldn't get over how smooth he was. He had a great handle on the audience. He was just so smooth on that dais. I never saw anybody like that before. I traveled to some banquets with him and Al Abrams in the same car. They could get each other going. It was great. They were both well-respected on the banquet circuit.

"I got to know him even better after he was let go. His language was different in the bar than it was in the broadcast booth. I don't know how he was so disciplined when he was working that he never said a swear word. He never wore socks, that's something you remember. He could wear the things he did because he was tan, and had a nice, slender body.

"I don't know how he could control his tongue on the air. When we won the division in 1970, we beat the Cardinals in St. Louis. Prince had said he was not going into the clubhouse to join in the celebration. We wanted to make sure he was involved.

"Little Freddie Patek got a bucket full of ice water, and went out on the field where Bob was standing, doing a post-game show. Freddie got up on a stool behind Bob and threw the bucket of ice water on him. Bob was surprised and the cold water must've stopped his heart momentarily. He came real close to swearing on the air. I knew he was miffed. He was working with a live mike. We might've electrocuted him; we never thought about that.

"He forgot real fast, and he was picking up dinner tabs for us soon after."

Ginny said she and Dave both liked Jack Buck, but didn't care for Harry Caray during their stay in St. Louis. "Harry Caray said unkind things about a lot of players on the air," recalled Ginny. "One of the wives sent him a telegram to complain. I remember one time when Dave was pitching, Harry Caray cried out, 'Do you mean to tell me we traded six guys to get him?' Stuff like that. We liked Harry Kalas. We liked Nellie King. He was kind and so philosophical."

"My baseball heroes were Stan Musial and Ted Williams."

I asked Giusti to explain a 'palm ball,' which was his favorite pitch, and to tell me where he learned how to throw it. Giusti mentioned Jim Konstanty to me, and gave me a little test. I knew that Konstanty had worn glasses and that he had pitched for the Philadelphia Phillies "Whiz Kids" team back in the late '40s and early '50s. Giusti gave me a point for that on his sportswriter I.Q. scoresheet.

It was Joe Page and Konstanty who had begun the new era of the tireless relief specialist, the pitcher who could pitch every day and save a game if the starting pitcher faltered. Both men helped win pennants, and changed the way the game was played. Konstanty, a check of the records later revealed, appeared in 74 of 154 games his team played in 1950, when he was the NL's MVP, and then started the World Series.

"He went to Syracuse, ahead of me," said Giusti, getting to the point of his Konstanty story. "He learned it from the same coach who taught me the pitch, Jim Kleinhans, who had spent some time with the Yankees. I had a good hard fast ball and a palm ball. It was a change of pace pitch. You threw it with the same delivery and motion as the fastest pitch a person throws. If it's thrown effectively, the ball will sink. It has a lack of rotation, like a knuckle ball. It throws off the timing of the hitter.

"As a kid, I really didn't think of myself as a pitcher. I played several positions, and just wanted to be on the field as often as possible. My baseball heroes were Stan Musial and Ted Williams. I liked the Cardinals and the Red Sox. I could have signed as a position player, but I thought my best shot at getting to the big leagues in a hurry was as a pitcher.

"I pitched in the College World Series and did well during my senior year (1961) at Syracuse. The Cubs and Cardinals were interested in signing me."

276

I asked Giusti to tell me about some of the other people who influenced his career. He said when he was with the Astros there were a lot of guys who had a lot of talent, but burned the candle at both ends, and he didn't think you could do that and have a long career in baseball. "I don't know how they did it," he said. "Guys like Turk Farrell really lived it up."

He was there when a veteran Robin Roberts, near the end of his career, joined the Astros. "He told great stories," recalled Giusti. "I learned a lot from him. It was 1966 and he was 39 years old (he turned 40 on September 30 that year). He pitched back-to-back shutouts against Pittsburgh and Philadelphia. The thing I admired the most about him was that he never had a derogatory remark or statement about anybody. I had a lot of respect for him. I see him at oldtimers games from time to time. I was 25 at the time I first met him and very impressionable."

I remembered Robin Roberts as a pitcher on the Phillies staff, along with Curt Simmons. I told Giusti I thought Roberts had gone to Michigan State University, something I must have read in *SPORT* magazine as a teenager. Giusti gave me another point on his scorepad.

I asked Giusti about pitching on the same staff in St. Louis as Bob Gibson, a Hall of Famer and a much-feared fireballer. Many former Pirates say Gibson was the toughest pitcher they ever faced. "In 1968, the year before I came to the Cardinals, Gibson threw 11 shutouts in one season and had a 1.12 ERA," said Giusti. "I don't care if you're pitching in the Little League, that's pretty good. He was a great competitor. They talk about his great attitude, but he also had great stuff. There are a lot of great competitors out there, but they don't have the ability he had.

"He pitched when he was hurt; he'd go out there when his leg was bothering him or something. He was known as a ferocious Don Drysdale type who never gave in to a hitter. He backed you off the plate. But I was not a big fan of Bob Gibson. He was a great pitcher; I'll give him that.

"I missed playing with Stan Musial in St. Louis. He was the executive vice president when I was there. I ran into him once when I was with my daughter at some golf tournament after I was out of baseball. I told him how I played for the Cardinals. I'm not sure he really remembered me. He handed me some of his cards which were signed. I still have them, but I thought that was sort of funny for him to do that."

Giusti just shrugged his shoulders, and gave Ginny a look, like she might offer some insight into Musial's gesture.

"He meant a lot to me when I was a kid," said Giusti, "so I was still glad to shake his hand. Sports was big in our family. My dad played semi-pro ball, and my uncle went to school on a football scholarship, but also played baseball. I always had some kind of ball in my hand.

"When I was in Syracuse, I used to see Dave Bing working out at Manley Field House on our campus. I was utterly amazed by how good he was. He was a helluva basketball player. Dolph Schayes was my hero. He was the star of the Syracuse Nationals." Giusti gave me another test and I told him some of the other players on that team. "Who was the bald-headed guy?" Giusti asked. That was George "Bird" Yardley, who's in the Hall of Fame with Schayes. They also had Johnny "Red" Kerr, Al Bianchi, Red Rocha, George King, Earl Lloyd, Ed Conlin, Paul Seymour and Jim Tucker, who had played with Dick Ricketts (Dave's older brother) and Si Green at Duquesne. I remember stuff like that better than some of my history lessons in school. The Nats, not with all the players mentioned here in their lineup, won the 1954-55 NBA championship. The players all had magic names, Giusti agreed.

Now that he's retired, Giusti has the time to do more things with his family. "I'm making up for lost time," he said, "for time I was away on the road." Ginny said he's great about visiting his mother several times a week at Country Meadows, where she resides in the assisted-living building of the seniors residence. He's also helped her with her own mother who lives in Waynesboro, Virginia, extending himself countless times.

"He's very thoughtful, very generous," said Ginny.

Jim O'Brien

Dave Giusti visits his mother, Mary, on "Pirates Day" at Country Meadows, a retirement/personal care home in Bridgeville.

An opener at Country Meadows
Pirates Alumni in action

"We get some good things done."
— Dave Giusti

A driveway full of earthworms, a certain smell in the air, flowers everywhere, greener grass, all signals that spring was here. Judging by the temperatures, in the high 70s, so was summer. Daylight savings time and the opening of the baseball season also tipped us off that better, brighter days were with us.

While the present-day Pittsburgh Pirates opened the season on April 1, 1998 at Olympic Stadium in Montreal, where there was snow piled up on the streets outside the domed facility, the Pirates of the past opened the season at Country Meadows in Bridgeville on a bright, sunny day.

There was a gleam in the eyes of most of the seniors in the audience at the assisted care building in the beautiful residence facility former Governor George Leader built on a hillside that can be seen by travelers on I-79.

Standing before them, performing for them, were some of the best pitchers and broadcasters the Bucs ever boasted. Two of the best relief pitchers in baseball history, Kent Tekulve and Dave Giusti, were there, though they conceded that ElRoy Face, the former pitching ace and carpenter at Mayview State Hospital, was still "The Baron of the Bullpen."

Two World Series stars were there in Nellie Briles, now the director of corporate sales for the Pirates, and Jim Rooker, who owns a bar-restaurant in Ambridge. Briles came through big in the 1971 World Series and Rooker in the 1979 World Series for the Pirates.

Giusti had been one of the most valuable performers for the Pirates when they won the World Series in 1971, and Tekulve had the same role as the closer when the Pirates captured the World Series in 1979.

Nellie King of Mt. Lebanon, like Rooker a former broadcaster and pitcher, was working with Bob Prince when the Pirates won the World Series in 1971. "It's a delight to see so many young people here," cried out King, who just turned 70 the previous month.

There were five former Pirates, all pitchers, and they could all throw strikes and get people out. "When people ask me what my best pitch was," said King, "I say a strike."

They were there because Tekulve and Giusti, who live in nearby Upper St. Clair, both had parents in residence. Giusti, who rounded up the players, regularly visited his mother, Mary, and Tekulve came to see his dad, Henry.

"We go to a lot of places like that," said Giusti. "We get some good things done. Nellie Briles does a great job as our president, and we have the most active alumni association in all of baseball. We meet our objectives. We thought the people there would enjoy it. Our guys will go out of their way to help somebody. Bob Prince would be proud of us; he always did things like this wherever he was wanted."

Tekulve pointed to his father, who was suffering with leukemia and was sitting in a wheelchair.

"All of you people who wondered why I threw the ball from such a weird sidearm angle," said Tekulve, "well, you can blame this fellow here. That's the way he taught me to do it in our backyard. Then I went to Marietta (Ohio) College and played ball, and now my son goes there."

They all spoke of dreams they had as kids in backyards and sandlot ballfields. They told stories of their days in the big leagues, sang some songs, gave away T-shirts and autographed baseballs and cards with their likenesses as young men in Pirates uniforms to their long-time fans.

After Briles sang, "Take me out to the ballgame" and "Won't You Come Home, Bill Bailey," King turned to me and said, "All the old ballplayers could sing. When we rode the buses, we'd all be singing and telling stories. Guys would talk to their roommates. Now they don't want roommates. They don't know how to sing or talk anymore. I go to a match with my golf team at Duquesne University and as soon as we get in the van they put on their headphones and listen to music. I get after them. You guys oughta be talking to each other."

They passed around a heavy baseball bat once wielded by Willie Stargell, and showed "The Roberto Clemente Story" on the TV screen. There were black and gold balloons everywhere, a special cake, and the staff at Country Meadows had done itself proud with its preparations.

The five speakers told stories about how tough it was for them and their wives, back when baseball players didn't make as much money, and when they didn't have as much to say about where they were playing.

"We had to move 20 times in 14 years," said Giusti.

"It was a tough life for a woman," said King.

Some questions from the audience opened up some interesting avenues for anecdotes and shared stories.

"Most of our fun and achievements were in Pittsburgh," said Rooker. "Yeah, I'm the idiot who walked all the way from Philadelphia to Pittsburgh because I opened my big mouth too much.

"This was when I was announcing. The Pirates were on a bad streak where we had lost six in a row. Now we get off to an 11-nothing lead in Philadelphia, and I said if we lose this game I don't want to be on the plane with the team going back to Pittsburgh. I said I'd walk home. Sure enough we lost. So people started calling the ballclub and the radio station, asking if I had walked back to Pittsburgh as I said

I would. So we had the Jim Rooker Unintentional Walk (in October of 1989) and raised over $40,000 for various charities. I learned my lesson that if you're going to say something, you better be ready to back it up.

"The trip was 320 miles and it took me 13 days. It took me two days to walk through Lancaster County and it was fertilizer season there, so you can imagine what that smelled like to walk down those roads between the farmfields."

Tekulve related a story about Rooker getting the call to pitch the fifth game of the 1979 World Series, when the Pirates were trailing the Orioles three games to one. "Nobody ever comes back from a 3-1 disadvantage, but we did," said Tekulve. "Jim came through for us that day.

"I was on the mound at the end of the seventh game of that series, and got the final out. That was the highlight of my career. Every kid, when you start out at age 9 or something, dreams about hitting a home run to win a World Series, the way Maz did, or getting the last out. Pat Kelly flied out to Omar Moreno. No one was happier in the entire stadium than I was. I had pitched a lot that year (a total of 98 games) and was down to about 155 pounds. I was gassed out. Every team in baseball begins the season hoping to win the World Series. Only one team gets to accomplish that goal. And I threw the last pitch."

Briles told the audience, "I pitched in the majors for 14 years with five different teams. I just couldn't hold a job. My boyhood dream was to be a major league player, and I was fortunate to realize my dream.

"When most of us played, the minimum salary was $5,000. Today it's $175,000. Next year it will be $200,000.

"I was traded to Pittsburgh in 1971 for Matty Alou, who had won a National League batting title here. Giusti was one of the guys instrumental in getting me here. We had played together in St. Louis. I can see my mother's face in every one of your faces, and I can remember how proud she was that her son was a big league baseball player.

"I was lucky enough to come here in time to pitch for the team that won the 1971 World Series, and like Jim (Rooker), I came through in a key game. Everyone who's had a taste of winning it all like that will never forget the feeling.

"The losing manager, Earl Weaver of the Orioles, was quoted as saying 'the only thing I have to say about Nellie Briles is I hate his guts.' That will sure make a fella feel good.

"When I was traded to Baltimore, I walked into the Orioles clubhouse and hoped to be greeted warmly and Weaver looked up at me and said, 'I still hate your guts from '71.'

"Turns out, I had to pitch that first night, and I did a good job. So I went to Weaver's office after the game, and I said to him. 'Before the game, you told me you hated my guts. But you love me now.' He grabbed me and kissed me on the lips."

281

When the former pitchers started to talk about their hitting prowess, King came clean. "I was 0-for-4," he said, "0-for-four seasons. I was 0-for-27 as a batter in the big leagues, and I thought I could hit the ball pretty good."

Someone asked each of them to name the toughest batter they ever faced.

King said it was Stan Musial. "One game he got three hits off three different pitches," recalled King, "and when he came up the fourth time I didn't have any other pitches to show him.

"Musial was amazing," continued King. "He had 3,630 hits and he had the same number of hits at home and on the road. In 22 years (1941-1963), he batted .331 for his career. He was .331 against left-handers and .331 against right-handers."

I was so fascinated by what King said about Musial, one of my all-time favorites, that I checked further and found out that Musial played in 3,026 games. He came up to the plate and wiggled and jiggled and swung the bat in a lazy arc, coiled and set for the pitch 10,972 times. He crossed the plate 1,949 times for St. Louis. They were all league records.

He won the batting crown an average of one out of every three years. He led the league in long hits seven years and had 1,377 that were not singles — 725 doubles, 177 triples, 475 home runs!

He led the league in most two-base hits for eight years, hitting fifty or more three seasons. He led five years for triples, six years in most base hits. In 1946, he led in seven batting categories. He led the league in most total bases 13 seasons, 10 consecutively. His lifetime total was 6,134. He batted in 100 or more runs in ten seasons for a career total of 1,951.

No wonder he was one of Bob Prince's favorite players. Prince emceed a dinner in his honor in Donora back in 1941, his senior year in high school. That's how far they go back.

Briles said Rod Carew of the Twins was his toughest opponent. "He didn't care whether you were a right-hander or a left-hander, either. He hit you either way."

Rooker could relate to that. "One time Carew broke a bat against me, and the bat came out and hit me. I threw part of the bat back at him. I think I ticked him off. He got a new bat, and he hit one over the wall."

Rooker also mentioned how Montreal catcher Gary Carter had a habit of hitting a ball and letting his bat fly, and how the bat often ended up flying into the other team's dugout.

"One day I grabbed the bat when he did it a second time, and I slammed it down on the dugout steps and broke it. I threw what I had in my hand back at him. He had been thrown out at first base, and as Carter came by our dugout he glared down at me and said, 'I'll remember that.' I remember saying, 'Big deal!'

"The next game in Montreal, he had three home runs off me. We still won the game, 5-3. Teke saved it for us, as I remember. Carter hit another shot off me that day that Phil Garner caught at third base. Garner nearly got killed."

Giusti's toughest out was Billy Williams, and I recalled that his buddy Steve Blass had always said Williams was the toughest batter for him to face. "We put him in the Hall of Fame," said Giusti.

Tekulve recalled that he couldn't get Pete Rose out. Murray Cook was the general manager of the Reds in 1989, and wanted Tekulve to consider finishing his career in his hometown of Cincinnati. He suggested in January that Tekulve call Rose in Florida and see what he thought of the idea. "Rose told me that my life would be easier when I came to the Reds because I wouldn't have to face him," said Tekulve. "Rose said to me, 'Do you know what my batting average is against you?' I had no idea. 'I'm batting .628 against you,' Rose snapped. I looked it up and he did, indeed. And he knew it! I wondered if he knew what he hit against all opposing pitchers. Or just me! He hit a lot of people pretty good."

Jim O'Brien

Five former Pirates pitchers pay a visit in April, 1998 to Country Meadows, a retirement/personal care home in Bridgeville. They are, left to right, Jim Rooker, Nellie Briles, Nellie King, Dave Giusti and Kent Tekulve.

Dick Groat
Prince paved the way for his wedding

"He was part of us.
He wanted it as badly as we did."

Bob Prince played the role of cupid when Dick Groat met his wife, Barbara, so Prince not only took credit for their long-standing marriage but also for their three beautiful daughters. Groat was grateful and always considered Prince a pal and one of the best people he met during his wonderful baseball and broadcasting career.

Groat is one of the greatest competitors to ever come out of Pittsburgh or Western Pennsylvania, a college and pro basketball standout as well as an accomplished infielder and batter who won National League MVP awards at both Pittsburgh and later St. Louis with the Cardinals. He'd give you all you could handle on a golf course as well, or playing cards in the clubhouse.

He was the Pirates' MVP and won the National League's batting title during the 1960 season when the Pirates won the World Series against the heavily-favored New York Yankees in seven games.

Groat grew up in Swissvale, a suburb just east of Pittsburgh, and loved playing in his hometown. "I was reared in Western Pennsylvania and never had any desire to leave this area, but Joe Brown had other ideas," he said. Groat still keeps a home there. He had a bad fire at his home a few years earlier, and lost many of his photos and keepsakes in the blaze.

He lost a lot in that fire, but he's never lost the fire that beats in his breast. This is a proud man.

He still has that hard-nosed well-chiseled look about him, though he moved stiffly because of back surgeries in 1996 and 1997, and he still has the look and demeanor of an individual who is about to clean your clock. He wears eyeglasses these days, and they only enhance the gleam in his eyes.

An opinionated person, he lets you know exactly how he feels about anybody he's ever met — it's usually off the record if it's a negative regard — so if he praises Prince you can accept it as gospel. The gospel of Groat, anyhow.

He always considered himself a better basketball player than baseball player. Baseball was America's pastime when Groat was growing up, and the money was better. He played in the NBA and the NL one season (1952-53), playing for the Fort Wayne Pistons (averaging 11.9 ppg in 26 games as his team's third-leading scorer) as well as the Pittsburgh Pirates.

His coach at Fort Wayne was former Duquesne University standout, Paul Birch, later the coach at Rankin High School. "I loved Paul Birch," recalled Groat.

Former Pirates ElRoy Face and Dick Groat sign autographs for fans outside Three Rivers Stadium at Pirates game in April, 1998.

Pitt basketball broadcast partners Bill Hillgrove and Dick Groat get together at Groat's Champion Lakes Golf Club on July 29, 1997.

Photos by Jim O'Brien

Bob Prince's jaw was broken playing polo in his youth. Surgery left him with a stiff upper lip, ala Humphrey Bogart. "When I smile, it looks like this," he said, grimacing. "That's why I'm always licking the lip."

Red Auerbach and Red Holzman, two NBA coaching legends, will attest that Groat was as good a guard as there was in the NBA at the time, that he could hold his own with Bob Cousy, Bill Sharman, Dick McGuire, Bob Davies, Slater Martin, Andy Phillip, any of them. Groat played only on weekends in the NBA, while finishing up at Duke, and didn't practice with the Pistons.

Branch Rickey, the general manager of the Pirates, made Groat give up playing pro basketball. He thought basketball would wear him out before the baseball season even started. "I was disappointed, but I didn't want to do anything that would mess up things for me in Pittsburgh," he said. "Mr. Rickey was probably right about that."

Groat loved playing for the Pirates, but tells everybody that playing for Augie Busch and the St. Louis Cardinals was better because it was a classier organization. He never forgave Joe L. Brown, the Bucs' GM at the time, for trading him to the Cardinals when he was in his prime.

A Groat smile or "thank you" note — he was one ballplayer faithful in expressing his gratitude to writers or broadcasters for good reviews — can make your day. He can be charming. He can also freeze you with a stern steely-eyed look. If you're competing with him, you're in trouble.

"Prince was an influence on me in having me write 'thank you' letters to sports writers," said Groat with a grin when I asked him about his considerate correspondence habits.

Prince promoted Groat as a hometown boy who made good, and helped make him one of the most popular athletes in the area during the late '50s and early '60s. Since he retired as a ballplayer, Groat has worked hard to make Champion Lakes a first-class golf club. He succeeded better than most ballplayers of his era in making the transition to the real world without skipping a beat.

Groat's life has been less satisfying since his wife, Barbara, died June 12, 1990. There is a memorial to her near the clubhouse at Groat's Champion Lakes Golf Course just outside scenic Ligonier in Westmoreland County. Groat would be 68 on November 4, 1998, but he was a young man again when he talked about his early days with the Pirates when he returned home to play for them after winning College Player of the Year honors for the basketball team at Duke University.

I caught up with Groat on July 29, 1997, when he was hosting an annual media day golf outing for the University of Pittsburgh department of athletics. Groat was looking forward to his 19th season as the analyst and color commentator on Pitt's basketball network. WTAE's Bill Hillgrove, pointing toward his 29th season as the play-by-play man, was among the guest golfers that day. He and Groat are fellow travelers and each refers to the other as "my best friend" at speaking engagements.

"Traveling with the Pitt basketball team and Bill Hillgrove is something I truly love," said Groat. "It's my good fortune to work with the best play-by-play announcer in the business." At a dinner later that day, Groat would tell the gathering, "I love the University of Pittsburgh. . ." His older brother Charley had been a championship runner for the Pitt track & field team in the mid-'30s.

"My brother took me to the top of the Cathedral of Learning one day when I was about five or six years old," said Groat. "You've seen the poster showing people looking down from the Cathedral of Learning into Forbes Field. Well, that's how I saw my first Pirates game."

Groat grew up following the Panthers. Dodo Canterna and Bimbo Cecconi were two of his all-time favorites.

He was less enamored with Pitt's All-American basketball player Don Hennon, probably because they were both feisty, fiercely-competitive guards during the same period and, to Groat's chagrin, often compared. If you want to see Groat grind his teeth, mention Don Hennon to him. Groat thought he was better, at both ends of the court. It's that simple. Who's to argue with Groat on that account? Groat remains an intriguing study. He brought a passion to every pursuit.

Dr. Billy Soffa, one of the top administrators at Pitt's School of Engineering, was an outstanding basketball player at Carnegie Tech in the late '50s. He'd come from Homestead and was a 5-9 scoring dynamo for Mel Cratsley's club. Soffa remembers what a fierce competitor Groat was in those days.

"Some of the Pirates used to come over to our gym at Tech," said Soffa. "Skibo Hall was pretty close to Forbes Field, just across the bridge in Schenley Park. I was always going up against Groat, and he gave me more than I could handle. I thought we were just going one-on-one in the gym, but Groat took it quite seriously. It was an education for me."

"You think I'm crazy?"
— Bob Prince

Dick Groat loved his late wife and their children and grandchildren and life on the road with the same sort of zeal.

The memory of meeting Barbara, and the life they shared together, remains vivid for Groat. Asked to reflect on Bob Prince, Groat promptly goes back to that memorable day when the Pirates were playing the Giants at the Polo Grounds.

Barbara Womble, who was from Wilmington, North Carolina, had come to New York as a big-time model, and accompanied her father to a Pirates-Giants game at Coogan's Bluff. It was Groat's good fortune that they crossed paths that fateful afternoon.

287

"We met in May of 1955 in New York, (three years after he had signed with the Pirates)," said Groat. "I was warming up at the Polo Grounds, and I heard somebody calling me by name from the third base seats. It was a mature voice. This nice, gray-haired man said he wanted to meet me. So I went over by the rail to shake his hand. He said, 'This is my daughter; she's modeling here. Her name is Barbara.' The gentleman had gone to Duke, I learned, and he had followed my career.

"He asked me, 'Did you marry Rachel?' You see, Rachel was a woman I had gone with in college. I told them I had not. I was on the Laraine Day Show on TV the day before and she had also asked me if I was married.

"I chatted with them awhile, and then watched as they went back to their seats. There wasn't a big crowd at the ballpark that day; the Giants weren't drawing that well. So I could track them.

"I got hold of Bob Prince. I said, 'Bob, I need a favor. Would you mind going up there and getting her phone number for me? I want to call her.' He said, 'You think I'm crazy?' I said, 'She's with her father.' He said, 'That's worse.' But he did it. I can still see him walking up the steps toward them, wearing one of those wild plaid sportscoats he wore, and he got me the telephone number.

"That's why Bob and Betty Prince always took credit for Barbara and my three children and my six grandchildren.

"I guess that's why New York and the Polo Grounds were always special to me. I got my first major league hit there. I got my first home run there and, more importantly, I met my wife at the Polo Grounds.

"The ballplayers thought I was crazy," said Groat, "because I was buying all these fashion magazines at the airport, because Barbara was on the cover and in the pages in some of them."

They were married the same year they met, on November 11, 1955.

His daughters are Tracey Lynn Goetz, 42, who owns a real estate company in Durham and is married to former University of Richmond head basketball coach, Lou Goetz; Carol Ann Borkovich, 40, who lives in Murrysville and is a fifth-grade teacher at Woodland Hills; Allison Morrow DeStefano, 35, who lives in Latrobe and manages her dad's Champion Lakes golf course.

It was an idyllic day in the Laurel Highlands when I visited with Groat. There were blue skies, large white clouds that looked like cotton candy, temperatures ranging from 73 to 77 degrees. Landscapes don't come any more beautiful. Groat's course, which he and former teammate and partner Jerry Lynch cut out of the rolling hills with bulldozers they operated themselves, provided a beautiful backdrop. Champion Lakes is rated one of the best public layouts in the area. Prince played there many times in his life.

The Pittsburgh Steelers had just returned from Ireland and had resumed practice at nearby St. Vincent's in Latrobe. On the way to Groat's golf course, I drove by Ligonier Valley Country Club and the

Laurel Valley Country Club. Arnold Palmer's Latrobe Country Club was nearby.

There were horses and cows on the horizon, rolling hills in the Laurel Valley, famous for Arnold Palmer, the Mellon and Scaife estates, Rolling Rock beer, Fort Necessity, where General Forbes and General Washington once held forth during the French-Indian Wars. The Champion Lakes Golf Club and Bed & Breakfast is located on RD 1, Bolivar, Pennsylvania.

Lynch is no longer involved with the ownership, but remains a good friend of Groat. Dick and his daughter, Allison, had upgraded the place in recent years.

They refurbished the upstairs of the home above and beside the clubhouse and converted it a few years earlier into a bed & breakfast inn, with nine comfortable rooms. Each has the name of a former Pirate engraved on a plate affixed to its door. "I named them after my closest friends on the Pirates of the '60s," explained Groat.

The rooms were named in honor of Jerry Lynch, Bill Virdon, ElRoy Face, Bob Purkey, Bill Mazeroski, Bob Friend, Bob Skinner and, of course, Dick Groat. Those rooms all contain framed photographs and signed memorabilia about its namesake. The ninth room is called the Players Lounge, and it includes framed photos of Forbes Field, and Groat's two favorite broadcasters, Bill Hillgrove and Bob Prince. There were baseball cartoons drawn by Bill Winstein and Jack Berger Sr., who had worked for *The Pittsburgh Press.*

Touring the rooms with Groat was like visiting a mini-museum of Pirates baseball, a wing of the Hall of Fame at Cooperstown. There was no room at the inn for Roberto Clemente. The Pirates Hall of Famer was pictured, however, in the hallway. Groat didn't say it, but Clemente simply wasn't one of his "best friends," though Groat had great admiration for his ability.

Groat showed off his place to Pitt's first-year football coach Walt Harris, who remembered Groat playing for the Giants at the end of his career when Harris was growing up in the San Francisco area. "I was always a Giants fan," said Harris. The new coach impressed Groat with what he accomplished his first year at Pitt. "I've always been a Pitt fan," Groat told him. Former Pitt athletes are always showing up to play, and they're still on scholarship with Groat.

"He was so much fun to be around."
— Groat on Prince

Dick Groat grabbed for a cigarette, as he talked about his buddy, Bob Prince. "He was so good with all of us," said the former Pirates All-Star shortstop. "He was part of us. He was a part of the team. He wanted it as badly as we did.

"He kept us loose. He was so much fun to be around. He was an integral part of that '60 success. He was so happy in '58 when we turned it around.

"During the last week in July of 1958, we were tied for first with the Dodgers. Our ballclub just matured, it grew up suddenly. Branch Rickey was drafting good ballplayers and bringing in good ballplayers. We learned how to play, and how to win. Bob was thrilled to have a winning ballclub to talk about.

"After we finished second that season, our slogan the next year was 'You Were Great in '58.' In 1959, we picked up Burgess, Hoak and Haddix in a trade with Cincinnati, and that really solidified our ballclub.

"So many things people don't realize when they look at a team. I became a better shortstop after that trade. The pitching staff got better, you see. You have pitchers who did what they wanted to do. You could position yourself better, knowing they'd do what they were supposed to do.

"Yet our record slipped in 1959, and we finished fourth. We were heart-broken. But we had improved our ballclub for the run we made the next year."

Groat was one of four Pirates picked to play in the All-Star Game in 1959. It was his first appearance in the mid-summer classic. Smoky Burgess, Bill Mazeroski and ElRoy Face represented the Pirates as well. Those four were joined the next season in the All-Star Game by Roberto Clemente, Bob Friend, Vernon Law and Bob Skinner.

The Pirates had eight players in the All-Star lineup in 1960, the most in club history, and they have never had more than four (in 1964 and 1971) since then. It's also one of the most beloved and best known ballclubs in any sport in the minds and hearts of Pittsburgh sports fans.

"Bob came up with a nickname for everybody," said Groat. "I don't know if any broadcaster had as great a relationship as Bob did on a personal level, and he made us even more popular with Pirates fans the way he talked about us. He could sell anything.

"I can remember how I always had my own hit and run signal, something I devised on my own. Bob would come up to me and he would want to know what my hit and run signal was for that game. I'd tell him. He wanted to know so he could alert the fans on the broadcast to what was coming. Danny Murtaugh didn't even know it. Bill Virdon knew. He was our leadoff hitter. When you're doing radio, you have to paint a picture. Bill (Hillgrove) does a magnificent job, whatever sport he's covering. Bob did the same thing. He made the fans feel like they were there.

"One of the reasons he was so popular and so well-liked by every-one is that I don't remember him second-guessing the ballplayers or the manager. Bill and I have said this many times: if you think we're prejudiced toward the Pitt basketball team, we are. And we inherit-ed that approach from our idol, Bob Prince.

Dick Groat is proud of the Champion Lakes Golf Club he developed near Ligonier.

Photos by Jim O'Brien

During tour of his Champion Lakes Golf Club, Groat points to photograph of friend and former teammate Bill Mazeroski scoring game-winning run after hitting home run to lead off bottom of ninth inning in 7th Game of 1960 World Series.

> *"Bob Prince touched many people one by one, so many hands he shook, so many things he did. That's why his life was so significant."*
> — Lanny Frattare,
> Pirates broadcaster

"He was my kind of guy. When he did our games, he'd be out with us after games. He was the most generous guy in the world. In Mt. Lebanon, where he lived back then, he sponsored the Wildcats football team and underwrote the program. He did so much for the kids in Mt. Lebanon. I still run into guys at banquets who played for the Wildcats, and love to talk about their experiences with Bob Prince. He didn't just pay the bills, he traveled with the ballclub and was their biggest cheerleader.

"I was out one night with Bob, at the Cork & Bottle downtown. He was 55 or 56 at the time, and I was just a kid. Some guy came in and started to get on him. 'Didn't you swim on the Pitt team?' the guy asked. He gave Bob some crap. The guy said he could beat Bob. It was raining that night and Bob said, 'I'll swim you right up that gutter and it'll be no contest.' He was ready to swim against the guy right there, on Oliver Street.

"Bob had an excellent record as a swimmer, and he was proud of it. He always thought he could outswim anybody he came across.

"Everybody on our ballclub loved Bob. He was almost a surrogate father for all of us. He was most supportive. We were terrible when we first came up, but he boosted us anyhow."

I mentioned to Groat that he came to the Pirates in time for the 1952 season. That's the year the Pirates had the worst record in the club's history. Under Billy Meyer, whose No. 1 uniform is retired for some mysterious reason (he had a losing record every one of his five years as bench boss of the Bucs), the Pirates posted a 42-112 record. They finished eighth and last in the National League. They finished eighth and last the next three years under Fred Haney, before he gave way to Bobby Bragan and they moved up to seventh for the next two seasons.

"My rookie year, I was just happy to be in the big leagues," said Groat. "That record didn't ruin it for me.

"I was always happy to be playing in the big leagues. When I made that little spurt to be the leading hitter in '64, I was playing in St. Louis in old Busch Stadium. On the last day of the season, I walked up out of the dugout and Walker Cooper was coming down. He said, 'Kid, you're doing all right.' That's the way I always felt, no matter where I was playing. It was great to be playing in the big leagues."

Looking back at the bed & breakfast part of his clubhouse complex, Groat offered, "Jerry (Lynch) raised his kids here. I lived there for years by myself after Barbara died. I think Allison decorated it so well. Those pictures of my best friends on the ballclub in there bring back only the best of memories.

"Bob Prince was always so special with all of us. He treated me so super. The only time he upset my father was in 1964, that final game of the season. He was hoping we'd lose the final game and then the Phillies and Cardinals and Reds would all be tied for first. He didn't realize that they had already set up pairings for playoffs.

"Our Jim Bunning shut out Cincinnati in the final game, and we went on to beat the Yankees in the '64 Series.

"One night I was furious with Bob Prince at Fitzgerald Field House. We were playing an exhibition basketball game for Children's Hospital. Bob was refereeing. I backed away from Don Hennon and let him shoot. Prince called a foul on me. I was nowhere near him. I had shut him down completely. After Bob called that foul on me, Hennon makes two free throws and tied the game. Prince called the game off with a tie. I was furious with Prince."

Back in his military service days, Groat came to Pittsburgh and played for the Fort Belvoir basketball team. Paul Arizin, a future Hall of Famer, came to the Field House to play for the Quantico Marines. I remember seeing them play there in the mid-50s, when I first started to go to games at the Field House. I remember seeing Sihugo Green and Dick Ricketts, resplendent looking in long camel hair overcoats, so tall, so regal-looking to a pre-teen fan.

Groat played in one game as a teammate of Hennon and got on him for playing a one-way game. "I don't care how much you shoot, but you better play both ends of the floor," Groat growled at Hennon. "You better get back on defense. I'm tired of being on the backend of three on two and two on one situations. If you can't do that, don't play with me."

Groat recalled how Prince and Ralph Kiner, one of his all-time favorites, his roommate in his rookie year, often got involved in business ventures together. "He and Kiner owned that UHF station," said Groat, "and they owned the Cameo, a bar/restaurant on Craig Street in Oakland.

"When we (Fort Belvoir) came up to play Duquesne, and we were playing at Fitzgerald Field House, Prince put the game on his TV station. He sold commercials, but all the money was going to Children's Hospital. He lost money on the deal. It was typical of Bob; he'd help anybody, often at his own expense. They went bankrupt at the station.

"One of his bartenders bought the bar from him, probably with the money he skimmed off the top.

"He was married to one of the finest ladies who ever walked this earth. Betty Prince. What a beautiful lady she is. She was great with my daughters and with my wife. She was like Mother Superior, the perfect lady. She's a fantastic lady; I'm glad she's doing well.

"After he and Nellie were fired, he said to me, 'Now I know why you don't like Joe Brown.' Bob supported Joe L. Brown when he was under consideration for the GM's job.

"Ed Wallis at KDKA wanted to get rid of Bob. They'd have never gotten rid of him if Joe L. Brown had come to his support. Tom Johnson was always a Bob Prince supporter, but even he turned his back on him in the end."

Mentioning Brown's name brought another bad thought to Groat's mind. There is a painting of the Pirates' All-Time team and one of the prints hangs in the lobby of the Pirates' offices at Three Rivers Stadium. Groat is not pictured. He truly belongs.

"That had to be a Joe L. Brown production. That's why I wasn't in it. I won a batting championship and MVP when I was here, but I'm not on the all-time team because Joe L. Brown kept me off it.

"That's because I had said I was never treated better in baseball than I was by the St. Louis Cardinals, which was the truth. Bill Virdon told me that Murtaugh told him that I buried myself with the Bucs when I made that remark."

Groat had some errands to run, so he invited me to tag along with him as he drove into downtown Ligonier, just a few miles from his golf club.

He was listening to WJAS on his radio as he drove to the bank in Ligonier. It was music from the '50s and '60s, for the most part. The host deejay was Bill Cardille.

"I love Bill Cardille," said Groat. "He's such a good guy."

Groat doesn't forget the good guys he's come across in his travels, or the bad guys for that matter, and the former are far more numerous than the latter. There was a long period when Groat stayed away from Pirates' functions and was seldom seen at the ballpark. It's good to see Groat back at Three Rivers Stadium.

"I'm back with the Pirates," he said proudly. "I like McClatchy and what's he's trying to do. I want to see major league baseball stay in Pittsburgh. I'll do whatever I can to help. Actually, I'd been back with the alumni really since Mark Sauer was in charge. He invited me to be part of the Pirates once again.

"They've done so many great things recently. McClatchy has done a magnificent job. They have some great promotions."

Merle Haggard was pictured on a poster behind Groat, promoting the Westmoreland Agricultural Fair that was coming to the area. There's two legendary figures, I thought.

Another legendary figure came into the conversation, namely Ralph Kiner. "I roomed with Ralph Kiner when I first came up and he helped me break in, teaching me a lot of things. I still have a tremendous respect for him.

"I roomed with Virdon from '56 to '62. Bill and I still keep in touch. Skinner and I roomed together in St. Louis. I don't know what you'd do without a roommate. Had breakfast together. Go over the game the night before. Look out for each other. You had someone to eat with.

"The ballplayers today make more money and they don't want to room with their teammates. But our roommates were important to us when I was playing. We helped each other through the bad times and the good times.

"And there was always Bob Prince. He got stuck with more tabs than anyone else. It was always the big tabs, too, whether he could afford it or not.

"People don't appreciate what he (Prince) meant to the Pirates. Worst move they ever made was getting rid of Prince."

"You ought to retire."
— George Sisler

When I asked Groat about his grittiness, and how the fires seemed to still burn in him, he nodded.

"It's always been a major deal to lose," he agreed.

"That's the reason I don't play golf in these outings anymore. With my back the way it is, I can't play competitively. I can't do the things I used to be able to do.

"In baseball, that's why it was easy for me to retire. I just couldn't play. My pride wouldn't permit me to stay any longer than I could get the job done. You have to have a great deal of pride to get to the major leagues in the first place.

"I finished up in San Francisco. I played for the Giants when they had Mays, McCovey, Jim Ray Hart. It was a selfish team, everyone for himself. It was altogether different in St. Louis when we had Bob Gibson, Tim McCarver, Stan Musial, Ken Boyer, Bill White and Joe Torre.

"When I went to the Phillies, I changed my hitting style because I had a bad year in St. Louis. I tried to make myself a pull hitter. When I was with the Phillies, I was hitting .180 in this one stretch, and thought I was through. I couldn't sleep. I was miserable. I talked to George Sisler, who was our hitting instructor when I was with the Pirates. 'I'm going to retire,' I told him. And he said, 'You ought to retire, the way you're hitting. You go back to your old style of hitting.' Ray Kelly, the baseball writer for the *Philadelphia Evening Bulletin*, later told me I hit .328 the rest of the season. I finished up at .260 and decided to stay with it.

"Today the product is so diluted. If you chose up 16 teams from the present talent — if you put them all in a pool and drafted them, then you might have some good teams.

"I think I played baseball at a great time. It was post World War II, and the best athletes in America played baseball. It was the national pastime. Now the best athletes go to the sport they do best, the one they can play best or the one where they're gonna make the most money.

"When I was playing in the NBA, George Mikan, Bob Cousy and I were the only players making $10,000 or more. I was offered a bigger contract to come back, but Mr. Rickey wouldn't permit me to play anymore. That hurt, because, in my heart, I knew I was a better basketball player."

Dick Groat was given a special gift at a "Pitt Day" program hosted by The Fellows Club at Jimmy Blandi's LeMont Restaurant on Mt. Washington on Saturday, March 28. Groat knew he was going to be honored by the civic group as "the greatest athlete in Western Pennsylvania history," based mainly on his having played on a high level in two professional sports.

What he didn't know was what Armand Dellovade, a devoted Pitt booster, had in store for him. Dellovade, an Avella native who owns and operates a national construction firm out of Canonsburg that does steel sheet covering work across the nation, had learned that Groat's two World Series rings — from the Pirates in 1960 and the Cardinals in 1964 —had been stolen from Groat's golf club some years earlier. Dellovade had a new 1960 Pirates ring cast especially for Groat, and gave it to him at The Fellows affair.

"This means a great deal to me," said a suddenly subdued Groat.

"I think Dick was genuinely touched by this gesture," noted Nellie Briles, a former Pirates and Cardinals pitcher who'd been a big key to the Pirates' 1971 World Series success and now served the club as Director of Corporate Sales and the President of the Pirates' Alumni Association.

"They talk about Maz belonging in the Baseball Hall of Fame," said Dellovade. "Well, I think that Maz and Dick Groat both belong in the Baseball Hall of Fame."

Jim O'Brien

Dick Groat flashes new 1960 World Series championship ring and Forbes Field model given to him by Canonsburg construction magnate Armand Dellovade, left, as Pirates Alumni president Nellie Briles lends his support.

Paul Long
A voice on high

"The man was absolutely fearless."

That voice. Paul Long is on the telephone and I feel like I've made a direct connection to a higher power. Long is God on a radio ad aimed at selling automobiles heard on the Pittsburgh airwaves. He speaks from on high to a woman who is supposed to be the quintessential Pittsburgh woman. In short, she chews gum, probably wears a babushka, and uses words like "yunz" to get your attention. Long is the only saving grace in this Godawful radio commercial.

Long's talents were put to much better use, and abuse, when he was paired with Bob Prince in the Pirate broadcast booth from 1957 through 1962. The two also often sat next to each other in Long's single-engine Cessna 180 airplane. "Bob just wanted to fly it," recalled Long. "He loved to fly. The problem is he didn't care that he had never taken any flying lessons. The man was fearless."

When I told Long an oft-told story about Prince taking over the controls of an airplane when a licensed pilot was flying him and Pirates' publicist Jack Berger to a sports banquet in Warren, Pa., Long released a loud laugh.

"Jack was really scared of planes in the first place," he said. "He hung onto the door. He was not an airplane guy. Having Prince at the controls would not be good for Jack's heart, or anyone's heart for that matter. Bob didn't know details, like that you had to wait for the airplane to be going at a certain speed before you could pull up the wheel on take-off. He didn't realize that if you do it wrong it'll kill you. You can fall out of the sky. You have to keep that nose up in the air. Prince didn't care about the small stuff. He was absolutely fearless when it came to most things.

"Prince . . . I'll never forget him. He was a memorable character. He was basically a good-hearted individual. He took a great interest in the Allegheny Valley School. I'm not sure why. Why did he pick that as his pet fund-raising project? (The Hillman family enlisted Prince's help to promote fund-raising to augment its own strong support.)

"I was added to the Pirates broadcast team in 1957. That's the year that KDKA went to all-color on TV for the first time. They were going to be doing a number of games on TV as well as radio and they needed another announcer. Dick Bingham was Prince's partner at that time."

Bingham had come from Chicago at the start of the 1956 season. He filled the gap in the announcing team caused by the death of A.K. "Rosey" Rowswell, who was an institution as the Voice of the Pirates. Long was basically used on weekends when games were on television and radio. He continued to do his news reports during the week and would be running to join Prince and Bingham somewhere on Fridays.

"They needed another talking head," recalled Long, now living in retirement at the Presbyterian Senior Care Center Retirement Home in Washington, Pa.

He was living in a condominium along with his wife, Elaine. "We've been married 50 years as of August 21 (1997)," he said proudly. "She's my child bride. She was one of the Kinder Sisters. Do you remember the Kinder Sisters? They were singers with the KDKA orchestra."

That's a tip-off to how far back Long goes with Pittsburgh broadcasting. The KDKA orchestra! He grew up 15 miles outside of Como, Texas, which he said was not named after Canonsburg's Perry Como. He came to Pittsburgh in June of 1946 to begin his Pittsburgh career. He met Elaine Kinder and they were wed the following year. She liked the way he talked.

Long worked at KDKA Radio and TV for $22\frac{1}{2}$ years, and then shifted on October 30, 1968 to WTAE where he remained another 30 years before retiring. When I asked him how old he was, he said, "Very old." He then disclosed that he had been born January 28, 1916, which made him 82 and counting. Paul Long likes to poke fun at himself.

Long said he worked with Bingham only one year, and then Jim Woods came from the New York Yankees to work with Prince. "They were a great team," allowed Long. "I stayed with them through 1962.

Long was there when the Pirates beat the Yankees in the seventh game of the World Series on Bill Mazeroski's home run in the bottom of the ninth inning. "That was a special time," said Long. "It was great to be a part of it. There's never been a time quite like it in the city of Pittsburgh.

"Prince was colorful, unique to me. Joe L. Brown was an interesting guy to work for. He was the son of Joe E. Brown, one of my favorites in the movies as I was growing up.

"I never expected a rich man's kid to grow up and communicate and entertain and manage ordinary, common people. I expected him to be at a party, or at a swimming pool with topless waitresses handing out food and drink in a Hollywood setting. Joe was a great manager. He got down and dirty.

"They had great guys like Bill Mazeroski on the team. I knew him. I remember telling him that a guy with the Yankees, probably Mickey Mantle, was going to be making $40,000. He said he didn't care. He said, 'I'd play for nothing if they let me.' I went to the ceremony somewhere out on Rt. 30 when Bill married Milene Nicholson, who had been working in the Pirates front office. She was from Braddock. They were both sweet people. Bill Mazeroski was never a philosopher. Just give me a bat and a glove or a golf club and I'll entertain myself. Dick Groat was another guy I found to be a first-class individual."

Paul Long was Bob Prince's co-pilot and the "third man" in broadcast booth from 1957 to 1962.

"When you remember me, it means that you have carried something of who I am with you, that I have left some mark of who I am on you. It means that you can summon me back to your mind even though countless years and miles may stand between us. It means that if we meet again, you will know me. It means that even after I die, you can still see my face and hear my voice and speak to me in your heart. For as long as you remember me, I am never entirely lost. If you forget me, part of who I am will be gone."
— Frederick Buechner,
Pittsburgh-born author
A Room Called Remember

"Prince wanted something and I didn't know what to give him."

"I never knew why Bob Prince was finally fired," allowed Long, as we continued our conversation. "He was always in hot water with management. He spoke his mind. He wanted to make friends with people if they were big shots and he often invited them to sit in the back of our broadcast booth. He had some illnesses along the way. But he was damn good at his job.

"He spent a lot of time scratching the backs of big-shots, but apparently he never tried to do the same with the KDKA executives. He belonged to at least two country clubs, which cost a few bucks. I spent some time with him at Chartiers Country Club, and I know he was a member at St. Clair Country Club.

"He was always popular. Everybody liked Bob Prince, most everybody anyhow. He couldn't remember names, but he always called people by their names. We'd be walking along somewhere, and he'd spot somebody approaching us. He'd say, 'Hey, Paul, what's the name of that guy over there with the red tie.' I'd tell him, or somebody else would tell him, and Bob would bellow, 'Hey, Joe, how ya doin'?' He was a politician in that sense. Most politicians would like to be that way. He could charm the fur off your back.

"Sometimes he was a little tough. He was the star, and he reminded you of that from time to time with things he said. He catered to big shots. He'd take someone like Benjamin Fairless, the CEO of U.S. Steel. He knew him well, and he'd yell at him across the stadium if he could see him. He'd mention his name on the airwaves.

"He'd say, 'Benjamin Fairless just walked in, so we can start the ballgame now. Hello, Ben!' I can hear it as I'm talking to you. And, of course, Ben Fairless enjoyed hearing his name kicked around on the air."

"How was Bob Prince to work with?" I asked Long.

"Just the things he'd say at times," responded Long. "He was on TV with Jim Woods and I was usually on radio. Sometimes he'd tell me before the ballgame, 'You better be prepared to do nine innings. I don't think I'll get over there today.' That's when he had somebody in the booth that he wanted to impress. He'd give them the full V.I.P. treatment, instead of him relieving me after three innings, as was the usual routine. He had his way; he was the boss over there. That was my No. 2 job, not my No. 1 job. I had a lot of news to do at KDKA. I'd be doing it right up until the time I had to leave for the airport. I did about 35 or 40 games a year, and we didn't televise games too far west. I enjoyed it. I was also a baseball fan."

> *"My dad would be in one bed and I'd be in another and the radio would be on between us. We'd listen to the Pirates in the dark. The only light in the room came from the radio."*
> — Pirates' fan

Long possesses a commanding, compelling voice. I asked him how he rated Prince's voice.

"It's not the tenor of the voice that counts," said Long. "It's the way you use it to express yourself. He didn't have a stentorian, basso profundo (a loud or deep heavy bass) voice. It was the way he used it that was remarkable.

"He was a bright fellow, a bit neurotic. You always sensed that he wanted something more from you than you were giving him. Groat's one of the world's nice guys; he didn't want anything. Prince wanted something and I didn't know what to give him.

"You take someone like Art Rooney, the Steelers' owner. He was everybody's friend. I don't know if he had an enemy. He was a perfect gentleman. When Art Rooney would be walking my way when I worked at KDKA in Gateway Center and he was working out of the Steelers' office when they were at the Roosevelt Hotel . . . we had a ritual.

"I'd reach in my pocket and pull out a cigar. And Art would have one of those eight-inch cigars in his hand. I'd say, 'Morning, Art,' and he'd say, 'Morning, Paul,' and we'd exchange cigars as we passed. That was it. It was a ritual with us. There was something about him. He had the common touch. He'd know me from a block away.

"It wasn't hard to recognize Prince when he was approaching on the street. Prince wore some of the wildest clothes I ever saw. I remember once at Wrigley Field we were about five or ten minutes away from 'play ball' time. Prince had gone down to the dugout to get the lineups. He started walking up the center aisleway. He had on a wild shirt — it had 49 colors in it — and shorts. I'd never seen him in shorts before. People began applauding him, and soon there was a real applause swell, and then a standing ovation.

"Prince had these crazy legs. He had legs that weren't invented by God. They looked like they were broken in 16 places. Plus, he was bow-legged. But he didn't care. He was putting on an act, waving at people, hollering out to them. In time, there was thunderous applause. He had played to the crowd and he had done so successfully."

A history lesson is appropriate here. It's important to know how things were different in the mid-'50s when Long teamed up with Prince. Back then, a page of the daily newspapers was devoted to half-hour by half-hour radio listings for all the local radio stations as well as the TV stations. There were only a half-dozen TV stations. There were hardly any sports events on TV at the time. There was no cable TV, no ESPN or all-sports stations.

There were five major radio stations in Pittsburgh: WWSW (970 on the dial), KDKA (1020), WCAE (1250), WJAS (1320) and KQV (1410). Sterling Yates, Art Pallan and Rege Cordic were on KDKA, Jay Michael and Dave Tyson on WCAE (now WTAE), Barry Kaye and

Bill Brant on WJAS, and shows like Jack Benny and Our Miss Brooks, The Shadow, and Inner Sanctum were nightly features.

Fred Remington was the radio and TV editor at *The Pittsburgh Press*, which had a special Sunday supplement for radio and TV coverage and listings.

In the issue for June 9, 1957 — the year that Long became a part of the broadcast team — Prince and Dick Bingham were featured on the cover. In the cover story, Remington described Prince as "perhaps the most controversial figure on the Pittsburgh airways.

"The Pirates have no more heartfelt a rooter. He dies a thousand deaths as the team is losing, an emotional state which sometimes distracts from his spoken account of the game.

"At such times, he tends to go into rambling circumlocutions because, consciously or unconsciously, he finds events on the field of play too painful to deal with in detail. His ramblings have an inflammatory effect on audiences."

Prince's response to such criticism: "When you're losing, you have a tendency to be irrelevant."

Long recalls those days. "Everybody knew those two guys," he said of Prince and Bingham. That's when KDKA was the only show in town. They had no competition. That was a period that marked the end of radio domination and the beginning of TV domination.

"DuMont television had begun on January 11, 1949, and there was no other television station for the first five or six years. Whatever was on KDKA was it. KDKA had the television audience."

That helps account for the popularity of KDKA newsman Bill Burns as well. Bill Burns and Bob Prince were the prime broadcasting personalities in Pittsburgh. Then came Cope, Myron Cope, and he captured the attention of radio and TV audiences like no one since.

"Cope was unique," said Long. "Nobody is like Cope. He's Cope's worst critic. He can walk into a crowd and take it over. That voice fools a lot of people. 'My God, he's on television with that voice!'

"By God, he was sharp. He could describe a scene, a personality, and use those crazy words he dreamed up, then hit you with a 'Yoi!' at the end. I liked him a lot.

"But even Myron Cope was never as big as Bob Prince in Pittsburgh. If you said Bob Prince in a crowd, everybody knew his name. There are still people who don't know who Chuck Noll is, hard as that might be to believe. But I know people like that. It's true. But everyone knew Bob Prince. The bottom line is he was a friend. You could always depend on him."

> ***"Bob Prince was an event looking for a place to happen."***
>   — Jack Bogut

Bob Friend
He lives up to his name

"Bob Prince built up a very positive image of us over a long time."

Bob Friend was flipping through photo albums. The former Pirates pitcher was pointing to people he figured would be instantly recognizable. They were some of the greatest sports and political figures to ever grace the city's landscape, and there were also some prominent statewide and national figures in these well-maintained albums.

Bob Friend could be found somewhere in all the photos, and Bob Prince appeared in many as well. Friend's always been a photogenic fellow, a goodwill ambassador for the Bucs and baseball, a respected politician in his day, and once a successful securities salesman and more recently a successful insurance sales representative for Babb, Inc., one of the city's most respected agencies.

He was one of the best singers on the ballclub back when, according to teammate Nellie King, all the players could sing and tell stories. Friend sang in barbershop quartet competitions. He can still carry a tune or a tale, and a well-stuffed brown briefcase. Bob Friend is what the best ballplayers used to be all about.

Friend is a fellow who worked just as hard off the field to develop a solid career as he did as one of the most reliable pitchers in Pirates' history. He and teammate Dick Groat were rare in their day because they had college degrees, and both of them carved out sound careers beyond the baseball diamond. Friend has always been an affable, decent fellow.

"Bob proved he has determination by spending eight winters to get his degree from Purdue," said Dick Groat, who'd gone to Duke and starred in basketball as well as baseball before signing with the Pirates in 1952. "He's one of the hardest workers I've seen."

Bob Prince promoted them both in that light, and popularized them throughout Pennsylvania and its adjoining states. They came to appreciate Prince's contribution to their success after they hung up their uniforms and discarded their spikes.

Friend's name is still in the Pirates' recordbook. He is first among starting pitchers with 568 appearances, innings pitched with 3,481, strikeouts with 1,682. He is fourth with 191 wins, third in shutouts with 35 and first in losses with 218. So much for his stats.

Bob Prince used to say Friend struck someone out with "a slip pitch," and Friend was confused by that because he didn't have "a slip pitch," but was willing to acquire one because he liked Prince so much.

Everything about Bob Friend's office was neat, even though there were framed photographs everywhere, on all the walls, on his desk, on the coffee table, mantel and every nook and cranny. The decor was Early American Organized Clutter. He could look around and have his memory jogged about the most important events in his life.

"Let's see here," offered Friend, "how about this? You know who this is, don't you?"

Jack and Jim McGregor were in several pictures, and that reminded me that Jim, who is a Common Pleas Court Judge, has an office in the City-County Building that is similar to Friend's because of their shared passion for Pittsburgh, sports, politics and golf, and not necessarily in that order. They are both proud of the people they've kept company with, but not in an overbearing manner. Their offices are extensions of the Heinz History Center in The Strip, and they just want to take you on a tour.

I wondered what became of Jack McGregor. He was a handsome, smart young politician who had the kind of looks Jack Kennedy put to great use on and off the field in his political life, and McGregor had been one of the leaders in landing the Pittsburgh Penguins and Pittsburgh Phantoms when the National Hockey League and pro soccer franchises were established in Pittsburgh back in 1967. McGregor left town and faded from the local scene. I got to know him when I was starting my own professional career back in the mid-60s, and thought he was going to get so much done in Pittsburgh.

In writing other books about the Pirates, I had visited Bob and his wife, Pat, in their home in Fox Chapel, and it's also a museum to the Friend family's lifelong involvement in sports. There are lots of famous folks, plus plenty of the most popular Pirates in the team's history, hanging on the walls throughout their home. The Friends have two children, Missy Alexander and Bob Jr., and young Bob was making his mark on the PGA tour, so his photos were finding their way into prominence as well.

Back in 1992, young Bob's rookie year on tour, when he took the opening-round lead in the New England Classic, an article in *USA Today* referred to him as "son of the late Pittsburgh Pirates pitcher of the same name." Bob and Pat Friend took a lot of ribbing about that at the Oakmont Country Club where they were working as volunteers at the time with the U.S. Women's Open.

There was a silver framed photo showing young Bob just to the left shoulder of Arnold Palmer as they played a practice round on a Wednesday at the U.S. Open Golf Tournament at the Oakmont Country Club in 1994. I didn't know at the time I was talking to Friend that I'd be having lunch that same day at the hallowed Oakmont Country Club. The photo was displayed at the end of a coffee table where our knees were pressed as we sat on a couch in the nicely-appointed office.

There was a rocking chair nearby that Friend had been given, according to a gold plate that was affixed to the top of it, a souvenir of his participation in an oldtimers' game.

Bob Friend is flanked by Dale Long and Mickey Mantle at 1971 reunion of 1960 World Series opponents at Three Rivers Stadium.

Bob Friend and Willie Stargell share memories at Three Rivers Stadium. Friend was veteran when Stargell broke in with Bucs in 1962.

Reunion at Roberto Clemente Foundation golf outing June 4, 1998 includes, left to right, Frank Thomas, Bob Friend, Bobby DelGreco and Bill Mazeroski.

The first photos Friend showed me were taken during his political campaigning days when he was elected County Controller on the Republican ticket in 1967 and re-elected to the position in 1971. The McGregors and Elsie Hillman, the chairperson of the Republican Party, were in most of those.

It was Tom Johnson, a Pittsburgh attorney who was one of the owners of the Pirates when Friend was a star pitcher, who got Friend into the political arena and it was Mrs. Hillman, wife of industrialist Henry Hillman, the richest man in Pittsburgh, who promoted and supported his efforts. "She knew I could win and she really got behind me," said Bob.

Friend said Tom Johnson was constantly standing up for Bob Prince whenever he got into jams as the Pirates' broadcaster, as well as getting players out of run-ins with the law.

Bob Prince popped up here and there. In one photo, showing Friend and his foursome at a celebrity golf outing that Prince sponsored at his St. Clair Country Club, there is a handwritten message that reads: "Thanks, Bart — For all you've done on my behalf. Bob Prince."

Friend smiled when he saw that. "He always called me 'Bart,' because my middle name is Bartmess. He loved that. So I became Bart, which I preferred to 'Porky,' which he also called me on occasion."

Friend's nicknames never stuck with him, however, the way "Tiger" did with Don Hoak, or "Dog" with Bob Skinner, or "The Great One" with Roberto Clemente. Prince also called Groat "Chrome" as in "Chrome Dome," because of his thinning hairline, but that never stuck, either, to Groat's great satisfaction. One of Friend's business associates, Bruce McGough, often refers to him as "Friendly," and it's most appropriate. Friend, like Prince, lives up to his name.

Friend showed up in photographs with the late Frank Gustine, one of my all-time favorites. When I once asked Ralph Kiner what kind of guy Stan Musial was, he said, "Frankie Gustine with a better batting average."

Friend was smiling with Groat and Bill Hillgrove, with Perry Como, the pride of Canonsburg; Del Miller, the late Hall of Fame harness racing icon from The Meadowlands; Les Biederman, the baseball beat writer for *The Pittsburgh Press* from 1937 to 1969; U.S. Senator Hugh Scott; Pennsylvania Governor Bill Scranton. Friend was also pictured with his arm around billionaire Malcolm Forbes. Friend was always comfortable with people of power and money.

Above the mantel there was a wonderful black-and-white photograph of Branch Rickey, who had been the general manager of the Pirates when Friend came to the team and a man who had made his mark building the Brooklyn Dodgers of the Jackie Robinson, Pee Wee Reese, Roy Campanella and Duke Snider days.

Flanking the photograph of Branch Rickey, shown smoking a cigar, was a color photograph of Friend with former President Ronald

Reagan and a black-and-white profile of political legend Everett Dirksen. Friend moved with giants in his heyday.

That was also evident in a series of snapshots a pal, Melvin Rapport, had taken of Friend during a 1971 reunion of players from the 1960 World Series — a personal disaster for Friend following a super season because he just couldn't keep the Yankees off the bases, or some of their hit balls in the park — showing him with a cast of stars at Three Rivers Stadium. Friend is pictured alongside Willie Stargell (then a player with the Pirates), Whitey Ford, Harvey Haddix and broadcaster Tom Bender, Mickey Mantle and Dale Long, Wilver "Vinegar Bend" Mizell, Yogi Berra, Bill Mazeroski. What a lineup. Those were all color shots. There was also a black and white in that bunch, showing him with Roberto Clemente. Another with Danny Murtaugh. Those were the best of times.

But Friend isn't one of those guys who's always looking back, or living in the past, even though one of his co-workers at Babb, Inc., the insurance brokers, often introduces him to people by saying, "He used to be Bob Friend." He remained involved in the community, is still in demand at civic events and on everyone's list for celebrity golf outings to raise money for many good causes throughout the tri-state area.

This was Friday, March 27, 1998, an idyllic early-spring day with the sun out and temperatures in the 70s. Friend, always the professional, had come prepared for the interview. He had made some notes, as I suggested when I called him the week before to make an appointment, and he was ready to talk about Bob Prince.

I told him I had been with Betty Prince and Nellie King the previous Friday, and that we had lunch at the P.A.A. "That's Bob Prince's place," offered Friend. "His favorite place there was the steam room. He used to tell me, in the early days, 'Bart, you keep pitching this way, and I'm going to take you out to dinner at the P.A.A. If you stink, you can forget about that invitation. You'll know you've made it when you get to the P.A.A.'

"When he finally took me there, he said, 'Bart, this is when you know you've arrived, when you get to a place like this.'

"Or we'd be walking through Downtown Pittsburgh, and people would be calling out to him, 'Hey, Gunner, how's it going?' or heads would be turning as we passed, mostly because of him, believe me, and he'd say, 'You know, Bart, you can tell you're something when people turn around and look at you. You know you've arrived.'"

> *"This is for those men of magic who sat above the action to bring clearly and concisely the sounds and the smells and the sights of sports to young and old across the land . . . to any place on this earth where a small boy could sneak a radio into his history class on an October day and be reprimanded by a teacher and then requested to turn it up so all could share the drama of the game."*
> — Maury Allen,
> *Voices of Sport*

"I felt like I belonged."
— Bob Friend

Friend was in his huge, high-ceilinged office at Babb, Inc., an insurance brokerage that dates back to 1929. His office was on the second floor of a beautiful brownstone building on Ridge Avenue in the city's North Side, just across the street from Community College of Allegheny County's main buildings, right in the center of the campus, a few miles from the Pirates' home field at Three Rivers Stadium. Students were streaming by during my midday visit.

The street was once home to the city's millionaires when the area was known as Allegheny, and was a city separate from Pittsburgh. The home of Art Rooney Sr., now occupied by his oldest son, Dan Rooney, was not far away. The late owner of the Steelers always referred to the neighborhood as "Old Allegheny," or "The First Ward." A baseball park and a football stadium were scheduled to be built at the bottom of the hill to usher Pittsburgh into the 21st Century.

The three-story brownstone was a baronial mansion originally owned by William Penn Snyder (1862-1920), who was associated with Henry W. Oliver in developing the Lake Superior iron ore area, and he also owned the Shenango Furnace Company. William Penn Snyder III has served as chairman of the board of nearby Allegheny General Hospital and all its health, education and research facilities. There is a Snyder Pavilion on the first floor of that hospital.

The Babb building is a magnificent edifice with a rich heritage, and it's a great building for someone in the insurance business. Its fortress-like facade has a feeling of security about it. It's a point of pride to Babb's principal owner and president, Ron Livingston Sr.

The building is full of heavy brass doors, beautiful stained glass windows, wood paneling, grand staircases and state rooms, a bank-sized vault, a garage where horses and buggys were once stored, and a French ballroom in the basement with sparkling chandeliers that remains intact as a showcase as much as anything else. Its opulence resembles that of the *Titanic.* Livingston hosts his annual Christmas party for staff there.

"It's something when you consider that the Olivers, Carnegies, Fricks and Mellons once moved across that ballroom floor," said Russell Livingston, Ron's son and the executive vice president of the firm. His brother, Ron, has a similar role in the firm's Philadelphia office.

"It's so beautiful," said Ron Sr. "It's a historic landmark building, so we're encouraged to keep it just the way it is."

Robert Bartmess Friend — Bartmess was his mother's maiden name — was born on November 24, 1930 in Lafayette, Indiana, and he was 67 when I visited with him on March 27, 1998. His brown hair was thinner, but his blue eyes still had a twinkle. It's unlikely he was still six feet, 190 pounds — his playing weight in 1960 — but he looked just fine. He looked and sounded just like Bob Friend.

Pat and Bob Friend enjoy 1989 Jesters Ball, sponsored by one of Bob Prince's favorite organizations.

Bob Friend models one of the "Prince sayings" sport coats given to those who played in Prince's golf outing for ten or more years.

Bob Friend is flanked by Russell Livingston, left) and Ron Livingston Sr. on majestic stairway of Babb Inc. offices on North Side's historic Ridge Avenue on March 27, 1998.

He had cut back considerably on his schedule, but still served his established clientele. "I've been here since 1976," he said. "Ron Livingston and I have had a great relationship. He's been doing a good job of running this, and I've always enjoyed my association with the firm."

Livingston is a big sports enthusiast himself, and has season tickets to the Pirates, Steelers and Pitt football games. Livingston has a picture showing him with Steelers' owner Dan Rooney near his desk, and he remains a big fan of Bob Prince.

Friend remembers the first time he laid those blue eyes on Bob Prince. It was at the Parris Hill Ballpark in San Bernardino, California in 1950. Friend was a 20-year-old rookie.

"I was sitting in the clubhouse and this guy comes walking in with cowboy boots and dark glasses," recalled Friend. "I didn't know who he was. He hollers out for everyone to hear, 'I just got back from the Springs.' That turned out to be Palm Springs. He's shaking hands with people. I'm wondering, 'Who is this guy?' He looked like he was pretty important. I thought he owned the club.

"He went around the room, patting the veterans on the back, and talking up a storm with all the old guys. That's when I learned he was Bob Prince, the Pirates' broadcaster.

"When we trained in San Bernardino in 1950 and 1951, Bing Crosby, the movie actor, would come around, too, but he never stirred up any more of a commotion than Bob Prince. Rosey Rowswell was there, too.

"Prince was very close to Ralph Kiner, the star of the team who came from California, and knew a lot of people out there. He and Prince were real buddies.

"I had put in two years at Purdue. I was very confident. No doubt about that. I felt like I belonged. I knew that I was going to Waco, Texas for my first year, to learn what pro baseball was all about.

"When I first reported to the Pirates, Billy Meyer was my manager and he really liked me. I knew that. I was a real greenhorn and I needed some seasoning. I had a good sinking fastball and I had a good arm, but I didn't know how to pitch yet. My arm was strong; I could throw every day. I was not awed; I was relaxed in that environment.

"There were a lot of veterans on that team. We had Kiner and Wally Westlake, Mel Queen, Bob Chesnes, Gus Bell, Pete Castiglione, Jack Phillips, Ted Beard, John Berardino, Ed FitzGerald, Joe Garagiola, Johnny Hopp, Clyde McCullough, Danny Murtaugh, George Strickland."

When Friend came back to stay in 1951, a check of the Pirates' press guide reveals that the roster also included the likes of Cliff Chambers, Dick Cole, ElRoy Face, Paul LaPalme, Vernon Law, John Lindell, Dale Long, George Metkovich, Ron Necciai, Johnny and Eddie

O'Brien, Ed Pellagrini, Paul Pettit, Howie Pollett, Dino Restelli, Tom Saffell, Bob Skinner, Paul ("The pride of Wilkinsburg") Smith, Max Surkont, Frank Thomas, Bill Werle, and a little later Tony Bartirome, Bobby DelGreco, Clem Koshorek, Vic Janowicz, Curtis Roberts, Lee Walls.

The Pirates had a Heisman Trophy battery on their all-time roster in Janowicz, a catcher, and Paul Giel, a pitcher, though they were years apart. Janowicz had won honors as the best football player in college ball at Ohio State and Giel gained similar honors at Minnesota. Neither was a first-rate baseball player, though. Bartirome and DelGreco grew up in The Hill District, right where the Civic Arena was later built, and they got a lot of ink from Al Abrams in his column because he had come out of the same neighborhood. Both were good glovemen who couldn't hit consistently in the bigs.

These were all magical names for a kid in Hazelwood, however. These were the first Pirates I came to know and recognize from reading about them each morning in the *Post-Gazette*. I wondered whether we were related to the O'Brien twins from Seattle, second only to Groat in basketball ability on that ballclub. Imagine having pitchers named Paul Pettit, Howie Pollett and Paul LaPalme all on the same staff. Cliff Chambers and Vernon Law were good names, too. Restelli was a real sensation, hitting home runs out of all the parks his first time around the circuit, then coming down to earth in a hurry when opposing pitchers found his weaknesses. Goodbye, Dino Restelli, it was good to know you.

Bob Friend and Vernon Law were the mainstays of the pitching staff back in the late '50s and early '60s for the Pirates. Friend was presented the UPI's Comeback of the Year Award in 1960.

He made the All-Star Game that year. He remembers striking out Ted Williams on a curve ball with the bases loaded at Griffith Stadium in Washington, D.C. He was the team's winningest pitcher at the break (Vernon Law would end up topping the team with 20 wins) and struck out more batters (183) than any right-handed pitcher in Pirate history. He won 18 games and had a team-best 3.00 ERA. He led the Pirates' pitchers in victories seven times in one nine-year span (1958-1963).

Friend felt Henry Aaron of the Braves was the toughest batter he faced during his pitching career, yet Aaron has listed Friend as one of the toughest pitchers he encountered. Friend takes some solace in that. "He really ripped me a few times," said Friend. "Stan Musial was a tough out, too. He could sit back and wait."

The Pirates thought they had something special in Friend, right from the start. He struck out 21 of 22 batters in his hometown of Lafayette, Indiana, prompting the Pirates to pay him a $15,000 bonus in 1950.

In his first spring training game in San Bernardino, California in 1950, he pitched six scoreless innings to defeat Cleveland's Bob Feller, one of his boyhood heroes. He pitched a no-hitter at Waco his first year and by September he was promoted to Indianapolis.

In 1955, when Pittsburgh was last in the league, Bob was a 14-game winner and became the only pitcher ever to win the ERA title (2.84) with a cellar team.

In 1958, he was the winningest right-handed pitcher in the majors with a 22-14 record. The following year he tied Washington's Pedro Ramos for the most losses (19) in the majors.

Friend took fierce pride in his ability to be on the mound every fourth day. He threw every day and was the backbone of the Bucs' pitching staff for several seasons.

"Prince was a helluva loyal guy."

"Prince was pretty good with all of us," offered Friend. "He never knocked anybody, or us, on the air. He gave us great names in the community. When I got involved in politics, I realized what he had done for us. You never appreciate people like that when you're going through it as a ballplayer. You accept it as part of the package.

"He'd say, 'Hey, Bartmess, the Iron Man. There's a guy who can pitch every fourth day.' He built us up. He was able to do that because we stayed with one ballclub in those days. We weren't bouncing around like they do today.

"He created our images. He built up a very positive image of us over a long time. After I was through with baseball, and traveled throughout western Pennsylvania, I realized what he had done for us. People knew me, they knew so much about me, my family, my background, where I'd come from, that I was a Purdue graduate, stuff like that.

"Prince was a helluva loyal guy. That's one thing I liked about Bob. He had some ups and downs; now there's a guy with real resilience. He overcame a lot of adversity, businesses and investments gone sour and such.

"He had good character. He bounced back. You'd never know he was having problems. Lots of stuff he brought on himself, I realize, but he never lost faith in his ability to make a buck, or win over a fan. You hear about players' managers. Well, Bob was a ballplayers' broadcaster.

"I mean guys like Harry Caray got on people. He got on Stan Musial and Ken Boyer. One time, Caray came on the air and said, 'We've got Tracy Stallard warming up in the bullpen. We must be giving up.'"

Friend showed me a program he had on his desk that featured a drawing of Dr. J, Julius Erving, the basketball star, on the cover for an annual dinner put on by the Norfolk (Va.) Sports Club. "It's like the Dapper Dan here," said Friend. "Every top sports figure from Virginia is there.

"I went there a few times with Prince. This one time he was the emcee. Bones McKinney, the former basketball coach at Wake Forest, was on the program, and he was so good, a real pro. It scared Prince. 'Bart, what the hell am I doing here?' he said. 'This guy is so good.' He was worried that he couldn't top that. 'I'm concerned about this one,' he said. In the end, Prince was fantastic, as good as I'd ever seen him. And he was the best. But he was worried, no doubt about it."

The feeling Friend described sounded familiar to me. I feel that way every time I'm on a dais at any sports luncheon or banquet. Everybody else is so great, or so it seems anyhow. But it brings out the best in you. Prince was a competitor, no matter the game.

"That same weekend, Bob was supposed to present an award to an outstanding local athlete in front of the statue of General MacArthur. Prince was a stickler for honoring military heroes and veterans because his dad had been a career officer in the military. He sees this young fella coming to accept his award, and the kid is wearing sweats. The guy is a well known pro today, but I'm not going to identify him. I don't want to embarrass him now. We're all dressed in suits, and Prince is upset. He's saying to me, 'I can't go through with this. I'm not going to dishonor the General by giving this kid anything in the presence of his statue. It's not appropriate.' Prince didn't think this kid was showing any respect or dignity for the occasion or the memory of MacArthur. He was upset, no doubt about it. Prince could get up on his hind legs like that. He was a stickler for saluting the flag, or paying proper attention during the playing of the National Anthem, stuff like that.

"I got closer to Bob after I got out of the game. We were in some clubs together. We were both in the Royal Order of Jesters, and Bob loved that club. I remember Bob didn't get into the Duquesne Club. He said his sports coats were too loud for them. But we went places together. Bob did a lot of great things around here for the game of golf, amateur players, and raised a lot of money getting ballplayers to play at golf outings. As a player I wasn't particularly close to him; neither was Groat. Bob kept his distance from the players away from the locker room. For some reason, he was close to Virdon. But not the way he'd been with Kiner earlier in his career.

"In 1956, I was pitching for the National League in the All-Star Game at Griffith Stadium in Washington, D.C. I remember I was with my mother when Prince and Al Abrams came along. I introduced my mother to them. My mother, whose name was Anna, was all of four-foot-nine, and she was close to 80 at the time. We'd been squeezed in an elevator on a hot day in D.C. 'This is Bob Prince,' I said to my mother. 'I know who he is,' she came back sharply. 'I know I don't like what he says about my son.' And I said, 'What did he say?' And she came back, 'That you were knocked out and that you weren't very good.' Prince loved it. He thought she was the greatest person he ever met. She was four-nine and she stood up to him.

"Most of the writers were good to us, too. We didn't have any bad relationships. I remember the Rinky-Dinks got roughed up once. We lost 112 games in 1952. Davis J. Walsh of the *Sun-Telegraph* critiqued all the players, and he got on Branch Rickey. No doubt, a lot of us were rushed on the scene too soon. At the time, of course, we didn't think so. We thought we were ready.

"It must have been good stuff, because we kept a lot of the clippings in scrapbooks. Pat and I and my sisters all kept scrapbooks. I lost a lot, though, when we had a small fire in our basement at our place on South Highland.

"I've been to a lot of banquets. I haven't missed many Dapper Dan Dinners since 1950, maybe a half dozen at best. Bob Prince was a great emcee, the best ever. Lanny Frattare and Bill Hillgrove do a great job, too, but no one was in the same class as Prince in that respect. There was just something about him.

"Some people have that charisma, and Prince had it. When Prince walked into a room, everybody turned around.

"He liked to live good. In Chicago, our team would be staying at the Knickerbocker, and Bob would have a suite at the Drake Hotel. He wanted his space from the baseball people. Prince and Kiner were really tight, but very seldom did Prince hang out with ballplayers. He'd go around the clubhouse, but his time was his time. He didn't think it was real smart to stay in the same hotel as the players.

"For some reason, he liked Warren Spahn and Lew Burdette of the Braves. Every time they came to town, they went out together after the game. He got tight with Don Hoak. Whatever he did, he did it right. You don't stay in one town as long as he did unless you've got some special pizzaz.

"You learn a lot about people away from the ballpark. We were talking earlier about what a great competitor Dick Groat has been all his life. Donny Brown, the son of Joe L. Brown, went to Mercersburg Academy and he arranged for us to play the Mercersburg Academy basketball team.

"I was playing for the Pirates, and we had Nellie King and Ronnie Kline and Dick Groat, and I can't remember who else for this particular game. Groat was the only one in shape. The other team was in good shape and they had played together all year. Dick scored most of our points, like he was a sophomore at Duke or something. They beat us pretty good. After the game, their coach comes over to our locker room and he's shaking our hands and thanking us for coming up. Dick wouldn't shake his hand. When I asked him about it, he said, 'We didn't come up here to lose.' I think you'll find that attitude in most professional athletes. We compete all the way; that's the way we are. That's what you find out about people in sports; they'll compete in anything, golf, marbles or checkers. Golf is often a very humbling situation for guys who've played other sports, but it's a great game once you learn how to play it.

"Pat and I have been married since 1957. We have two children. Missie is 38, and she lives in Midland, Michigan. She has two children, Michael and Brynne. Bobby Jr. is 34, and he's been out playing golf on one circuit or another for ten years. He has two children, Charlie and Mary Elizabeth. She was just born this past October. Being a grandfather is a great experience. It gives you another dimension in life. Thank God they're healthy.

"Bobby's been a late bloomer. Tom Lehman was like that. He made a major breakthrough at 34. That would have been considered old back in the '60s and '70s, but players are staying with it year round now, and staying with it later because of the money involved. Bobby was on the PGA Tour in 1992 and 1993, and he had moderate success. Then he lost his confidence and struggled. He came on last year and now he's doing fine. He shot a fantastic 63 to get his (PGA Tour) card back. He did that at the qualifying round at Green Leaf West in Haines City, Florida. Everything is falling into place now. Maturity is kicking in. Who knows? He's a solid pro right now. He's had some good finishes. He's 70th on the prize money list. He's moving back here because he wants to raise his family here — he loves Pittsburgh — but he'll be in Florida for the winter, and he'll be traveling quite a bit.

"There's a lot of sacrifice involved. But this is what he wanted to do since he was seven or eight. There's been a lot of heartache. Pat and I go out and see him play two or three times a year."

(In mid-May, 1998, young Friend finished sixth in the Byron Nelson GTE Classic in Dallas, his best showing. He was the leader after the first day, one stroke back after the second day. He won $83,000. "I thought he was going to make the putt on the 18th," offered his father. "He'd have won another $13,000 . . . but you can't get greedy. This was a real confidence booster for him.")

As a youngster, Bobby wrestled and played football and baseball, but eventually he chose golf. He learned to play at Oakmont and took lessons from head professional Bob Ford. "He's a good competitor," said his father. "I could see it when he was growing up."

"He was always practicing longer than anybody else," related his mother, Pat. "Everybody else would quit, and he would be out there another two hours."

When Bobby went to Louisiana State to play golf, his college teammates came up with a nickname for his father: Pitch.

Before I left his office, Friend opened one of the drawers in his office to show me all the postcard size pictures he had of himself for signing sessions. "I told Bruce McGough I needed some for public appearances, and I ended up with over 5,000 of them. That should hold me for awhile."

> *"Back in the '60s in our neighborhood in Squirrel Hill, you could walk down the street and you wouldn't miss a word of the game. People were sitting on their porches listening to the ballgame on the radio."*
>
> — Herb Soltman
> Scott Twp., Pa.

"I'm putting my dream on hold."
—Billy Anderson,
Oakmont C.C.

I drove from Babb Inc. to Geyer Printing Company on Bigelow Boulevard for a meeting with Bruce McGough to discuss details for the printing of this book. In addition to doing all the books in my "Pittsburgh Proud" sports book series, Geyer Printing also does the Pirates' press guides and some other promotional material. They also do the annual yearbook for the Baseball Hall of Fame in Cooperstown, New York.

McGough, an avid golfer, took me to Oakmont Country Club for lunch. He was planning on playing in a member tournament the next day, a Saturday, and wanted to see how the course was shaping up. He would bump into Bob Friend and his son, Bob Jr., on Sunday when the Friends played nine holes there. Bob Sr. is a lifetime member at Oakmont.

Going to Oakmont is always a treat. I was first there in 1962 to see the upstart Jack Nicklaus knock off Arnold Palmer in a playoff for the U.S. Open title. I was an intern on city-side that summer at *The Pittsburgh Press*, and had volunteered to write photo captions for photographers so I could attend the Open. I had the best seat in the house, often crouching next to a photographer inside the ropes with a close-up view of all the activity.

Bob Drum, who was the golf writer at *The Press* at the time, introduced me to many of the nation's top sportswriters, including Dan Jenkins, one of the finest golf writers in the history of the game. I also met Oscar Fraley, a nationally-syndicated columnist who gained fame as the author of the book "The Untouchables" that inspired a TV series of the same name, which dealt with Elliot Ness and his federal crime fighters and Al Capone and all the mobsters in Chicago.

I had also been to Oakmont in the summer of 1997 for Frank Fuhrer's Family House Invitational. I thought about what a shame it was that UPMC had pulled out as the sponsor of the event, which brought so many great players to Pittsburgh each year.

There had been so many great golfers in the 1997 event. As I approached the Oakmont Country Club with McGough, I recalled how I had passed on an opportunity to take a close-up photograph of Justin Leonard because I didn't know that much about him, and he looked so young. He won the British Open soon after, and that same weekend I was there with McGough, I would be a TV viewer as the 25-year-old Leonard would charge from 5 strokes back on the final round once again to win the Players Championship at Sawgrass, in Ponte Vedra Beach, Florida. He won first place money of $720,000, just beating out Tom Lehman, who had also performed in Fuhrer's Family House Invitational.

Bob Friend, with sidekick, 8-year-old Bob Jr., signs autographs at Pirates' 1960 World Series Reunion promotion at Three Rivers Stadium in 1971.

Bob Friend Jr., a tour golf pro, offers tips to Matt Bahr, former place-kicker with Penn State and Steelers, during "The Second Mile" outing at St. Clair Country Club on May 26, 1998.

> *"I'm a dyed-in-the-wool Republican. When I go to the Duquesne Club, I wear a dark, pin-stripe suit. I'm not seeking attention then. I joined a lot of clubs over the years. I thought the best thing was to belong where the doers and shakers belong and somewhere along the line they'll help you."*
> — Bob Prince

The field at Oakmont had also included Ernie Els, Tom Lehman, Phil Mickelson, Craig Stadler, Bob Tway and Jim Furyk. It was fun to watch Arnold Palmer playing with Bill Cowher, the coach of the Steelers, in the pro-am. Hometown hero Danny Marino of the Miami Dolphins was there, too. As I was walking through the men's locker room with McGough nearly a year later, I could still see Palmer as he appeared there to talk to the press the previous summer.

Matt Bahr, the former Penn State and Pittsburgh Steelers place-kicker, was a guest having lunch in the men's grill following a golf game with club members. Because of his short stature, he was an unlikely looking former pro football player, but he'd kicked for 18 seasons in the National Football League and had always been a class act.

They still tell stories about Bob Prince at Oakmont, and his heritage lives on, it seems, in his namesake, Bob Jr. Ed Prebor was another familiar face to be found in the men's grill. He's the vice-president for corporate sales at Sargent Electric, and I've bumped into him at many golf events. He knew I was working on a book about Bob Prince. "His son still comes here to play once in a while," said Prebor. "He's a real character, too."

McGough and I sat nearby at the same table where I'd sat with Frank Fuhrer a few years earlier. We were joined by Billy Anderson, the top assistant pro on Bob Ford's instructional staff who also serves as the director of tournaments at Oakmont, and would soon be acknowledged as one of the area's hottest young golfers.

Anderson, 26, is reputed to be a fine young talent. He was planning to compete for a spot on the pro tour when he was promoted to his present job. "If it wasn't a place like Oakmont, I'd have gone," said the bright-eyed Anderson. "This is too good a job to leave right now. But it's still my dream to be on the pro tour. I'm putting my dream on hold." There are hundreds of thousands of talented young men and women who have the same dream. He's already a year older than Justin Leonard. It is so difficult to realize that dream. "I talked to Bobby Friend the other day," he said. "He's moving back here, and he'll be out here more often. He's doing what I dream of doing."

Bob Friend faces Stan Musial in June 16, 1956 game at Forbes Field when he shut out the Cardinals, 2-0. The year before, Friend became the first cellar-club pitcher in history to lead his league in earned-run average.

At the wall
October 13 still special

"We had 'em all the way!"
— Herb Soltman

A baseball fan forever, Herb Soltman still has his ticket stubs from the seventh game of the 1960 World Series. It cost him $7.70 for each of his first level reserved seats.

His seats were so close to the diamond at Forbes Field that he was among those who mobbed Bill Mazeroski at home plate after the Pirates' 24-year-old second baseman hit a home run over the wall in left-center field leading off the bottom of the ninth inning to beat the New York Yankees, 10-9.

Soltman is somewhere in the mob of a blurred photo he carries with him.

It was a home run for the ages. Right up there with Bobby Thomson's home run that won the National League playoff for the New York Giants over the Brooklyn Dodgers in 1951. It was a home run that was shown during the telecast of a 1997 American League playoff game between the Cleveland Indians and Baltimore Orioles. It's shown every year during the World Series.

Mazeroski's home run, still the single most significant moment in Pittsburgh sports history, came at 3:36 p.m. on Thursday, October 13 in 1960.

When Mazeroski was at the Pirates' Fantasy Camp a couple of years ago, one of the attendees hit a home run. Maz met him in the dugout afterward and said, "I can give you some tips on how you can live off one home run for the rest of your life."

Soltman was among the seventysome die-hard baseball fans who gathered on the same date, in 1997, at what remains of the ivy-covered, red brick outfield wall of Forbes Field at the southern end of the campus of the University of Pittsburgh. A resident of Virginia Manor Apartments in Scott Township, Soltman is a salesman for Babcor Packaging, in the paper bag business, working out of a building on South Canal Street on the city's North Side, and he bagged his work activity for the afternoon to go out to Oakland.

He said he had a grandmother who died at 105 years of age who had attended only one baseball game in her life and it was the 7th game of the 1960 World Series. And she lived at Webster Hall, just down Fifth Avenue from the ballpark.

He was showing his tickets, and a ledger in which he had logged a pitch-by-pitch account of that memorable seventh game in one of the wackiest World Series in history. The heavily-favored Yankees outscored the Pirates, 55-27, in seven games, winning by lopsided scores of 16-3, 10-0 and 12-0. "They set all the records, but we won the championship," cried Pirates' outfielder Gino Cimoli.

319

The fans made this annual pilgrimage to the wall from some far-away places: Illinois, New Jersey, Ohio and Tennessee.

It is an annual gathering of hard-core ball fans. There's no admission. No tickets, unless you bring some you have kept from the 1960 season. Some stop at the Original Hot Dog Shop — The "O" — before they settle in at the wall. Some bring lawn chairs. Some bring gloves and balls and play catch. Some bring memorabilia to share. Everybody brings stories. Many wear Pirate caps and T-shirts, and dress for the occasion.

Doug Snyder used to come in from Schaumburg, Illinois, and now he comes from Bedminster, New Jersey. He schedules his business trips so he can be in Pittsburgh on this date every year.

A teacher from Waynesburg, Herb Carpenter, brought his teenage daughter, Leah, with him, taking advantage of the Columbus Day holiday. They brought a baseball board game and played it while everyone listened to a taped broadcast of the entire seventh game.

Joe "Mr Baseball" Landolina of Squirrel Hill brought his son, Chris, a second grader, so he could appreciate his dad's passion for the game.

Renee and Enos Abel of Moon Township, who met each other at a post-game celebration of that World Series victory, returned once again. They had gotten engaged on October 13 a year after they met.

Sol Finkelstein was the first to make this an annual pilgrimage. Sol, a resident of Squirrel Hill, brings a tape of the seventh game of that 1960 World Series and plays it in sync with the actual game time. Finkelstein has tapes of Bob Prince broadcasting other Pirate games, and makes copies for fans. He's usually the first to show up and sits at the base of the flagpole that remains at the 457 foot mark in deepest centerfield.

The game started at 1:05 p.m. and ended at 3:36 p.m.

Those who gathered at the wall cheered at appropriate times, and spoke aloud of their concern about the Pirates' chances when the Yankees would come back to take the lead in the wild battle. That's when guys from Oakland ask if anybody who bet on the Yankees wants to double their bets. Everyone laughs.

They cheered like crazy when the Pirates scored five runs in the bottom of the eighth inning to regain the lead. Hal Smith hit a three-run shot over the wall in left-center in that inning, described by the broadcaster as "one of the most dramatic home runs of all time."

It was an idyllic day, with bright sunshine and temperatures reaching 80 degrees, ten degrees higher than it was back in 1960. Soltman said the Pirates of 1997 had recaptured his interest in the game. He had attended 19 games during the 1997 schedule. "These playoffs have been great, too," said Soltman. "We'll have a good World Series no matter who plays."

When Maz hit a 1-and-0 pitch by Ralph Terry out of the park, those who had gathered at the wall were jumping up and down and cheering like it had just happened. Soltman shouted out, "We had 'em all the way!"

At the wall...

Enos and Renee Abel of Moon Township return to The Wall on October 13 to mark their first meeting — at post-game celebration after 1960 World Series triumph.

Bob Friend met super fan Sol Finkelstein at The Wall on October 13, 1996.

Doug Snyder and Joe Landolina get best seats for replay of 1960 World Series broadcast.

Reflections on the firing
What happened behind the scenes

"We got hurt by that."

Lou Slais, former president,
Pittsburgh Brewing Co.:

"I was the president of the brewery from 1967 to 1979. I hesitate to say anything about this, but, yes, I represented the brewery at the meeting where Bob Prince was fired. We were the prime sponsor of Pirates baseball back then. I defended him any number of times. I liked Prince, personally. Prince was a friend of mine. We knew the Westinghouse people were unhappy with the way he was doing the games.

"We didn't want Prince removed as the broadcaster. We were afraid of the backlash. We didn't think it would go down well with the public, with our customers, and it sure as hell wasn't accepted well. It hurt the Pirates and it hurt our business. I was criticized by my board of directors for letting it happen.

"One thing I always kept secret was who fired Prince. But Ed Wallis (of Westinghouse) was the key man. What happened at the meeting, I hesitate to divulge. Tom Johnson might have saved Prince, as he had in the past, but he didn't this time. You say Joe L. Brown now says it was a flat-out mistake, and that he wishes it wouldn't have happened. Well, I agree with that. I just don't want to talk about it anymore. What good would it do? I don't want to stir up anything. I'm sorry, but that's all I'm going to say."

*   *   *

Dan McCann, Assistant to President,
Pittsburgh Brewing Co.:

"I've been with the brewing company for 37 years this June, and I never had more fun than when Bob Prince worked for us, in a community relations role. We hired him to work for us about a month after he was fired as the Pirates' broadcaster. Our president at the time, Lou Slais, liked Prince and wasn't too pleased with what happened to him. Lou was at the meeting with Westinghouse officials and Joe L. Brown of the Pirates when Prince was let go. Lou knew there would be negative repercussions aimed at the Pirates and the brewery, as well as KDKA, because Prince was popular with the fans. He didn't push the idea, but he went along with the majority. He knew there'd be a backlash. And he was right. We got hurt by that.

Bob Prince takes a smoke break.

At age 60, two years after he was fired by the Pirates, Bob Prince became the play-by-play announcer for ABC's Monday Night Baseball, teamed with Warner Wolf and Bob Uecker. It didn't work out. "You watched the playoffs," explained Prince in talking about his release. "They never shut up. My cup of tea is to say, 'Ball one' and let you see it. If a guy swings and misses, I don't have to tell you he swings and misses. You can see that. I had too many people talking in my ear, 'Do this, do that.' I kind of feel I know the game after 30 years in it."

"I used to go with Bob to weekly visits to clubs in communities on the outskirts of Allegheny County. They were called the 'Iron City Beer Steeler Huddle,' and we had them in places like Butler, Johnstown, Altoona and Greensburg. We'd go out on Tuesday nights each week. We'd take the Steelers' highlight film, and one week we'd have Rocky Bleier and the next week it would be Jack Ham. Bob Prince was the emcee. Bob was just as popular with the public as Bleier and Ham. People just liked him. He treated people good. He was funny as hell. He liked to drink a little bit, he was a real Pittsburgh guy. He worked for us right up until the end, with the Curbstone Coaches luncheons and those Huddle sessions with a different cast of Steelers. He was always a big hit."

*　*　*

Tom Johnson, attorney and minority partner, Pittsburgh Pirates:

Bob Prince was often criticized for hob-nobbing with the rich guys and power brokers of the city, but he felt it was an effective way for him to get things accomplished.

"No one knew this for a long time, but I got the Pirate job through my Harvard connection," he said. "I graduated from (the University of) Oklahoma in business administration in 1938 and, let's face it, I was a ne'er-do-well. I didn't want to go to work.

"I had three uncles and a couple of cousins and an older brother who graduated from Harvard Law School. Why shouldn't I go? I did OK, but I gave it up after a year. I never intended to be a lawyer. One of my classmates was Tom (Thomas P.) Johnson.

"Uh huh, you get it. Tom Johnson became one of the Pirate owners in August 1946. He got the play-by-play job for me in 1947, and I started broadcasting with the 1948 season. Connections and associations are important."

Barney Dreyfuss, the original owner of the Pirates, died in 1932, and the ballclub was taken over by Bill Benswanger. The club was sold in 1946 to a syndicate that included Frank E. McKinney, an Indianapolis banker, and John W. Galbreath, Ohio financier and sportsman; movie star and singer Bing Crosby and Pittsburgh attorney Tom Johnson.

Only Johnson survives. He still holds a minority interest in the team, and is a frequent visitor to Three Rivers Stadium to see the Steelers and Pirates play. He had a setback in January of 1998 with the death of Jane, his wife of nearly 64 years.

"I got Bob out of hot water a number of times with Westinghouse management, just as I got a number of well-known Pirates out of one kind of trouble or another through the years," Johnson said. "Bob was a great guy, but he could often be his own worst enemy. He didn't always use good judgment, and sometimes the drinking clouded his thinking.

"He pulled one once around Easter time when he offended everyone who was listening to a broadcast. He said, 'There's never been a perfect man except Jesus, and he was Jewish.' I called up Jim Woods on a special telephone to the broadcast booth, and I screamed, 'Tell that sonofabitch to get off that air before he kills us.' That was the sort of stuff he'd do. He didn't mean any harm, but how would you like to hear that? He finally got Joe L. Brown angry, and this time I was not going to tell Joe what to do, though I did appeal to him not to dismiss Prince. This time I couldn't save him. Joe admitted to me later, after all hell had broken loose, that he should have listened to me."

Pirates minority owner Tom Johnson, a former classmate of Bob Prince at Harvard Law School, visits The Wall that remains of Forbes Field on October 13, 1996.

"If you don't play to win, why keep score?"
— Vernon Law,
Pirates pitcher

Joe L. Brown
The General Manager

"How could you not like Bob Prince?"

It was like listening to the "Joe L. Brown Show" on KDKA Radio prior to one of the Pirates' games back in the '70s. The mellow voice was unmistakable, coming from his home in Monarch Beach, California via the telephone. This was Saturday, May 2, 1998, and it was a weekend when I would also talk over the telephone with Paul Long and in the visitors' TV booth at Three Rivers Stadium with Vin Scully. All of their voices were theirs and theirs alone. God had been good to all of them when it came to handing out vocal chords.

"Bob Prince was a gregarious, fun-loving, talented man," began Brown. "My interaction with him was always good. We were friends. How could you not like Bob Prince?"

Brown had been the general manager of the Pittsburgh Pirates during some of their best days, as well as some of their worst days.

The Pirates enjoyed some tremendous highs under his leadership — as Brown built three championship teams — but Brown is also remembered as one of the bad guys in the Bob Prince Story. After warning Prince over a long period of time that he had to make some changes in his baseball broadcasts, Brown was among the powers-that-be who handed Prince his head after the 1975 season.

"I wish it hadn't happened, of course," said Brown. "No question. It was a flat-out mistake."

Talking about Bob Prince wasn't a fun way for Joe L. Brown to be spending a day, but he obliged. Brown has always been a stand-up guy.

He was the Pirates general manager for 21 seasons, from 1956 to 1976, and served as a special assignment scout up until 1992. He was an interim GM in 1985 when Prince came back, all too briefly, to the Bucs' broadcast booth.

Brown says the decision to bring Prince back was made before he was put in charge. "I would have approved the decision," he said.

Mostly, his teams were pretty good. At times under his direction, the Pirates were a powerhouse. He was originally hired on October 25, 1955 to replace the venerable Branch Rickey as the front office boss of the Bucs.

He had worked briefly with Rickey during Rickey's stay in Pittsburgh. Brown was working with the farm team in New Orleans when he got the call to come to Pittsburgh. It was in New Orleans that Brown became enamored with Danny Murtaugh, and they would, on several occasions, work magic together.

Some thought that one of Brown's faults was that he thought Murtaugh was the only man who could manage the Pirates properly, and put him in charge of the club on four different occasions.

Joe E. Brown, the Hollywood comedian/actor and father of Pirates GM Joe L. Brown, entertains some of the most popular Pirates of the late '50s, from left to right, Bob Friend, Dale Long and Frank Thomas.

Bob Prince and Joe L. Brown present plaque to Bill Mazeroski at his retirement ceremonies in October, 1972 ceremonies at Three Rivers Stadium. Maz performed for 17 seasons as a classy second baseman for the Bucs.

The best biographical sketch on Brown is offered by Bob Smizik, the *Post-Gazette* sports columnist who worked the baseball beat when Brown was in charge of the ballclub, and has always held him in high regard.

"Having failed with the most renowned men in the baseball business, the Pirates went after one of the most obscure, a bright, talented, energetic general manager," Smizik wrote in his book, *The Pittsburgh Pirates — An Illustrated History.*

"He had a famous father and almost shared the same name. The father was actor and comedian Joe E. Brown. His son was Joe L. Brown, but he was better known in Hollywood than in Pittsburgh.

"Yet, this obscure baseball man with the famous father was to have an impact on Pirates baseball that would last for more than 30 years. He was to pick the franchise up with his own special brand of stern but caring administration and turn the Pirates into a contender throughout most of the 1960s and all of the 1970s. And when the franchise was in disarray again — this time in the 1980s — he was called out of retirement to save baseball in Pittsburgh."

Brown said he first dealt with Prince on a professional basis when Brown was doing some promotional work for the movie "The Babe Ruth Story" and came from Hollywood to Pittsburgh during a national p.r. tour. Actor William Bendix played the part of Babe Ruth in that less-than-remarkable movie that still pops up on TV in the early morning hours. "It was terrible," said Brown.

"Bob was very kind to me," said Brown. "He couldn't have been more accommodating. He helped me promote the movie in Pittsburgh."

Brown said he also spoke to Prince when the Pirates were training in San Bernardino, California, and later when Brown was working with Pirate teams in Waco and New Orleans.

I asked Brown how his father was associated with the Pirates or with Pittsburgh teams, in general. I had seen Joe E. Brown in photographs, along with actor Pat O'Brien, with Pitt's legendary football coach Jock Sutherland back in the late '30s. His father appeared with O'Brien and Sutherland in one of my early books, *Hail to Pitt: A Sports History of the University of Pittsburgh.*

"My dad was never really associated with the Pirates, though he was a good friend of Bing Crosby, who had a minority interest in the ballclub," said Brown. "My dad was a good friend of Jock Sutherland.

"Regis Toomey, another actor, was a dear friend, too. He had been an 880-yard runner on the Pitt track team. Dick Powell, the actor, was a good friend of my dad. He worked with my dad. My dad came here to appear at the Sheraden Theatre. Powell, who was from Pittsburgh, was an emcee there for stage shows. My dad was a good friend of John L. Harris, whose father opened the first movie theatre in the country right here in Pittsburgh. Harris owned the hockey team and started his ice show here. So my dad had a lot of ties with this town."

I asked Brown what it was like to be the son of a famous show-biz star. I mentioned that both of Bob Prince's children, Nancy and Bob Jr., had talked about the difficulties they encountered as children because their father was a famous and controversial celebrity. They didn't like having a father in the public spotlight, or sharing him with his fans.

"I loved it," said Brown. "I didn't feel I was any different from anybody else. People liked my dad. I always admired my dad greatly. I loved him. If you try to get into competition with your dad, or your mother, if they happen to be established stars, you're asking for trouble.

"As long as I lived, I couldn't have been what my father was. I deliberately went away from his line of work, though I didn't realize I was doing it at the time. I enjoyed the stage. I was involved in plays all the time when I was in school. But I'd rather do what I ended up doing."

With the possible exception of being a party to firing Bob Prince, that is. I had read and been told that Brown had instructed Prince to give up broadcasting the Steelers and Penn State football to concentrate on baseball if he truly wanted to be the "voice of the Pirates." Bob's wife, Betty Prince, related that as well.

Brown said that wasn't so. "I never mentioned it to him," he said. "I had no problem with his other on-the-air activity. He still represented the Pirates, whatever he did."

I had also read, and heard, that Bob was not blameless when it came to his dismissal by officials from the Pirates, KDKA and the prime sponsor at the time, the Pittsburgh Brewing Company. He had been warned, in a series of meetings with high-level officials over an extended period of time, to clean up his act and concentrate more on the baseball action on the field rather than telling long-winded tales of yore.

"That was one of the causes," said Brown. "It doesn't do much good to get into all the reasons at this time. What good will it do now? I wish it hadn't happened. I think it was inevitable. Bob could have corrected the problems that were cited. He had aggravated the management of KDKA. They were very strongly upset with him.

"He had been warned several times that unless he made some changes in the way he handled the baseball broadcasts that changes would be made.

"KDKA was the catalyst for his dismissal. I agreed with their decision. The Pittsburgh Brewing Company was leery of it. They were afraid of a public backlash. They got it. And we got it. We felt we had to do it at the time.

"I think it's important to point out something else. I think Lanny Frattare has done a marvelous job for the Pirates. He's different from Bob, but good in his own right."

Brown had told Nellie King that his contract was not being renewed before they pulled the plug on Prince. Yet Milo Hamilton, who replaced Prince, had told me that King could have kept his job if he hadn't berated everybody concerned over the firing of Bob Prince. In another conversation, King said that wasn't so.

"If Bob had not been fired, Nellie would not have been fired," said Brown. "KDKA and the Pittsburgh Brewing Company felt if we were going to make a change we should make a complete change. It just happened that I told King about the change before I told Prince.

"We had a meeting with Bob at the end of the previous season (1974). Ed Wallis of KDKA discussed the changes he wanted Bob to make. He wanted fewer long anecdotes and more concentration on play-by-play. Bob said he would. But, of course, he had told us before he would go along with our wishes, and gone back on his word. Time and again, Bob would go right back to doing it the way he had always been doing it, not the way we wanted him to do it.

"When you are managing a ballclub, or in charge of a business, you have to do what's right, whether people like it or not. You can't worry what the news media is going to say or how the public is going to react. If you let your business be run by fans and don't do what's right, then you're a coward."

I have a little problem with Brown's business theories, as advanced above. Certainly you must consider the public and news media reaction if they are your customers and, respectively, the carriers of the news about your business operation. You can be brave, but stupid, if you ignore the wants of your customers. KDKA and the Pirates both suffered from their decision to fire Prince, and the Pittsburgh Brewing Company experienced a serious drop-off in beer sales. They would later hire Prince as a public relations representative for the brewery to offset that early backlash. Prince represented the brewery in many ways, appearing on behalf of Iron City at many public gatherings.

"If you have good beliefs," Brown said, "that should be the way you live your life."

When Bob Prince died in 1985, Brown was asked to comment on the man. Many felt and expressed the thought that Brown's words in eulogy sounded hollow because he had been involved in the decision to can Prince ten years earlier. Many, including Betty Prince, felt that Bob Prince had actually died in 1975 when he lost his job as "voice of the Pirates."

"There is no doubt about it now, ten years later, it was a colossal mistake to fire Bob Prince," Brown said upon learning of Prince's death. "I was a part of it. It was a flat-out mistake."

Brown said his sentiments were heartfelt and sincere. "If I didn't feel it, I wouldn't have said it," related Brown. "I sincerely liked Bob. He was a friend, a good man. You couldn't be around Bob and not have fun."

If getting rid of Bob Prince was a bad move by Brown, trading away hometown favorite Dick Groat was another. On November 19, 1962, he traded Groat and pitcher Diomedes Olivo to the St. Louis

Cardinals for pitcher Don Cardwell and infielder Julio Gotay. Groat took the trade hard. "It was the biggest hurt I ever experienced," said Groat. "It was my hometown. I never wanted to play anywhere else."

Groat has said that going to St. Louis turned out to be a great break for him, but he still never forgave Brown for unloading him. Groat also recalled Brown cutting his salary once when he felt it was unwarranted, and that Brown never considered him when there were openings for a manager.

"We haven't been hit on by anybody but Dick Groat," said Brown. "There was no outpouring of critical letters when we made that trade. Dick Groat thought I got rid of him because he was through. That wasn't so.

"I thought that between (Dick) Schofield and (Gene) Alley we could replace Dick Groat. Alley was a year or two away from being a full-time shortstop. He and Maz were a great double play combination. Gene Mauch, the manager of the Phillies whom I always regarded as an astute judge of talent, told me that Alley was the best shortstop he ever saw over a two-year period. Cardwell didn't come through for us. It was not a good deal. But I never made it because I thought Dick Groat was through. He took that personally.

"I had a great regard for Dick Groat. I thought we had a great relationship until I traded him. I think he felt he'd always stay in Pittsburgh. But those things don't happen that much.

"Dick hasn't gotten over it to this day. It didn't work out, that's all. I dealt a lot of other fellows who were good players, and some who had Pittsburgh ties. I traded Bob Purkey. He was a good friend. He had a good career in Cincinnati. I traded Frank Thomas.

"We traded guys who had been good for us. Dale Long. Dick Stuart. Bob Skinner. Jerry Lynch. Don Hoak. Some of them worked out in our favor, some of them did not. But I remained friends with most of them. That's part of the game.

"So was making the change with Bob Prince. I'm not proud of it, the way things turned out. At the time, we felt we had no other recourse. I think he was a great announcer.

"When he paid attention to the game, as he usually did, he lent so much drama to the game. He was so colorful. He could explain complicated plays, and tell you where three different players were positioned, all in the same sentence.

"He brought fun to the listeners. He clearly loved baseball. He did all sports, but baseball was the game he did best. He was a great announcer. I had many wonderful moments with him."

Brown said retirement suits him well. His first wife, Din, died nine years earlier. "I have a lovely new wife; her name is Paulita," said Brown. "We went to high school together. I'm in love again. I'll be 80 in three months (August, 1998), and I'm in good health.

"Monarch Beach is a beautiful community, just south of Laguna Beach. We're about a quarter-mile from the Pacific Ocean. We can look down there and see the ocean."

The view is great. Even so, Brown can still see Pittsburgh from his perch as well. He remains in touch with people in the Pirates front office.

"I can always see Pittsburgh," he said. "I've just about spent as much time here as I did in Pittsburgh. I was there a total of 23 years. I have a great love for the city and its people.

"The Pirates are just as important to me as when I was the general manager. They are kind enough to keep me informed of what's going on there. I go to spring training every year for a week and spend it in Pirate City. I see Kevin McClatchy every time he comes to the West Coast. He truly cares about Pittsburgh and the Pirates.

"I think Cam Bonifay has done a fantastic job under difficult circumstances. I've seen their young prospects and I think good things are ahead. It could be wonderful. They need the new ballpark. I don't know how they can continue to exist without one."

Note conservative attire on Bob Prince as he participates in military ceremony when Roberto Clemente joined the U.S. Marine Corps in 1958. Marine officers, left to right, are Frank A. Gunner Jr., Luther A. Reedy and Keith Lynn.

> *"Baseball survives because guys like Clemente still play it."*
> — Jimmy Cannon,
> *N.Y. Journal-American*

Audrey Woods
The Possum's wife

"They were like brothers."

Audrey Woods was on the telephone from her home in Oviedo, Florida, not far from Orlando, talking about Bob Prince and her late husband, Jim "Possum" Woods.

Prince and Woods formed one of the most fun-loving, yet respected baseball broadcast partnerships for 12 years (1958-1969). Woods also worked as a broadcaster for the New York Yankees, the Oakland A's and the Boston Red Sox. Woods died, at age 71, on February 20, 1988.

He gained the nickname "Possum" from pitcher Whitey Ford when he was a member of the Yankees' broadcasting team because Ford felt Woods resembled a possum with his close-cropped silver-gray hair.

Woods worked for the Yankees prior to coming to Pittsburgh to do the Pirates' games. In his third year in Pittsburgh, the Pirates were playing those same Yankees in the World Series that won't soon be forgotten in Pittsburgh.

I called Audrey Woods in early May, 1998, at the suggestion of Sally O'Leary, who said she had spoken to her the week before. No one kept in touch with people who had been associated with the Pirates through the years as much as O'Leary, who had worked for the ballteam over 30 years in its public relations office and coordinated an alumni newsletter. Audrey had been living in Florida for 22 years.

At first, Audrey felt she didn't have much to offer because surely all the Bob Prince stories had been told by others. As she talked, however, she had much to offer about the special relationship her husband and Prince had enjoyed. She told me she had recently spoken on the telephone to one of her relatives for nine hours, but I assured her that an hour with me would suffice.

"We had some exciting years in Pittsburgh," she said. "Jim was there for 12 years, and I was there for eight of those 12 years. They were pretty exciting times.

"Jim was very fond of Bob. They were like brothers. I think it was a sad time for both of them when Jim left to go to St. Louis. I don't know how Bob felt about that. Bob was one terrific guy, the funniest guy I ever met. I just laughed and laughed when I was around him. There were no two like them.

"Jim went to the St. Louis Cardinals for two years (1970-71), and that was a big mistake. Jim wasn't happy there. He was trying to replace Harry Caray. People didn't think Jim was enough of a character, or that he wasn't like Harry Caray. But we know why

Harry was fired; you know, too. Jim worked with Jack Buck for two years, but they just didn't click the way Bob and Jim had clicked.

"From there, Jim went to the Oakland A's. Charlie Finley owned the A's, and he was a colorful character himself. They won the World Series twice (1972-1973) while we were there, and we had so many exciting times from that.

"We spent the last five years with the Boston Red Sox. I loved Boston. It was a great season in 1975 when they went to the World Series. The only thing bad was that Jim didn't get to work the World Series. I had my bags packed, ready to go, when Jim told me we wouldn't be going. 'You've got to be kidding,' I said. That hurt. That spoiled things there. We had gone to the playoffs together. We won the playoffs in Oakland, and spent time with old friends there. We ended up losing the World Series in seven games to Cincinnati.

"I just wish Jim were here to talk about Bob. I used to try and get Jim to write a book about his experiences. I got him a tape recorder and tried to get him to do it, but he never did.

"There was such a looseness, and a camaraderie about their relationship. They were always funny together. I don't think I ever laughed as much as I did during those years in Pittsburgh. I loved Betty, too. We didn't socialize a lot together, but we always went to their house on New Year's Day with some other people and we'd eat and watch the college football games together.

"One time when Jim was in Pittsburgh, Bob talked Jim into taking me along on a West Coast road trip. Bob was taking Betty on a three-city trip to San Diego, Los Angeles and San Francisco, and Bob wanted me to go to keep Betty company.

"It was an education for me. I recognized how hard those guys worked. I was exhausted after that trip. I didn't go along that much. Charles O. Finley once had a party at his big ranch near Chicago, and all the wives were there on a command performance.

"Bob was such a great guy. I met a lot of people in baseball, but nobody like him. It was so different in St. Louis. Bob and Jim always got along so well. It was not the same with Jack Buck. They didn't accept Jim in St. Louis. Everywhere else was so great."

Then Audrey Woods reminded me of Betty Prince the way she talked about her husband, with such great glee.

"There was nobody on this earth like Jim Woods," Audrey went on. "Women loved him. All the ballplayers loved him. The fans loved him. Jim always called Bob 'The Gunner.' I've heard different stories about why he called him that."

I told her the ones I had heard. One was because Bob had such a rapid-fire delivery. The other was because some guy got mad at a night club when he saw Bob talking to his wife. The guy had a gun on him, but Bob managed to talk his way out of the confrontation. After that, Woods called him "The Gunner."

"I've heard all those stories," said Audrey, "but Jim never told me why he called him that."

Being a peacemaker was not a new role for Woods. During the five years he worked with the Yankees, he sat in the broadcast booth between Mel Allen and Red Barber. "He said they never got along," said Audrey, "and that's why he sat between them. He was there when they had Mickey Mantle, Billy Martin and Casey Stengel. And Jim said it was a lot of fun.

"I first met Jim in 1961. I was a secretary in the radio-TV station offices that carried the Milwaukee Braves games. I went to Chicago once to see Jim. I'd been going with him a while. And I was sitting in the broadcast booth behind Bob. Bob leaned back and put his elbow on my knee, and said, 'How do you think you're gonna like living in Pittsburgh?' I just smiled. I thought he was needling me. 'Yeah,' he went on, 'you're coming to Pittsburgh.' They were both so much fun, the two of them together. You could just listen to them on the air, and you knew they got along well.

"I've got a tape now, of the two of them re-creating the 1960 World Series. They used to talk to each other a lot on the phone after they parted ways in Pittsburgh. I met Jim in the first place because he was a good friend of my boss at WTMJ, a radio/TV station. They had worked together earlier in Iowa. I heard my boss talk about Jim Woods a lot. Jim called this one day, and I asked him if he wanted to talk to my boss, whose name was Blaine Walsh. He was the Braves' play-by-play man. Jim said, 'No, I want to talk to you.'

"I loved my job, and I was never going to leave Milwaukee. We went out that first night, and I had a good time. Blaine Walsh came into the office the next day and said, 'I understand that you had a date with Jim Woods.' I said, 'Yeah, I had a lot of laughs. He's a funny man.' And my boss said, 'You know what he told me? He said he's going to marry you.' And I said, 'What? Where'd you get that?' And we got married in 1962.

"It was a most exciting life. It's like a dream now. Now my life is rather quiet. And I miss Jim. Yes, I wish you could talk to him."

Pittsburgh Pirates

Jim Woods, left, and Don Hoak have a laugh with Bob Prince in Forbes Field dugout in summer of 1962. They worked together in Pittsburgh for 12 years.

Vin Scully
Dean of baseball broadcasters

"Bob Prince was the most colorful
baseball announcer in the country."

Vin Scully was sitting with his back to me as I slipped inside the visitors' television booth at Three Rivers Stadium on Sunday, May 3, 1998. A plate enscribed with KTLA-TV was on display in an insert frame at the doorway.

The Los Angeles Dodgers had just defeated the Pittsburgh Pirates, 10-5, winning three of four in a weekend series, and Scully was wrapping up the game telecast from his seat high above home plate. A fine rain started falling on the field in the late going, just as it had all morning prior to the start of the contest.

Scully had a raincoat on a hook at the back of the TV booth. He knew how to dress for every occasion. He'd been around. A press box wag had told me earlier to tell Scully that he brought rain to Pittsburgh every time he was in town.

When Scully spun in his chair to face some bright lights that had just been turned on for a post-game show, I was struck by how good he looked, especially under harsh lights. An assistant, probably his producer, pushed a strand of Scully's red hair into place. Scully patted his hair on both sides of his head, did a voice check, and wet his lips as he readied himself for a five-minute close-up segment.

How many times had he done this before? Yet he seemed to be concerned about his appearance and his presentation the way he primped and prepped himself. His pride was evident. He motioned to me that it was okay to come forward into the broadcast booth.

When I mentioned to Scully that I was working on a book about Bob Prince, he smiled, showing a full set of bright white teeth, and announced, "The Gunner." The way he said it was just right. He enunciated all three syllables just so. "The Gunner." He sounded just like Vin Scully, one of the most respected baseball broadcasters in the history of the game.

I recalled hearing that same rich voice one night as I drove through dark mountain roads in West Virginia. He was doing the playoffs with Johnny Bench, and he was so good at it, simply the best in the business at describing a baseball game, offering only significant stats, sparingly, and telling the right stories at the right times. Bench, a Hall of Fame catcher, missed most of the soft pitches Scully delivered his way. Tim McCarver would be better at Scully's side, I thought at the time, better able to respond to Scully's suggestive cues.

Scully smiled and posed for me when I asked him if I could take some pictures of him. He couldn't have been more gracious or more accommodating.

Jim O'Brien

Vin Scully gets ready for post-game show May 3, 1998 for finale of four-game series at Three Rivers Stadium.

"A broadcaster has to be a shill. He has to sell tickets, be factual and entertaining. There may be things you don't like about a club, but you better sell the product. A broadcaster can help attendance by making the game interesting enough that listeners will come out to the ballpark."

— Bob Prince

Scully was 70 years of age, though he'd never tell you that, and in his 49th consecutive season as the "voice of the Dodgers" — the longest run of any major league broadcaster with one team. He was the same age as Nellie King, whom Lanny Frattare, the "voice of the Pirates," had mentioned in his broadcast that same afternoon, yet King hadn't been a color analyst for Bucs' baseball since 1975. Scully was still going strong.

Scully was resplendent in a Dodger blue blazer, a blue and gold paisley tie knotted perfectly and in place against a well-pressed light-blue dress shirt. He wore gold cuff links. There was a three-pointed gold pocket handkerchief sticking out just so. When I touched the pocket handkerchief and said that Prince always recommended that you wear such a hankie that complemented your tie, Scully smiled and said, "I've always had these. I've always dressed like this."

The same was true of Ross Porter and Rick Monday, the other announcers who worked with Scully. It was the same with Fred Claire, the executive vice-president of the Dodgers, who had gone from being a sportswriter covering the club to becoming its publicist, then its general manager. Hard to believe a guy could go from covering a team for a newspaper to running the team as a front-office executive. (Claire would be canned in June, giving way to Tommy Lasorda, soon after Rupert Murdoch purchased the ballclub.)

The Dodgers dressed the part of champions. In that respect, they reminded me of the Dallas Cowboys. Dress standards may have slipped considerably in the press box in the past 25 years, but not so with Scully & Co. from the Dodgers.

What struck me was how fresh Scully appeared after a two-and-half hour stint behind the mike. He did the first three innings on TV, the second three on the radio, going downstairs to the next level to do that, then hustling back up the stairs to complete the final three innings and then the post-game show for TV. He looked so neat, so dapper, so calm and cool. And his voice sounded as strong as ever, which was not the case when I last heard Jack Buck, one of his famous contemporaries with the St. Louis Cardinals.

"This is going to be a brief post-game show," Scully told his audience. His opening spiel was smooth, absolutely flawless. He's been heralded as a master of the English language. It was intriguing, just listening to him close-up. It was a pleasure to shake Scully's hand.

He gave the highlights of the contest, accounted for some of the scoring. "The Dodgers won three of four games . . . at the expense of the hapless Pirates," said Scully, "and they should have won all four. They had a 4-1 lead Friday night . . . and lost it in the late innings, 5-4." I wondered how Pittsburgh's faithful fans would have felt if they heard Scully brand their ballclub as "the hapless Pirates." It wasn't likely to turn up as a slogan in any of the home club's promotional efforts.

Scully posed for pictures, autographed the game scorecard for the young man who had been keeping stats for him, spoke and shook hands with everyone who approached him, and seemed quite happy about being Vin Scully.

He warmed quickly to the request to reflect on Robert F. Prince.

"Bob Prince was a great friend of mine," said Scully. "He was so much fun to be around. He was a left-handed golfer, you know, and I'm left-handed. So he'd take me out to the St. Clair Country Club, and we'd go around together. I'd play out of his bag. When he came to LA, he played out of my bag.

"I watched the evolution of Bob Prince in this business. He broke in with Rosey Rowswell. When I first saw Bob Prince he was prim and proper. He wore dark suits, white dress shirts and dark thin ties. He could have been mistaken for an undertaker.

"The original Bob Prince was so different from 'The Gunner.' He started wearing the craziest color combinations, those wild plaid sportscoats. He became such a colorful character. And, of course, he did that dive out of his room into the swimming pool at the Chase Hotel in St. Louis. Everybody remembers that.

"Since the first day I started back in 1950, he was good to me. He had started with the Pirates two years before I was hired by the Dodgers back when they were in Brooklyn. He was a wonderful guy. I used to love him.

"I scolded him a few times, too," Scully continued. "He took a few liberties with drinking before ballgames, and I thought he could get himself into trouble that way.

"When he was let go here and became the first announcer for Monday Night Baseball on ABC, I was rooting for him to succeed. I wanted the nation to discover what a great announcer Bob Prince was.

"But when I heard him on TV, he wasn't the same Bob Prince. He wasn't anything like the Bob Prince of Pittsburgh. I called him and asked him, 'What are you doing? That's not Bob Prince I'm hearing.' And he said, 'They've really intimidated me. Someone's always talking in my ear, telling me to do this and that, telling me not to do this or that. They're not letting me be me.'

"And I said, 'Bob, if you're going to lose your job, or get fired again, better you should get fired for being Bob Prince.' But it didn't work out. And that was a shame. He wasn't the same guy I knew. They stripped him of his personality, of all the things that made them special. Here they had the best, most colorful baseball announcer in the country, and they took the life out of him."

Of course, the same could be said, and leveled with a much more indignant charge, against KDKA for canning him in the first place. They had done the same thing to him — taking the life out of him — when they fired Prince after the 1975 season, after he had been the "voice of the Pirates" for most of his 28-year stint in their broadcast booth.

At the time of his release, Prince was the dean of the industry, as far as serving with one team longer than any other broadcaster in baseball. Scully, of course, has since surpassed him, and then some, in that regard.

Scully, coincidentally enough, was at Three Rivers Stadium when Prince was brought back to the Pirates' broadcast booth in May of 1985. The Pirates were playing the Dodgers. That was the last time Scully saw Prince, and he didn't sound or look like the Bob Prince he had known in his heyday. Prince died a few weeks later.

Announcers like Prince, Scully, Buck and Harry Caray, who had died only a few months earlier in the 1998 season, were as much a part of baseball as Babe Ruth, Lou Gehrig, Ralph Kiner, Stan Musial, Honus Wagner, Jackie Robinson, Willie Mays and Roberto Clemente.

There were 18,674 fans in the stands at Three Rivers Stadium for the fourth and final game of the series. Management had expected 26,000. But it rained all morning and the Pittsburgh Marathon was run that same morning in a fine mist, and that always created traffic nightmares around the city, and kept non-Marathon fans at a safe distance.

Even though their Pirates trailed 10-0 at the seventh inning stretch, the fans sang "Take Me Out To Ball Game" with great gusto. Vince Lascheid, the stadium organist, provided the music, and the words were on display on the scoreboard screen in centerfield. Singing that song had become much more of an in-thing to do in the wake of the much-publicized death of Harry Caray, who delighted the faithful at Wrigley Field by singing that song over the p.a. system from his broadcast booth during Cubs' home contests.

Scully had been at this a long time since he came out of Fordham University and joined Red Barber and Connie Desmond as part of the Brooklyn Dodgers' broadcast team in 1950.

He had called 25 World Series and 12 All-Star Games, but said he had never worked with Bob Prince.

He called three perfect games (Don Larsen in the 1956 World Series, Sandy Koufax in 1965 and Dennis Martinez in 1991), and 18 no-hitters.

Along with Milo Hamilton, then with the Atlanta Braves, Scully had called Hank Aaron's 715th career home run that broke Babe Ruth's major league record at Atlanta's Fulton County Stadium in 1974.

He had won numerous awards throughout his career, capped by being inducted into the National Baseball Hall of Fame as the Ford C. Frick recipient in 1982.

After 49 years, was there anything Scully hadn't seen in a baseball game?

Yes, and that's the beauty of baseball. You never know when something is going to happen at the ballpark that you have never witnessed before. You never know when Pirate pitchers are going to combine for a no-hitter over ten innings, or when a Mark Smith is going to step up to the plate and hit a three-run homer to win it. That's what happened the previous July 12 at Three Rivers Stadium.

On this particular Sunday, the same Smith extended his hitless streak for the 1998 season to 0-for-29. And, with the Pirates trailing

9-0, Turner Ward did something in the sixth inning in right field that no one in the Pirates' press box had ever seen before, and, even more impressively, Scully had never seen before.

That's when Ward leaped for a long drive to the wall off the bat of Dodgers' catcher and power-hitter Mike Piazza, struck the seam of the padded barrier and slipped between the crack and completely disappeared from view.

You've heard about guys who will run through a wall for a coach, well Ward is one of those guys. "That'll be on the highlights film," Scully told his radio audience. Greg Brown said something similar on the Pirates' wrap-up show. Ward, a free agent from his home state of Alabama who had a reputation for all-out effort, bruised his right forearm but held onto the ball. Ward came back to throw the ball into the infield after a runner had tagged up and scored and another advanced to second base. A fearless outfielder for the Dodgers named Pete Reiser had shortened his major league career in the '40s by constantly running into the walls and fences in pursuit of fly balls. Scully said he had seen a taped TV highlight of a minor league player going through a wooden slat fence, but that he had never seen a major league outfielder disappear like that, going through the outfield barrier.

The Gunner would have gotten a kick out of that, for sure.

Wearing his beige raincoat, Scully left the press box with co-worker Rick Monday, a former major league outfielder with the Kansas City Athletics, the Chicago Cubs and the Dodgers. I had been stationed at the U.S. Army Hometown News Center in Kansas City back in 1965, and moonlighted in the evenings and weekends in the A's press box at Municipal Stadium. That was the year when Charles O. Finley's franchise made Monday, an All-American at Arizona State, the first player picked in the initial major league free agent draft.

Scully also was thinking back to his early days in the business when he and Monday stepped into the media elevator to go down to the visitors' clubhouse after the game. Scully is one of those guys who can't help but share stories.

"I went down to the Dodgers' clubhouse at Ebbetts Field when I'm fresh out of Fordham," Scully is telling Monday. "I was supposed to get the lineups for the broadcast. I go into the manager's office and Leo Durocher is lying flat on his back on a table, sleeping.

"I wasn't about to wake up Leo Durocher. I turned to walk away, when I hear his voice, 'What can I do for you, son?' And I turn around and now he's sitting up on the table. I said I was sorry to disturb him, but I was looking for his lineup. He put his arm around my shoulder, and he's talking to me . . . now this is The Lion. I was in heaven..."

> ***"Baseball isn't statistics, it's Joe DiMaggio***
> ***rounding second base."***
> — Jimmy Breslin,
> New York writer

Jim Rooker
Still pitching in Ambridge

"I never saw a broadcaster treated as well as Bob Prince."

Jim Rooker was ready with a question as soon as I stepped inside the door at Rook's East Side Saloon in Ambridge. The handsome host who once pitched for the Pirates and later broadcasted their ballgames grabbed me firmly by the elbow. He steered me from the saloon side of his establishment into the dining area, and pointed to a lineup of larger-than-life-size photographs high on the near wall. "Is that Rosey Rowswell?" he asked, zeroing in on the photograph to the far right.

"Yes, that's him," I replied.

Rooker smiled in relief, as if somebody had challenged him about the identification of the old fellow as he appeared bent over a microphone fiftysome years ago when he was the Pirates' premier broadcaster. Rooker thought he was right, but my reaffirmation helped.

"Our customers are always asking us who that is," said Artie Brown, who along with Bill Renie, has been a partner of Rooker in the restaurant-saloon business for ten years. All three of them were present, looking after a full room of lunch time customers on Wednesday, April 8, 1998. It was Holy Week, when some people pass up lunch as part of their Lenten fasting, so the full house was impressive.

So was a large fried fish sandwich that came on a bun that was big enough to serve as a catcher's mitt, and was a point of pride to Rooker & Co. The food and the atmosphere at Rook's East Side Saloon should satisfy any hungry or thirsty sports fan, especially with four large TV screens, two on each side, showing all variety of sports wherever one looked.

There are framed photographs and posters all over the place, inviting stargazing among the visitors, along with placards with famous quotes from famous ballplayers — like Willie Mays, Roy Campanella, Ernie Banks and Yogi Berra — about sports and life. Old favorites such as Stan Musial, Ted Williams, Carl Yastrzemski, Ara Parseghian stood out.

Customers are in good company at Rook's East Side Saloon, or so it appears.

Rooker had been one of the heroes in the 1979 World Series as a tough left-handed pitcher who came through in the clutch in the critical fifth game, after the Bucs lost three of the first four games to the Baltimore Orioles and were on the brink of elimination. He had become even more popular as a Pirates' broadcaster, though he irritated some with his penchant for analyzing every pitch as if it were

Jim O'Brien

Jim Rooker takes a break from tending bar at Rook's East Side Saloon in Ambridge, on April 8, 1998.

a rocket launch to the moon.   But he did know his stuff, no doubt about it.   Rooker remained part of Pirates' broadcasting history, indeed, a direct descendant of Rosey Rowswell and Bob Prince.

Rowswell was the pioneer broadcaster of Pirates' baseball on a regular basis, working first with Jack Craddock and later Prince. Rowswell was the Pirates' first full-time announcer. He was at the post for 19 years (1936-1954), surpassed in service time only by Prince (1948-1975) with 28 years, and Lanny Frattare (1976-1998), who was starting his 23rd year in the Pirates' broadcast booth.

The new season was also the start of the 15th season as a Pirates broadcaster for Steve Blass. Next was Rooker himself, with 13 years (1981-1993). That was a year longer than Jim Woods with 12 years (1958-1969) Nellie King with nine years (1967-1975) and John Sanders with nine years (1981-1989).

For the record, KDKA Radio broadcasted the first baseball game ever, when Harold Arlin was behind the microphone on August 5, 1921 when the Pirates played the Phillies.

There were four photographs grouped together on the wall in the dining room of Rook's East Side Saloon. From left to right, they were Rooker, Prince, King and Rowswell. They were the only photos in that particular area.   There was no photograph of Frattare to be found there, or anywhere else in the establishment, not even in the rest rooms.

The absence of a Frattare photograph points up the ill feelings that Rooker harbors for his former co-worker in the Pirates' broadcast booth.   Suffice to say, Rooker is no fan of Frattare.   He blames Frattare and Mark Driscoll, the former VP for broadcasting in the Pirates' organization, for his dismissal from the booth following the 1993 season.

Rooker was released along with Kent Derdivanis and they were replaced, respectively, by Bob Walk, another former pitcher for the Pirates, and Greg Brown, who grew up as a broadcaster in the Pirates organization.

In a way, Rooker reminds one of how Bob Prince behaved after he was fired from his post as the prime Pirates' announcer back in 1975. In a word, badly. He can't let go.

For his part, Frattare prefers to take the high road, saying he still regards Rooker as a friend — "we had 12 good years together out of thirteen" — and would hope that Rooker would feel the same way about him.

Rooker said that Mark Driscoll had criticized him for not being involved enough in off-season promotions, but thought he was satisfied with his on-the-air efforts, and felt he didn't deserve to be dumped.

I felt uncomfortable as Rooker ranted about his unhappy relationship with Frattare because, personally, I like Lanny and I've enjoyed Jim's company as well. So it was no fun getting caught in the crossfire. A ranting Rooker, with that well-chiseled chin of his jutting out over his chest, can rival Steelers' coach Bill Cowher as a

Harold Arlin did the first baseball broadcast in history when KDKA carried the Pirates-Phillies game at Forbes Field on August 5, 1921.

Bob Prince and Tommy Rodgers teamed up for KQV show on Decenber 17, 1940.

Pirates first full-time broadcaster Rosey Rosewall went for a ride at Forbes Field.

"Inasmuch"

A poem by Pirate broadcaster Rosey Rowswell:

"Don't let it be said that you turned a deaf ear to the plea of a youngster in need.
"Don't let it be known that your heart was cold when you should have been giving it heed...
"It's little the world will care what you say of a good intent betrayed;
"It's the things undone that will leave a scar when the final count is made."

formidable figure. Those granite chins only enhance their competitive appearance.

The comparison came to mind because Cowher, of course, was pictured on Rook's Walls of Fame.

Heroes of the Pirates, Penguins and Steelers share every available space, and Pitt and Robert Morris are represented as well on those walls. There are national sports figures there, too. Wherever you sit in the spacious dining area at Rook's, you'll be joined in the booth or at your table, in a sense, by some of the city's favorite athletes.

Where I sat, talking to Rooker, our company included Steelers' Kordell Stewart, the Penguins' Mario Lemiuex, who lives behind a wall in a mansion in nearby Sewickley, and in the next booth were the autographed likenesses of Dave Giusti and Chuck Tanner and Tony Bartirome. Nearby were Willie Stargell and Roberto Clemente. Carnell Lake and Levon Kirkland were close as well. Ralph Kiner and Bob Moose are among those pictured elsewhere.

The place is impressive and irresistible, a cross between Froggy's and Frankie Gustine's, for sports fans who have frequented those sports hangouts in Market Square or out in Oakland. It doesn't have a lot of curbside appeal, as the realtors like to say, when you approach it on Fourth Street. It blends in with a nondescript lineup of buildings that also house the Serbian Club and, catty-corner, the Fraternal Order of Eagles.

Rooker tells you proudly that he belongs to both of those clubs, and has membership cards to prove it. He's associated with the Ambridge Chamber of Commerce, and other civic groups. "We belong to everything," he said, "and we get as much of our food and supplies as possible from local businesses. We get our fish at Nappy's, out by the airport, our provolone cheese sticks from Anthony's right around the corner on Maplewood Avenue, and we get much of our food from Jubilee, a supermarket here in town. We get the freshest bread and rolls." He firmly believes there's a future for him and his partners in the Beaver Valley community.

"This is our 10th year in Ambridge, of all places," related Rooker. "Why Ambridge? Why not? Why shouldn't Ambridge have a nice place? We get a tremendous amount of Sewickley customers here. There's nothing else around here."

Only Leetsdale and a short stretch of Ohio River Boulevard separate Ambridge from Sewickley and Sewickley Heights, more affluent neighborhoods.

There used to be a lot of mills associated with the steel business in Ambridge and nearby Aliquippa, along the Ohio River. Many of those mills stand empty today, but some of those old buildings have been refurbished and have come back as smaller, but vital industrial companies.

There was good news in the *Beaver County Times* and the Pittsburgh *Post-Gazette* that very day, in fact, regarding new business development in the area. USG Corp. announced the day before that it had chosen a former steel mill site in Aliquippa for a $112 million plant to manufacture construction wallboard and employ from 190 to 400 people.

Chicago-based USG was the second major wallboard maker to choose Beaver County as the site for a new plant. National Gypsum, a USG competitor, had broken ground the previous month for a $79.1 million facility in Shippingport.

Then, too, a "permanent no-strike, no-lockout agreement" had been voted in by the United Steelworkers union at the WorldClass Processing plant that can be seen from the sidewalk in front of Rook's East Side Saloon. The old mill site has been cleaned up and renamed Port Ambridge.

The plant used to house U.S. Steel. Ambridge is named for U.S. Steel's once-flourishing American Bridge Division. U.S. Steel and Crucible Steel are mostly memories, but the area is now home to a ever-growing number of specialty steel and related businesses, and it all bodes well for Rooker and his persevering partners.

It was his partners, by the way, who named Rook's East Side Saloon before he ever showed up to tend bar. "I said, 'What's the East Side mean?'" Rooker recalled. "They told me we were located on the East Side of the Ohio River."

Another famous former strong-armed saloon keeper on New York's East Side, Joe Namath, grew up in nearby Beaver Falls. This is an area with a rich sports tradition, turning out the likes of Mike Ditka, Joe Walton, Tony Dorsett, Jim Mutscheller, Tito Francona and his son, Terry, John Michelosen, the Zernich Brothers, "Pistol Pete" Maravich, Vito "Babe" Parilli, Simmie Hill, Norm Van Lier, Denny Wuycik and Dick DeVenzio, Candy Young, Mike Lucci, Po James, Skippy Doyle, Terry Yarosz, Mickey and Brad Davis and George "Doc" Medich among others.

"They like to remember when they were young."
— Jim Rooker

Jim Rooker and his partners at Rook's East Side Saloon had sponsored a charter bus for the Pirates' 1998 home opener the night before my visit. The bus was full, and Rooker says the trip took only 25 minutes from his bar to the ballpark parking lot, just so no one thought his bar was near Siberia.

Rooker had related war stories and jokes during the journey to and fro, regaling his customers with twice-told tales. I've been to banquets with Jim Rooker and he can be a very funny fellow. One of the old timers on the bus, Benny from the Eagles Club, was going to see the Pirates play at Three Rivers Stadium for the first time. This gentleman had given up on going to games after the Pirates left Forbes Field in favor of Three Rivers, a familiar tale in too many similar towns around Pittsburgh.

Benny was one of the guys who enjoyed talking about Bob Prince. "They like to talk about him," said Rooker. "They like to remember when they were young. They still like to hear Prince's voice. It's his legacy."

So instead of addressing Pirates' fans everywhere, as he once did on radio and TV broadcasts, Rooker was playing to a much smaller audience in a bus, 43 in number, as he once did in his early days traveling the highways in the minor leagues.

Rook's East Side Saloon on Fourth Street used to be the Misbehavin' Saloon, featuring a follies kind of dancer on the sign outside. "It was a real steal," said Rooker. It was a real find by Artie Brown. "We bought it by basically paying for the liquor license," added Rooker.

The impressive backbar came with the liquor license. "We've had lots of offers from people who wanted to buy that backbar," said Rooker. "But we're keeping it."

The tip-off that the bar belongs to Rooker and friends is a sign posted on the front door that reads: "Gentlemen — Please No Tank Tops After 5 p.m."

Rooker was 56, but his blond hair and smooth, clean-cut appearance belied his age. His blue eyes, white teeth and wide smile could still light up a room, and break a few hearts. He was in the midst of divorce proceedings after a long separation from his wife, and he was sharing a home with Becky, a woman he said he hoped to marry. They were living in Bradford Park Square, a housing plan in Economy Boro.

His oldest son, David, 37, who once pitched in the Pirates' organization, was helping out in the restaurant that day. Rooker said David was going back to school for computers to train for a new career. His daughter, Stephanie, who would be 35 in July, was working as a secretary in the Bethel Park School District, and his daughter, Jamie, 20, was going to beauty school in Pittsburgh and living with her mother in South Park. Jim had been married for 38 years.

Once in a booth, not the kind Rooker would really prefer, he warmed to the subject of Bob Prince.

"Being in the American League and coming to Pittsburgh, I didn't know who Bob Prince was," he began. "This was in the '70s, and I wasn't that close to any announcers in either league. You said, 'How's it going?' and that was about it when you passed them. There was no history of being tight with announcers, so I never gave much thought to it.

"I saw the way Prince mingled with the players here, though, and I could tell it was different. I never saw a broadcaster treated as well. The more you were around him, the more you realized this was a fine guy. He'd shoot the bull, tell you stories you couldn't tell or write, entertain you with the raunchiest jokes you ever heard in your life. Before you had a chance to say hello, he had a drink up on the bar for you.

"He was the kind of guy a lot of people probably wanted to be. There had to be some envy. If there was a guy who had it all, Bob Prince was that person. He was so beautiful.

"He had that way about him. He had to be respected and liked. But there's always a percentage out there who don't like you, no matter what you do. He made mistakes; we all make mistakes. I'm sure he pissed off some people.

"I grew up in Southern California, listening to Vin Scully, and he was my favorite. Still is. There were some real biggies in the business, such as Scully, Jack Buck, Harry Caray, Ernie Harwell, Lindsey Nelson, Bob Murphy, Ralph Kiner, guys like that. There was a long line of them, but their number is dwindling.

"Bob and I got along well, right from the start. I got a tremendous kick out of him. When Bob Prince buys you a drink, you feel like you've been brought into the in-club. I was coming to a new team from Kansas City. I was coming from an expansion club to a contender, a team that could go all the way. It was like walking down the street and finding money. You want to prove you're good enough to belong. Bob helped me feel like I belonged.

"So did the fans. Pittsburgh is different from any other city in baseball, from what I've learned. Fans send more cookies and cakes to the clubhouse here than anywhere else I've been. The guys never lack for sweets.

"When he got fired three years after I got here, I hear they're going to have a big parade in downtown Pittsburgh. My first thought, I admit, was 'God, he's only a broadcaster.' Well, I soon realized he's not just a broadcaster. He's Bob Prince. Those of us who were there — I remember Willie Stargell was with us — rode on a platform truck. We all stood up, one car behind Bob and Nellie King.

"The streets were jammed. It was a lot like an Opening Day Parade. People were throwing stuff out of their office windows. It was almost a parade of celebration. I honestly thought the parade would change the minds of the powers-that-be. To me, the fans had made a statement, 'No, you can't do this.' But it was a done deal.

"I was at a banquet with Bob a year after. I think it was in Verona, or some place like that. There was a big turnout in a small town. Bob said in front of the crowd, 'If I were the Pirates, I'd have fired Bob Prince, too.' He told them that.

"I was with him when he came back for one last time. Prince made it fun. This is not brain surgery; it's a baseball game. Just sit back and relax; enjoy the game.

"The Pirates were not very good at the time, yet they scored nine runs in the first inning that Prince was at the mike. I remember Tommy Lasorda came out of the Dodgers' dugout and looked up at our booth. He gave this look like 'Why me?' We all started laughing. Bob started laughing, too.

349

"Jerry Reuss, who had been a Pirate, was now with the Dodgers. Bob started talking about how Jerry had met and married this beautiful girl named Terry. I wrote the word 'divorced' on a card and slid it in front of Bob. He wrote back, '0-for-1' and smiled at me. He shrugged his shoulders. He always said that if you made a mistake like that, just keep talking and they'd forget it.

"I remember that his wife, Betty, was up there behind us in the booth. He'd do the middle three innings. She asked me to stand behind him and rub his neck. It hurt him. I knew it didn't look good at that time.

"He brought an atmosphere to the broadcast booth that should be there. This is the way it's supposed to be done, he was saying in his own way.

"After eight years (1973-80) as a player with the Pirates, and helping them win a World Series, then 13 more as a broadcaster, you feel like you're part of the veins of the organization. So, yes, I was hurt when I lost my job.

"But, as I told Paul Meyer of the *Post-Gazette* the next day, 'They fired Bob Prince. They can fire me.' It hurt just the same. You build your life around what you're doing. So the question arises: What am I going to do?"

Rooker caught on with ESPN, the all-sports cable network, and had provided analysis on baseball telecasts during the four seasons after the Pirates pulled the hook on him. "ESPN had tried to recruit me earlier, and now I was really interested," he said. He did about 30 games a year for ESPN. Rooker didn't know what his ESPN schedule was going to be like for the summer of 1998, nothing had been firmed up yet, but he was hoping to have some games again.

He was planning on getting into politics. He was running for the seat from the 16th District State Legislature. He was running unopposed on the Republican ticket in the primary, and would probably be pitted against five-term incumbent, Susan Laughlin, in the next year's election. Rooker had planned on running for a political office the previous year, but was chased off by some negative media reaction.

"My first day in spring training... I knew it would be different."

Jim Rooker was born on September 23, 1941. He broke into the big leagues for the first time, just briefly, in 1966 as an outfielder for the Detroit Tigers. He was up and down from the minors to the majors for a few years, before sticking for good as a pitcher with the expansion Kansas City Royals as a third round draft choice in 1969.

We started swapping stories about our respective days in Kansas City. I put in a year in Kansas City in 1965. I was a private in the military, serving as an editor at the U.S. Army Home Town News Center at 601 Hardesty Avenue in Kansas City. I was not far from Municipal Stadium, and used to work in the evenings as a go-fer in the press box for the A's and later as a spotter for network announcers like Charlie Jones and Paul Christman with the AFL Kansas City Chiefs. It was an unforgettable experience.

The A's were owned by Charles O. Finley. And Charley O., the mule, used to chew grass on a knoll alongside the outfield fences. The Chiefs had a terrific football team and a first-class owner in Lamar Hunt. Many of the same players would represent the team in a Super Bowl I would be covering for *The Miami News* at the outset of 1969. Finley moved his A's to Oakland, California, and an expansion team replaced them in Kansas City.

It wasn't a very good team and its manager, Sid Gordon, had been out of baseball for 20 years and, in Rooker's view, was a good guy, but out of touch with the times. "It was difficult to play baseball there," recalled Rooker. "You were always looking over your shoulder; it was always your fault the team was losing."

Bill Virdon, Danny Murtaugh and Chuck Tanner were his managers in Pittsburgh, and they all ran a looser ship than what he had encountered in Kansas City. There was just a better atmosphere and attitude that was to his liking. "My first day in spring training I knew it would be different," said Rooker. "Players were joking with each other. I couldn't believe it. The way the players were treated . . . and it was that way in the '70s and into the '80s.

"Willie (Stargell) was the lead man. He never led by rah-rah stuff. He went out and played and you followed suit. When he was taking a day off, I'd sit next to him in the dugout and talk to him. You'd learn how to pitch by listening to him. You'd pick up on his mind, play mind games. You could lean on him.

"Phil Garner had come over from Oakland, and he was a leader, too. So was Dave Parker in his own way. He and Garner would go at it in the clubhouse. They'd be in each other's face. They could say all kinds of things, relating to race and so forth, and somehow it was okay. No one really took offense.

"They'd have the clubhouse in stitches. I'm told it was like that with Giusti and Blass and Clemente before I got there. Giusti liked to joke, but he could get serious, too. Blass was the funny guy. Bibby, Candelaria and Reuss were good pitchers, but no one took them too seriously."

Rooker was credited with 11½ years in the major leagues, and had started taking his baseball pension the year before. Later on, he would also be eligible for a pension from his broadcasting career. Then Social Security would kick in. So Rooker was doing all right.

Now Jim was part of another team, in his 10th year with partners Artie Brown and Bill Renie. "I'm here just about every day through lunch, from 10 a.m. to 2 p.m., and then I come back in the evening, but not all the time. Artie and Bill usually handle the evenings. It's a sharing situation. If it weren't for them, we wouldn't be here. Most of the years, I was on the road a lot broadcasting Pirates baseball.

"When I was doing the baseball broadcasts, Bob Prince called me. He was very supportive. It was good hearing from him, just as it had been as a ballplayer. He advised me to a have a good time, to let the fans enjoy the game."

There was a tear sheet of the first page of *USA Today* for those who wanted to catch up on the day's sports news while standing tall at the urinal. It pointed up how things had changed since Rooker was working in the big leagues.

The headline reported that Rupert Murdoch was watching as his Dodgers won their season opener by 9-1 over the San Diego Padres. Murdoch, a media magnate from Australia, had purchased the Dodgers for $311 million from Peter O'Malley. It was the first time since 1950 that someone outside the O'Malley family owned the Dodgers. In the same story, it was reported that Mike Piazza, the All-Star catcher and Dodgers' star, had rejected a six-year $81 million deal. He wanted a cool $100 million for his services over the same span. He was booed by the fans, but said they didn't understand the concept of fair market value in sports these days.

I had worked for Rupert Murdoch for a brief time, back in the late '70s. He had bought *The New York Post* from Dolly Schiff, and he and his underlings were looking for hotter, more controversial stories. Over 70 percent of the editorial staff left in less than two years, not interested in digging up dirt for a living. *The Post* is still in business, though, while three other papers where I was employed, *The Philadelphia Evening Bulletin, The Miami News* and *The Pittsburgh Press,* have gone by the wayside. So there's a sound method to Murdoch's madness and I have no doubt the Dodgers will prosper under his management.

"When he's healthy, he can beat anybody."
— Chuck Tanner

Rooker remembers the best of times when he pitched for the Pirates. He averaged 13 wins per season in his first five years as a Pirate (1973-77). He is best remembered for his performance in Game Five of the 1979 World Series.

With the Bucs down three games to one, Rooker was pitted against Mike Flanagan, one of the aces of the Orioles staff. Rooker had been bothered by arm problems throughout the 1979 season and twice was put on the disabled list.

He had a 4-7 record and a 4.59 ERA that summer. Chuck Tanner was questioned about the wisdom of going with Rooker as a starter. Bruce Kison, who had pitched in the opener, had been scheduled to start but his throwing arm had gone numb from throwing on a cold night the first time out.

"I don't care what people think," Tanner said. "I have confidence in Rooker. When he's healthy, he can beat any club."

Rooker insists he wasn't stressed out by the assignment. "There was no pressure on me because I wasn't supposed to win. We're down three games to one. There was more pressure when we were struggling against Montreal late in the season."

Steve Nicosia was the catcher that day and he called for Rooker to throw his sinker and let it run in on the right-handed batters, just the opposite of what the Orioles were expecting. "I pitched every right-handed batter inside, jammed them with a fast ball," said Rooker.

"Eddie Murray of the Orioles went to their dugout and said, 'Sore arm my ass!' They got a bad scouting report. They were expecting slower stuff on the outside. I busted them good inside. I nailed them to the wall. Our whole pitching staff was under-rated because Baltimore's was thought to be so outstanding."

On the eve of the fifth game, Rooker packed for an elk hunting trip with former teammate Goose Gossage for after the season. "I cleaned my gun," reported Rooker, "then went to bed about 11 o'clock, then I got up in the morning, had a fight with my wife, and came to the ballpark." It was that simple.

He retired the first nine batters, the best start of any of the more-publicized pitchers in the Series. He didn't give up any hits in the first four innings. After five innings of three-hit pitching, Rooker was finished for the day.

"I didn't have a good year," related Rooker, "but when September and October rolled around my arm was at full strength. I don't think I pitched 100 innings all year, so I may have been sharper than I normally would have been at that time of the year. I was cranked up and ready to go. I had pitched in relief in the first game, and had good stuff."

He remembers when the championship rings were passed out before the opening game in 1980. "It was an incredibly exhilarating feeling," said Rooker. "It didn't really hit you until you got the ring. A lot of guys had tears in their eyes. Yeah, I was one of them. If you even talk about it too much you get choked up about it. As a kid playing Little League, you dream about stuff like that. To have it happen to you . . . what else is left? I can still remember how special it was.

"We had so much talent in the '70s," said Rooker. "We were always knocking heads with the Reds to get to the Dodgers. I played with and against guys who are in the Hall of Fame. That's part of dreaming as a kid."

Rooker also remembers the worst of times, when drugs started finding their way, along with bad guys, into the Pirates' locker room. "I saw Dave Parker and John Milner going into a little equipment room right next to Tanner's office and snorting cocaine," said Rooker. "I couldn't believe they'd do it right next to Tanner's office. They'd come out with the stuff on their noses.

"I really don't think Tanner knew what was going on, in defense of him. Tanner always gave you credit for knowing your job, and he didn't bother you. When I was the player rep, I used to ask him why he let certain guys take advantage of him. He was a manager who kept one eye and one ear closed.

"In 1980, I went into that room and hid behind boxes so I could observe what was going on. I saw it myself. After I was done playing, and I came to the clubhouse as an announcer, I couldn't believe some of the people who were coming in there. There's a sign outside the clubhouse door that bars people without proper credentials from coming in. There's a good reason for that. These guys were bad news and they had the run of the clubhouse. It didn't make any sense. I think Dave Parker blew a Hall of Fame career. He had so much talent. He's coaching now with St. Louis and I hear he's really grown up. I'm told he's like he was at the beginning here, when he was so excited about his prospects and how great it was to be playing in the big leagues."

Rooker related stories that pointed up how special he thought Pittsburgh was because of people like Bob Prince and Chuck Tanner, and even tossed former Steelers owner Art Rooney into the mix.

"I suffered a broken arm in an auto accident in 1978," said Rooker. "I'd been drinking too much, it was my fault. I spent about four or five days in the hospital. Art Rooney sent me a card. I didn't even get a card from the Pirates.

"After I got out of the hospital, I went to see Mr. Rooney to thank him. He told me it would be okay for me to rehab my arm in the Steelers' training quarters. We didn't have the kind of machines and equipment they have in the Pirates complex these days. Ralph Berlin, the Steelers' trainer, looked after me real good because of Mr. Rooney."

Art Rooney was just one of the reasons Rooker liked Pittsburgh so much, and is happy he remained here.

He certainly preferred Pittsburgh to his hometown of Compton, California. "That was a bad, bad town," he said. "I think that's where the first drive-by shootings started. It's a badass town. It was a toughass place to grow up. Plus, my mother had two different husbands who weren't worth a damn. So for me, Pittsburgh is paradise by comparison."

Voices in sport
Reflections on Prince

"He has one of the biggest hearts
of anyone I've ever known."
— Jim Woods

Stan Savran, Fox Sports:

"I came to Pittsburgh from Cleveland in 1976. I met Bob Prince about three months after he got fired. I never heard him do Pirates baseball and that was my loss. Everybody told me about Bob Prince, though. It's like when I came here everybody told me about Bill Burns, but I had never seen him. I was working for Bob Dickey at KQV Radio and he wanted me to meet Bob Prince. I had him on my talk show one night and then the three of us went out for drinks afterward. We went to the Harvard-Yale-Princeton Club. I had a drink, that's all I could handle. Bob had a few screwdrivers, like it was nothing. Prince had approached Dickey about helping him put a syndicate together that would bid for Pirates' baseball for KQV and take them away from KDKA. They were able to do that, but I heard that the Pirates officials simply showed the bid to KDKA and all they had to do was match the offer to keep the Bucs on their station. But this was the way Prince hoped to get back on the Pirate broadcasts. I might have been working with him, which excited me. I didn't realize it at the time, but Bob really colored my thinking about KDKA and the people who were running the station. I based my opinion strictly on what he was telling me. It clouded my view and I often made some critical remarks about them on the air. In a sense, though I didn't know it, I was being used to serve Prince's purposes. He felt they had been unfair to him, and I was willing to go along with that. This was his way of getting back into baseball. From what he was telling me, I never doubted he'd come back. I was sure he'd be back. On reflection, I thought it was sad what happened to The Gunner. He got a job here and there, usually short-lived, at different stations around town. The same thing happened later on with Bill Currie. When I got fired at WTAE, I wanted to make sure that didn't happen to me. They were throwing scraps to a name, looking to capitalize on his fame. This guy had been a giant in the industry for over 30 years. He told me two things that stayed with me. He said if you're going to make a career in this town then you should get yourself allied with some charity. Do something to help other people, and you'll help yourself at the same time. He also told me to always wear a coat and tie, and use a pocket hanky that matches your tie. I've listened to him in both of those ways."

"Bob Prince . . . the sound of summer."
— Frank Aiello, N. Huntingdon, Pa.

Mal Goode, late national network reporter:

"Young reporters don't understand how bad things were in the early days. I was one of the first black reporters who got a shot on a network basis, and I knew what the barriers were like as I made my way up the ranks, first in Pittsburgh, and then in New York and D.C. Management didn't want a black face or voice on the air. But Bob Prince fought to have me as a guest on his show, and as a host when he was out of town. He helped break down a lot of barriers."

* * *

Jim Woods, Prince's broadcast partner (1958-1969):

"I had heard so many times about the swimming pool incident, where he dove from his third story window into the pool at the Chase Hotel in St. Louis. We were with the Pirates in spring training and we were staying at the Marlin Beach Hotel. We were coming in late one night, as we usually did in those days, and our rooms were on the second floor.

"We were walking along the balcony and it looked down on the swimming pool. I said, 'Gunner, do you think your act would go over here?' The next thing I know, he was going right over the balcony, and into the pool — with his clothes on!

"Another time, we were in St. Louis and it was about 95 degrees. He just declared, 'To hell with this. It's too hot,' and broadcast the game in bikini underwear. And I'm talking about a very brief bikini. He used to wear those bikinis around the hotel swimming pools, too. They didn't leave much to the imagination.

"Once during spring training, we were walking around a golf course in Fort Myers. It was really hot and Bob had taken his shirt off. A very stuffy lady came up to us and said to Bob, 'Young man, I wish you would put your shirt on!' Bob turned to her and said, 'Why? I don't care if you take yours off!'

"At the same time, he has one of the biggest hearts of anybody I've ever known. When he'd see a player who was down on his luck, he'd give him $50 or $100, or the shirt off his back. And in a lot of cases he never got it back, because the player would be sent to the minors or something and just forgot about it."

* * *

Lynn Cullen, WPTT Radio, PCNC:

"I was new at WTAE, and was feeling a little lost in Pittsburgh. One day at the station, I bump into Bob Prince in the hallway. This was past his heyday, but he was still a big media figure in Pittsburgh. He was a national figure as well. I was in town a short while, but I had heard about him. I meet this tall, lanky guy and he was so friendly. He did not assume that I should know who he was, big as he was. He introduced himself to some young person as if they were important. He showed an expansiveness and generosity that was uncommon in this business. I was so new, bereft of friends, changing my place of employment, and I was so grateful to this man, who happened to be Bob Prince, for the way he was treating me. He engaged me, he really talked to me. I was the new girl in town, a nobody, when he was a Prince, a true Prince. I mentioned that I was happy to be in a city where they had a big league baseball team. I had come from Green Bay, Wisconsin, a football town. Soon as I mentioned that, he immediately brought up his friend, Ray Scott, who had been the 'Voice of the Packers' during the Vince Lombardi championship run. I can't say I ever saw him again. I never talked to him again. He just had such a wondrous impact on me that day. I just had a sense of a nice man who made my entrance into Pittsburgh a little easier. I guess I had a buoyed sense of being in Pittsburgh that lasted for a few days. What a nice guy."

* * *

Art McKennan, Late P.A. announcer at Forbes Field and Three Rivers Stadium, Summer of 1993 in an interview with Rick Sebak of WQED-TV:

"Rosey Rowswell built up interest in baseball among the women, and Bob Prince continued to do the same thing. Rosey did that stuff, corny stuff, like telling Aunt Minnie to raise the window when a ball was about to leave the ballpark. Then Bob Prince or somebody would break some glass. This was in radio, before the TV ever came along.

"Bob Prince used to talk about everything: the trees in Schenley Park and some misfortune he had during the daytime, or something, but the people — the baseball purists — didn't like all that.

"I remember one time, Joe L. Brown used to monitor him. Because Bob was, you know, a little bit strange in some of the stuff he put over. I loved him. I miss him very much. He began to talk about the tree blossoms out over the left field fence. They were honey locusts. And he was talking about those beautiful trees, and they were, it was an evening in the spring. And, finally, he wanted to know what they were, and I didn't know what they were. So I called our Director of Parks, who I worked for on a full-time basis, at his home and he told me what they were. So Bob told the listeners about that. And after he talked about them several times, Bob got a telephone call from Joe Brown, and Brown said, 'For God's sake, Bob, give the score once in a while. To hell with those honey locusts.' That actually happened.

"I think one of the funniest things that ever happened to me out there, just listening to conversations after Harvey Haddix had pitched his 12-inning no-hitter. Harvey got a letter from a guy, and he brought it up to the radio box. And he was reading it to Bob and everybody broke up. And I finally got a look at it, after I asked Bob to let me see it. You know what it said? 'Dear, Harvey. Tough shit!' That's all it said. Absolutely all it said. I'll bet Harvey still has it. He was one of the nicest guys around here, typical farmer.

"Of course, Bob was an institution. He was something to sit next to. And, if there was nobody in the ballpark, or something like that, or there weren't too many writers with our team, the visiting writers sat beside me for the most part. Bob would talk to me, right through the window there. And I'd nod or something. And he'd say something, some statement, and I'd say, 'Yeah, yeah.' And he'd just go on talking.

"I went to the PAA after we won the 1960 World Series. I had a disability at the time and I went there to get in my swimming exercise. I was on my way out of the side door of the PAA when Bob Prince came along. He took me by the shoulder and guided me by the dining room. He was going to the dining room to eat something or have a drink, I guess.

"And when he got to the opening of the dining room of the PAA, the big dining room, he got a standing ovation. The place was jammed with people. They stood up and applauded for him. I'll never forget standing there with Bob."

* * *

Bob Smizik, columnist, Pittsburgh Post-Gazette:

"When I think back of the great people I've met in sports, his name is near the top. Despite the flashiness and flamboyance, Bob Prince was a down-to-earth guy. When the papers went on strike in the early '70s, he approached Charley Feeney and myself and offered interest-free loans. To me, he was going to give us a stipend to live on. I don't know of too many people who think about him in that light. We both turned him down. We still think about him. His name will come up in our conversations in the press room, 'What if the Gunner were here? What would he say?' I've been around some special people in this business — like Buzz Ridl and Bill Virdon — mostly people I met early in my writing career, who were first class, decent people. Joe Brown would be another. I'm lucky to have known Prince and those kind of people."

"He was a homer, he was for his team, he was for his people and he was for the players, regardless of their color or background. Prince just didn't announce the game, he shared it. He brought it home."

— Rev. Laird Stuart
At memorial service

Greg Brown, Pirates broadcaster:

"I remember being at a meeting in 1985 with Rick Starr, the general manager at KDKA, and Chris Cross, the program director, and they said 'we want to bring back Bob Prince.' I got a rush when I heard that. I got chills when they said that. Steve Greenberg and I went right to Joe Brown to see if he'd sign off on it. Brown said, 'Let's do it.' It was great to have been part of that, even though it didn't work out the way we had imagined because Bob's health was worse than we knew at the time. He was only able to do a few games before he was hospitalized and died soon after.

"As a kid, I was a Pirates' fan. I really got interested during the 1971 World Series-winning season. My father was in the coal business in the Harrisburg area. He was the president of Keystone Bituminous Co., and he had to come to Pittsburgh on business. We'd stay at the Hilton Hotel downtown. While he was at business meetings, I'd run around the lobby getting autographs from the visiting ballplayers. We could pick up the baseball games on the radio in Harrisburg, and I used to listen to Bob Prince and Nellie King and Don Hoak. That's the broadcast team I remember best."

Jack Wheeler, disk jockey, WJAS Radio, Pittsburgh

"I celebrated my 50th year in the broadcasting business last January (1998), and I started working in Pittsburgh in 1968. So I've been here for 30 years. Bob Prince and I were very close. He was a super guy. I was the one who promoted the parade for him and Nellie King after they got bagged by KDKA. I'm the one who's been after City Council to name that little street that has no name at Three Rivers Stadium in his honor. They could have a Bob Prince Boulevard, but they're too wishy washy about doing anything. It's a damn shame.

"Bob and I opened up the Allegheny Club at Three Rivers Stadium, and I'm sure the waitresses there can tell you some good stories. I was just talking to Nellie King the other day at a funeral, and I reminded him of how Bob would leave the broadcast booth during a game and come to the Allegheny Club and forget he was doing a game, and leave Nellie alone for five or six innings.

"I used to do a show every morning at WEEP with Joe Brown. Bob asked me what I was going to do when the season was over and Brown wasn't around as much. He called me 'Wheels.' He suggested that he take his place. So we gave him $150 a week and he called me from everywhere he was in the country. That was fun.

"Bill Currie was in his heyday at KDKA and I didn't know he wore a toupee. Until Bob came up to him in a hotel where we were staying with the Pirates, and spun his toupee around. Bob would do anything for a laugh.

"One night he was doing a game in San Diego and it went into extra innings. Ed and Wendy King had a show every night on KDKA from 9 till midnight called 'Party Line' and they never got on that night. Bob told the listeners to call me at the station with any questions they had on the game. All of a sudden I got real busy when I didn't want to be busy. I had an all-night show on KDKA at the time. So when I came on, I gave the listeners Bob Prince's telephone number at the hotel and had them keep him awake all night. We used to do things like that to each other.

"He was a lovely innocent. He had a halo around his head, but it wasn't on straight. He was like a naughty little boy. But he was good. He did things for the Pirates that no one has done since. He made a dull game interesting; he talked about other things.

"Bob was a little arrogant, and he bothered some officials at KDKA. He could always turn to Don Burnham, the chairman of the board at Westinghouse, and get him to get them off his back. When Burnham retired, though, the jackals got him. Candidly, the Pirates could have fired him back in the mid-'50s. But they didn't and they shouldn't have done it after they let him go all that time. They let him spin in the wind, and they cut his heart out. I've had no use for them ever since."

Art McKennan

Stan Savran

> *"You don't have to explain everything. They understand the basics. Tell 'em a story or two, and then shut up and let 'em watch it. And don't forget the score. Mr. Branch Rickey told me, 'I want you to remember that you get 10,000 new listeners every minute.' I give the score with every batter, every 3-and-2 count, and every out."*
> — Bob Prince

Other voices
Princely reflections

"The light went on when
he walked into a room."
— Dick Enberg, NBC Sports

"Bob Prince was defiantly partisan. He couldn't be a disinterested observer if he tried. I remember the broadcast of the classic Harvey Haddix 12-inning no-hitter in Milwaukee and how Prince was literally cheering for him all the way even though it was supposed to be an unwritten law that you never breathed the words — no-hitter — while the no-hitter was in progress. Prince was never fettered by such superstitions, and that was part of his appeal. He defied the usual conventions. Of course, at times he did this to a fault, but that was always forgivable. Lovers are always given to excesses, and Bob Prince was a Pirate baseball lover."

— Sam Hazo, President
International Poetry Forum
Pittsburgh
March 23, 1998

*　*　*

On learning of his death:
"What a sweet guy Bob Prince was. The Bucs' mike man got along with the newspapermen when broadcasters and reporters generally hated each other's guts. I don't know if Bob took the up or down elevator the other day, but he'll have them laughing wherever he went. Pleasant dreams, sweet Prince.

— Dick Young, columnist
Baseball Hall of Fame
New York Daily News
June 16, 1985

*　*　*

"Bob Prince was a once-in-a-lifetime guy. He'd come into a room like this and take over the table, telling one story after another. I loved the guy. Once, he took me to a celebrity golf outing at the St. Clair Country Club. The fellow in front of us at the first tee was taking a long time before driving the ball. Bob hollered out, 'For Christ sake, hit the friggin' ball!' The guy turned around and it was the Rev. Billy Graham. He was visibly shaken. He said, with his voice quivering,

'Robbb...bert, Robbb...bert!' To which Prince replied, 'Well, c'mon, Billy, hit the friggin' ball.' The rest of us wanted to run and hide."
— Jack Buck
Baseball Hall of Fame Broadcaster
St. Louis, Mo.
Interviewed at Three Rivers Stadium in the fall of 1997

* * *

The following was from an interview at Steelers' offices on January 12, 1996, prior to their AFC championship game with the Baltimore Colts, when Dick Enberg was in town to do the game for NBC Sports:

"I was working in the American League, but the story of him diving from the window of his room into the swimming pool at the Chase Hotel in St. Louis made its way to us in the other league as well. I don't know what happened, but there just aren't as many characters in our business now. He just commanded attention; he was such a delightful person, a great story-teller. I got to see him at All-Star Games and World Series, stuff like that. As a young man, you were just glad you were included in the session. The light went on when he walked into a room.

"Prince was from a different era. I remember Don Drysdale telling me stories about being with Bill Veeck in Milwaukee, and he told stories about what that was like. You wish you had a tape recorder when guys like Prince and Veeck were telling their stories. They'd come to the press room and they'd talk with anybody and everybody.

"I did the California Angels for 12 years and the managers and front office people didn't want to go home after the night games. They'd just sit around telling stories. It was the celebration of the game we all loved. We loved our wives, but we loved baseball, too. It's sad that we've gotten away from that. Something's been lost. We're missing the whole heartbeat of what we craved when we came into this business in the first place. It was that passion that made you fall in love with the game.

"The 'Watergate' hangover helped create a different atmosphere. No one trusted anyone anymore, and people were afraid to let their hair down in front of the media for fear it would get out to the public. The biggest difference was that in the '50s we grew up still in awe of the game and its people, and we were looking positively. Now they're looking for the negative side.

"Now it's getting to be just a sports event. I'm here to do business. So I dress the part. I dress better on game day. You should look the part. Prince was from another era; he dressed to draw attention and it added to his zaniness.

"He had that strong voice. There was a style about him that brought you in. He had that little mischievous spirit that crept into his comments. He just found that manure pile and pulled stories out of it. He had a great partner in Jim Woods, who was a first-rate announcer on his own, 'The Possum.' Prince always seemed to know more than the rest of us.

"I never found him conceited. He never looked down at you. There was a gamesmanship about him that made him unique. Few have it. I don't. Some of his compatriots came close. He was probably a little crazy. He was bright and crazy.

"I've worked with some great people, like Merlin Olsen. Curt Gowdy has been my hero. I learned so much from him. You have to paint the whole picture, and there are different ways to do that. Red Barber was the antithesis of Bob Prince. I think of him as being an academician. He taught us how to report a game. I listened to him as a kid. My MVP in baseball is Vin Scully. He's the best.

"I grew up in Michigan, and I heard Van Patrick and Ernie Harwell. They were terrific. This is my 20th year with the NFL and I'm still trying to get better. I learned my craft on radio. I remember Prince doing the '60 World Series on TV. I remember Mazeroski and Danny Murtaugh and Mickey Mantle and the Yankees. Prince came out to Hollywood and did some recreations of that series, and I spent time with him in the green room (pre-show reception area at TV studios). I was doing UCLA and Rams games then. Prince could paint pictures and tell stories. He was a storied character. I'm just glad I had a chance to meet him."

— Dick Enberg, NBC Sports
Santa Fe Rancho, Calif.

*   *   *

Gil Lucas, Fox Sports, Pittsburgh

"The next to the last day I ever saw Bob Prince was at a press conference held on the infield portion of Three Rivers Stadium. It was well attended with all of the usual media suspects showing up. The purpose of the conference was to announce that Telecommunications (TCI of Pennsylvania) had acquired the cable rights to the Pittsburgh Pirates.

"Everybody was in a festive mood...except for the lonely figure of a man slumped in a camel hair topcoat, trying so hard to find comfort on a hard fold-up metal chair. The coat, a vibrant orange and yellow, seemed out of place on this warm April afternoon.

"Hordes of media types went over to offer congratulations to the man who was finally coming home to do the play-by-play for his beloved Pittsburgh Pirates. The man, of course, was Bob Prince, aka The Gunner, the most loved and hated man to ever announce a baseball game in Pittsburgh up to that time.

"The memories of Bob diving out of his hotel window in St. Louis to win a $20 bet or seeing that reed-thin body running around the city in a garish outfit which consisted of paisley shorts and a wild sport coat. Those images were hard to summon when you saw this shell of a man who at that time was being ravaged by the most insidious of diseases . . . cancer.

"It was finally the time I most dreaded. That was to go over and say something uplifting to Bob, as well as for myself. Anything I could say would ring false, as both of us knew in our hearts he was dying right before our eyes. I leaned over to Bob with his tyrolean hat half-mast over his drawn eyes, a scarf over his throat and mouth, that distinctive crooked mouth, that now couldn't be controlled from drooling.

"That same voice and crooked mouth that announced thousands of innings to millions of people all over the world. I whispered in his ear the only thing that I thought could bring a small smile to this man of once unbounded dash and energy. I leaned down and said, 'I have seen you look worse.' He looked up at me with eyes that were still alive and he softly kissed me on the cheek that was now drenched from tears streaming from my eyes.

"Nothing was said by Bob, but I knew he understood my feelings and all of a sudden, I felt better and Bob's eyes told me he felt better. The irony of Bob's cancer is that it was in his mouth, a place that cancer rarely strikes. That mouth and voice brought baseball to his fans and he will be remembered as 'the voice of the Pirates' as long as baseball is played in Pittsburgh."

* * *

Ray Scott, Sports Broadcaster:

"Bob Prince and Rosey Rowswell were both unique broadcasters. They didn't fill the role of what another city's ideas might be of a baseball broadcaster. But they're a part of Pittsburgh style. Pittsburgh is a unique city and they were perfect for it."

* * *

Curt Gowdy, Sports Broadcaster:

"I didn't know why he wanted to come back at the end like he did, and I can't understand why they let him go in the first place. Bob was a homer, sure, but people like that. I always thought I wasn't hired to be a cheerleader. When I started with the Boston Red Sox, the biggest criticism of me was that I didn't root for the Red Sox. Sure, you root for them, I lived and died for them, but I thought my job as a broadcaster was to report down the middle."

"I don't want to be a millionaire. I just want to live like a millionaire. Why should I retire? You tell me something I can do that's better than being a sportswriter."
—Dick Young,
New York Daily News

Bob Prince and Gil Lucas relax at Toftrees Resort after Pitt beat Penn State, 31-11, on November 23, 1984.

When Bruce Kison learned of the death of Bob Prince in the summer of 1985, he was then pitching for the Boston Red Sox, but he'd never forget "The Gunner's" generosity.

After the Pirates won the seventh game of the 1971 World Series in Baltimore, pitcher Bruce Kison had a date he had to keep. That very day he was to be married in Pittsburgh.

He and his best man, pitcher Bob Moose, were whisked away by helicopter out of the parking lot at Memorial Stadium to the airport where they caught a private jet back to Pittsburgh so Kison could be married as planned.

"The ballclub has always wanted to take credit for that," said Kison, "but the truth of the matter is that Bob Prince made all the arrangements. Now, Bob Moose is gone and Bob Prince is gone. It is very sad for me.

"You don't see his kind in broadcasting anymore, a legend who will allow himself to come down to the players' level."

Bill DiFabio, WTAE Radio, Sportscall:

"This is a hairy story. The year was 1982 . . . The Gunner was working for HSE, the local cable outlet. Prior to the start of the game, several media types gathered in the press room. I was sitting by myself when Gil Lucas and The Gunner walked in and joined me. So the three of us are sitting down. A few minutes later, a guy walked in with a bad hairpiece. I mean this piece was really bad, like someone melted one of those old black telephones over the guy's bald head.

"The Gunner looks at Gil and says, 'Now that's a bad head.' He asked me what I thought. I said, 'Gunner, there are some good ones out there.' Bob shook his head. 'I can spot them a mile away,' he snapped. So I said, 'Well, Gunner, what do you think of mine?' Gunner shot up from his seat, and said, 'What? That's not your hair?' My reply: 'You got it!' And, with that, I pulled the hair off my head and said to The Gunner, 'Here, check it out."

"I tossed it into his lap. He must have jumped ten feet up in the air, fumbling my hairpiece. Dizzy and George, the guys behind the bar in the press lounge, said they'd never seen The Gunner look so scared.

"So a couple of hours later, The Gunner is in the middle of his play-by-play and the camera is panning fans seated behind home plate. The camera zooms in on this bald-headed fan. Gunner yells that what the guy needs is a DiFabio. For the next two or three minutes, Gunner explained to the audience about Bill DiFabio and his new rag-doo. My phone never stopped ringing. The look on the Gunner's face when I threw him the hairpiece was worth a million dollars."

Bill DiFabio, left, is a guest on WMBA (Ambridge) Saturday sports talk show with hosts Randy Cosgrove and Bob Pompeani during 1998 NFL draft.

"The Prince of Pittsburgh"
The Gunner was his own man

"A million people are waiting to turn me off."

Once one of the most respected sports writers in the country, Myron Cope was a regular contributor to The Saturday Evening Post, True, Sport and Sports Illustrated. The following article first appeared in SI's September 13, 1965 edition, and was reprinted in a collection of Cope's best stories in a book published in 1968 by Prentice-Hall called "Broken Cigars." Cope was a contemporary and good friend of Bob Prince, and always admired his ability to make people laugh.

By Myron Cope

From his bony knees right up to his protruding ribs and his pebble-sized shoulders, his form was perfect — even if emaciated — as he crouched to dive. Many years before, he had been a collegiate swimmer, and he was proud of it. Now, when a man had offered to bet him $20 he could not make this dive, he had snapped up the wager without a moment's hesitation. By rights, he should have been given odds, for it is a tough dive into the pool at the Chase Hotel in St. Louis when you are making it from a third-story window.

"He had to clear about twelve feet of pavement," recalled Danny Whelan, the Pittsburgh Pirates' trainer, who along with the Pirate team had been staying at the Chase that day. "It was strictly a blotter job, believe me."

The man perched up there on the windowsill was Bob Prince, a broadcaster of Pirate games. It is safe to say that had the scene been broadcast back to Pittsburgh, it would have evoked three reactions. At least a dozen radio and television men would have raced to apply for Prince's job, which along with sidelines pays him approximately $70,000 a year. Second, prayers for his safety would have been offered by bankers to whom he has owed money for twelve years. And third, a sizable number of baseball fans who bristle at his rambling, didactic, partisan style, would have cried, "Miss!" One of Prince's longtime friends, recalling a boisterous party at which a burly sportswriter seized Prince bodily and threatened to hurl him out a seventh-story window, half the people in the room would have been for it and half against.

At any rate, there he was, poised to dive. He sprang, and then his body stiffened beautifully, and he descended straight and skinny as a spear. "I cleared the concrete by four or five feet," Prince said.

Thus baseball's most incorrigible exhibitionist, a man who in his home territory dwarfs the athlete celebrities he chronicles, lived to see another and yet another birthday. His 49th, celebrated a few months ago, was called to the attention of Forbes Field patrons by the public-address announcer and was, as might have been expected, thunderously booed.

For a variety of reasons, the popular five-word expletive — "Why doesn't he shut up?" — enjoys public usage far above the nationwide norm during Bob Prince's broadcasts. Dining one evening with Kasper Monahan, a Pittsburgh drama critic, Prince rose from the table and said, "I've got to get to the booth. A million people are waiting to turn me off." As it happens, the jest was needlessly modest, for the very people who urge Prince to drop dead usually listen to him right up to the last out, when — if the Pirates have won — he insufferably crows, "We had 'em all the way!"

Part of the fascination of listening to a Pirate broadcast is waiting to hear Prince's next high crime against the English language, which he occasionally mangles in earnest pursuit of elegance. "Our booth," he has stated from Philadelphia's Connie Mack Stadium, "must be more than 100 feet high, according to my metric calculations." Intending to explain why he does not trifle with batting averages, not even metrically, in the opening weeks of the season, Prince has informed his audience, "They don't mean a thing at this time of year, so we deign to use them."

Another stimulant of audience fascination lies in Prince's propensity for jamming his foot into his mouth, to wit: "I know what *I* gotta do here, I gotta walk Mr. Frank Robinson . . . Don't get me wrong now — I'm not the manager, they don't pay me to manage . . . Strike one! . . . Well, that's all right, let's get Robinson out of there . . . You gotta pitch to him . . . Nothing else you can do here."

Although Prince is adequately supplemented by two co-broadcasters, listeners frequently get four or five voices for the price of three. Cries of "Shut up, Prince!" hurled by nearby spectators pierce the play-by-play. Nonetheless, when Prince is not carrying on a running argument with his hecklers, he is — and this surely is a third reason for his ability to retain his audience — one of the most effective play-by-play men in the business. For all his faults, he possesses a sharp vocal quality that cuts through crowded saloons and can be heard distinctly from the patio next door. As unjaded as the day he broadcast his first game, he makes difficult plays and tense games come alive with excitement. "He's controversial," said Jack Berger, the Pirates' public-relations director, "but he's one of the very best."

In the final analysis, the main reason for Prince's vast, if disgruntled, audience is that Prince is an individual, a larger-than-life figure who dives out of third-story hotel windows and is shaped so distinctly in his own mold that every listener feels that for better or worse he knows him. Tall, bespectacled, and so scrawny that his sponsors ordered him to cease wearing Bermuda shorts to the ballpark, Prince lopes about in outrageously loud sports jackets said by some to have been cut from blankets taken from the backs of Pirate owner John Galbreath's thoroughbreds. Conspicuous as Prince manages to be, it is no wonder that he easily is Pittsburgh's most recognizable personality. The nature of baseball broadcasting being what it is, however, the rewards are mixed. On the one hand, Prince could say, "I'm privileged to be able to call the presidents of every major corporation in Pittsburgh by their first names, and they'll do anything for me within reason." On the other hand, he is accustomed to having sideburned punks pull alongside his Lincoln Continental and shout, "Hey, there's Bob Prince!" So saying, the sideburned punks pass him with a roar, then slow down to a snail's pace, and then, as Prince tries to pass them, cut in front of him.

"This happens quite often," said Prince. "I've ridden them off the road. I nosed my car bumper-to-bumper with one wise guy and rammed my pedal to the floorboard and took him as fast as I could through stop signs, stoplights, everything I could take him through. I put another guy into a culvert and watched the sand fly out."

Obviously, it takes a man of derring-do to tolerate the kind of fame Bob Prince enjoys in broadcasting, but Prince seems wholly willing to take risks that only his listeners would wish on him. Publicist Berger vividly recalled a day he accepted an invitation to share a single-engine plane that big-spender Prince had chartered for a trip to a banquet in Warren, Pennsylvania, a distance of about 150 miles from Pittsburgh.

"We're no sooner airborne," said Berger, "than Prince asks the pilot if he can take over the controls. He doesn't have a pilot's license but he tells the pilot he's got a number of flying hours. Prince takes over, and everything goes smoothly for a while. The weather on our path is fine. But Prince looks way to the left and sees a storm center and says to the pilot, 'Why don't we fly through that storm?' The pilot was agreeable, so into the storm we go, and I'm sitting there saying Hail Marys. We come out of the storm okay, and then Prince decides to fly the plane upside down. Finally, as we're approaching Warren, Prince said, 'Can I land here?' The pilot, as usual, says okay, even though we have to fly down the side of a mountain and across a river and hit a landing strip that is just a few feet above water level. Well, Prince is flawless. He puts the plane down nicely. Then he says, 'You know, that's the first time I've ever landed a plane.' I went back to Pittsburgh on the bus."

"What the hell," said Prince. "Maybe I could have been a lawyer and made a couple hundred thousand dollars a year, but I wouldn't have had half as much fun."

Prince got into broadcasting after his father had more or less thrown him into the street, damned if he would tolerate a career play-boy. The late Colonel F.A. Prince, a onetime West Point halfback, raised his son on half-a-dozen army posts and saw him through four universities. At last, with a B.A. from Oklahoma, Prince entered

369

Harvard Law School, where he flunked Procedure in his first term. "I probably could have gotten back in the next term," said Prince, "but my old man went to the movies in Montgomery, Alabama, and looked up at the newsreel and started swearing. I was up there competing in a jitter-bugging contest. He said, 'You're just spending my money at Harvard. You're going to work. Here's $2,000 to get started. Go make a living.'"

Instead, Prince went to Zelienople, Pennsylvania, near Pittsburgh, and settled comfortably in his grandmother's home. Colonel Prince phoned and said, "Throw him out of the house." It seemed only natural, then, that the prodigal son would turn to sports-casting, for he had been a frustrated athlete all his life, and to this day still is. "When I was young I rode in a rodeo in Cheyenne," said Prince. "I came out of that chute on a big, black sonofabitch and rode him for about five seconds and then got the living hell kicked out of me. My old man said, 'You gotta be an idiot — why'd you do it?' And I said, 'Cause somebody said I wouldn't dare try to.'" Rising to other challenges, Prince had his mouth caved in by a polo mallet and his face scarred from fencing without a mask. When his skill as an eques-trian was questioned, he responded by galloping a fox hunt trail — jumps and all — at 3 a.m. in a driving rain. When invited to appear with show-business personalities in a benefit stock car race, he fin-ished first by furiously crowding a terrified disk jockey off the track.

Prince had a cousin who obtained a Pittsburgh radio station, so he was able to obtain a job as a sportscaster. He quickly decided that the best ticket for his fifteen-minute evening show was controversy, and for a starter he harassed boxer Billy Conn for ducking tough fights. Conn's next fight was an easy one, lasting only the few moments it took his friends to pry him off Prince's throat. Pressing on, Prince conscientiously attended Pirate games, carrying a type-writer with which he made notes. Both sides of his typewriter case bore his name in giant letters — a display of ostentatiousness that was not lost on the working press. One afternoon, while Prince sat behind the Pirate dugout, the chairman of the local chapter of the Baseball Writers Association dropped a bag of water on him. "I was sort of a brash individual," Prince explained.

Pirate owners, impressed by the following Prince had built with his fifteen-minute show, foisted him upon play-by-play announcer A.K. (Rosey) Rowswell, a shriveled old man who had no use for Prince. Throughout 1948, their first season together, Rowswell permitted him to speak only when commercials had to be read. Otherwise, Prince's duties consisted of executing a Rowswell sound-effects trademark known as the Big Drop. Each time a Pirate hit a home run Rowswell would cry, 'Get upstairs, Aunt Minnie, and open the window. . .'" The idea was that the baseball was screaming toward Aunt Minnie's bedroom window. Prince, standing on a chair, dutifully would hurl glasses, ashcan lids and cowbells to the floor. "She never made it," Rowswell would conclude.

370

Bob Prince checks out Billy Conn, right, at exclusive press showing of "The Pittsburgh Kid" at Fulton Theatre in 1941.

Roberto Clemente honored Bob Prince by presenting him his most cherished trophy, the silver bat, emblematic of the National League batting championship in 1961 when he batted .351. The bat was returned to Clemente's family after Prince's death.

Feeling more abused than Aunt Minnie's house, Prince braced Rowswell at the end of his first season, demanding, "What do you got against me?"

"You're nothing but a fresh punk," replied Rowswell.

"Look," said Prince, "all I want to do is succeed you when you retire or die. Even if it takes thirty-five years, all I want to be until that time is your assistant." The next season Rowswell would let Prince share the play-by-play and, before Rowswell's death five years later, Prince's exposure as assistant broadcaster multiplied his broadcasting assignments and personal appearance fees. He became a business adviser to Pirate slugger Ralph Kiner and was, said a Forbes Field regular named Maniac McDonough, "the reason Ralphie has to work today."

Together, Prince and Kiner roared over the countryside in twin silver-gray Jaguars and just as dizzily plunged into business deals. Borrowing heavily against their combined income of $150,000, they invested in a new ultrahigh-frequency television station, and in a three-story restaurant. A storm blew down the station's tower, putting the shaky broadcasting company out of business, and the next day Kiner — on whose Pittsburgh exploits the restaurant relied for survival — was traded to the Chicago Cubs. "In the space of forty-eight hours," said Prince, "we dropped $100,000." With a number of dry wells thrown in, Prince's debts amounted to $120,000.

Although married and the father of two children by now, Prince was scarcely fazed. To his bankers he piped, "It's not every guy my age who can owe this much money."

A man of honor, Prince had no taste for declaring bankruptcy. "Gentlemen," he said, "if you allow me to continue to belong to all my clubs and drive expensive cars and live in the manner to which I'm accustomed, you'll get dollar for dollar." Today, Prince belongs to ten toney clubs, leases a new Continental every year, tosses down double Canadian Clubs with Cokes, and brandishes forty credit cards. He still owes the bankers $12,500, but few men have suffered the shorts in such grand style. Prince has sent a tailor around to Forbes Field to measure trainer Danny Whelan and equipment manager John Hallahan for $125 sports jackets. Impressed by the athletic skill and good character of All-America basketball star Don Hennon of Pitt, Prince bought him an $800 microscope to help him in medical school. "When people ask me how much Prince makes," said Maniac McDonough, "I tell them I don't know, but it's a thou less than he spends."

Through all these affluent years Prince has waged a continuous battle on the air with listeners who write letters demanding he cease yakking about the wind and quit reminding them five times a night that Forbes Field is "the house of thrills." Umpire Bill Klem denounced Prince as "an ill-bred apple head" for second-guessing umpires over the air. Ballplayers like him but accord him little respect. On one occasion, while he was conducting a pregame radio

372

show in front of the dugout at Forbes Field, pitchers Lew Burdette and Warren Spahn — then with the Milwaukee Braves — undid his $126 alligator shoes. Spahn hurled one atop a screen behind home plate while Burdette raced to centerfield and tossed the other over the wall. Another time, in the midst of a dugout telecast at Milwaukee, Burdette crept beneath camera range and sprayed Prince's left leg with ethyl chloride, turning him numb from the knee down, and then touched a match to the anesthetic, setting Prince and his $75 slacks afire.

No amount of abuse, however, is enough to deflate Prince's vision of himself as a dashing figure. "My second year in the big leagues," Bob Friend recalled of his Pirate pitching days, "I pitched the home opener and shut out the Reds. On the day I was to make my next start, Prince comes into the clubhouse and says, 'Look, kid, if you pitch another game like you did the other day, see me after the game and I'll take you to the Pittsburgh Athletic Association and introduce you to some important people.' I said, 'What if I lose?' He said, 'Then forget it.'"

Much to Friend's surprise, however, he grew fond of Prince. "He's always flashing his money," said Friend, "and he loves to show off his credit cards. But if a guy's down to his last ten bucks, Prince will always come through." The Bob Prince that listeners neither hear nor see is a man who helped found a school for retarded children and turns over to charities about 90 percent of the fees he earns as a toast-master. Black ballplayers regard him as a genuine friend. He regularly has them to his home for dinner and a swim, warning them with exaggerated gruffness, "You'd better behave yourself or I'll put lye in the pool."

Such admonitions closely resemble Prince's style as a toastmaster. Sports fans who insist they cannot stand the sound of his voice pack banquet halls to hear him put down guests of honor and assorted celebrities. St. Louis invited Prince to deliver the principal speech at a retirement banquet for Stan Musial. "I think it is ridiculous," he told the assembled hero-worshippers, "that we are gathered here tonight to honor a man who made more than 7,000 outs."

In 1964, and continuing into the early part of the current '65 season, Prince toned down his outspoken style, sensing that because the Pirates had declined into the second division Pittsburghers were in a surly mood. Then, when the club roared back into the pennant race, Prince became his old loquacious self, rooting hard, aiming guarded but prickly needles at umpires, and generally irritating his audience. Only once in his broadcasting lifetime have the Pirates won the pennant, and, even in the moment of triumph after Bill Mazeroski hit a ninth-inning home run to beat the Yankees in the seventh and last game of the 1960 World Series, Prince managed to set his listeners' teeth on edge. It had been decided that if the Yankees led after eight innings the Yankee announcer would head downstairs for the clubhouse to be ready for postgame interviews; if the Pirates led,

Prince would go. At the end of eight, the Pirates led, so Prince scrambled from the television booth. By the time he reached the clubhouse the Yankees had tied the score and he was told to get back upstairs. He reached the booth just as Forbes Field shook with a great roar. Network men spun Prince around, crying, "Get back downstairs! The Pirates won!"

Breathless and not having the least idea how the Pirates had won, Prince fought his way into the clubhouse, hopped on a platform and took up his microphone. A helpful aide had maneuvered the hero to Prince's side. Prince pulled Mazeroski to the microphone and asked him automatically, as he would a third-string catcher, "Well, Maz, how does it feel to be a member of the world champions?"

"Great," Mazeroski began.

"Congratulations," Prince said and then shouted, "There's the president of the National League!" Briskly ushering Mazeroski off camera, he called, "Will you come up here, Mr. Giles?" His audience shook with frustration.

A sensitive man beneath his brass, Prince acknowledges from time to time that he has a special gift for enraging people. "The worst thing I ever did," he sighs, "was name my son Bob Prince, Jr. That poor kid has led a rough life."

Jim O'Brien

Myron Cope shares Steelers broadcast booth with Bill Hillgrove. Both were big fans and friends of Bob Prince.

> *"It's almost as if your childhood and Bob Prince were synonymous."*
> — Myron Cope

When Prince's Wildcats roughed up The Hill Boys

"We beat 'em."

By Charley Feeney
Pittsburgh Post-Gazette

March 21, 1971

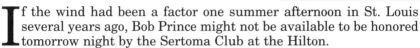

If the wind had been a factor one summer afternoon in St. Louis several years ago, Bob Prince might not be available to be honored tomorrow night by the Sertoma Club at the Hilton.

Prince's famous swan dive from the third floor of the Chase Hotel in St. Louis gained him national recognition among the kooks of the world. Fortunately for Prince, Dick Stuart wasn't supposed to catch him when the Pirates' broadcaster made the leap and landed in nine feet of water in the hotel swimming pool.

It was Stuart who instigated Prince's leap. "Dr. Strangeglove," who made every ground ball his way an adventure because of his suspect fielding ability, bet Prince $20 that he wouldn't attempt to jump into the pool from his hotel room.

"It was 90 feet up and seven feet out," Prince said yesterday, "and Stuart never paid off the bet."

Tales of Bob Prince on the baseball circuit are numerous. He has been known to blame the wind for Pirate defeats and he has been known to force people to ask for color-blind tests when he dresses for a twi-night doubleheader on a hot summer night. He also originated the Bob Prince cocktail. After one drink, the wind becomes a factor.

For 25 years, Bob Prince has been broadcasting Pirate baseball games. He has his critics (Who doesn't?). In his profession, he is known as a first-class announcer. The Sertoma group of Western Pennsylvania is honoring Prince for his "service to mankind."

Now to people who may think that Bob Prince is strictly a fun and games guy such an honor may seen like some kind of bad joke.

Bob Prince is a charitable man. He is not the type who will lend his name to charity and let it go at that. "I'm not a member of a charity in name only," Prince says with pride. "Many people join these organizations just to see their name in print and to say they belong."

He works for charities. He is one of the founders of the Allegheny Valley School for Exceptional Children and this school will receive much of the proceeds from the dinner honoring Prince.

Prince is a worker on and off the mike. Prince gets a boost out of helping youngsters. He has been doing it for more than 25 years.

Back in the forties, Prince organized teenage baseball and football teams in Mt. Lebanon. The Mt. Lebanon Wildcats they were called. Now these weren't underprivileged kids. They were the sons of lawyers, bankers, doctors, and shopkeepers. They had the best of everything. They wore silk football jerseys, satin pants and had plastic headgears when they were still rare sights on local sandlots.

Everybody was eager to challenge those big rich kids — "cake-eaters," they were called in ridicule — from Mt. Lebanon.

"Our club wasn't made up of sissies," Prince said. "A team from the Hill District challenged us. I remember Tony Bartirome and Bobby DelGreco played on the Hill team. The Hill boys had tough backing. The bookies, some of the mob, made sure these Hill boys had football uniforms and gear. The game drew four or five thousand people. We passed the hat and paid for our football program in one game."

Prince remembers three things about the game.

"We beat 'em," he said. "It was a clean game, no fights, few penalties and the start of the game had to be held up because one of the Hill team's coaches — Charley Affif, the former pro boxer, who was a wine salesman — had to attend a Syrian wedding.

Through the years, Prince, between an occasional double Canadian Club with Coke (ouch!), has done a lot of good for youngsters.

Bob Prince talks a lot about the good things other people do. Tomorrow night at a dinner in his honor, people will talk about the good things Bob Prince has done.

It could be a long show.

Tony Bartirome

Bobby DelGreco

Pittsburgh's Lovable Voice
Prince wrote his own rules

"How sweet it is."

By Beano Cook

TV Sports/Washington Star

September 14, 1975

(Editor's note: It's ironic that this column appeared during Prince's last season as the Pirates' announcer.)

When the Federal Communications Commission took time between reviewing the scripts for "All In The Family" and the different innovative ways the bad guys commit murder in "Hawaii 5-0" to issue a proclamation that all play-by-play announcers must declare to the world that they are hired with the approval of the home team, Bob Prince, the lovable voice of the Pittsburgh Pirates, took the notice in stride.

"I have never denied that I'm for the Pirates," said Prince, whose vocal descriptions make it evident that the opponent rates below Hitler's SS, at least in Prince's opinion. "Ninety-nine percent of my viewers and listeners are Pirate fans. And my style of announcing doesn't bother them.

"I keep hearing that I couldn't do this in New York, but I disagree. I might not start that way, but I could work my way into it. The people who listen to baseball broadcasts are basically for the home team."

The Pirates are practically assured of winning the Eastern Division of the National League for the fifth time in six years. And part of the reason is a Prince gimmick — "babushka power."

"It means grandmother in Polish and Russian," Prince said. "Remember that Pittsburgh is an ethnic community. So on a road trip I mentioned that all the women should come to the next Pirate game in Pittsburgh wearing a babushka. I know that women are the most powerful group of people in the world."

When the Pirates returned from the road trip, ten babushkas had been mailed to Prince. "I knew I had them," Prince said. And he did. Pittsburgh drew 43,000 fans for one game, the largest turnout of the season.

"It's an offensive weapon," Prince pointed out. When Joe Garagiola asked Prince for a demonstration of "babushka power" on national television, Prince waved one. Unfortunately, Cincinnati was at bat and promptly scored eight runs.

"It's devastating," Prince said, "but never again will I demonstrate it when the other team is at bat."

Prince will start his 29th season with the Pirates in 1976, which is an FCC record. "No announcer in the history of baseball has been with one club as long as I have," Prince said. "A few baseball announcers have been around longer, but not with one club."

And doing this nearly three decades, Prince has given more to his listeners than batting averages and the ERA of the starting pitchers. Take 1960.

Pittsburgh won its first pennant in 33 years. And along the way, the Pirates won a game in extra innings, tying the game with three runs in the ninth after two outs. Prince said, "We had 'em all the way. How sweet it is."

Prince doesn't write down his adlibs. "You can't think of things to say," Prince said. "Most expressions just fall in." Apparently comedian Jackie Gleason liked "how sweet it is" so much that he took it for his own routine.

In 1966, Prince came up with the Green Weenie. "It was a hex weapon," Prince said. "It wasn't used as an offensive weapon, just a hex weapon." It was merchandized, and Prince took his share of the royalties and gave them to the widow of Jack Hernon, who was a popular baseball writer for a number of years in Pittsburgh.

Sometimes Prince's phrases get him into trouble. A few years ago, when the opposition got men on base, Prince would yell, "We need a Hoover (a quick double play)." Somebody complained to the FCC about free advertising for Hoover vacuum cleaners so Prince had to change his routine. No problem. Prince went one better. "We need a J. Edgar." But now Prince is back to just Hoover and nobody complains.

Prince describes a ground ball on the artificial turf as a "bug on the rug." He nicknamed the late Don Hoak "Tiger" and has given the name of "Cobra" to outfielder Dave Parker. Prince also delivers messages to shut-ins. "I inherited this idea from the late Rosey Rowswell," Prince said. "I mention 20 or 30 names a game. I also mention towns all the time. The Pirate fans come from towns like Wheeling, West Virginia, Steubenville, Ohio and Clairton, Pennsylvania. I think it's important to the Pirates organization to mention these towns. You better pronounce Monaca and Monessen and Zelionople right. Names are important. Also birthdays. Also saying hello to somebody in the hospital and mentioning an older person who can't come to the game is very important. At least, I feel that way."

Prince never has had the urge to work in New York. "I don't need it," he said. "Everybody hates everybody else in New York. Nobody trusts anybody. That isn't for me."

Like most oldtimers, Prince notices the change in players. However, the biggest difference concerns women. "When I first started announcing, a wife of a player would never think of saying anything to her husband about something I said. Now it happens all

378

ESPN's Beano Cook, KDKA's Bob Pompeani and Dan Edwards, former publicity director of Pittsburgh Steelers who joined Jacksonville Jaguars when that NFL franchise was formed, get together at the Grand Concourse at Station Square.

Norm Vargo of McKeesport Daily News, Joe Gordon of Steelers, and Dave Ailes of Pittsburgh Tribune-Review, enjoy a good time at Gordon's retirement party.

the time. Players come to me and say, 'Bob, my wife said you said this.' I usually ignore it."

When the local newspapers shortened the boxscores to save space, Prince complained repeatedly about it on the baseball broadcasts. The owner of the *Post-Gazette* called Pirates' GM Joe L. Brown and lodged a formal complaint about Prince's criticisms. Brown was warned that if the criticism didn't cease the *Post-Gazette* would cut the space allotted to the Pirates. Newspapers believe in the first amendment, but only for themselves.

Recently Prince entered the hospital for an operation. During his stay he decided on his funeral. "I want to be buried in Three Rivers Stadium," Prince said. "I want the multitudes to have the chance to see me. I want the casket open, so they know I'm in it."

Pittsburgh Pirates

Bob Prince appealed to many women fans, recognizing that "Babushka Power" could help the Pirates.

Bob Prince was never boring...

"We grew up with him."

By Phil Musick
Columnist, The Pittsburgh Press

May 6, 1985

This was written when the Pirates and KDKA called Bob Prince back to the broadcasting booth in May of 1985 to work their games once again:

His voice still sounds as though he'd spent all week gargling nail files. It's still raspy and easily capable of making you feel like his incisors are at work chewing on your inner ear.

His ego is still hitting a solid .350 and when he talks about "the wind being a factor," you're sure that the next time he says it, that you'll be sick all over your shoes.

The nickname is the same as it was when most of us practicing this craft were certain he got it for shooting down objective reporting. The sports jackets remain expensive and the stuff of rainbows. And nobody has ever discovered why he's always paired them with skinny ties that look as though they've been drawn on his shirt with a felt-tip pen.

Sometimes, Friday night, he talked too much; sometimes not enough. And you can hear it in his voice that he continues to be saddened by the fact that he didn't really invent the game.

But, as it has been for as long as most of us can recall, baseball in this town is still a guy with a razorish voice, an Adam's apple you could cut paper with, and a way of saying "we had 'em all the way" that never ceased to make you wonder what time the next day's game began.

Bob Prince returned to the scene of the crime last night at Three Rivers Stadium and everyone in the place stood up at once and beat their hands together until they were pink. By comparison, Gen. Douglas MacArthur making good on his famous promise, "I shall return," was tame stuff.

One of those present even snuffled a bit. For a lot of us, Bob Prince was part of our youth. Like '51 Fords, and Marty Robbins singing about white sport coats and pink carnations, and penny loafers, and lowering your eyes when you asked a girl to go to the drive-in.

We grew up with him. Acquired crabgrass and kids and myopia and pot-bellies. And grew comfortable with him. Maybe it was a love-hate relationship. I never could figure that one out. But he was there on KDKA, had always been there and, we were sure, would always be there. Like that old, soft sweater you put on when the world's trying to take your head off.

A guy named Paul Chidester, who lives in Clarksburg, West Virginia, understands. He's seen maybe three games in 15 years and probably didn't miss that many on the radio when Prince was gabbing about Hoovers and bugs on the rug when he wasn't being maybe the most knowledgeable announcer in baseball.

"He always made it interesting," Paul Chidester has said for years.

A decade ago, the yummies running KDKA at the time didn't think so. Prince and Nellie King got sacked in a manner so ungracious as to be indescribable, other than to say that those who wielded the ax couldn't even have spelled the word style.

A guy sitting around a newspaper office that day, who grew up assured that the smart thing to do was set the radio dial at 1020 and tear the knob off, counted the telephone calls protesting the firings. When his pencil broke, the number was in the vicinity of the one that will be used by the Super Bowl in the 26th Century.

The bill of particulars against Prince and King was never clear, KDKA and Pirate officials coming down with terminal lockjaw. A lot of people in this town never quite forgave either the station or the ball club.

Over the years, the Pirates, as a civic institution, seemed boring. And, whatever the rap against Robert Prince, he was never boring. That was, is, his charm. Incensed. Irritated. Excited. Delighted. Any or all of those. But not bored.

You listened then, you will listen now, because either he made the game sound as thrilling as The Sensuous Couple, or because you could list for co-workers the next morning the crimes against the language and The Grand Old Game that the jerk had committed the night before.

Robert Prince has been a lot of things on local airwaves for a lot of years. Boring wasn't one of them. And probably never will be. It only took a radio station and a baseball team 10 years to figure that out.

When they managed that keen intellectual feat, and when the fans had dwindled to a precious few, they conspired to return him to the broadcasting booth. A pox on them both.

Still, Bob Prince once again has baseball on the lip and we shall be far the better for it.

Nice to have you back, Gunner.

"I'm a lucky bum, getting paid to see what the rest of the people are paying to see."
— Bob Prince

They said goodbye to someone special
Memorial service for Bob Prince

No one was ever a pauper around him.

By Bob Smizik
The Pittsburgh Press

June 17, 1985

All that set it aside from the other bronze tablets in the courtyard of the Westminster Presbyterian Church in Upper St. Clair was a small corsage — a pink and white rose. Beside the flowers the inscription on the 4-inch square tablet read:

> **Prince,**
> **Robert F.**
> **1916-1985**

Beneath the tablet rested the cremated remains of Bob Prince, the flamboyant beloved Pirates announcer, who died Monday.

With a simplicity that was in radical contradiction to his lifestyle, his family, friends and fans said a final goodbye to Prince last night.

The rich, the famous and the unknown were in the crowd of about 700 who attended the 30-minute service conducted by Rev. Laird Stuart.

The Pirates were represented by owners John and Dan Galbreath, General Manager Joe L. Brown, vice president Joe O'Toole and most of the front-office personnel. Former players attending included Dock Ellis, who flew in from Los Angeles, Dick Groat, Bill Virdon, Bob Purkey, Ron Kline, Jim Rooker, Steve Blass and Nellie King, Prince's broadcasting partner for many years.

The list of famous also included Steelers owner Art Rooney, Judge Emil Narick, Pirates minority owner Tom Johnson and many of the heavyweights from the town's three television stations.

The common man was there, too. There were men in shirtsleeves, women in slacks, and Radio Rich, the orphan, now in his 50s, who became almost like a son to Prince.

In a 10-minute eulogy, Stuart called Prince "no saint," but added, "he had a heart as big as center field."

No saint, indeed. He lived a life that would have killed lesser men 20 years ago. He loved a good time and made sure he had one every day.

He was a man of incredible charisma. He was at ease with bank presidents and rookie reporters, and treated both the same — like his best friend.

He was loved by every waiter, doorman, cabbie and bartender he ever met. It was said he did not bother to carry one dollar bills with him. His tips were always five or more.

The last time I saw him, he was dying, but I didn't know it. It was March in Bradenton, Florida. He was sauntering around McKechnie Field in a pair of pants no one else would wear, loafers and, of course, no socks. He was slapping backs, shaking hands, snorting and guffawing at his own stories. He didn't look good — more frail than ever — but, really, he seemed to be on a steady, ever-so-slight decline ever since KDKA ripped out his heart and fired him following the 1975 season.

Always — always — the first question: "How are those kids of yours?"

That was Bob Prince. He remembered the right thing. He came at you from the heart.

Was his heart bigger than centerfield? At least. Even at Forbes Field.

His work with charity, especially the Allegheny Valley School for Exceptional Children, is well known. Lesser known is how he bankrolled Radio Rich through his hard times and how he helped hundreds of others with twenty here, fifty there. Bob Prince's money was meant to be spent — if not by him then by someone else.

There was the time both newspapers in this town has just gone on strike. The last time that happened, the papers were out for four months. Prince cornered two writers in the press lounge at Three Rivers Stadium and asked if they needed interest-free loans.

The offer was refused, the gesture never forgotten.

He was at his best at center stage. He needed only to move into a room to take it over. But he wasn't content with just that.

One time stands out. There was the night in Chicago, after a day game with the Cubs. He insisted on taking a small group, about ten writers and Pirates non-playing personnel, to dinner. Not just any restaurant would do. Prince made reservations at the Pump Room of the Ambassador Hotel — at the time, 1975, just about the classiest place in Chicago. The bill would come to close to $500.

Not even this gesture was enough. There would be no cabs to this dinner. A limousine was ordered. It was no ordinary limo. Half the Pirates team was in front of the hotel when the limo arrived. Prince had promised them something special. The car was about a half a block long and as the driver pulled up in front of the hotel he tooted the horn. It played, "The Colonel Bogey March."

384

Prince snorted, guffawed and slapped backs for five minutes. He got a larger charge out of that than being treated like the Secretary of State when he arrived at the Pump Room 10 minutes later.

Sure, he was the master of the bawdy story. But he could have the manners of a butler in the company of women.

He was one of a kind, an American original, but few of the mourners last night could have pictured Prince in the role Rev. Stuart described him.

Bob Prince, Stuart told the mourners, taught Sunday school classes at Westminster Church. His favorite dealt with the story of David and Goliath. He told it not so much in Biblical terms as in baseball terms. David was a rookie pitcher, an unknown; Goliath a slugger, a combination Babe Ruth and Willie Stargell.

"Heaven only knows how many kids went through our church school and had that old story come to life, indelibly etched in their minds forever because of the way Bob told it," Stuart said.

With Prince's wife Betty and children, Bob and Nancy, seated in the front pew, Stuart said, "He was determined to be Bob Prince. He was determined to be himself. He was beloved — no saint, he'd want that said now — but he was beloved."

A saint? No.

A warm, caring, wonderful, big-hearted gentleman, who gave us thrills and chills and laughs and tears and brought baseball alive for us? Yes.

From Bob Smizik family album

Bob Smizik was on Pirates' beat for The Pittsburgh Press when Chuck Tanner was managing the ballclub in March 4, 1977 spring training session.

When Prince was king

"He made the Pirates part of life on the front porch"

By Tom McMillan

Columnist, Pittsburgh Post-Gazette

June 11, 1985

W e turn back the clock this morning. It is 1971. We have the Pirates. We have the Giants. We have Game Three of the National League championship series.

"Now, Richie Hebner." says the voice in the booth, a jagged voice, popping out over the airwaves. "Well, he gave one — do you suppose he can grab one? How 'bout a ding-a-long? He giveth and he taketh away.

"He hits one out of here now, this would be some kind of pandemonium. And why not?

"Here's the 1-2 pitch from Marichal — and there's a ball hit deep to right field! Back goes Bobby Bonds! And he can't get it! Kiss it goodbye!

"Well, what'd you hear me say? He giveth and he taketh. And he just gave us the lead."

It is a sad morning this morning. We walk to work. We shuffle our feet. A piece of us is missing. Bob Prince is dead.

Bob Prince was as Pittsburgh as the inclines and the streetcar tracks and The Bridge To Nowhere and a pound of chipped chopped ham at Isaly's. He was as Pittsburgh as the orange construction barrels on the Parkway East. Twenty-eight years we listened to him as the Voice of the Pittsburgh Pirates, as the man who said, "That was as close as the fuzz on a tick's ear," as the man who said, "You can kiss it goodbye." Some of us, the lucky ones, grew up with him.

"I've had three or four guys tell me that — they grew up with him," Myron Cope said on his WTAE talk show last night. "It's funny. It's almost like your childhood and Bob Prince were synonymous."

"Eyeball to eyeball, now. Five to five. Right now, Oliver, who's 0-for-3, is in a very key situation. Two on. Two out. And there's a ball hit very deep to right field! Going back! You can kiss it goodbye! Oh, did he plant that little baby!"

The Gunner died at 5:35 p.m. in Presbyterian-University Hospital. He died of complications following cancer surgery. Players and writers and club official-types were hanging around the Pirate dugout at Three Rivers Stadium when the word came down, and there was some silence, some bowed heads, and there were some tears.

"My first reaction is I wish he was around so I could ask him what to do tonight . . . how to react on the air," said Lanny Frattare, the Pirates' play-by-play man. "I've leaned on the man so long. I've looked up to him. I'd like to say, 'Bob, what do I do?' This gives you kind of an empty feeling."

Jack Buck was walking down the corridor from the visitors' dugout to the visitors' clubhouse. Jack Buck is the announcer for the St. Louis Cardinals. Jack Buck is the Bob Prince of St. Louis. "This tears me up," he said. "This makes me cry.

"Bob was a funny guy. I remember the time in St. Louis when he dived out of a hotel window into a pool. He was a character in the nicest sense of the word.

"He would sit there in his undershorts in the booth, eating an apple, reading a book. And he would tell you about the game. He pulled no punches. He knew his stuff!"

The TV stations were going live from Three Rivers Stadium on the 6 o'clock news. One TV station — KDKA — had Joe L. Brown of the Pirates as its guest. Joe L. Brown was the general manager in 1975, when KDKA and the Pirates and the stuffed shirts at Westinghouse Broadcasting said, "We are going to fire Bob Prince." Frattare asked Joe L. Brown last night if firing Prince had been a mistake. "No question," he said. "A flat-out mistake."

"Let's spread some Chicken on the Hill with Will. One on. One out. Here comes Willie the Starg!"

He talked to us. He made the Pirates part of life on the front porch. He would root for double plays ("What we need right here is a Hoover. Everybody think Hoover.") and we would root for two-run rallies ("What we need right here is a bloop and a blast.") One year, in a stroke of genius, or craziness, or both, he invented the Green Weenie.

You could buy a Green Weenie from your favorite Forbes Field vendor. You could shake it, and you could make some serious noise; official Green Weenies had lots of little particles inside. The idea, Bob Prince said, was to shake hundreds and thousands of Green Weenies at the other team's pitcher. He went on the air to warn the pitcher, fair and square, that "The Green Weenie Whammy will getcha."

There's a ground ball to short. Alley. To Maz. To Robertson. We had 'em alllll the way!"

They brought Bob Prince back to the broadcast booth May 3 (1985) at Three Rivers Stadium, and in his first inning — the fourth inning — the soft-hitting Pirates scored nine runs. "It was like a 21-gun salute," Lanny Frattare remembers of that night against the Dodgers. "It was like the ballclub was welcoming him back." But Prince was frail, and weak, and 68 years old, and the cancer was beginning to chew at him. Two games later, on Sunday, May 5, he left the booth for the last time.

"I was hoping, really praying, that there were going to be some more games for him," said Jim Rooker, the former Pirate pitcher, now Frattare's partner on the broadcast team.

387

"It's hard to react to something like this. You're afraid it's going to happen, you know it's going to happen, but you still can't believe it. You're shocked. I was walking off the field today and I was looking up at the booth. I kept thinking I was going to see him there."

Bob Prince gets excited during Bucs' broadcast in '70s at Three Rivers Stadium.

> *"I never take risks I can't handle."*
> — Bob Prince

You thought he'd always be there
Bob Prince was the Pirates

"You don't look tough enough to be a baseball writer."

Phil Musick
Sports Columnist, The Pittsburgh Press

June 12, 1985

I guess he wasn't indestructible after all. I always thought he was. That, somehow, he would always keep at bay the tiger that lived ever at his gate. That he could burn the candle at every possible point, and he did, and that he would still continue to thrive on a lifestyle that would've killed a man 20 years younger in a matter of months. That he was just a shade larger than life and, thus, an inch beyond death. Or, at least, that he would be while I was still around.

He'd always been there, hadn't he?

Didn't he get an autographed Pirates ball when I was 9 and living next door to his mother in Los Angeles? Didn't his mouth fall open years later, when I told him how I'd known him since I was a kid, and he hadn't believed it until I told him his mother's address on Menlo Avenue?

Wasn't he part of my youth, like '51 Fords, and Marty Robbins, and penny loafers, and eight-ball, and breathing hard at the drive-in?

Hadn't he been there the day I got my first big job, covering the Pirates for *The Pittsburgh Press*. And he'd laughed and said, "You don't look tough enough to be a baseball writer." And I had grinned back and said, "I'm tougher than I look," and he'd spent the 1969 season toughening me up, anyway?

Hadn't we shared a dozen daises at banquets, me playing Sancho Panza to his Don Quixote? "You forgot to acknowledge so-and-so" . . . "Don't worry, Kid, I'll get him up later for a bow."

Hadn't I fed him cue cards and slurped down half of his screwdrivers while he held the Dapper Dan banquet right there in the palm of his hand? Or needled him unmercifully while co-hosting the Curbstone Coaches luncheons, because it was the only way I could get a laugh and he could get a million just by standing there and scanning the audience with that crooked, lusty smile.

Yeah, he's dead. But nobody gets off this earth alive and, he took a lot of killing and he'd like that. And, as Frank Sinatra sings, he did it his way. I never saw him when he wasn't having a good time and when that was happening hadn't galvanized around him, so that he got to spend his whole life at center stage. And he wasn't a guy for the wings.

So, let's call a halt to the laments, the eulogies that painted a different guy from the one I knew, and I knew him for years. Let's put a period behind all the contrived utterances that made a saint out of him, when he was as much a sinner as most, and hearing them would've surely made him snicker out loud.

Instead, let's remember something a friend of Roberto Clemente, Phil Dorsey, said after the Pirates star died, "He wasn't all angel and he wasn't all devil . . . but I'd like it to be remembered that he was a lot more of the one than the other."

So, sing no sad songs this day for Rapid Robert Prince.

For 68 years, he held life by the throat and wrung every last drop from it. He was a swashbuckler, and he liked being one. Like the rest of us, he had some vices. The difference, I always thought, is that his were more interesting than most. So were his virtues, and he had his share.

One of them was pure generosity — with his time, his money, himself. Another was that indefinable stuff called class. Some broadcasting people, who couldn't have picked up his Jockey shorts with two hands, misused him 10 years ago. When they fired him and took the heart out of him, and when he could've put his foot down on their necks without appearing churlish — because he had that capacity — he never said a word. Style, they call it. Grace.

Best thing I ever heard about him was said by one of his broadcasting partners, Nellie King. Their personalities were polarized. Prince, garrulous and a lover of any old spotlight at all; King, sensitive and restrained. One night Bob got outside one too many glasses of orange juice and his ego was unleashed. In truth, he became tiresome.

Nellie King looked at him and said, "Bob, you know, you don't need all that B.S. You're a hell of a guy without it."

So he was. For a very long time in this town, no one will say the name "Bob" without triggering one memory or the other of a man named Prince.

Anyone who wants to pay him honor, go out and hoist a glass of orange juice for him. Remember how deeply he is ingrained in the fabric of his town. Tell a ribald story. Make someone laugh. Have fun. Recall him with the affection he richly deserves and will get for as long as any of us is still around.

Come to think of it, maybe he was indestructible, after all.

Prince on national pride...
"During the playing of the National Anthem, you will not talk to me. You stand at attention, look out at the flag and think of your country. If you don't think of that, at least LOOK like you're doing that!"

Helping a new guy on the baseball beat

Prince lived up to his name

"You want a good story."

By Dave Ailes
Sports Editor
The Tribune-Review

June 12, 1985

Shed no tears for Bob Prince. The Gunner milked a minimum of 26 hours out of every day, squeezing at least two average life-times into his 68 years. The Almighty didn't cheat the spindly-legged, perpetual-motion sports announcer out of a single second.

He dressed loud. Talked loud. Collected friends the way J. Paul Getty collected long green.

He smoked too much. Drank too much. Stayed up too late too many nights as a center-stage attraction wherever he went. He was one of those rare individuals who, without really trying, dominated every situation, every setting.

More than an announcer, he was an entertainer — one of the most sought-after banquet speakers, especially at stag events where his blue language was uproariously funny rather than offensive.

"He didn't have an act," said Nellie King, who shared a booth and microphone with The Gunner for nine seasons. "He was himself, on the air and off. Bob was a little crazy sometimes, and always uninhibited."

The Gunner paid for his excesses, the way we all do. But it's a good bet that if you asked him, on his death bed, if he regretted burning a Cathedral full of candles on both ends, he'd wink, and say, "Good buddy, I loved every $%# minute of it."

Each of us whose lives he touched has a personal story about him. Mine unfolded one pleasant morning at Pirate City in Florida. It was my first year at spring training, first day as a reporter of a Chuck Tanner major league team. Such a setting can be intimidating when you barely know the difference between Richie Hebner and Enrique Romo.

Prince walked up, shouting good-natured insults at a couple of his friends, then plopped down next to me on a bench behind the training camp locker room. "You want a *good* story, something that has nothing to do with balls and strikes?" he asked. "Stay right here."

Prince, slapping backs as he went, wheeled into the locker room. A minute later, he reappeared, his arm around Tanner's shoulders.

Prince implored Tanner to talk about the old days . . . when the manager had a reputation for breaking furniture, long before he became "Mr. Sunshine." Tanner was a hellion. With Prince egging him on, laughing all the while, Tanner told about the time he kicked over a tall locker after his first Quad Cities team (Midwest League) lost a close one. He slapped a player with a $50 fine for leaving his baseball spikes on the bench in front of his cubicle.

"I was a madman, not a manager," Tanner said. He and his coaches used to crawl up fire escapes and peek in hotel windows when they made bed checks on the road. Each story had a punch line and Tanner, with Prince's help, spiced them up as they went . . . like the time he sneaked back into a corner of the dugout after getting ejected from the game by an ump. The session lasted nearly an hour, producing the funniest and most interesting story of spring training. Prince did it for me, a nobody who, as far as he knew, was writing for a Podunk weekly. His was a gesture I'll never forget.

More than his kindness and treatment of everyone as an equal, I'll always remember Bob Prince as one of the most colorful men in sports. He was a fun guy who never took himself or baseball too seriously. He loved the game, but always kept his sense of humor about it. Owning a large ego that he jealously protected, Prince had faults. Human failings. He also had a special gift of gab, an unrivaled raconteur.

Sports needs more truly unique individuals like Bob Prince. He'll be missed by fans, players and media alike. With true affection, we kiss you goodbye, Bob.

Pittsburgh Pirates

Chuck Tanner, congratulating Kent Tekulve for coming through in relief, helped Dave Ailes get off to a good start at spring training at Pirate City.

Did Prince Have Idea His Days On Earth Were Already Numbered?

"We're the last of the dinosaurs."

By Norm Vargo
Sports Editor, Daily News, McKeesport, Pa.

June 11, 1985

Just a few months ago — on the cold, snowy night of January 31, to be specific — Bob Prince showed up at the Thompson Run Athletic Association, late as usual for his annual toastmaster duties which had become a tradition for the West Mifflin organization's always sold-out sports night.

Somehow, something was missing. The inimitable Prince's entrance didn't have its usual flair. In fact, a skinny, haggard Prince was rather subdued as he greeted friends, well-wishers and celebrities who would be honored that evening.

Bob Prince just wasn't Bob Prince, but the show went on to keep the tradition going. It was the 23rd consecutive appearance by Prince at the West Mifflin fete.

Afterwards, sportscaster Myron Cope — who played straight man for Prince's jokes that evening for what must have been the umpteenth time during their long friendship — remarked, "Prince just doesn't look good. I'm worried."

And it wasn't long after that the storied "Gunner" sought out this writer, another long-time friend. "We're the last of the dinosaurs," Prince chuckled. "You know that, don't you?"

Prince talked, more than usual. About his dream of returning to the Pirates broadcasting team, back to the job from which he had been so unceremoniously fired almost a decade earlier.

"You know, I'd give anything to be back in baseball . . . with the Pirates," Prince confided between sips of a screwdriver, the mixed drink with which he became synonymous.

A few months later, on April 18, Prince's dream came true. He returned to the Bucs' broadcasting team. A dream, short-lived that it was, did come true as Prince waged a difficult battle with throat cancer.

Bob Prince could deal with the situation. He always could.

But Prince's parting comment as he left the Thompson Club last January told a story, in retrospect. "Norm, this is the last time I'll be back here . . . so long, buddy."

Many overheard the remark. None gathered the significance.

Did Bob Prince know his days were numbered, even then?

Prince, 68, the voice of the Pirates for nearly three decades and one of baseball's best known play-by-play broadcasters, died Monday of complications following cancer surgery.

Nicknamed "The Gunner" for his rapid-fire delivery, Prince became a Pittsburgh tradition, renowned for his unabashed rooting, colorful colloquialisms and his equally loud sports jackets.

"To many, Bob Prince was more than just the voice of the Pirates. He was the Pirates," said Joe L. Brown, the Pirates' interim general manager. "There is no doubt he was one of the great sports announcers of all time."

Brown referred to Prince as a "person person." A guy who was also concerned with the welfare of others, many of whom he helped down through the years. He was active in charity fundraisers, mainly for the Allegheny Valley School. Often, he requested that his honorariums be donated to the school.

"You've given me back the only thing I love in the world, besides my family," Prince said during a news conference announcing his rehiring.

Honored on "Bob Prince Night" at Three Rivers Stadium on May 3, Prince was able to take part in only three game broadcasts because of his health problems.

He reported to Three Rivers Stadium on May 17 for a Pirates-Cincinnati Reds game, but became ill while enduring a 2 1/2-hour rain delay and returned to his home. He was readmitted to Presbyterian-University Hospital three days later for dehydration and pneumonia in both lungs and doctors decided to stop his radiation treatments.

A moment of silence was held in honor of Prince before Monday night's Pirates-St. Louis Cardinals game. A memorial service will be held at 7 p.m. Sunday at Westminster Presbyterian Church in suburban Upper St. Clair.

Prince waved colorful black-and-gold scarves called babushkas and shook Green Weenies, plastic noisemakers which he claimed brought good luck, to boost the team he referred to as "My Bucs."

He invented nicknames for many players, "Cobra" for Dave Parker and "The Great One" for Roberto Clemente. And he once had to pay an $800 bill when he promised to buy chicken for all at Willie Stargell's restaurant if the slugger hit a home run — and Stargell did just that.

Prince gleefully screamed, "We Had 'Em All The Way" after a Pirates victory and often rooted for a "Hoover" (double play) or a "bug on the rug" (a ground ball double).

He once attributed his success to a gift for gab.

"Whatever you call it — glib — or whatever. I was born with it," Prince said.

Prince often ignored the game action on the field, or only casually mentioned it, in order to spin stories and tell anecdotes. It was this incessant story-telling that led KDKA executives, with the approval of the Pirates and the Pittsburgh Brewing Company, to unexpectedly oust Prince and broadcast partner Nellie King on Oct. 28, 1975.

"There is no doubt about it now, 10 years later," Brown said, "it was a colossal mistake to fire Bob Prince. It was a flat-out mistake."

Prince, who often called himself "a Pittsburgh guy," joined the Houston Astros' broadcast team in 1976 and was the first play-by-play announcer when ABC-TV debuted Monday Night Baseball that year. But he seemed out of his element when he couldn't root for the Pirates and returned to Pittsburgh at the end of the season to launch a free-lance career. It's hard to accept Bob Prince's death, even though it appeared inevitable to those closest to "The Gunner."

"I just can't put Bob's death into perspective...," said an emotional Dick Groat, the former Pirates shortstop, when contacted last night. "I can't imagine Pittsburgh, and baseball, without Bob Prince."

Bob Skinner, who along with Groat was a member of the Pirates' 1960 World Series championship team and is now the Bucs hitting coach, said, "Yes, it is a shock. We all knew Bob was real sick, but he's always been such a fighter against the odds, we expected him to pull through. Baseball just won't be the same without Bob Prince..."

Everybody has "Gunner" stories to tell. Mine deals with a caustic, very critical column about Prince doing a telecast of a Penguins-Rangers hockey game from Madison Square Garden in New York. Prince was out of his element that night.

"We have the puck, they have it, we have it, and, uh, I don't know the guy, shoots," Prince went on, obviously unprepared for doing a play-by-play account of a game, any game.

In short, the column criticized Prince for his shortcomings, and advised strongly he find a job doing baseball. A "natural" for baseball, Prince — who used to do the old Pittsburgh Hornets hockey games from the Duquesne Gardens — had slipped miserably.

Naturally, Prince heard about the column. His wife, Betty, was upset. It wasn't too long afterward that Prince came to the Thompson Club sports night. Darrell Hess, the dinner committee chairman, whispered in my ear, "better watch out, Prince is gunning for you."

Okay. Prince got up to the microphone as the program began that night and stared at me in my seat just off to his side. He continued to stare, and then pointed. I was admittedly uneasy.

"See that guy?" he began. "He ripped me a new butt in his column. And you know what? I deserved it . . . he was telling me something that only a friend would have nerve enough to say. That column made me take another look at myself. Thank you."

What a relief. But that was Bob Prince.

> *"I did a lot of banquets with Bob Prince. I had some fun experiences with Bob, as did everyone who was ever with him."*
> — Jim Meston, humorist

"The Gunner" Was On Target At Thompson Club
He made it a big banquet

"Prince stood behind his word."

By Darrell Hess
Sports Columnist, The Valley Mirror

June 20, 1985

The Gunner was special to me. . . "Bob Prince is dead." It was only fitting that I should be told of his death while I was preparing for a high school banquet at the Thompson Club. For I had met Bob Prince for the first time at the same club 25 years earlier. A relationship was formed that continued until he was struck down with cancer.

I often thought of that first meeting. The Thompson Club Sports Night banquet was sold out for the first time in its fifth year of existence because he was headlining it.

The Pirates had won the 1960 World Series in October. Dick Groat was the National League MVP and he was coming. Steelers linebacker John Reger would be there. And the "Voice of the Pirates" was making his first appearance in the West Mifflin area.

The Lowell Smith Agency handled the arrangements and I was told that the Pirates highlights film would be brought to the banquet. Naturally, I was a nervous wreck when the banquet started at 6:30 with three empty chairs at the head table — no Prince, no Groat, no Reger. At 7:30 p.m., just as dessert finished, the threesome arrived. After the usual exchange of greetings, I asked Prince where the Pirates World Series films were.

"I don't know anything about movies," The Gunner replied.

"Well," I said, "we advertised the Pirates and World Series films would be shown and I have a sellout crowd in there that's going to be disappointed."

Prince replied, "Somebody made a mistake, but don't worry about it. I can handle the crowd."

In his opening remarks, Prince apologized for the oversight of the films. "Don't blame Hess," he said. "I'll get the films and a projectionist out here another time and there won't be a penny charge."

After an evening of laughs and sports stories, Prince left. He had a basketball game to do at Ohio State the next night. I called the Smith Agency the next morning to tell them of the film oversight and to see what could be done. "Bob Prince was already here this morning," the person at the Smith Agency told me. "Tell us when you want the films and you have them." Prince stood behind his word.

Bob Prince was special to a lot of people. I liked him because he treated everyone the same. He respected me — the chairman of a little sports banquet in West Mifflin — just as much as the chairman of the Dapper Dan, or a much larger banquet in Erie, or Naples, Florida.

It didn't matter to Bob Prince whether you lived in Mt. Lebanon or Munhall, or whether you belonged to the Duquesne Club, the PAA, the St. Clair Country Club, the Thompson Club or the Homestead Elks. He made you feel important. And you were important to him.

Bob Chopnak and I were at Oakmont when the U.S. Open Tournament was held there a few years back. Rain came and we sought shelter in the clubhouse and finally moved into the locker room. The Gunner was seated there with Stan Musial.

He called us to his table. "Sit down," he said, then added, "Stan, this guy runs the funniest banquet in America. Maybe someday he'll invite you."

I'm sure Ruth and Ken Mayher, of the Duquesne Golf Club, recalled the evening Bob and I stopped in after an Iron City Huddle at the Homeville Fire Hall. Bob chatted with the young couple for at least an hour, discussing everything from his experiences as a son of an Army officer to the challenges of marriage.

Bob visited the Duquesne Golf Club a number of times, serving as emcee for its Sports Day. His answer each year to my invitation was the same, "I'm tied up that afternoon for golf, but if you need me for the dinner, I'll be there."

The Boy Scouts of the East Valley Area needed a luncheon speaker and I was asked to get Prince. Bob was in Florida at the time and I called him there. "When are you coming back?" I asked. "April 10," Bob replied. "What do you want?"

"The Boy Scouts need a luncheon speaker on April 11, so I guess you can't be there. It's the day after you get back and I'm sure you'll be busy."

"I'll be there," Prince said.

"Wait," I said. "There's no speaker's fee involved."

"It's for the Boy Scouts, isn't it?" Prince came back. "I don't want any money." Prince was there, as promised.

Bob Prince served as emcee of the Thompson Club Sports Night for 23 consecutive years. He made it an annual sellout. After his first two years at the club, he asked me to deal directly with him rather than the booking agency.

From that day on, money was never mentioned when the banquet arrangements were being made. Whatever we decided to pay him was okay. I found out later he gave most of his speaking fees to charity.

He told me many times he would do the Thompson Club banquet without charge because he liked the people there and he could "let his hair down." As time went on, Prince would fly up from Florida to do the banquet and the Dapper Dan banquet in the same stretch.

Yes, The Gunner was special to me. And he was special to so many, many people. That's why there will be a permanent void at the Thompson Club banquets and all the other banquets in the Pittsburgh area in the future.

Bob Prince will be inducted into the Pennsylvania Sports Hall of Fame at the Sheraton Hotel in Station Square in November. He belongs there. And he belongs in Cooperstown. So long, Gunner. Thanks for everything.

Thompson Run A.A.

Bob Prince holds forth at January, 1977 edition of the Thompson Run A.A. Sports Night banquet where Hall of Famer Sam Huff was among those who paid tribute to Andy Russell, another top linebacker, upon his retirement from Pittsburgh Steelers.

Toastmaster Bob Prince is flanked by two former great relief pitchers of the Pirates, Kent Tekulve and ElRoy Face.

Bob Prince yuks it up with Jim Flanagan, the Pitt-Green Bay Packers star from West Mifflin, and humorist Jack Henry at January, 1967 edition of Thompson Run A.A. Sports Night.

Winning one for The Gunner
Thrilling Pirates game brings back memories of that voice

"The man who drew me to baseball"

By Mary Anne Lewis
Free-lance writer/KDKA Radio talk show host

July 19, 1997

How many other kids listened to Bob Prince until the wee hours of summer mornings in 1970, 1971 and 1972? Those years marked the beginning of the end of an era for Major League Baseball: an era remembered for cheap seats, old-fashioned pinstripe uniforms and colorful radio announcers whose signature antics and phraseology left a permanent mark on the history of the teams that employed them.

But it was the beginning of an era for young baseball fans like me, too young to have remembered Bill Mazeroski's fabled home run in 1960, but old enough to have possessed their own AM transistor radios, hoping against hope that some night history would repeat itself in a game that would forever be remembered.

It never really happened. But something about last Saturday's no-hitter (the combined no-hitter by Francisco Cordova and Ricardo Rincon against the Houston Astros) came close, transporting me back to the days when baseball really seemed as American as apple pie, and the Pirates were a team known for coming through in the clutch.

Cliches like that were the province of Prince, "The Gunner," the man who drew me and countless others not only to baseball, but to the magic of radio. The folksy raconteur possessed the power to create a theater of the mind as wide and deep as the newly opened Three Rivers Stadium.

Last Saturday was my 37th birthday and, like thousands of others in the region, I seriously considered attending the game between the Pirates and the Houston Astros, a game that turned out to be the first ever extra-inning combined no hitter.

But reports of a sold-out game, the Pirates' first two scoreless losses in the series with Houston, and the fact that I had to work all night prompted me to stay home and listen on the radio. I had talked myself into doing the "sensible" thing, to my regret later.

At midnight, I had the privilege of once again sitting in the KDKA "air chair," for the weekend overnight shift, to hash over the victory and to hear fans express an excitement I haven't heard for 25 years. The first caller claimed to have caught Mark Smith's home run, and it went on from there.

During the course of the six-hour program, I had much chance to reflect on the miraculous nature of baseball recounted in theatrical productions from "Damn Yankees" to "The Natural." I also had cause to reflect on Prince, and the era that brought him fame and a loyal following.

"Prince had no inhibitions about kidding players of a different race."

In the days before free agency, Bob Prince worked hard to create enthusiasm for a bunch of players who were generally out-of-shape and not earning a great deal of money. The current Pirates announcers do a fine job with play-by-play, copious statistics and tough questions for coaches and players. They obviously have fun at their job.

But it's impossible for anyone on the air to recapture the spirit of a game before it was taken so seriously by so many people. Sure, the fans were serious about baseball, and so was everybody on the field. But the game didn't generate much controversy outside the sports pages. And nobody was tremendously concerned about tax money being spent to support the game.

Back then, racism in sports wasn't discussed much — and neither was salary. Both were undoubtedly an issue to players. One sports magazine ran a story about catcher Manny Sanguillen's troubles on the road in a southern town, where he was unable to rent a room to share with his white wife. The same story noted Sanguillen was earning about $35,000 a year.

Prince, though, had no inhibitions about kidding players of a different race. Today, his favorite bromide about Willie Stargell spreading "chicken on the hill" might easily be construed as racist. Back then, most people simply smiled about Stargell's prolific ability to smack home runs into the upper decks.

For me, the magic of baseball started to fade after the 1972 season. First, the Pirates lost the pennant on that awful wild pitch from Bob Moose. I cried that day. I cried harder a few months later, when Roberto Clemente died in a plane crash off the coast of Puerto Rico.

Teen-age concerns eventually overshadowed the fate of the Pirates in those years for me. The Bucs seemed to falter, Prince lost his job in 1975, someone threw a battery at Dave Parker in the outfield in 1978 after he signed a $1 million contract.

During the course of his career with the Pirates, which started in 1948, Bob Prince taught a lot of people a lot of lessons. Only as an adult professional in broadcasting can I appreciate his ability to spin colorful tales and educate at the same time.

Any pitch narrowly missing the strike zone was off by "a gnat's eyelash," one of Prince's more powerful and easily remembered metaphors. He also invented the "Green Weenie" to engender fan support, a forerunner of the Steelers' "Terrible Towel." But one of my callers Sunday morning noted that Prince expanded his young fans' vocabularies with phrases that sounded rather stuffy: "sartorial splendor" and "inclement weather." Callers were also using words that aren't often used in the same sentence with baseball anymore — words like innocence, honor and humility.

The Gunner was smiling

Some callers wondered whether divine intervention was at work on the night the Pirates drew the largest regular-season crowd to the stadium in 20 years. What kind of message does a game like Saturday night's send to baseball team owners and players?

There was much discussion of what to do about a new stadium, as well as the Pirates' future for the rest of the season and the rest of the century. Wouldn't it have been nicer to see the same game in an intimate setting similar to Camden Yards? Or, do we really need a new stadium if we can sell it out in the middle of the season? Would Kevin McClatchy *really* move or sell the team with a 110-year history in this town?

It's tough to speculate what Bob Prince, who died in 1985, might have to say on any of these issues. But it's not too difficult to imagine the good words he might have shared about the game itself.

From the Jackie Robinson tribute to the fireworks and the postgame show, the airwaves would have exploded with Prince-isms, all designed to draw a fan into the excitement over witnessing a piece of Pirates history — even if it was only on the radio. You had to know that wherever he is, the Gunner was smiling. And, as far as divine intervention is concerned, we can only hope he has a little influence.

"Calling a game with cold dispassion is a cinch. You can sit on your can, reporting grounders and two-base hits lackadasically. You've got no responsibilities. But rooting is tough. It requires creativeness. It also fulfills your function, which is to shill. You are the arm of the home club who is there to make the listener happy."
— Bob Prince

They were the best of times...
these are the worst

By Vic Ketchman

Sports columnist, Standard-Observer

June 12, 1985

As each bad day brings more bad times for the Pirates, the man in his mid-30s reaches back a little harder for his fondest memories. Today, they own the worst record in baseball. Twenty-five springs ago they had the best.

It was baseball as it will never be again in Pittsburgh. The 1960 season was life at its best in these parts. The river towns were alive with soot. Everyone had work. There was prosperity. And the nine-year-old boy who, for the very first time would follow closely and emotionally the fate of a baseball team, would have a summer to remember for the rest of his life.

He would have a summer so great in drama and spirit he will tell its tale to his grandchildren. Some day he may say: "We had a baseball team here in 1960..."

We had a team of destiny then. We had a team in a charming old ballpark that was the stage for great players, and for those who were only playing great because something drove them to that end that particular summer.

And, we had Bob Prince 25 springs ago.

Prince's body died Monday. His presence was laid to rest 10 years ago. But his spirit will live forever in our memories of 1960.

Somehow, it will always seem that Prince contrived the whole drama in 1960. Actually, he was only the right man in the right place at the right time, seizing the moment to win over Pirate fandom. He was "Beat 'Em Bucs" and "We had 'em all the way," and exuded the kind of wild and crazy spirit that embodied the '60 team.

Prince was personality. He was not cast in the corporate image that is so popular today. He worried not about making a mistake. He tried to hit home runs. He tried hard to sell baseball and the Pirates. He was outrageous. He was fun. He never took himself too seriously. He made you laugh and he made you cry...for your favorite team. He made the Pirates a religion in 1960. And, for the nine-year-old boy, Prince was God.

Ironically, the fondest memory of Prince was the day he was anything but God. On a cold and windy day in Chicago's Wrigley Field, in the ninth inning of a crucial day in the 1970 pennant race, Prince would commit his greatest gaffe.

Pirate centerfielder Matty Alou was trotting under a fly ball that surely would be the final out in a big win. Attempting to seize the moment, Prince came forth with: "It's a can of corn...golden bantam."

402

Then, all of a sudden, Alou's step quickened as the Wrigley wind began to knock the ball down. Alou was in full gallop when the ball fell to earth. "My God, he dropped it!" Prince said in almost the same breath in which he was describing the short fly as an easy catch. The Pirates went on to lose the game.

Some hated Prince for feeling a need to be outrageous . . . to pursue greatness. But most appreciated Prince for what he and his sport were meant to be: entertainment.

The eulogies come many now. The best is by the fans: "I grew up with Bob Prince." And, we did. It is the greatest tribute that can be paid him. We reserve in our time on this earth a place for him. He was a big part of our lives, especially for the boy with the transistor radio under the bed covers, where the temperature on a steamy July night soaked the sheets, but the Pirates were playing on the Coast and if you wanted to listen into the early-morning hours, you didn't dare let mom or dad hear Prince kiss one goodbye.

Yes, the best eulogies come from his fans. Certainly, they don't come from within the Pirates who, for all intents and purposes, killed this man 10 years ago when they took away his very soul. Ironically, they killed themselves, too.

Listening to Joe Brown speak in eulogy rings a bit hollow, for ten years ago Brown allowed Prince to be fired. Don't blame it on a wayward radio executive named Edward Wallis. It was a combined effort by the Pirates and KDKA. Shame on them for not having enough foresight between themselves to see they were severing the very blood line that had existed between themselves and the Pittsburgh community. Shame on them for having deprived us of Prince's final years. Shame on them for having taken away the tradition that signed on for each game with, "It's Pirates baseball time . . . the first three innings are brought to you by Iron City beer..."

So now it has come to pass. This is not 1960. Everything is in sharp contrast. It was the best of times. These are the worst of times.

We have not a team of destiny. We are without spirit or slogan. No nine-year-old boy in his right mind hides a radio under the covers. No one's quite sure if the team will even be here next year. We've come full circle. Only Joe Brown remains. Imagine his hurt.

"I grew up with Bob Prince. I started following the Bucs in 1948 with Bob and Rosey Rowswell. I met Bob and Jim Woods when I was a student at Florida Southern and the Pirates were playing the Tigers in Lakeland. Every time I saw Prince after that he remembered me and where we met."
— Rich Corson, McMurray, Pa.

Prince inspires a young Virginian
Bob turned fan into a poet

"Bob Prince brought the game to life."

By Dave Crawley
KDKA-TV Feature Reporter

April 24, 1998

My career in broadcasting — the very fact that I now work for KDKA — is due in large part to a man I never met. I first began listening to Bob Prince early in the Pirates' magical 1960 season — having found him by accident while searching the radio dial for baseball games.

I was 13 years old, living in Hampton, Virginia, and had never been to Pittsburgh. But my old neighbor down the street was a Pirates fan and, lacking a local team to cheer for, I became one, too. It was the first year I followed baseball, and will always be the best.

Despite the miles between us, I was able to pick up KDKA's signal at night. I loved listening to the rumbly growl of Bob Prince and his sidekick, Jim Woods. Bob Prince brought the game to life. The mental images he created could never be matched by televised reality.

We moved to Alaska the following year (my dad was an Air Force man), and I never heard Bob Prince again. But his catch phrases of years ago still ring clear in my mind. "How sweet it is!" "We had 'em all the way!" "Kiss it goodbye!" And, of course, "Arriba! Arriba!"

I had envisioned a career as a newspaper reporter until I heard Bob Prince. But listening to his broadcasts throughout that wonderful season (I followed the west coast games with the radio under my pillow so my mother wouldn't know I was staying up so late) turned me in the direction of broadcasting.

My initial inclination, to be a sportscaster like my idol, later gave way to feature reporting. I'm glad it did, because the ballplayers of today would never measure up to my idealized images of childhood. But it was Bob Prince who started me on my career path, without ever knowing it. I wonder how many others he might have affected in the same way.

Thanks to Bob Prince, the players and critical moments during that 1960 season have crystallized in my mind. I remember the night a Pirates runner was called out on a questionable play at the plate in the bottom of the ninth. Instead of tying the game, it was the final out. Pirate players stormed out of the dugout, prompting Jim Woods to say "the Bucs are really mad!" To which Bob Prince replied, "I'm mad, too!"

Bob Prince was clearly biased in favor of his team — and I loved it. I became a much bigger fan than the neighbor who had gotten me interested in the first place. Far from a city I would not visit until much later, I heard Bob Prince talk about a home run ball traveling so far it would land in the Monongahela River. The way he savored each delicious syllable, he made that river, and so much else in Pittsburgh, seem like magic.

We listened to the seventh game of the 1960 World Series on the radio in algebra class. I believe Chuck Thompson had the honor of announcing Bill Mazeroski's historic shot. I must have jumped five feet into the air — at which point the teacher told me I had just earned an unsatisfactory citizenship mark on my report card. I could not have cared less. I knew that the glow of that moment would linger in my mind long after that mark was forgotten (to this day, I'm not certain if the teacher really followed through on that threat).

The season that culminated in Maz's home run led to my first foray into journalism. I wrote a poem about that seventh game (with Bob Prince announcing, of course) and sent it to the Newport News, *Virginia Daily Press.* To my surprise, columnist Charles Karmosky printed the entire 13 stanza poem in his column! It was, and still is, one of my most exciting moments.

Perhaps it was inevitable that, years later, I would come to Pittsburgh and work at the very station that Bob Prince brought to life for me so many years ago. Those legendary call letters still have a special magic for me, as I remember Bob Prince announcing them across the miles on summer nights of distant memory.

I came to KDKA in 1988, a couple of years after Bob Prince passed away. It was because of him that I first became published as a journalist. It was because of him that I decided to become a broadcaster. In some measure, it is because of him that I now find myself at KDKA.

I only wish I had the chance to thank him.

AN ODE TO THE BUCS

As it appeared in the column by Charles Karmosky:

Tribute will be paid to the Pittsburgh Pirates in a thousand ways from now and as long as baseball history is written, and it's a good bet their thrilling conquest of the New York Yankees already has or will find its expression in verse, but we haven't seen any yet, so it's with a great deal of pleasure that today we turn this corner over to the youngest (we think) poet laureate of the Buccaneers. Quite appropriately, since the Bucs' World Series win was such an upsetting affair to some people, something like David slaying Goliath, our poem today was composed by little David, a 13-year-old better known to his friends and neighbors on Yorkshire Terrace as David A. Crawley.

Tis a sad and gloomy day in Pitt
The Bucs trail, seven-five,
As they try to win their first World Series
Since nineteen-twenty-five.

The Pittsburgh Pirates led the Series
Three games to two, you see,
But the Yankees won the next game
To tie it, three to three.

Pitt won the Series, in '25
And hadn't won it since.
To broadcast this important game
Is our old friend, Bob Prince.

"It looks pretty bad for the Pirates
In the Smoky City,
If they should lose the Series now
It sure would be a pity.

"There's two on, one out, in the last
Of inning number eight
And clean-up hitter Rocky Nelson
Strides up to the plate.

"Rocky Nelson hits a fly to left.
The fans all give a shout.
But Yogi Berra makes the catch.
And now two men are out.

"Bob Clemente hits a grounder
Which he beats out for a hit,
And the New York Yankees' pitcher
Is about to have a fit.

"A run just scored, it's seven to six
Hal Smith is at the plate;
He'd like to knock the very next pitch
Out of Pennsylvania State.

"There's a long, high drive into deep left field.
He's really tagged the ball;
She's going, she's going, just kiss it good-bye!
It's o'er the left field wall!

"For the New York Yankees in the ninth
It then was do or die,
But the New York Yankees bounced right back
With two big runs to tie.

"The Bucs will win the ball game now
If they can only score.
If they do not they'll have to play
An extra inning more.

"Up to the plate steps Mazeroski
With all his might and brawn;
He gives that ball a mighty whack
She's going, she's going, she's gone!

"Mazeroski rounds the bases
Amid the mighty cheers.
The Bucs are now WORLD CHAMPIONS!
It's been thirty-five long years."

Sports editor's note: Our thanks and congratulations go to young David who happens to be an eighth-grader at Jefferson Davis Junior High, and next time, David don't hesitate or wait so long. Certainly don't wait as long as the Pirates did to come through, "thirty-five long years."

Pittsburgh Pirates

Bob Prince, Jim Woods and staff fill Forbes Field broadcast booth in early '60s.

My memories of Bob Prince

He was a very special man.

By Sally O'Leary

Assistant Director of Public Relations (1964-1996)
Retired, Cranberry Township, Pa.

May 1, 1998

I grew up a baseball fan, listening to games on the radio in Sheffield, up in northwestern Pennsylvania. My mother was a great fan and really got me interested in the game. Growing up in a small town like that, I certainly never dreamed of going to the big city and working for a major league baseball club. But fate has a way of directing you.

I first met Bob Prince when I was working for an advertising agency, Fuller, Smith & Ross. Mellon Bank was one of our clients, and they were a sponsor of the Pirate games at the time. I was in charge of trafficking commercials, and my name was on the commercial scripts as a contact for any problem. That prompted Bob to call me one day and we became great friends.

He knew of my interest in baseball, and my desire to work for the Pirates some day. He kept telling me that some day there would be an opening and he would see that I got an interview. I had written letters a few times to the sports teams in the city, seeking employment, but always got the form letter back that there were no openings, however, they would keep my name on file.

In early May of 1964, I heard that the young lady who had the secretarial position in Public Relations at the Pirates was leaving. Before I could do anything, Bob called to tell me that he had arranged an interview for me with Jack Berger, who was the PR director at the time. He also told me that if I got the job he knew the ball club would never pay enough for me to leave my position at the advertising agency. But, if I would be his baseball secretary, he offered to pay me year-round to supplement the salary so I could afford to make the move.

I had my interview in the stands at Forbes Field on a Saturday afternoon and the following Monday was told that I was hired, to start on May 24. Thanks to Bob this all developed and I think Bob was my personal PR man! He would use my name on the baseball broadcasts so often, as his "Gal Friday," that even today, many people who meet me for the first time remember my name from those days at the Pirates.

Not only did I do the baseball fan mail for Bob, but he very often would pose a statistics question on the air, and know that I would somehow look up the answer and get word to him in the broadcast booth. I had the private phone numbers of all the booths in the National League, so I could reach him if necessary. Notes that were prepared for the press in those early days were not as copious as they are today and Bob depended on someone to be on top of things for him. That was good for me because it forced me to keep track of records that might be set or broken. And it made him look good on the air to have up-to-date information.

His scorecards were a work of art. You could look at one of them years later and recall the entire game. He had simple ways of keeping score and yet could detail plays that read like a book.

Bob's generosity was well known. He had a sympathetic ear to anyone who would approach him and there are many people who experienced his generosity in one way or another. For several years, he paid for my vacation each year. It was first class airplane seats and good hotels, wherever I chose to go. It was quite often to California in the fall of the year. In 1971, Bob went to South Vietnam on a tour with former players and I happened to be in San Francisco when he returned from that trip with Willie Stargell and Ed Watt. We all had dinner together one night at one of Bob's favorite places in Marin County. What tales they had to tell of that trip.

Keeping track of get-wells and birthday greetings for Bob to use on the air was a monumental job in itself. His fans were legion, and especially the women and the elderly. The shut-ins were very dedicated fans and listening to Pirate baseball was sometimes the only thing that kept many of these people going. When the season ended it was always a tremendous letdown for them. They always listened for their names to be mentioned on the air and, oh, they were so grateful.

Bob was asked to promote everything on the air, from a bingo party or card party to a church festival. If Bob mentioned it during a ball game the public would know about the event and probably support it. However, these announcements eventually got to be a little too much and he had to cut back on many of them. He was *supposed* to promote the Pittsburgh Pirates and their up-coming promotions and home schedule. We eventually had to prepare a schedule of in-game announcements for him to use.

His volume of mail was huge. Some people wrote to praise him, some to read him the riot act, some to thank him, some to suggest things the team should do. And we answered every piece of mail. And the letters were all original letters — not Xeroxed copies, and we didn't have computers to maintain a basic reply letter that could be called up and personalized from the system.

The day Bob was fired, along with Nellie King, is still vivid in my memory. It was late October and the Pirates were not in post-season games, so the office was in a relaxed mode. I very seldom went out to lunch, but I did that day. And my boss at the time, Bill Guilfoile, had taken a vacation day. He was in town, but, of course, not in the office.

When I came back from lunch, there was Bill preparing a press release and he showed it to me immediately. Needless to say, I was floored. The phone calls were overwhelming, as well as the mail. The move was not a popular one, as we all know, and for many, many years a lot of people felt that things in the Pirate broadcast booth were never the same.

My phone at home rang constantly for the next several days and nights with people expressing their opinion about the firing. It reached a point where I didn't even answer the phone. Personally, it affected me as well because of our personal friendship and because of the salary Bob was paying me. Suddenly, that was gone, and I really wasn't sure if I could hang on working for the smaller income at the Pirates. Bob worked for the Houston Astros for a year as their broadcaster. When he returned to Three Rivers Stadium to do games for the Astros, it was a "homecoming" for his fans. They were constantly watching the booth on the fourth level to get a glimpse of Bob and to cheer him. The visiting announcers' names were usually put on the scoreboard sometime during the game, welcoming them to Pittsburgh. Of course, when that message went up on the scoreboard there was a tremendous reaction.

One of the really nice nights at the ballpark after Bob was fired was the night he returned to do a TV game for USA Network. His broadcast partner that night was Jim Woods, and what a great reunion it was for those two guys. One of my prized photos is of Bob and Jim, taken that night. He wrote this inscription: "Sal, darling, my memories with you are filled with nothing but great thoughts and much, much love. I'm blessed with your friendshp. Bob Prince."

And one of the saddest nights was when he returned — very ill — to do a game for KDKA Radio in May of 1985. We played the Dodgers that night and scored nine runs in the first inning — the fourth — that Bob was at the mike. He had a way of working miracles. All of his gimmicks over the years — the green weenies, the babushka, the cardboard fans — were so well received and are still in the hands of many of his fans. I remember a few games at Three Rivers Stadium when we had to delay the start of a game because the fans were still trying to get in on a night when Bob asked all the women to come and wave their babushkas, or when we gave away green weenies. His fans had great fun at the ballpark!

One night at Forbes Field, cardboard fans were given away as a promotion. Don Drysdale was the starting pitcher for the Dodgers and, to distract him from pitching his usual good game, all the people started waving their fans. The game was halted several times, asking the fans to cease their actions.

One of the nicest tributes to Bob was done by Bill Guilfoile when he was the public relations director for the Pirates. In 1971 when we prepared the World Series program, Bill thought it would be a good idea to use all of Bob's clever sayings over the years on the cover of the program. That program is a collector's item today and shows the really unique character that Bob Prince was. In later years, a sports coat was designed for Bob with all his sayings stitched into patches on the coat.

For many years, a very active sports boosters organization in my hometown in northwestern Pennsylvania had an annual sports dinner honoring high school athletes. Because of my sports connections, I was asked to help secure speakers each year. My good friend, umpire Tom Gorman, a very funny man, was always at the dinners.

I also got Bob Prince to come one year. Bob was noted for getting someplace at the EXACT time, maybe even a little late, but never early. He suggested that I ride up to Sheffield with him, which was fine. Of course, he set a time to pick me up, and he was late doing that. Then, on the way, he wanted to stop a couple of times for "refreshments" and all the time I'm looking at my watch, knowing that the people in Sheffield are starting to panic. There was a reception planned before the dinner that we were supposed to attend. Yes, we made it, with probably five minutes to spare. Of course, he was a hit with the crowd. We all know he took command of a room when he appeared.

The last time this banquet was held, it was promoted as a "reunion" type banquet and several of the former speakers returned to be a part of a special evening. And Bob returned, too, and was as big a hit as ever. I was very proud to be able to have him there both times.

There are very few, if any, play-by-play announcers like Bob Prince today. He was a natural and made the game a joy to listen to. You never knew what was going to be said. I marvel at the way he was able to control his language on the air! He certainly was "The Voice of the Pirates" and when he was fired it was never the same. NO ONE sold the Pittsburgh Pirates like Bob did!

The nicknames that Bob gave to players are still a part of those players today. Several of them live in the Pittsburgh area and, from working with the Pirates Alumni, I know these fellows are asked to make personal appearances. Many times they are called by the nicknames Bob gave them many years ago.

Betty Prince is a class lady. She has a great sense of humor and really had to put up with a lot over the years. She was a devoted wife and mother and had to raise Nancy and Bob in the shadow of such a famous husband and father. This was not an easy chore. Both Nancy and Bob had their share of difficult times growing up and hearing people make nasty remarks about their father. But they were both very proud of their Dad and I know they miss him so very much. His early death deprived them of some happy, relaxed fun years.

One of my proudest days was to be present at the Baseball Hall of Fame when Bob Prince was recognized as the recipient of the Ford C. Frick Award. This prestigious award goes to a broadcaster for major contributions to the game of baseball and certainly there is no doubt that Bob was deserving of this honor. Unfortunately, it was presented in 1986, the year after Bob died. Ralph Kiner made the pre-

411

sentation and Betty very graciously accepted it. Kiner, of course, was one of Bob's closest friends in baseball, is a member of the Hall of Fame himself. I was in attendance with my sisters.

Bob's charitable works should never be forgotten. He devoted many hours and dollars to help so many different groups, organizations and just plain people. He made a difference in many lives. Quite often the fee he would be given for a personal appearance never reached his pocket. The check was made out to a special charity.

As I said at the beginning, I never dreamed that I would have the opportunities in life that I ended up enjoying. Personally, I was so fortunate in my lifetime to have met Bob. He was a flamboyant, charming man and a true friend. This very special man made my life in baseball possible and I hope that somehow he knows what he did for me. I am forever grateful.

Dave Arrigo/Pittsburgh Pirates

Pirates owner Kevin McClatchy presents "Pride of the Pirates" Award to Sally O'Leary for her long service to the ballclub, as her sisters, Katie and Louise, look on proudly.

> "He was always dressed up when he came into our station. I came to work here in 1978. His tie was always loosened, but that was about as casual as he got. He always called me Princess. He was so nice. I just loved him. He was so sweet."
> — Elaine Blye, WTAE receptionist

Prince impressed Pitt student

The Gunner was quick on the draw with his witticisms and wallet

By Sam Sciullo
Editor-Publisher, Inside Panther Sports

As a lifelong baseball fanatic and child of the '70s who grew up in Pittsburgh, it was impossible to escape the influence of Bob Prince. Playing baseball around the neighborhood, kids would yell out all his pet phrases — "Kiss it goodbye!" or "Foul by a gnat's eyelash!" or "Goodnight, Mary Edgerly, wherever you are!"

When you get to hear an announcer on a regular basis over a period of time, you come to think you know that person. This is especially true in baseball, where they play so many games, and listening to the games is more of an everyday occurrence — unlike football, basketball and hockey. Plus, there's so much time to kill, the pace of the game lends itself to story-telling and joke-telling.

I started to follow the Pirates on a serious basis in the late 1960s — great times — when Roberto Clemente and Willie Stargell, a pair of future Hall of Famers, were in their prime, and just before the great infusion of young players who helped the team dominate for much of the '70s: Al Oliver, Dave Cash, Rennie Stennett, Dave Parker, Richie Hebner, Manny Sanguillen, Richie Zisk, Bob Robertson. You look at the current Pirates' roster, and I'll always be a loyal fan, but you have to shake your head at the difference in talent. I know the old saying about how the older you get the greater they were, but you can look it up, as Casey Stengel was fond of saying. All those guys I mentioned . . . they hit from the first day they were in the majors.

But back to Prince. My earliest recollection was probably the 1966 season, when the Pirates made a serious run at the National League pennant, but ended up in third place, behind Los Angeles and San Francisco. You want to see some impressive offensive numbers, check out what that Pirates' team did. Clemente was the NL MVP; Matty Alou was the batting champion (.342),and Stargell hit about .315 with 33 home runs and more than 100 RBI. Clemente led the club with 202 hits and 119 RBI.

And those were just the outfielders! Prince made it all so exciting. "I Got The Fee-Vah!" he would shout. The Green Weenie also made its comeback in 1966.

The real, significant personal encounter I had with Bob Prince was in October of 1979, the first semester of my junior year at the University of Pittsburgh. I was covering Pitt football for *The Pitt News*, plus I was one of the spotters for Bill Hillgrove on the Pitt broadcasts. Talk about perfect timing: the three years I worked as a spotter, and got to see all the games, were 1979-81 under Jackie Sherrill. The records for those three seasons were 11-1, 11-1 and 11-1 (I had paid my dues, though, since I also saw every home game at Pitt during the three consecutive 1-9 seasons under Dave Hart from 1966 through 1968).

The Panther football team was playing at Washington and, because of the time difference, the team left Pittsburgh on Thursday, two days before the game. Coincidentally, the Pirates had defeated the Baltimore Orioles in Game 7 of the World Series the night before in Baltimore. Both Prince and Hillgrove had been in Baltimore doing reports for WTAE-TV. As I recall, Channel 4 was going to telecast the Pitt-Washington game as a local production, and Prince was going to be the play-by-play man. I don't remember who the color analyst was. I do remember that when Prince walked into the gate area at the old airport, all heads turned. The man had an unbelievable presence — an aura — and right away he dominated the conversation, dropping names, treating everybody as if they were old buddies.

When we got to the hotel in Seattle, I remember milling about in the lobby with Bill Kelly, who has since passed away. He was the producer/director for the Pitt games on radio back then.

Prince came over, and was admitting how completely unprepared he was to do the telecast in two days. He didn't have any rosters or spotting charts made up. Hearing that, I told him I'd be happy to draw them up for him, which I did. He told me which room he was in, and to bring them up when I was finished.

A couple hours later I went to his room and knocked on his door. He opened it without asking who was there, and there stood Bob Prince, naked except for undershorts and a lit cigarette in his hand.

"C'mon in, let's talk awhile," he said.

First, he grabbed $50 from a wad of bills atop his dresser and gave them to me. That was a lot of money for a college kid back in 1979. We talked about the Pirates, of course. Clemente, Stargell and the rest of the heroes from my youth. The specific thing that struck me odd was when he told me he had sponsored Dick Leftridge for West Virginia back in the '60s. He later served as Leftridge's agent when he signed with the Steelers as a No. 1 draft choice (1966). He was a real stiff for the Steelers and remained only one season.

A year after I graduated from Pitt, Jackie Sherrill offered me a job at Texas A&M, where I worked in the sports information office from 1982-1987. One year early in my stay, Milo Hamilton was in College Station to broadcast a Southwest Conference basketball game involving the Aggies, so I decided to introduce myself to him in the press room prior to the game. I told him that I had felt badly that he was treated so shabbily in my hometown of Pittsburgh.

"He refused to give up the ghost," said Hamilton, talking about Prince. You could see and hear the bitterness and frustration that still haunted Hamilton. It was a shame. Both were Hall of Fame announcers.

I have a hundred stories. . .
Old friend talks about Bob

"He was without peer."

By Bill Wilson

Retired sportscaster, WJAC-TV, Johnstown, Pa.

April 18, 1998

I first met Bob Prince in the late '50s when I was the Atlantic weatherman on WJAC-TV in Johnstown. I didn't take over as sports director until 1963. Because Atlantic Refining was the main sponsor of the Bucs in those days, I attended many affairs with Bob and we became very close for some reason or another, and he never came to Johnstown without getting together for a few "ice teas" at some watering hole or another.

Bob used to invite me to join him in the booth several times a season and it was during one of those visits in 1959 I'll never forget. The Bucs were up, 3-1, in the top of the ninth with one out and Dodgers on first and second.

Dick Stuart, who could hit it a mile but defensively was called "Dr. Strangeglove," was playing first base. A Dodgers' batter, whose name escapes me, bounced one down the line at first for what looked like a game-ending double play.

Well, Stuart pulled a Bill Buckner and the ball rolled into right field, scoring one run, and only Clemente's arm kept the lead runner from going to third. Now it was 3-2 Pirates and still only one out with two on.

Now Prince never did like to make one of his beloved Bucs look bad, but this time he went ballistic. He gave his radio engineer the "cut the microphone" sign and proceeded to snap his scoring pencil in half, toss it into the air and proceed to replay the Stuart error, peppering his outburst with a torrent of blue words, if you get the drift. Then he signaled for the microphone to be turned back on, and proclaimed the ball may have just taken a bad hop through Stuart's legs.

Anyway, Pittsburgh held on and won it, 3-2. Fortunately for Prince, he only had to describe Stuart's play from 1958-1962.

When I became sports director in 1963, Bob and I spent much more time together, both at home and at the Pirate spring training camp. We played a lot of golf together in Florida and it usually took about five-and-a-half hours to play a round because it was always "hit the ball and talk to someone on the course for about 15 minutes." He knew everyone at the Bradenton Country Club and you know how he liked to talk. Before the round started, "The Gunner" would indulge in a screwdriver or two, take one to go and say, "OK, Billy, tee it up." Bob was one of only three people who ever called me Billy. The others were my grandmother and a certain blonde romper room teacher.

Two other golf stories . . . As you know, Bob held the Prince Celebrity Classic at the St. Clair Country Club back in the early '80s, and he always invited me as one of the celebs. In 1983, I was lucky enough to win "closest to the pin" on one of the par threes. At the post-tourney banquet that night, Bob presented me with a fine watch and I never wore another one until the day he died in 1985.

Now, for the kicker. As it happened, I was driving to State College for an interview with Penn State football coach Joe Paterno and when I looked at my watch it had stopped. It was about 9:15 a.m. on the day (June 10, 1985) Bob died, about eight hours before his death. But the irony of that day bonded me to Bob in a way I can't describe. He was always like a big brother to me and I could never wear the watch again. It remains in my safety deposit box.

In March of 1985, I played what turned out to be Bob's last time on the links. It was at Gator Creek in Sarasota, and we headed to the 14th tee. Bob said, "Billy, I can't go another hole . . . I'm just worn out." That night, my late wife, Ruth, and I joined Bob and Betty at the Sand Bar on Holmes Beach along with two other couples. When we got into the car to leave, Ruth began to sob and I asked her why. She told me Bob had admitted to her that he had "the Big C" and it turned out to be the last time I ever saw him alive. Ironically, we didn't know that my wife was in the early stages of cancer herself. She died in January of '86.

In 1965, I almost got the job I dearly wanted. Bob called me in February and asked me to join him in the radio booth. Jim Woods was still there, of course, but they were after a third member of the broadcast team. Prince said he wanted me. At the time, the N.W. Ayer ad company in Philly handled the Atlantic account that ran the show.

So Bob sent my resume, a photo and a tape to Ayer and said, "This is the guy I want." He called me back about a month later and said it was a "done deal." Then the roof fell in. He called a couple of days later and told me they had decided to go with an ex-player and Don Hoak got the job. I was very disappointed, of course, and Bob was embarrassed. But ten years later, when he and Nellie King got canned, we would joke about the fact that at least I was still working at WJAC-TV. But that's another story.

As you know, being fired by the Bucs was a severe trauma to Bob, and it almost did him in. Betty Prince told me that Bob went into seclusion in his bedroom for several days with the shades closed and that she feared he would never be the same again.

Well, you couldn't keep Bob down and he went on the air for the Houston Astros the following year. But it just wasn't the same. I did a twenty-minute film with Prince several months after the Pirates dropped him, and he told me he blamed two men he thought were his friends for letting him down. Bob always felt that part-owner Tom

Johnson and GM Joe L. Brown could have saved his job, but that they buckled to the powers that were at Westinghouse Broadcasting.

Incidentally, I was with Bob in the booth for a Cubs game at Three Rivers one day, and a certain Westinghouse exec had about a dozen or so VIPs from Chicago in the same booth. How Bob ever got through that game amazes me, because it sounded like the Cubs cheering section the entire day. That's one reason Bob complained about such things that got him into trouble with that certain exec and it led to his firing.

In 1965, we started a Cambria County Sports Hall of Fame here in Johnstown, and there was never any doubt who we wanted as the master of ceremonies. I called Bob and he said simply "where and when?" He never asked for a dime in the seven banquets he did for us, although we always sent some money to his favorite charity as a way of saying thank you. These were big-time affairs, with top names from the world of sports as guests. And Bob Prince's introduction of Jesse Owens in 1969 was one for the ages. Even before Owens got up to speak, Bob had the crowd of some 1,400 at the War Memorial on their feet cheering. It was the most emotional intro I've ever heard and only Prince could have done it. He was without peer.

When there was a stage and a microphone involved, Bob feared no man. Including Bob Hope. Hope appeared at Penn State on his 80th birthday. I recall that Bob and Betty, Joe and Sue Paterno and my wife and I sat in the front row for the event because Bob was to introduce Hope. And he certainly did. Hope was laughing as he came on stage from some of Bob's quips and they went one on one for quite awhile before Hope went into his routine. Many thought Prince was funnier, even without a teleprompter. It was quite a night.

Bob Prince could hold his own with Bob Hope or anybody else who ever took the stage. Bob was a beaut, a class act.

Bill Wilson and Bob Prince were headliners at Johnstown Hall of Fame banquet for years.

Prince helped him get a job

"He wanted to know what I liked to be called."

By John Duffy
Free-lance broadcaster/reporter

November 12, 1997

As a young broadcaster attending and working at the radio station at Duquesne University, I also was a talk show producer at WJAS Radio. In 1982, WJAS decided to hire Bob Prince to do daily sportscasts and commentaries.

Management at the station decided Prince should have someone to help compile scores from the night before and also record his broadcasts that were done via telephone from his home every morning. I lucked out and was chosen for the job.

The first time I met him was in the station manager's office and, needless to say, I was in awe. The skinny man not wearing socks and destined for enshrinement in baseball's Hall of Fame said he was looking forward to working together. Then he asked me a question that really surprised me. He wanted to know what I liked to be called.

I answered with "Duff," still amazed that he was that concerned about what I preferred instead of just going ahead with what he thought was best.

The work went well although he would sometimes call the station late and really cut things close. It really just added to the excitement. As time passed, I would give him ideas for commentaries and other information that he would use on the air and credit me for it. That made me feel more like an equal than a flunkie.

Eventually, the time came when Bob wanted some time off. Since the shows were sold, the station wanted them done, but the question was who would do them. Bob had an answer and the answer was me. I was once again surprised by Bob and very gratified that he thought that much of me. At the time, I remembered that when I was hired I was told that I would not get on-the-air work at the station. It's great when things work out in your favor. I later became the station's sports director.

Bob helped me in the radio business and also helped me get a job in television as well. Warner Cable used to be the company that covered the City of Pittsburgh. They also started a sports channel, Home Sports Entertainment (HSE), that began operation in 1983. Bob, along with Steve Blass and Willie Stargell, were hired to announce Pirates games. Prince wanted a statistician for the games and that ended up being yours truly. In addition to doing the stats work for some sixty or so

Bucco games, I would also end up on the air occasionally reading promotional announcements and out-of-town scores.

Not everything Bob did for me involved business. The night Three Rivers Stadium opened, July 16, 1970, was also a day I was in Children's Hospital undergoing surgery on my legs. The game was telecast locally, a rare event at the time, and I fought through a medicated fog to see the Pirates' new uniforms. I saw the double-knits but conked out for the night soon after the first pitch and was out for the night. When I awoke the next morning, just about everyone from my roommates to the doctors and nurses making their rounds, were referring to me as a "big shot." I didn't know why until I was told that Bob wished me well from the broadcast booth. To this day, I have no idea who told him, but I'm happy he found out.

Another time Bob surprised me was my first trip to Bradenton, Florida for spring training. I was at McKechnie Field watching the team work out before a game when Bob came in and noticed that my rather large forehead was turning red. He told me to go into the clubhouse and get a hat.

When John Hallahan, the Pirates equipment man, heard that Bob told me to see him I didn't have to wait very long. Later that day, wearing the cap mind you, Bob gave me a piece of paper and said, "This is just to make sure you have a good time while you're down here." The piece of paper turned out to be a check for $300. After I picked my jaw off the ground . . . I had a great time.

I also had a great time at the annual Dapper Dan Dinner, thanks to Bob. He was emcee for the event and asked if I wanted to attend, no work involved, just go and have a good time. Needless to say, I was there, planning to go to both the Saturday luncheon and Sunday dinner. As luck would have it the luncheon was sold out when I arrived at the Presidential Suite at the Hilton. I figured I got to see the suite and would come back the next day for the dinner. Then Prince stepped in. Yes, all the seats were sold, but he did know of someone who wasn't going to be able to make it and said I could take his seat. He was Steelers' placekicker Gary Anderson and his seat was on the dais.

At first, I was nervous sitting between ballplayers Tom Paciorek and Grant Jackson. Then I realized what could happen when Prince was in command, so I just sat there and had the time of my life. The dinner and after-dinner party the next night were a lot of fun, too, but they didn't seem to have the Gunner's touch the way that Saturday experience did.

I, like many others, owe a lot to Bob both professionally and personally. He taught me a lot about the radio business. He taught me to remember who the audience was and to report to them what they need to know. He also would remind me that the people tuning in are more concerned about the story than the person reporting it. In other words they probably don't really care who you are so don't constantly tell them.

The most important thing he taught me was the attitude that "what goes around comes around," meaning that in the end people always get what they deserve. It makes it a lot easier to get through life when you quit worrying about others and what they're doing because it will catch up to them, good or bad, at some point.

Whether listening on my own radio while playing whiffle ball with my friends or hearing his broadcast come from just about every house in the neighborhood on summer nights, he was a big part of the soundtrack of my young life. I was fortunate enough to enjoy his broadcasts, then later in life I found out that he was just as good a friend and mentor as he was a broadcaster.

The last time I saw Bob was at Three Rivers Stadium the night of his final appearance on KDKA Radio shortly before his death. After a magical inning in which the Pirates scored nine runs against the Dodgers, Bob was sitting in a corner of the press room. I sat with him for a while and we talked about nothing very memorable. I do remember, however, what I said on my way out and I'll close by saying it here. "Thanks, Bob."

Bill Kovach

Civic Arena media lounge gathering includes John Duffy, Jim O'Brien, Nellie King and Bill Hillgrove.

Recalling The Gunner
Letters from fans

"I loved the man and miss him to this day."

"Back in the late '50s and early '60s, I was a young boy learning the game of baseball, especially influenced by my dad. I idolized Maz, nobody was like him, still isn't (Hall of Fame, where are you?). My dad always tried to impress upon me the things that made a great player, so I was always looking for these things in mostly everyone coming up to the majors. Well, here comes the year that Dick Stuart comes up from the minors after hitting, I believe, 66 home runs at Lincoln, Nebraska.

"We Pirate fans have all of these hopes and dreams that he is the next Babe Ruth. Well, he turned out to be merely home run or no hit most of his career and was probably the worst fielding first baseman of all time.

"One night at Forbes Field, my dad and I were sitting in the first row of box seats right alongside first base. I don't remember what year it was, but they were playing the St. Louis Cardinals.

"Joe Cunningham, a dead pull left-handed hitter, was up at bat. Now remember, The Gunner used to brag about this guy Stuart as if he was the greatest thing since sliced bread and I'm a pretty knowledgeable little baseball fan. I knew better and used to get so angry with Bob whenever he would say these things about Big Stu that obviously weren't true.

"So back to Cunningham's at-bat. Dead pull hitter. So Stuart plays him right down the line on the bag. Maz is playing him, favoring him to hit closer to first than the average hitter. Cunningham hits a ball on the ground no more than three feet from the first base bag. Stuart never moves, simply stands on first, no effort to go for the ball, and the ball goes into the right field corner and the run scores.

"Cunningham gets a double, and if it weren't for Clemente, probably would have had a triple. Guess what Stuart does? He looks at Maz and says, 'Why didn't you get that ball?' Well, I have to tell you the whole section we were sitting in went crazy. We really gave it to Stu, me looking up towards The Gunner shouting something to the effect, 'Did you see that Prince? What do you think of your big ham now?'

"My related story is so I can tell you my feelings for Bob Prince after all these years. I, like many, did not appreciate Bob Prince when we were kids as much as we do since he's been gone. Back when we were youngsters, we were so busy learning the game and trying to recognize quality play, we didn't appreciate that The Gunner was only doing his job, being the Bucs' greatest promoter, even if he stretched the truth now and then.

421

"In these days of '90s baseball, when the things we loved so much about the game have been forgotten about, I have come to appreciate the greatness of a Bob Prince. His knowledge of the game, his ability to tell stories to keep your interest during a dull game, and mostly his humor. I didn't realize it when I was 9 or 10 years old, but as a 49-year-old man, many years later, I loved the man and miss him to this day."

— Bill Nudo, Uniontown, Pa.

"I remember when Bob Prince announced with Rosey Rowswell until Rosey's death in 1954. The games were broadcast on WWSW Radio at that time. What made Bob Prince such a good announcer is that he made the Pirates exciting even though they weren't. That's until they turned it around in 1958. Also he would travel throughout the whole Pirates' area promoting the team all the time. Bob and Rosey would always mention people's names on broadcasts, such as for wedding anniversaries, people sick or hospitalized, shut-ins and made a lot of people feel better. But the best memory of Bob Prince is his enthusiasm for baseball and the Pittsburgh Pirates."

— Thomas Chuey,
San Francisco, Calif.

"The Princes lived in the same apartment on Shady Drive East as my parents when I was born in January, 1942. We moved out in September, 1945, but I don't know where the Princes were or when they moved.

"I read several times that the Princes entertained black players in their home. The racial situation in the 1950s wasn't as good as people like to remember. At Mt. Lebanon High School, we occasionally got the 'Now-many-of-them-are-fine-people' speech. You can draw your own conclusions.

"As an announcer, Bob was about as impartial as Harry Caray was in recent years. My favorite memory on that point is a game the Pirates played against the Giants (San Francisco variety). Frank Thomas homered for the Pirates and Bob took off on how the Pirates should look more in their own backyard for talent, as Frank was from Oakland, that he had relatives on the South Side, his family had T&T Hardware on Carson Street, etc., etc., etc. Suddenly, he exclaimed, 'Folks, I mean to tell ya, Mays just sent one out of here like a rocket!' It wasn't journalism, but it was wonderful.

"Bob was a Pittsburgh legend. He was a very good announcer, but he was a better person.

*"On another subject, I'm enjoying your book, **Keep The Faith.** You have a remarkable gift for getting football and baseball players to talk candidly. I'm looking forward to the finished product on Bob Prince."*

— Jan Finkel,
Swanton, Md.

Bob Prince provided sound effects in early years when Rosey Rowswell would holler "Open the window, Aunt Minnie, here she comes..." She never got to the window in time, and Prince would drop items that sounded like a window breaking.

"The great thing about baseball is that triumph over difficulty repeats itself over and over. In every game there will be an eighth and ninth inning, and with two outs and two strikes it's still possible."

— Walter S.

"This was back in the '50s at Forbes Field. I was there with my brothers, Ray and Jack, and some friends. We were sitting in the second tier, right behind the reserved seats. There was a big walkway just below us. We were waiting for the game to start, and I spotted Bob Prince in the walkway. He was on his way to the broadcast booth. I hollered out, 'Hey, Bob Prince,' and he waved at us. Then I hollered, 'Hey, Bob, come on up!' And he did. He shook everyone's hand and he talked to us for a few minutes. He answered our questions, and he was so pleasant. He made us laugh. I always admired Bob Prince, and I felt bad when they let him go."

— Russ Schmidt,
New Kensington, Pa.

"Memories come back to me in bunches. The Gunner's colorful story telling impressed me even as a child. Bob used to come up here to Vandergrift with a few players every year from the mid-1960s to early 1970s for Vandergrift Community Days. Some of the players that came with him were Bruce Kison, Milt May, Maz, the late Bob Moose, Nellie Briles and my personal favorite, Kenny Brett. Brett came to the Bucs after the 1973 season from the Phillies for Dave Cash. He was a left-hander who is the older brother of soon-to-be Hall of Famer George Brett. Danny Murtaugh used him a lot as a pinch-hitter in 1974 and 1975, because he was a great hitting pitcher. Anyway, Brett had pitched in the 1974 All-Star Game in Pittsburgh and won that game. I was trying to get him to sign my All-Star program by his picture without much success. The Gunner took my program and knew what I wanted. He turned the program to Brett's photo, had Brett sign it, gave it back to me with a wink and a warm smile. I'll never forget it!

"I always enjoyed the Gunner's play-by-play of the Buccos, and also thought that Nellie King with his calm, smooth, in-control voice was the perfect complement to Bob's bombastic ways. When KDKA fired these two announcers, a big part of my childhood went with them. Thanks for bringing back so many great memories with your books.

— Tony Despotakis,
Vandergrift, Pa.

"Perhaps the secret was that Bob Prince could balance the bluster with the common touch. Every small town that had a sports banquet probably had Prince as a guest speaker or master of ceremonies more than once."
— John Mehno, free-lance writer

"One of the seasons I remember best about following the Pirates was the summer before Bob Prince and Nellie King were let go. My wife Barb and I had been married less than two years. I had finished up my time in the Army and was just beginning with TIMET in Toronto, Ohio. That is the plant where I still spend a lot of my time, although we have been assigned to Hartford, Pittsburgh and Urgine, France since then. We were renting an apartment in Toronto and saving for our first house. When we bought a two bedroom along the Ohio River, we moved all that we owned in a couple of trips with a borrowed pick-up truck.

"We had a bad TV that gave out on us that summer. I used to be able to smack it and revive it, but no more. So I started following baseball on the radio, and it has been my favorite way to follow the Pirates ever since. Something that stuck with me from that first season with Bob Prince was a comment he made to Nellie King during one of the games. He observed that there are few broadcasters who get to be the 'voice' of a major league baseball team. He held that it was quite a privilege to do what he was doing, and he added, 'Once you have earned the position, you are in for life.' After the season, when it was announced that their contracts would not be renewed, I remembered what Bob Prince had said. There is a lesson for all of us in that irony."

— Buzz Myers,
Upper St. Clair, Pa.

Nellie King and Bob Prince waved to their loyal fans during parade in downtown Pittsburgh after the two were fired following the 1975 season.

Letters from fans
Tributes to Prince

"He was the voice under the pillow."

My favorite Bob Prince memory happened in the winter of 1967. My dad worked for Mon River Towing Inc. in Belle Vernon. Mon River Towing is owned by the Guttman family. One of the owners, Jess Guttman, would get my dad and me tickets to the Big Ten high school conference banquet at the Twin Coaches, a supper club in Rostraver Township, near Belle Vernon.

Not only did the banquet honor the conference all-stars (who seemed like professionals to me) but also featured a line-up of guest speakers and special guests that often created a lifetime opportunity for a starstruck 11-year-old.

Guests such as Woody Hayes, Joe Paterno, Duffy Daugherty and Bud Wilkinson were regulars. Local sports personalities such as Ed Conway, Nick Perry, Red Donley and, of course, Bob Prince, rounded out the lineup, along with members of the Pirates and Steelers.

While I'm trying to get some autographs in the bar, in walks The Gunner. He's wearing a lime green and pink plaid sports coat and extremely loud lime green socks. The sports jacket made an impression on me, but the socks made a lasting impression on me.

All heads turned and everyone in unison responded to his entrance with "Hey, Gunner!" He ordered the bartender to "Set 'em up on me!" Everyone cheered. He looked at me and said, "Young fella, what'll you have?" I was shaking in my shoes.

"C-C-Coke, please," I answered.

"Atta, boy," said the Gunner. On top of that he asked me, "Do you want me to sign that?"

So that's the night Bob Prince bought me a round of drinks and graciously gave me his autograph. It's my best Bob Prince memory. And, oh, those lime green socks!

—Herb Carpenter,
Waynesburg, Pa.

Bob Prince was the president of St. Clair Country Club and chairman of the pool committee for a few years while I was responsible for the swimming program there. He was a great boss, and so supportive of what we were trying to do. He even gave the kids tips about swimming and diving. I thought he was a great man.

—Earl J. Birdy, Executive Secretary,
Western Pa. Country Club Swimming Assn.

Two young boys stood at the top of Mt. Washington Roadway, hoping every Saturday to hitch a ride to Downtown where they could attend the YMCA on Saturday. Often, Bob Prince would come flying up Merrimac Street and see these two young kids (approximately 12 years of age) and offer them a ride in his bright red convertible, with the top down! To say the least, we were thrilled just to get a ride with Bob Prince.

More often than not, he would offer us tickets. He would say, "How would you like to go see a hockey game?" Of course, in those days it was for the Hornets at the Gardens in Oakland. We always took him up on his offer.

So as you might guess we would often hesitate when others would say, "Do you want a ride, guys?" We would say, "Not today." We would patiently wait, hoping that Mr. Prince would soon be along in his red chariot and say, "Hello, hop in guys!"

My buddy's name was Stanley Cull. I have fond memories of "The Gunner." I don't think he even knew my name, but that didn't matter much. We always considered him a real friend. Later on, I sold pop in the bleachers at Forbes Field, but I never got to see Bob again.

— Miles K. Sherman,
Bethel Park, Pa.

*I have a complete set of your books. I have your autograph and Maz's autograph on your Bill Mazeroski book **Maz And The '60 Bucs**, which is my favorite. Listening to Thor Tolo the other night, I heard that you are writing a book on Bob Prince. It is important for the younger generation of Pittsburgh sports fans to know that Pittsburgh had the very best radio voice in all of baseball for many years.*

It was Bob Prince who educated me and created the passion which I now have for my Pittsburgh Pirates. He was the voice under the pillow for a little kid in New Castle, Pennsylvania, who simply could not miss a single inning of one of his Pirate broadcasts.

I must share this with you. When Bob Prince was fired, it was like the end of the world for me. Although by that point I was an adult, what KDKA did broke my heart. The evening of the news of his firing, I immediately began to walk through New Castle neighborhoods collecting hundreds of signatures on a petition that I hoped and prayed would undo this awful deed. It, of course, did not.

I recall sending a copy of that incredibly large petition to him with a letter that was straight from my heart. Several days later, I received a note from The Gunner which simply read, "Lou, thank you for what you did. It's great to be able to smell the roses. May God bless you. Bob Prince." That note is now a family treasure.

—Lou Zona,
New Castle, Pa.

Heard you are doing a book on the late Great Bob Prince, which I'm thrilled about. Bob Prince was and always will be my favorite announcer. See, The Gunner used to spend time in Clearfield and go deer hunting and I met Bob at the Dimeling Hotel when I was a bell-hop there. Looking forward to a book about one of my boyhood idols.
— Bill Knepp,
Clearfield, Pa.

*I received **Remember Roberto** as a Christmas gift, and read it cover to cover. It brought back a flood of memories of the Pirates of the '60s and early '70s. I grew up in a small town about 90 miles north of Pittsburgh. I was an avid Bucco fan and spent countless nights listening to Bob Prince and Jim Woods describe the action, as the Pirates either fought for the pennant or fought to stay out of sixth place.*

Once or twice a year, I was fortunate enough to attend a game at Forbes Field. I, like most fans, will never forget my first major league game. It was in September of 1960. The Bucs were in the middle of a pennant race and were playing the Dodgers. The first glimpse of Forbes Field was truly breath-taking. The grass was greener than I could ever have imagined. The scoreboard and the monument out by the 457 foot mark were just as I thought they would be.

It's amazing what we remember 38 years later. I remember Gino Cimoli (my favorite player) started in center field for Bill Virdon. He led off the game with a single and later in the game, with Ron Fairly at bat, made a long run into the left center field gap, only to have the ball glance off his glove for a triple. The guy behind me yelled, "Virdon would've had it!" I wanted to argue, but I was only ten years old so I kept my mouth shut. Bob Skinner ended up hitting a homer off the roof off Ed Roebuck to win the game. My family is always amazed that I can remember such details from a game played some 38 years ago, but I think every true baseball fan remembers his first game in such minute detail.

My fondest memory of the '60 World Series was not Maz's home run. It was Hal Smith's home run. And when you think about it, Smith's home run was more dramatic. Just as you know where you were when JFK was shot, you know where you were when Smith and Maz hit their homers. I was in fifth grade during recess when Smith hit his. I had brought my portable radio to school and, when he hit it, I got excited and knocked over the radio, changing stations.

*For a few excruciating seconds, we weren't sure exactly what had happened. I knew then the Pirates were going to win. Even when the Yankees scored two runs in the ninth to tie it, I still knew the Bucs would win. I wasn't sure how. I was just sure they'd win. Your books bring back memories of my childhood. In some ways, the Pirates **were** my childhood. Everyone should have such a childhood.*
— Carl T. Smith,
Salamanca, N.Y.

Bob Prince salutes his fans when he came back to broadcast Pirates games in May of 1985. Lanny Frattare, at left, was among those who cheered his comeback. Prince got sick a few days later and died on June 10.

Happy days: Prince presents Gold Glove Awards to (left to right) Bill Mazeroski, Gene Alley and Roberto Clemente in '60s at Forbes Field.

Pittsburgh Proud
Sports Book Series

Here is information relating to the series of books about Pittsburgh sports subjects by Jim O'Brien that are available to you by mail order:

KEEP THE FAITH
The Steelers of Two Different Eras

Interviews with Steelers of the '70s and the '90s to show what they shared in common, and what was different about the challenges they faced. These are the Steelers of Chuck Noll and Bill Cowher, or Art Rooney and Dan Rooney. Going to Ireland in the summer of '97 brought this all home. 448 pages, 200 plus photos. Hardcover: $26.95, plus sales tax and shipping charges. (ISBN # 1-886348-02-2)

DARE TO DREAM
The Steelers of Two Special Seasons

Profiles of the Steelers and their families from the 1994 and 1995 seasons, when the Steelers had two of the best seasons in the team's history, and even got to the Super Bowl under Bill Cowher. Family photographs and stories, especially those offered by their mothers, offer special insights into the Steelers of the modern era. 480 pages, 270 photos. Hardcover: $26.95 (ISBN # 1-886348-00-6). Perfect bound softcover: $16.95, plus charges. (ISBN # 1-886348-01-4).

WE HAD 'EM ALL THE WAY
Bob Prince and His Pittsburgh Pirates

Personal reflections on Bob Prince, who was "The Voice of the Pirates" for 28 seasons (1948-1975), and one of the most talked-about and controversial characters ever to grace the Pittsburgh sports scene. This book also catches you up on what's become of the Pirates of the same era who remained in the Pittsburgh area after they retired from playing the game. 432 pages, over 200 photos. Hardcover: $26.95, plus sales tax and shipping charges. (ISBN # 1-886348-03-0)

DOING IT RIGHT — The Steelers of Three Rivers and Four Super Bowls Share Their Secrets for Success

Tales of the glory days of the Pittsburgh Steelers. Interviews with the stars of the '70s, as well as players from the early days of the franchise, and those who followed the championship seasons. If you've wondered whatever became of some of your favorite Steelers, here are the answers. Terry Bradshaw, Franco Harris, Rocky Bleier, Jack

Lambert, Jack Ham, Mel Blount, Joe Greene, Lynn Swann, Mike Webster, Ernie Holmes, John Stallworth, Chuck Noll, L.C. Greenwood are all profiled here. 536 pages, with over 250 photos. Hardcover: $24.95, plus sales tax and shipping. (ISBN # 1-916114-09-0)

REMEMBER ROBERTO
Clemente Recalled By Teammates, Family, Friends and Fans
Pirates Hall of Famer recalled by those who knew him best. Interviews with his wife and sons, and his celebrated teammates during his 18 seasons as an All-Star rightfielder at Forbes Field and Three Rivers Stadium. This was the first adult book on Clemente to come out in over 20 years. 448 pages, over 220 photos, many borrowed from players' personal photo albums. Hardcover: $ 24.95, plus sales tax and shipping charges. (ISBN # 0-916114-14-7)

MAZ AND THE '60 BUCS
When Pittsburgh And Its Pirates Went All The Way
Interviews with all the living members of the World Series champion Pirates of the 1960 season, and five of the key members of the New York Yankees. Chapters on every one of the Pirates of that season. An intriguing reminiscence of what Pittsburgh, particularly Oakland, was like in the early '60s. Reproduced autographs of all the players. 512 pages, over 225 photos, many from players' personal family photo albums. Hardcover: $24.95, plus charges. (ISBN # 0-916114-12-0)

PENGUIN PROFILES
Pittsburgh's Boys of Winter
Stories reflecting on the history of hockey in Pittsburgh. Interviews with many of the recent stars, from Mario Lemieux to Jaromir Jagr and Ron Francis to Penguins of the past. 448 pages, over 200 photos. Hardcover: $24.95, plus charges. (ISBN # 0-916114-16-3)

For more information or to place an order please call Jim O'Brien at his home office (412-221-3580). Or write to: James P. O'Brien — Publishing, P.O. Box 12580, Pittsburgh PA 15241. Pennsylvania residents should add 6% sales tax to price of book, and Allegheny County residents should remit *additional* 1% sales tax on price of book, plus $3.50 for postage per book. Please provide signing instructions. Let us know who is receiving the book, who it is from, for what occasion, and any message you deem appropriate to go over author's signature. Books are mailed the same day the order arrives.

"I always look forward to the next book in your series. Reading your books makes me feel like I was there in person. Keep up the good work."
— Tim Hall, New Castle, Pa.

Pittsburgh Pirates

Bob Prince
1916-1985

"The Pirates were playing on the west coast and I was supposed to be sleeping. But I'd be in bed with the transistor radio under my pillow. You felt like you were there when you were listening to The Gunner. He'd talk about two-out lightning and you'd be excited. I'd be mesmerized. I'd make my own scorecards for the games when I was 11. I was a 162-game man. It was so much different then. Nothing much on TV, maybe the Game of the Week. I had a tape recorder and I did my own play-by-play, trying to be like The Gunner. He was my man."

— North Side baseball fan

Gene Baker

Joseph Gibbon

Joe L. Brown

Dan Narron

Joe Christopher

Gino Cimoli

Rocky Nelson

"Smoky" Burgess

George C. Witt